Corporate Social Responsibility Across Europe

André Habisch · Jan Jonker
Martina Wegner · René Schmidpeter
(Editors)

Corporate
Social Responsibility
Across Europe

With 7 Figures and 18 Tables

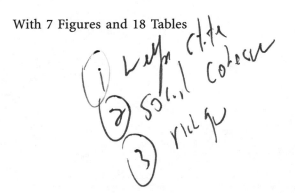

 Springer

Professor Dr. André Habisch
Martina Wegner
René Schmidpeter
Catholic University of Eichstätt-Ingolstadt
Ostenstraße 26–28
85072 Eichstätt
Germany

Dr. Jan Jonker
Nijmegen School of Management
Radboud University Nijmegen
PO Box 9108
6500 HK Nijmegen
The Netherlands

Cataloging-in-Publication Data
Library of Congress Control Number: 2004113533

ISBN 3-540-23251-6 Springer Berlin Heidelberg New York

Springer is a part of Springer Science+Business Media

springeronline.com

© Springer Berlin · Heidelberg 2005
Printed in Germany

Hardcover-Design: Erich Kirchner, Heidelberg

SPIN 11533948   43/3111-5 4 3 2 1 – Printed on acid-free paper

Foreword

Corporate Social Responsibility, or CSR, helps businesses to build up credibility and trust which are the key to hiring – and retaining – the best and brightest staff, and to a reputation which consumers and investors can identify with.

For the public at large, CSR plays another role. The impact of trade liberalisation and technological change brings concern about globalisation, economic restructuring and the ever growing power of multinationals. If corporations demonstrate a sense of social and environmental responsibility, they help to ease the transition towards the new economic order.

But why are governments interested in CSR? – Their task is to make sure that the process of global economic and social change is managed properly and fairly. Let me give you a simple but striking example. The ILO estimates that two hundred and fifty million children are currently working world wide in dangerous or degrading conditions. This can only be changed if the countries concerned ratify and apply the ILO instrument outlawing such practices. With proper CSR, we can at least ensure that European companies commit to respecting children's rights in all their global operations and thus send out a signal to others.

Moreover, CSR is a major contributor to Europe's employment and social agenda – the pursuit of more and better jobs. It is also an important driver of better global governance, reinforcing existing policy tools such as legislation and social dialogue.

For these reasons, the European Commission decided to launch a consultative paper on Corporate Social Responsibility in July 2001 and a policy paper in July 2002. In this paper we prepared the ground for a European CSR strategy, showing that the "agenda" of business and the "agenda" of public policy-makers can coincide. The policy paper aims to promote CSR practices, to ensure the credibility of CSR claims as well as coherence in public policy on CSR.

To respond to these challenges, a Multi-Stakeholder Forum was set up bringing together European representative organisations of employers, business networks, NGOs and Trade Unions. The Forum aimed first and foremost to raise awareness of CSR and secondly to promote innovation, convergence and transparency in the use of existing CSR practices and tools such as codes of conduct. The Forum also tackled the question of legal recognition of CSR benchmarks, such as labelling, both in individual jurisdictions and across borders. Public authorities at all levels are seeing CSR as a tool of government. More and more, CSR criteria are included in market regulation, the provision of grants, or tax incentives. However, unless government proceeds in an orderly way, it runs the risk of introducing new barriers to trade in the EU's internal market. Extreme vigilance will be needed here.

But ultimately, the EU's success in promoting CSR will depend on ensuring widespread "ownership" of CSR – by business, social partners, civil society and public authorities. We hope that the information included in this volume will help deepen all stakeholders understanding of each others' role and thus contribute to a European approach towards CSR.

Anna Diamantopoulou   Athens, August 2004

Member of the Greek Parliament
Former European Commissioner
for Employment and Social Affairs

Foreword

Over recent years the debate about Corporate Social Responsibility (CSR) has spread very rapidly across Europe as part of the intense discussion about sustainability and globalisation. CSR, a virtually unknown concept a decade ago, is today a topic for discussion not only for business people but also for politicians, trade-unionists, consumers, NGOs as well as researchers.

Europe is the most active and most vocal region when it comes to CSR. This could also be observed on the occasion of the CSR Colloquium in Wildbad-Kreuth in January 2004, where researchers from all over Europe presented national perceptions of CSR and where I had the pleasure to contribute the European Commission's view of CSR. Being based on this event, this book helps clarify whether Europe will be able to develop its own unique and distinctive model of CSR against a diversity of national concepts of CSR.

As this unique overview of 23 countries proves, CSR comes with different national characteristics resulting from diverse cultural traditions as well as heterogeneous social and economic backgrounds. Until recently ethical concerns played a dominant role in Anglo-Saxon countries. While environmental preoccupations ruled the CSR agenda in the north of Europe, CSR was perceived as a means to advance social issues in the south. Expectations from CSR have been less tangible in Eastern Europe. As approaches towards CSR are being taken further in the context of a globalised world, they are expected to increasingly bring together these social, environmental and ethical ingredients, shaping them into an ever more uniform European concept of CSR.

The dominant traits of this emerging European concept of CSR are its links with sustainability and governance. CSR is defined as a way of doing business which contributes to sustainable development, reinforcing competitiveness, social cohesion and environmental protection. CSR is therefore much more than philanthropy or ethics. Already today there is a wide consensus on this definition.

Corporate Governance, as the second common denominator, is more controversial. While the development of CSR initially was – and to some extent still is – based on unilateral company initiatives responding to market pressures, today multi-stakeholder approaches are clearly showing the way forward. This corresponds to the 2002 definition of the European Commission, stating that CSR is implemented in dialogue with stakeholders. However, the stakeholder approach raises political, regulatory and organisational challenges. Despite the recent European Parliament resolution on company law and corporate governance which points to the essential role to be played by stakeholders, there is still a wide gap between the actual practices of corporate governance and the CSR debate. Furthermore, the question of how to involve legitimate stakeholders' representatives is still an unresolved issue.

CSR is driven by market actors such as consumers, investors, as well as opinion leaders and reputation makers such as NGOs and the media. As CSR is about action taken by companies in reaction to market pressures, it also needs market rules to develop in a sustainable manner. So while CSR is essentially taking place at firm level, it is increasingly affected by national, European and international policies. Today CSR is becoming an established policy tool and most European governments are developing policies aiming at shaping CSR. It is important for businesses and their stakeholders that these policies be consistent with the CSR objectives of sustainable development and better governance.

The present volume illustrates twenty-three national CSR approaches discussing also the above mentioned objectives, and it is my conviction that it will thus contribute to strengthening and shaping a European understanding of CSR.

Dominique Bé   Brussels, August 2004

Directorate General
Employment & Social Affairs
European Commission

Foreword

One of the most important tasks in our globalised world is to find an equilibrium between economic success and social welfare. It is obvious that such a complex task requires all players on the market to reconsider their roles. Many players, such as NGOs and not-for-profit organisations, but also politicians ask especially companies to take on more social responsibility.

But why should a company do so? Such an approach only incurs cost and does not increase profitability – and this means that competitiveness is at stake.

This often quoted statement of economic hard-liners does not hold true. In the first place, companies were founded to serve people. As the Managing Director of betapharm I am convinced of this idea and this is why we are committed to social projects in the health care area. But companies will only assume social responsibility if their executives have the required mindset. Since they are responsible for the well-being of their companies, they will only commit themselves to community projects if this helps their organisations at the same time. And this is neither unethical nor an abuse of social commitment for profit reasons, but simply the above mentioned combination of the two crucial needs: economic success and social welfare.

Secondly, CSR has a key effect on the inside of companies. Employees do not only want to earn money: In an increasingly networked world without a set value structure they need an emotional platform, jobs with additional value. CSR is such a platform. As such it is able to motivate people. Socially responsible companies are more competitive, as they have highly motivated staff and as they are attractive employers for committed and qualified people.

Entrepreneurs deciding in favour of CSR need to be visionaries and have to understand that the assumption of corporate responsibility is more than advertising. However, at present many approaches towards CSR fail because the public and the consumer do not reward the efforts undertaken by socially responsible companies. This has to change. And this can only be done on the political level. Socially responsible and successful companies must not be punished but have to be recognised as organisations of special importance. Politicians have to make sure that these companies gain a superior image in public.

I am convinced that the social development, the increasing problems worldwide will force us to get involved in CSR – and it will bring benefits for all players, for society and the company itself: due to a better image, higher reputation of the brand, staff motivation and a competitive edge. Companies which excel due to their social commitment will win in competition – and this will be to the advantage of all of us.

Peter Walter   Augsburg, August 2004

Managing Director of
betapharm Arzneimittel GmbH

Acknowledgements

The idea for this volume arose during an international symposium on CSR that took place in Wildbad Kreuth, in the middle of the snow-covered Bavarian Alps in January 2004. We are grateful to the Hanns-Seidel-Foundation (Munich), which generously supported the Center for Corporate Citizenship in organising this first international scientific meeting on CSR in Germany. Special thanks also go to the event's initiator, Dr. Georg Stein and Prof. Dr. Siegfried Hoefling from the Hanns-Seidel-Foundation, who provided us with such valuable support during the conference.

However, we could not have realised this volume without the support of the Ministry of Economic Affairs, The Netherlands. It is through the Dutch National Research Programme on CSR that we have been able to get in touch with colleagues with a thoroughly European scope. We are grateful for their indirect yet important support.

The demanding editorial process of this volume was supported by an international board of colleagues from across Europe. The editors would like to thank Melsa Ararat (Istanbul), Maria Bohata (Prague), Domènec Melé (Barcelona) and Nigel Roome (Rotterdam) for their constructive and inspiring commitment to this process. Given the heterogeneity of contexts and approaches covered by the papers the task of our colleagues went far beyond the usual work of a reviewer.

The printing and distribution of the volume has been very kindly sponsored by betapharm Arzneimittel GmbH, Augsburg (Germany). We are grateful to Peter Walter (Managing Director) and Petra Kinzl (Member of the Management) for their ongoing support of the Center for Corporate Citizenship at the Catholic University of Eichstätt-Ingolstadt in general and this volume in particular. We also would like to thank the people from Philips and from CSR Austria as well as the Maximilian-Bickhoff-Universitätsstiftung for their generous sponsoring which helped us to realise this volume.

Last but not least we would like to give our sincere thanks to Dr. Martina Bihn from Springer Verlag.

André Habisch   Eichstätt, August 2004
Jan Jonker
Martina Wegner
René Schmidpeter

Table of Contents

Northern Europe

Western Europe

Eastern Europe

Southern Europe

Pan-European Approaches

Introduction

André Habisch and Jan Jonker

CSR – A Subject with Substance?

This is a unique book. It provides an empirically grounded and lively insight into an emerging movement across Europe; a movement labelled often as Corporate Social Responsibility (CSR) or Corporate Citizenship (CC). Under a variety of headings[1] we are witnessing a series of vivid debates questioning the role(s), functions and balance of – and between – institutions in contemporary society. This questioning addresses a thought-provoking variety of issues and themes. This book provides ample evidence of what is being questioned in different countries across Europe when raising and debating the issue of CSR. The debate is real; it has participants, outcomes and it has substance. It is sometimes unstructured and unfocused yet promising. In its bare essence it indicates how we are forced to have a fundamental dialogue concerning the (re)configuretion of the relations and balance between institutions that together make up our society. The embedded core issue is the challenge to question the role of business in contemporary society. This is not a debate that can be neglected or overlooked despite some observable criticism. The debate is in part initiated and structurally stimulated by the European Commission supported by initiatives, pave-way documents and institutions such as the Green Paper, the Dublin Foundation, the actual European Research Programme (KP6) and many other initiatives. Moreover, a rich variety of recent national and "private" initiatives can be found. They range from Business in the Community (BITC – UK), the Copenhagen Centre (DK), the Center for Corporate Citizenship (GER), CSR Europe (B) or the Dutch National Research Programme (NL) on CSR and many, many more. It is exciting to see how much political, organisational and institutional time and energy are devoted to give further substance and direction to this debate on a European scale. Still, it is our conviction that we are only witnessing the beginning of a movement that – either in its present form or in a transformed way and under new headings – will question fundamentally the fabric of society.

To understand more profoundly the roots of the debate across Europe a prerequisite is to investigate developments and transitions on a national scale. We take the viewpoint here that the European discussion at large is an amalgam of very heterogeneous national debates, often in different stages of development. These national debates are emerging against a background of historical, political, scientific, cultural – and of course – business developments. Trying to understand what the specific meaning of a term such as CSR is in a national context requires investigating those national roots and related developments. This book provides such an investigation, showing the richness of variety that can be found in different contexts.

CSR in essence addresses the reconfiguration of the balance between institutions that together make up society.

Why is CSR a subject with substance? Why is it appropriate to talk about CSR as a European movement at the beginning of the 21st century? CSR in essence addresses the reconfiguration of the balance between institutions that together make up society. This balance has come under pressure in the last decades of the previous century. During this period we have been witnessing the creation of what is now sometimes called the "open society": a society in which ideas, services, concepts, developments, labour, computer viruses, catastrophes are exchanged at the speed of light. Neighbours far away have become close by, what is happening here and today has immediate impact elsewhere. As a whole, interdependencies across people, across nations and across economic regions have been strengthened. Or, as Barber (1995) puts it: "Interdependence is not some foreign adversary against which citizens need to muster resistance. It is a domestic reality that already has compromised the efficacy of citizenship in scores of unacknowledged and uncharted ways." This growing interdependence is not an accident of history. Rather it is one of the results of many years of conscious and persistent work to remove national barriers within agreements such as GATT and WTO. In Europe the breakdown of the Berlin wall and the end of the Soviet Union provided other stimulating factors towards an ongoing process of interdependence and integration. The new generation of mass media with their constant and instant flow of information across borders should also be mentioned in that respect. Last but not least people themselves have become more familiar with a variety of foreign cultures in the past decades. This is partially due to the consequences of living in a globalised economy as a (world) consumer. "Globalisation thus is a complex set of processes, not a single one. And these operate in a contradictory or oppositional fashion. Most people think of globalisation as simply "pulling away" power or influence from local communities and nations into a global arena. And indeed this is one of the consequences. Yet it also has an opposite effect. Globalisation not only pulls upwards, but also pushes downwards, creating new pressures for local autonomy." (Giddens, 1999: 13). It leads to a vast array of interdependent, almost incomparable issues such as living with more emigrants within national boundaries, fresh fruit in the supermarket, being able to travel abroad more frequently, fighting terrorism on a trans-national scale or developing appropriate approaches to handling water problems. None of these issues just by themselves could be marked as the centrepiece; it is more the amalgam of the whole that creates a driving force behind the movement of CSR.

Institutions in Society

With that growing interdependence it also becomes clear that new and fundamental issues enter the societal debate; a debate that is complex in nature. It cannot be pursued by providing simple answers and quick fixes. Given the complex implications that arise out of that debate, no wonder also that the debate itself is conducted under a variety of headings such as the quest for Corporate Citizenship, Stakeholder Engagement or Corporate Governance. This explains why it makes no sense to search for just one common denominator, one common concept or just one direction once we speak about CSR in Europe. It is the richness of this debate we want to capture in this volume, revealing its development across nations.

Society could be understood as an equilibrium between various institutions and corresponding behavioural patterns.

We take the view here that society is structured on the basis of institutions. By institutions we mean sets of formal and informal rules based on common values specifying relationships and balances leading to agreed concepts and subsequent behaviour. Fundamental for the notion of institutions is their "hidden" yet guiding character. It is not common to question the existence and functioning of institutions daily. However, the moment their contribution to society is diminishing their importance becomes apparent. Crucial for the notion of institutions is that they are shared by a large group of people in order to provide a common denominator for acceptable social behaviour (including cooperation and competition). It is assumed here that there should be a certain threshold – a certain degree – of institutions and the acceptance of what they stand for, in order to create a dynamic fabric of society. A well-balanced framework of institutions creates the necessary fabric of a society. It is assumed that there is a certain equilibrium between various institutions and corresponding behavioural patterns one could call the "societal balance". This balance provides a certain order in the sense of a structured base for interdependent expectations of mutual behaviour. This degree of social order (often also called social cohesion) as a whole operates on a local, regional, national and an international level to a stronger or weaker degree (Ostrom, 1995). Societal fabric does not come about haphazardly but needs to be developed and maintained carefully.

We are assuming that the present CSR debate across Europe reveals that this institutional society balance is being questioned. Neither local nor national communities can any longer be just a world on their own. Interdependence and reciprocity blended with the open character of society show time and again that established societal practices are no longer apt to address the novel and complex questions at hand. Dealing with the safety of commercial aviation, for example, is no longer a national matter but can only be treated on a European scale. Pollution does not stop at borders nor does economic migration, water, asylum seekers or national security. Given those issues, the quest for a certain degree of social structure, rules, regulations and thus appropriate institutions becomes obvious. This obviousness is reflected in the various national debates taking place under the heading of CSR.

Drivers for Reconfiguration

Society can be described as a historically grown balance of three dominant clusters of institutions: government, civil society and the market, represented by commercial organisations. The fact that CSR is an issue as much on national levels as on a European level indicates that a fundamental transition of the long taken-for-granted balance between those clusters of institutions is taking place. On the surface this stems from a growing consciousness of the need to protect the environment, the depletion of natural resources and the awareness of social inequality creating a lack of access to opportunities. It hardly needs to be discussed that mankind is consuming its (global) natural resources at a pace never demonstrated before. Since the 1970s, protecting the environment has become an accepted priority fostered by rules and regulation. Nowadays any self-respecting organisation – whatever its nationality, nature or goal – has a system in place to take care of those environmental issues. The question remains whether we really invest enough in the protection of the environment. The answer to that question is not positive. But while working on those issues under the surface it becomes apparent that something much more fundamental is happening. We therefore would like to identify three fundamental transitions that are taking place.

1. What we are at present witnessing is a fundamental transition in the concept of "national governments". In the 20th century safety, language, culture and history all blended together in one melting pot called a nationality. But nowadays making adequate laws is no longer a question of national or regional concern only. Laws and regulations are more and more made "in Brussels". Furthermore, for a growing number of European countries the monetary system is managed in Frankfurt. More recently the EU has expanded into 25 nations under one flag and one administration. Or, as Scott (2001: 93) puts it: "The nation state, which historically has been the principal social unit, is … under pressure from economic forces beyond its control. Its relevance to a society characterised by devolution is arguably declining. National economies also have to a significant degree been overtaken by the global economy. But the global economy is not the real institute. The global system cannot supplant the national one, which is based on social values. A globalised market can never satisfy our need for belonging."

2. A second important transition takes place in what is called civil society characterised by words such as fragmentation, stakeholders, needs and expectations, rights and duties, new divides, disintegration of certain groups etc. In this transition we are witnessing a search for answers regarding social cohesion, common identity and safety. While recent developments are threatening this transition, it also offers ample opportunity to create new structures more apt to address these complex and novel issues. Citizens see themselves

as competent actors of a societal playing field, making use of the latest technologies to address (individual and collective) needs and expectations. Instantly groups and communities are created when novel issues arise. This can happen on a local level (sometimes also national) but with the same ease and speed at an international level. Recently a series of fine examples of this self-organising capability has been demonstrated across Europe.

3. In this context of transition it becomes apparent that business has an important role to play. For a long time the relationship among organisations has been conceptualised by drawing on a paradigm developed in the age of the industrial society. The business of business has been just doing business for a long time. The present political, societal and organisational debates indicate that a change of this paradigm is required. From this viewpoint business enterprises have not been perceived as actors really contributing to the creation and maintenance of social order. However, in contemporary society the way firms operate has become a critical issue, both in theory and practice. Businesses are confronted on a daily basis with issues, needs and demands emerging out of a social order that has long been taken for granted. Important variables of sustainable business success are not only cheap labour and liberal tax laws but also the quality of educational systems, a predictable legal and political system, a healthy natural environment, a supportable crime rate and so on. Assuming social responsibility means stimulating those groups and processes of institution-building in society that are apt to confront problems of social order in a broad general sense, nearby and far away. This quest currently appears as a simple and undefined appeal to organisations to generate profit while contributing to society, taking into account the needs and expectations of social and ecological constituencies. CSR is however a complex, multi-faceted and dynamic phenomenon that brings into question the function, role and position of the business enterprise in society.

Defensive strategies are no longer an adequate response to this new situation: business could gain importance for European policy projects.

At present we are witnessing a series of cyclical incidents about business – be it negative regarding environmental and health impacts or business frauds – leading to the downsizing of trust. Stakeholders – either legitimate or not – question the contribution of firms to the common good. Trust in business is an important prerequisite for its "licence to operate". Without a certain degree of trust no business can survive. Media and opinion leaders increasingly focus on the public role of business, thus threatening a traditional division of labour that attributes the responsibility for the provision of common goods only to politicians and public administrations. Defensive strategies of sticking to legal rules and the avoidance of a critical public are no adequate response to that situation. Here, for business to act responsibly is the only way to generate and maintain trust. Moreover, to generate and maintain trust also includes active entrepreneurial engagement to address common problems in society. When business is perceived as the principal gainer of economic integration but never apparently contributes to some of its costs, its profits appear illegitimate in the eyes of many (public) actors even if they are legitimate from a legal point of view.

In the transitional countries of Central and Eastern Europe additional issues can be recognised. In many cases the societal infrastructure is rather weak and not capable of providing public goods necessary for the sustainable development of these countries. A culture of distrust in corruptive public services and exploitative business is often dominant. If business enterprises as foreign direct investors want to make use of the advantages granted here (such as low salaries, modest tax rates and well trained industrial workers) they will have to invest in the human, cultural and institutional capital of their new business environments as well. Developing human and social capital is in that respect an appropriate strategy to augment the quality of its position and the sustainable success of its business activities.

Governments and public administrations should foster that investment process by providing an institutional infrastructure for partnership and for the emergence of networks of social capital. Only if they "allow" for business to assume social responsibility and join networks of civic cooperation will it be possible to provide public goods and overcome a disintegration of their society. It is obvious that governments and societies as a whole would immensely gain from a wide-spread culture of socially engaged business enterprises. One might even state that with a "professional" approach to CSR, business could bring about similar positive effects and externalities to their social environment as to the professional management of their "core operations". This does obviously hold true for the provision of educational services and the human rights situation, but also for hard-nosed social problems of certain groups, for tackling international environmental problems, for certain health care issues etc. For current European policy projects such as building infrastructure, addressing problems of social disintegration and building a more competitive environment in the global context (Lisbon summit), business is already an important partner.

Business as a Motor of a Self-Organising Civil Society?

The present CSR movement is not a clash of civilisations (as some tend to suggest) but the expression of surfacing tensions due to the ongoing "construction" of a "single" society on a European and also a more global level. The essence of the problem is to address the reconfiguration of a balance between institutions that together make up society. That reconfiguration will certainly imply a relative loss of weight of central government(s) as the "monopolist" in the provision of public goods and services. It also implies questioning the role and function of many other more nationally oriented institutions given the problems, issues and questions at hand.

CSR can be looked upon as a complex of symptoms referring to a society in the middle of a series of fundamental transitions.

The central argument in the CSR debate at large is that businesses ought to play a more prominent societal role, given their dominant (economic) position. This perspective is based upon the generally accepted recognition that an enterprise operates within a societal network of stakeholders, who influence directly or indirectly the results of the enterprise. It also seems to imply a more "responsible" behaviour of the business enterprise embedding a variety of nondescript social obligations. The contemporary debate regarding CSR can be looked upon as a complex of symptoms referring to a society in the middle of a series of fundamental transitions. It is the argument of this study that what we face under the unmistakably diffuse heading of CSR is a struggle within society. A struggle expressing the ambivalence within each (national) culture as it faces a global networked future and wonders what level of cultural and national autonomy can be – or should be – retained. It also expresses the dilemma faced by the individual trying to balance the clear benefits of individualism with its apparent extremely high costs. Last but not least it expresses a search for those institutions to keep, reinforce or (re-)create addressing the emerging issues in society; a society in the midst of a transition.

The Next Step

Although the debate has been promising so far, it has reached a point where numerous parties appear to agree that some fundamental action is required. Talk is far more prevalent then walk. Ideas and concepts abound, they take all kinds of shapes and sizes, ranging from traditional community sponsoring activities, zero-based material budgeting, socially responsible investment (SRI) to an international engagement in the protection of Human Rights or against child labour. There is little wonder that it is hard to define what CSR really means – as if in the end one ultimate definition would be the panacea to all (scientific, pragmatic, operational or organisational) doubts. At present a working definition is probably the most attainable. For that purpose, CSR can be defined as: the extent to which – and the way in which – an organisation consciously assumes responsibility for – and justifies – its actions and non-actions and assesses the impact of those actions on its legitimate constituencies. Those constituencies – or stakeholders as they are often called – represent the network of interactions an organisation maintains with its direct and indirect environment.

This definition raises some further questions with a potential fundamental impact. For example needs and expectations of various stakeholders do not necessarily correspond. Which interests should be taken into account in order to be a responsible corporation? This question is difficult to answer in a society in which every stakeholder seems to be entitled to have legitimate demands, leading to an array of expectations that cannot all be fulfilled simultaneously. As a consequence, an organisation intending to legitimate its norms, intentions and acts, cannot always refer to what it assumes as general and shared opinions.

It should be obvious that this represents a positive – not a normative – approach. It does not determine what business *should* do but instead carefully addresses the question of what *they are actually doing* and tries to understand these activities in the logic of business itself as well as its societal environment as a whole. Hence, as a kind of minimum requirement between observers, participants and critics of the various national CSR scene(s) it should be at least clear that – as a consequence of the fundamental transformations outlined above – new forms of (inter)organisational behaviour emerge. These forms can vary substantially across (national) cultures. In that respect CSR can also be viewed as a constructive element of a global multi-level governance network in which different elements of social order are provided by regional, national, international and global coalitions including businesses and NGOs, governments and international institutions. To outline these differences is a rich and inspiring source for better understanding. Nothing more – but also nothing less – is the key objective of this book.

About This Book

The most substantial part of this book will provide a series of national overviews of the following countries: [1] Finland, [2] Denmark, [3] Norway, [4] United Kingdom, [5] Ireland, [6] Belgium, [7] The Netherlands, [8] France, [9] Germany, [10] Austria, [11] Hungary, [12] Czech Republic, [13] Poland, [14] Lithuania, [15] Estonia, [16] Russia, [17] Ukraine, [18] Serbia, [19] Turkey, [20] Greece, [21] Italy, [22] Spain, and finally [23] Portugal. Each of these national overviews is written by one – sometimes two or even three – authors living and working in that specific country. Most authors are related to – or working in academic institutions in their homeland. In order to provide a structured manuscript the various countries are grouped into geographical sections, which, however, are not to be understood as definite categories.

For each country a contribution will basically be structured around the following issues:

1. Traditional roles of the economy, state and society focussing in particular on expectations of the role of business in society;

2. Traditional drivers for CSR such as religion, tradition, core values, culture or history as well as an outlook of their future development;

3. A concise overview of the recent history of CSR for each individual country followed by political, societal and economic drivers leading to a sketch of future trends.

Each contribution draws its individual conclusions and indicates (literature) references. In many cases national websites referring to institutions or initiatives focusing on CSR are included in the individual contributions. The editors of this book cannot be held responsible for the reliability and validity of the provided contributions including the websites. This remains the full responsibility of the individual authors.

The various contributions were collected on the basis of a format covering the above issues discussed at a Conference held in Bavaria in early 2004. The authors met for several days to present developments in the field of CSR in their respective countries and discuss the endeavour of this book. But as the countries differ extremely from each other, diversity in the contributions presented will definitely remain. Furthermore, the authors come from different academic disciplines such as economics, theology, business ethics, sociology and management. During the discussions it became clear that what was common practice in one country was hardly applied in another. It is also good to mention that the meaning of words and of certain notions vary from country to country. Although the utmost care was taken in assembling this material, we are aware of the fact that websites in particular have a tendency to change rather frequently. We therefore hope that the indications provided are still accessible, but we cannot be held accountable when that is no longer the case.

The last section of the book will provide three cross-country analyses regarding a comparative or integrating view of CSR issues. In the epilogue an attempt is made to provide an outlook of CSR developments for the near future. We do hope that the information given on a national and European level will provide the readers with a rich source of information as well as ample material, references and contacts to help move the debate forward on various levels. It is one – and not the least important – goal of this book to provide a contribution to the further development of CSR across Europe.

Note

[1] Just to name a few: Corporate Governance, Socially Responsible Investment (SRI), Ethical Entrepreneurship, Eco efficiency, Stewardship, Business Ethics, Operational Ecology, Social Cohesion, etc.

References

Barber, B. R. 1995. *Jihad vs. McWorld: Terrorism's Challenge to Democracy*. USA: Random House.

Giddens, A. 1999. *Runaway World: How globalisation is reshaping our lives*. UK: Profile Books.

Ostrom, E. 1995. *Governing the Commons – The Evolution of Institutions for Collective Action.* USA: Cambridge University Press.

Scott, M. C. 2001. *Heartland: How to build companies as strong as countries.* UK: Wiley.

Northern Europe

FINLAND

1 The Strength of a High-Trust Society

Jouni Korhonen and Nina Seppala

Introduction

Finland has often been governed by a coalition of political parties representing both the left and the right of the political spectrum. Such a tendency and ability to build coalitions across what can elsewhere be viewed as major political divisions characterises the post-war Finnish society that has sought consensus and cooperation among different political, economic, and social actors for the purpose of balancing its relationship to the European Union and the Soviet Union – subsequently Russia – with a sustainable market-based economy.

In comparison to Anglo-Saxon countries, the role of government in Finland has been extensive rather than limited in directing the economy and maintaining a welfare system. Finland is a corporatist country in which consensus is sought through a mechanism that brings together the government, unions, employer's organisations, and the representatives of agricultural producers in connection with annual budget negotiations. Labour unions have been strong particularly in the metal and forestry industries and they have participated in the setting and implementation of public policy. The involvement of Finnish companies in social activities has taken the form of sponsorships and donations and focused on sports and culture (The Observatory of European SMEs, 2002: 22).

The Context: Attitudes Towards Business and Other Institutions in Society

Finnish society is characterised by a high degree of trust in institutions. The latest *Eurobarometer* (2003) demonstrates that the Finnish trust the political system, the media, and other institutions more than Europeans do on average (Table 1). For example, 74% of the Finnish tend to trust the national legal system compared to the European average of 51% or the Belgians of whom only 36% trust their legal system. Similarly, 59% of the Finnish trust their national government compared to the EU average of 37%.

Private sector institutions such as big companies and charitable organisations enjoy a lower level of trust than the media and the state institutions. This tendency is demonstrated by the fact that only 40% of the Finnish trust big companies whereas the police and the legal system enjoy levels of trust almost twice as high. Still, the level of trust in big companies is significantly higher than the European average of 29%. Charitable organisations are the only institutions that enjoy less trust in Finland than in the European countries on average. This anomaly follows a tendency that divides Europe into, on the one hand, mostly Northern European countries where the legal system is among the three institutions enjoying highest levels of trust together with the army and the police and, on the other hand, Southern European countries and the United Kingdom where charitable organisations enjoy a higher level of trust than the legal system (*Eurobarometer*, 2003).

In sum, there is a high degree of trust in Finland towards institutions in general. Companies are less trusted than state institutions, but they still enjoy a higher degree of trust in Finland than elsewhere in the European Union.

Table 1. Trust in institutions

Institution	Finland		EU 15	
	Tend to trust	Tend not to trust	Tend to trust	Tend not to trust
The press	59	36	47	46
Television	74	20	57	38
The government	59	32	37	53
The parliament	62	31	42	46
Political parties	24	65	16	75
The legal system	74	22	51	41
The police	89	9	67	28
Big companies	40	48	29	57
Voluntary organisations	52	37	59	29

Source: Eurobarometer (2003)

Expectations Regarding the Behaviour of Companies

Despite the relatively high level of trust in governmental and private sector institutions including companies, a gap exists between the behaviour of business organisations and the expectations of the Finnish public. The vast majority of the Finnish (75%) think that companies do not give enough consideration to social issues. In other European countries, only 48% of people believe the same[1].

A study on the Finnish attitudes to ethical trading revealed that two thirds of the respondents thought that there are ethical problems in business and trade[2]. The use of child labour was considered as the most serious ethical issue concerning the behaviour of Finnish companies abroad. Other ethical issues viewed important in connection to trade included human rights violations and the protection of the environment. These findings imply that the Finnish public is concerned about the behaviour of Finnish companies abroad, particularly in developing countries.

Yet, according to another study[3], CSR is seen as the employer's responsibility towards employees. In particular, health and safety issues together with job security and equal treatment are viewed as important areas of CSR. In line with these expectations of the public at large, 82% of Finnish CEOs consider responsibility towards employees as a very important area of CSR (Keskuskauppakamari, 2003). However, CEOs view responsibility for products and services as well as compliance with laws and norms as even more important than responsibility towards employees.

To sum up, it seems that the Finnish public is concerned about different issues regarding the behaviour of companies in foreign countries and at home. Regarding business operations abroad, the Finnish public is concerned about core labour standards and human rights issues, whereas the treatment of employees is seen as the key component of responsible business conduct in Finland. These concerns of the public have been met by the emergence of CSR.

As a named and defined phenomenon, corporate social responsibility is relatively new in Finland. In terms of its formal acknowledgement, adoption, and documentation, CSR has gained ground only during the very last few years. Yet, in comparison to other European countries, a high proportion of Finnish companies is involved in activities that can be viewed as CSR. For example, a study conducted in 2002 on small and medium-sized enterprises (SMEs) and social and environmental responsibility demonstrated that 82% of Finnish SMEs are involved in social activities in communities in which they are located in comparison to 49% of the SMEs in the European Union on average and 44% of the SMEs in Greece where SMEs are least active in social activities (The Observatory of European SMEs, 2002: 20). It therefore appears that there is a relatively high degree of CSR activity in Finland even though it has not been acknowledged or explicitly defined as such until recently.

Beliefs of the Top Management Motivate Companies to Engage in CSR

Finnish companies currently engage in CSR because of top management's interest in and beliefs about CSR. CSR is also a response to stakeholder expectations. In a survey of 269 Finnish CEOs conducted in November 2002 (Keskuskauppakamari,

2003), the interest of the top management and owners in CSR was considered as the most important motive for engaging in responsible corporate behaviour.

As can be seen in Table 2 below, this interest of the top management and owners in CSR appears to be upheld by beliefs about the benefits that responsible conduct is expected to produce: The majority of Finnish CEOs believe that responsible behaviour enhances corporate reputation and creates economic value in the long term. Further, perceived expectations of different stakeholder groups motivate Finnish companies to get involved in CSR. From among the various stakeholder groups, the expectations of customers were viewed as a very important motivator for engaging in CSR by 46% of the respondents. Moreover, the expectations of employees, business partners, and the financial community were considered as very important by more than 30% of the respondents. In contrast, only 7% of the CEOs viewed the expectations of non-governmental organisations as a very important driver for CSR in Finland. This may be explained by the fact that the public profile of advocacy organisations such as Amnesty has been relatively low compared to their profile in countries such as the United Kingdom. What is more, as will be seen later, trust in voluntary organisations is lower in Finland than in many other European countries.

The important role of stakeholder expectations in motivating companies to engage in CSR was corroborated by another study on Finnish SMEs according to which the main three reasons for carrying out social activities included enhanced customer loyalty, employees' satisfaction, and relations with business partners (The Observatory of European SMEs, 2002: 28).

In sum, it appears that, at present, the adoption of CSR is driven by the perception of the top management that CSR improves relations with key stakeholders and produces business benefits in the long term.

The current motives of companies to engage in responsible business conduct do not explain the emergence of CSR as a phenomenon. As noted before, CSR has appeared as a named and defined business concern only during the last few years. The Finnish Chamber of Commerce (Keskuskauppakamari, 2003: 1) suggested in a recent report on CSR that the interest in CSR has been driven by the principles of sustainable development on the one hand and the internationalisation of the Finnish economy on the other. In contrast to some other countries, even though at least one major Finnish company has encountered allegations similar to those experienced by Shell and BP regarding their operations in developing countries, corporate scandals have not been viewed as a driving force for CSR in Finland, although they may have sensitised individual companies to CSR. In what follows, we will discuss the emergence and development of CSR in Finland in the context of environmental management and the internationalisation of the economy which we believe are the two most important single influences that have contributed to the rise of awareness of CSR.

Table 2. Factors motivating companies to engage in CSR as reported by CEOs

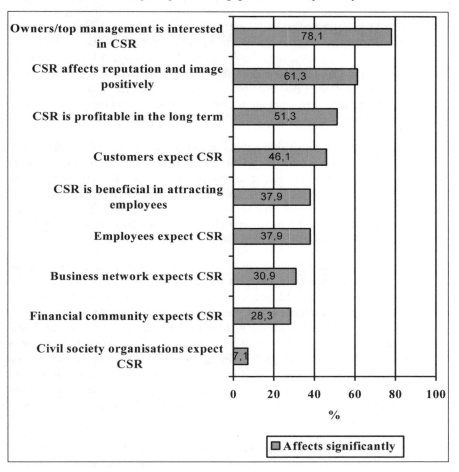

Source: Keskuskauppakamari (2003)

The Role of Environmental Management in the Emergence of CSR

Two thirds of the land area of Finland is covered by forests (Kauppi, Mielikäinen & Kuusela, 1992; Korhonen, Wihersaari & Savolainen, 2001) and one third by peatlands (Selin, 1999; Savolainen, Hillebrand, Nousiainen & Sinisalo, 1994; Lappalainen & Hänninen, 1993), that is, by renewable natural resources (in case of peat, this holds if integrated over all peat areas in Finland). The vast forestry and forest industry sectors have been and continue to be the cornerstone of the Finnish economy and exports. Finnish forest, pulp and paper products are sold and consumed worldwide. For example, approximately 90 % of the main product, paper, is exported, e.g. to Germany and Central Europe.

As Finland is a relatively cold country and paper production is an energy intensive area of industrial activity, the Finnish industrial structure is natural capital intensive both in terms of raw materials and energy and fuels used. Because of this natural capital intensive nature of industrial activity, Finnish companies have been exposed both to the international and domestic public eye of environmental awareness and scrutiny. Therefore, Finnish companies have had to pay attention to sustainable management of domestic natural resources and fuel sources as well as the waste and emission flows that are the obvious outcome of material and energy intensive activities.

The annual use rate of renewable natural resources in Finland is less than their annual growth. Finland is one of the three countries in the world together with Denmark and the Netherlands that have arranged their regional energy supply systems to a large extent into coproduction of heat and power (CHP), in which waste heat is utilised for industrial steam and for district heat in an eco-efficient manner. The EU average for CHP from national electricity generation is less than 10%, while this figure amounts up to 35% in Finland (Korhonen, 2001).

With these situational factors, the availability of resources on the one hand and the pressure to produce from raw materials and in an energy intensive way on the other, Finnish industry has achieved wide international recognition in its environmental and energy technologies and management. For example, approximately 70% of the fuels used in the national forest industry are derived from domestic wood waste and 94% of the fuels used are utilised in CHP (Korhonen, Wihersaari & Savolainen, 2001; Verkasalo, 1993). In the light of the coming EU legislation for emissions trading, the international climate negotiations and conventions, and the fact that 80% of the world's energy production relies on non-renewable fossil fuels, the Finnish experience in corporate environmental management and management of energy efficiency can be determined as significant.

The development of environmental management systems in Finnish industry has influenced the emergence and development of corporate social responsibility in general. Many companies have first conducted their environmental reviews, audits, environmental reports and gathered these under environmental management systems that nowadays take the familiar forms of the EU Eco-Management and Auditing Scheme (EMAS) or the International Standardisation Organisation's ISO 14001 standard. During the last few years, companies have been linking these environmental management systems to other dimensions of CSR. For example, Fortum, Finland's largest energy company, used to publish environmental reports, until it recently included information on its environmental policies and activities into its new Corporate Citizenship report.

The findings of a recent survey of Finnish CEOs show that environmental management is viewed as one of the six central elements of responsible business conduct in conjunction with issues such as responsibility for the products and services and compliance with laws and social norms (Keskuskauppakamari, 2003: 2). This finding illustrates the connection between the concepts of environmental responsibility and CSR in the minds of Finnish business leaders.

Above, we have discussed the evolution of corporate environmental management in Finland. It must be, however, noted that it is difficult to determine what triggered the adoption of environmental responsibilities by Finnish companies. We would like to argue that due to the cold climate, industrial structure induced energy demands, and the vast renewable natural resources, it has made economic sense for the industry in Finland to use domestic fuels and raw materials in a sustainable fashion and to develop energy-efficient and eco-efficient production technologies. Only during the last ten or twenty years have the firms "renamed" or "relabeled" the decades-old activities and production techniques as "environmental" and now eventually as part of the wider corporate social responsibility agenda.

In sum, CSR in Finland has had a strong focus on environmental and ecological issues due to the climate conditions and important role of the forestry and forest industry. It is only recently that Finnish companies influenced by international trends have begun developing policies and processes on the other aspects of CSR.

The Role of Government in Promoting CSR

The Finnish government has participated in the development of CSR policies as a member of international organisations, particularly the European Union and the OECD. It advocates these policies within the Finnish business community by, for example, encouraging Finnish companies to implement the OECD Guidelines for Multinational Enterprises and participating to cross-sector initiatives on CSR[4]. However, the government has emphasised that it views CSR as voluntary in nature (MONIKA, 2004: 7).

The main governmental forum for CSR is the Committee on International Investment and Multinational Enterprises (MONIKA) that was established within the Ministry of Trade and Industry to promote the OECD Guidelines for Multinational Enterprises. The Ministry plans to develop MONIKA into a multi-stakeholder body that advocates responsible business conduct particularly among small and medium-sized enterprises (MONIKA, 2004: 8).

Relations between the ministries, Finnish companies, and civil society have been mostly cooperative in the area of CSR. Non-governmental organisations have sought a dialogue with companies and the government. This dialogue is illustrated by the fact that the main associations in the area of CSR bring together organisations from the public and private sectors. For example, The Ethical Forum that was established in 2001 comprises a variety of organisations ranging from church organisations to labour unions. Similarly, the Finnish Business and Society association initially included the National Research and Development Centre for Welfare and Health as well as seven companies.

Future Trends

The role of the government has been central in providing free education, health services, and social security in Finland, whereas a good company has paid its taxes, complied with laws and regulations, and sponsored sports and culture. Society's expectations regarding the role of business and government appear now to be changing. The majority of Finnish respondents to a study on European attitudes towards corporate social responsibility conducted in 2000[5] was of the opinion that the role of companies in attending to social issues is increasing in relation to that of the government. Finnish companies do not seem prepared for these changing expectations. A survey on SMEs indicated that Finnish companies are likely to continue participating in social activities at their current level (The Observatory of European SMEs, 2002). According to the survey, 69% of the companies reported that they would "continue as it is". Moreover, 18% of the SMEs reported that they would decrease their participation in social activities, whereas only 9% claimed to increase their participation.

The discrepancy between society's expectations of a greater role of companies in addressing social issues and the plans of companies to continue their activities at their present level is unlikely to lead to confrontation. The Finnish are less likely to take action through consumer choice than people in other European countries. Only 24% of the Finnish consumers view themselves as ethical consumers[6]. Even when they do, they are involved in, for example, recycling and voluntary contributions to charities instead of altering their buying behaviour. Moreover, 69% believe that consumers have little influence on trade[7].

In turn, the situation with the environmental management themes of CSR is different. Because of the centrality of the environmental and energy questions in the international arena or in the EU, it can be expected that the Finnish industry will continue to increase its environmental activities exporting its technology and know-how around the world and attempting to further enhance its reputation and green image in the international scene. The ongoing discussion on the implementation of the Kyoto Protocol and the international climate conventions, the renewable fuel technologies and eco-efficient energy production methods will be important for the international community and Finnish industry. Environmental issues are increasingly the focus of investment also in academic and educational circles. Such developments create further domestic motivational factors for industry to develop and document its environmental practices.

In fact, our own experience indicates that there is a risk that the role of environmental management research and practical communities will become so powerful that due to normal academic fragmentation, it will become separate from the corporate social responsibility community. This is happening, although environmental issues have played a very influential role in the emergence of CSR in

Finland. We feel that the Finnish academic and practical environmental management and CSR communities should try to avoid this kind of a scenario of development in isolation from each other. In a small country and with such new topics as environmental and social questions of sustainable development, the different communities should cooperate.

The challenge for CSR in Finland, as a representative of the Ministry of Trade and Industry indicates (MONIKA, 2003: 13), is to link together initiatives and activities in areas that have until now been somewhat separate. For example, issues related to the rights of employees are attended to by different governmental bodies from, for example, trade issues. CSR requires the creation of linkages and cooperation across existing institutional boundaries.

Notes

[1] www.businessandsociety.net/uusi/tutkimukset +raportit, accessed 27.11.2003

[2] www.reilukauppa.fi/tiedote_tutkimus.html, accessed 27.11.2003

[3] www.businessandsociety.net/uusi/tutkimukset +raportit, accessed 27.11. 2003

[4] www.ktm.fi; www.eettinenfoorumi.org/foorumit_1_sasi.shtm, accessed 27.11.20031

[5] www.businessandsociety.net/uusi/tutkimukset +raportit, accessed 27.11.2003

[6] www.businessandsociety.net/uusi/tutkimukset +raportit, accessed 27.11.2003

[7] www.reilukauppa.fi/tiedote_tutkimus.html, accessed 27.11.2003

References

Eurobarometer. 2003. Public opinion in the European Union. Brussels: European Commission.

Kauppi, P. E., Mielikäinen, K., & Kuusela, K. 1992. Biomass and the carbon budget of the European forests. *Science,* 256: 70 – 74.

Keskuskauppakamari. 2003. *Yritysten yhteiskuntavastuu.* Helsinki: Keskuskauppakamari.

Korhonen, J. 2001. Co-Production of Heat and Power: An Anchor Tenant of a Regional Industrial Ecosystem. *Journal of Cleaner Production,* 9(6): 509 – 517.

Korhonen, J., Wihersaari, M., & Savolainen, I. 2001. Industrial Ecosystem in the Finnish Forest Industry: Using the material and energy flow model of a forest ecosystem in a forest industry system. *Ecological Economics,* 39(1): 145 – 161.

Lappalainen, E., & Hänninen, P. 1993. The Peat Reserves of Finland (in Finnish). Geological Survey of Finland, Espoo. Report of Investigation 117.

MONIKA. 2003. *Julkisen vallan haasteet vastuullisen yritystoiminnan edistamisessa. Seminaari yritysten yhteiskuntavastuun kehitysnakymista.* 2 April 2003. www.ktm.fi/monika, accessed 27.05.2004.

MONIKA. 2004. *Vastuullisen yritystoiminnan edistamista koskevat kauppa- ja teollisuusministerion linjaukset.* 11 February 2004. www.ktm.fi/monika, accessed 27.05.2004.

Savolainen, I., Hillebrand, K., Nousiainen, I., & Sinisalo, J. 1994. *Greenhouse Impacts of the Use of Peat and Wood for Energy.* VTT Espoo, Finland: Technical Research Centre of Finland.

Selin, P. 1999. Industrial use of peatlands and the re-use of cut-away areas in Finland. (originally in Finnish). *Jyväskylä studies in biological and environmental science,* 79.

The European Observatory of SMEs. 2002. *European SMEs and social and environmental responsibility.* Brussels: European Communities.

Verkasalo, E. 1993. Forest industry as a producer and consumer of wood-based energy in Finland. *Silva Fennica,* 26(2): 123 – 131.

2 Inclusive Labour Market Strategies

Mette Morsing

Introduction

Although issues of ethics and social responsibility have been on the agenda among Danish managers in private as well as in public organisations for a number of years, today these issues seem to appear with more urgency than before. While Danish companies since the 1980s have been exposed to strong environmental regulation, and as such have integrated environmental concerns into their business strategies for a number of years, many Danish managers also claim that ethics and social responsibility always have been an inherent way of doing business. Often the social initiatives were implemented in an informal and even implicit way as a response to current local expectations and demands. Lately the CSR discussions in Danish companies are engaging a new tone of international concern and calling for a systematic corporate commitment as Danish companies experience the consequences of globalisation.

This chapter will explore the societal and cultural drivers for the Danish perspective on CSR and in particular highlight the interplay between state and companies in "social partnerships" for setting the Danish national CSR agenda, which is the inclusive labour market. Finally, the future challenges for CSR in Denmark are discussed.

CSR in the Small Welfare State?

In Denmark, the notion of corporate social responsibility appears to raise modest expectations. In principle, incentives to engage in social initiatives seem low.

First, since the first comprehensive Danish social legislation in 1933[1], the state has been the main provider of social services. Denmark is a small country with 5 million people, a rather stable and homogeneous population and a long tradition of participatory democracy. Generally the Nordic welfare model (as compared to the Continental, Atlantic and Southern models) is characterised by the fact that citizens are granted extensive social rights (Berghmann, 1997). There is a strong emphasis on personal social services organised and financed by local authorities and transfer schemes financed and organised by the state. Local authorities are by tradition strong and relatively independent. They have the authority to spend local tax in ways they see fit, which provide them with a strong position as opposed to local authorities in other types of welfare models (Lund, 2003). In Denmark as in the rest of the Scandinavian countries, welfare expenditure is high. To accommodate these state responsibilities, citizens and companies are exposed to paying one of the world's highest taxes.

Second, many Danish company managers claim that acting socially responsible has always been an inherent part of the company culture. They say that their companies have since their establishment taken into consideration the implications of corporate actions in particular on local communities and other stakeholders, that may substantially affect or be affected by the operations of the business. The majority of Danish companies are small and medium-sized companies, and their embeddedness in local societies contributes to their interest in the "well-being" of those local societies. Let us take a few examples of Danish companies who take and show a social responsibility: the world's first ethical accounting statement appeared in 1989 in a collaboration between researchers at Copenhagen Business School and a Danish Bank, Sparekassen Nordjylland, as the bank's CEO decided not only to engage in dialogue with the local community about the company's social responsibilities but also to report on the outcomes of the dialogue in terms of social initiatives, because they found that "financial statements rarely provide a true or fair view of a company's real value", according to the CEO (Giversen, 2003). Novo Nordisk (www.novonordisk.com), the world's largest producer of insulin, is another Danish company with a strong reputation for having integrated CSR into its core business strategy. Novo Nordisk was way ahead of environmental legislation in the 1980s and is now taking the corporate lead on social responsibility. The company has won international prizes for its social initiatives and its sustainability reporting[2]. Green Network (www.greennetwork.dk) is a voluntary association of 275 public and private organisations in Jutland with the ambition to promote sustainability. Green Network held its 10th anniversary this year. Whether the Danish motive for being socially responsible is "the normative case" based on a founding father's belief that he wanted to "do good" for society and be perceived as a decent corporate citizen, or it is based on "the business case" in which management perceives a need to adapt to societal expectations in order to produce goods and develop a workplace in accordance with the local environment's expectations and demands, is not possible to decide. In fact, it is most likely a blend of the two motives (Smith, 2003). The point to make here is that many Danish managers perceive their companies as already rather socially responsible, and although one might object that this perception is based on managerial opinions rather than on facts and structures, the consequence is that these perceptions do not provide managers with an immediate incentive for further social engagements.

Third, "trust" is a key issue in current discussions on the drivers for CSR in international business[3]. In the light of extreme corporate financial power[4] and in the wake of corporate scandals, trust was a main issue at The World Economic Forum in Davos in 2003 and in 2004 – or rather the lack of trust in private companies. However, this scepticism and distrust does not seem to be the case in Denmark. Yet. Denmark has for a number of years been known to be one of the two least corrupt countries in the world according to Transparency International (Zadek, 2003), and according to research on national cultures, Denmark is a society characterised by a strong sense of egalitarianism and a low power distance (Hofstede, 1980, 1994), which in practice means that there is a perceived relatively small difference between "top" and "bottom" of the Danish organisational hierarchies. The relatively even distribution of income across professions contributes to the picture of an egalitarian society. According to a recent survey of the Downing Street Strategy Unit (Bibb & Kourdi, 2004: 11), the Danes are one of the most trusting people. In the survey people were asked: "Generally speaking, can others be trusted?" and the Scandinavians (Norway, Sweden and Denmark) were found to be the most trusting with nearly 70% saying that they trust others, compared to only 30% in the USA, Britain and France. Although a few corporate scandals have appeared in the Danish business environment, this does not seem to have developed a conspicuous corporate distrust among the Danes. The trust in managers may also be seen as a reflection of the managerial actions to avoid corporate scandals, for example a corporate governance guideline was initiated by a group of managers and the Copenhagen Stock Exchange in the wake of a Danish corporate scandal on Nordisk Fjer, and resulted in what is referred to as the Nørby Code (www.corporategovernance.dk)[5]. As such, the pressure to build trust is not perceived as impending among Danish companies. In fact, a recent comparative analysis by one of the weekly major Danish business magazines, shows that Danish managers are far more trusted than Swedish and US managers[6].

Alas, the Danish state with its participative democracy is relatively good at providing social services, Danish managers perceive themselves as already rather socially responsible, and there is no alarming distrust shown towards companies among the general public. So, why should Danish companies want to engage in further corporate social initiatives?

Government as the Driving Force for CSR

Recently the Danish welfare model has come under pressure. In the 1990s, the Danish state supported almost 25% of the able-bodied population. A large number of people found difficulties in maintaining a stable relation to the labour market, and this created social exclusion of those people who were unable to live up to normal workforce standards, e.g. handicapped, elderly, ethnic minorities and socially marginalised people. This meant a major increase in public expenditure and created an unsustainable pressure on the welfare system. In 1995, the Danish minister of social affairs, Karen Jespersen, in the then social-democratic government, was the first to call for corporate assistance in meeting the challenge, and for constructing a Danish agenda for CSR in what she referred to as "the inclusive labour market strategy". The ideal was social cohesion, and the means were to mobilise private companies and social partners in "social partnerships" to address the problems of unemployment and social exclusion. A comprehensive campaign labelled "It concerns us all" was initiated by the social minister in 1994, which tied together labour market and social issues and encouraged partners in the private as well as the public sector to join forces.

Although many Danish company managers will claim that their CSR initiatives concern many other issues, the inclusive labour market strategy is nevertheless still the predominant CSR issue on the Danish agenda. While the then social-democratic government set the agenda around 10 years ago to encourage private companies to engage, state institutions and trade unions have taken up the agenda simultaneously and enlarged it to comprehend also public organisations. Further, a recent study of the two largest business-oriented Danish newspapers' coverage of CSR issues during the last 9 years, shows the dominance of the inclusive labour market in the public discourse: 28% of all articles on CSR were concerned with the inclusive labour market, while the rest of the articles were scattered on various CSR issues[7].

State and Companies in Partnerships: The Inclusive Labour Market Strategy

One outstanding Danish company inspired Karen Jespersen initially. Grundfos (www.grundfos.com) is a major producer of hydraulic pumps and the company had for a number of years shown how a company can contribute to solving societal problems whilst serving its own agenda. Grundfos has established a number of special workshops for people with reduced capacity that serve to integrate minorities from the local community into the workplace, whilst contributing to the maintenance of a flexible workforce, and the minister realised that in order to rectify social exclusion, employers had to understand not only their moral obligation but also their advantages in creating special working conditions for this group of people. For a company like Grundfos, a flexible workforce is important in the prospective of a future labour shortage and for Grundfos there is a profound interest in integrating a larger number of people in the workforce. For Karen Jespersen it was vital for the inclusive labour market strategy, that it was more than an expression of corporate philanthropy: "the companies had to show more than the desire to do good. It was not merely a question of asking companies to do more but of finding ways in which the political system and the companies might finding ways in which the political system and the companies might join forces in addressing fundamental societal problems. Hence, the point was to build dialogue and cooperation between the political system, the companies and the local authorities. Partnerships were the essence" (Thyssen, 2003).

"It concerns us all" became the starting point of the Danish government's campaign on corporate social responsibility, in which social partnerships between private companies and state institutions are central. While the campaign encouraged and attempted to motivate companies to see themselves as part of the larger society, there was also a strong concern that the campaign would not meet its goals without the participation and commitment of companies. The campaign could not survive as a political vision, and the concrete formation of a National Network of Company Leaders became a central element in a functional and symbolic sense. The National Network consisted of company leaders from 16 of some of the most admired Danish companies (www.netvaerksprisen.dk). The purpose of the Network is to "contribute to the current debate about corporate social responsibility – to function as an advisory body to the Minister and to help inspire companies to take independent initiatives promoting social welfare among employees as well as in the local community. The primary goal of the National Network is to help limit social exclusion and increase the integration in the labour market"[8]. While the Network started a series of systematic and inspiring dialogues between private companies and public institutions, the Network also carried the message of positive will to help enhance the national social inclusion from some of the most admired managers in some of the most admired Danish companies, i.e. managers and companies known to be setting the agenda in many other areas also.

Nevertheless, the campaign met resistance and scepticism from the Danish Employers' Confederation (Dansk Arbejdsgiverforening) as well as from the largest employers' organisation, the Confederation of Danish Industries (Dansk Industri). They were concerned that the campaign was the first move towards regulation on CSR – a notion they were – and are – against. However, from the beginning it was clear that the main idea was that company commitment must be based on voluntary initiatives and efforts. The ministry, the Network and the companies emphasised this again and again. Experiences with regulation on CSR from other countries – and even from environmental regulation in Denmark – had shown how companies in many instances would pay their way out. This inhibits corporate reflections on the concurrent development of CSR issues and might even encourage a stop in the continuous re-assessment of changing CSR issues, agendas and contexts. The Danish social minister had higher ambitions. "Social involvement has many different faces", she said and the overall vision was a long term shift in the attitude towards new forms of interaction between state and private companies rather than short term results or regulations, and to redefine social policies as an investment rather than an expense to society or a regulation of social behaviour.

"Soft Law"

Although regulation never was the Danish state's agenda on CSR, administrative systems and frameworks have been developed as a kind of "soft law" for companies and social partners, which they themselves can interpret and set into practice according to the local context. I shall emphasize two initiatives: the *"social coordination committees"* and the recent framework agreement *"the social chapter"*.

In 1998 the social coordination committees became mandatory for all 269 Danish local authorities. It was the first – and so far only – "soft law" on CSR in Denmark, as the committees were included in the new social legislation. A social coordination committee is a forum of representatives from the Danish Employers' Confederation (Dansk Arbejdsgiverforening), the Confederation of Danish Trade Unions (LO), the Public Employment Agency (FOA) and other relevant organisations. The role of the local authorities in collaboration with the social partners and private companies is to map the status of unemployment and social exclusion in the local authority and to develop a strategy of how to integrate those socially excluded people into the workforce in private companies. The committees function as an institutionalised framework for the development of partnerships with a minimum of regulation: the committees function as a role model, they must be established, but how the individual committee decides to live up to the broadly defined role is up to the individual local agreement. As an indication of the willingness among Danish local authorities to support the campaign, it is interesting to note that 60 of Denmark's 269 local authorities had established these social coordination committees before it became mandatory in 1998.

In 1999, updated and reinforced in 2004, "the social chapter" (www.personaleweb.dk/rum-for-alle) was launched by the National Association of Municipalities (Kommunernes Landsforening), the National Association of Counties (Amtsrådsforeningen), the Trade Union for Public Servants (KTO) and Copenhagen and Frederiksberg Municipalities, who formed a "framework agreement" to encourage all Danish local authorities to participate themselves in employing socially excluded people. This was an enlargement of the inclusive labour market strategy as it encouraged local authorities not only to engage in social partnerships, but also themselves to employ people who cannot enter the workforce under normal conditions. The strategy is called "the social chapter" which refers to the agenda of prevention, retention and integration in the workplace. The social chapter is first and foremost a signal that the central labour market partners agree that not only private companies but also local authorities shall contribute in taking a social responsibility in terms of the inclusive labour market strategy. The social chapter is, like the social coordination committees, articulated in broad terms, leaving it up to individual authorities to develop a strategy that fits the individual local context. It is a framework agreement, and as such it may be referred to as the "softest of soft laws". Nevertheless, the current national campaign to promote the social chapter has already gained much interest.

Contributing to Setting the European Agenda

Although the initiative by the Danish government was primarily meant to serve the local Danish context, it was also envisioned to be involved in the promotion and development of social partnerships in a European context. Since the UN's World Summit for Social Development in 1995, which was held in Copenhagen, the issue of social integration and unemployment has been a priority not only on the Danish but also on the European agenda. The Social Summit was the largest gathering ever of world leaders at that time, and it emphasised the conquest of poverty, the goal of full employment and the development of social integration as primary objectives for future development. Two years later, in 1997, The Copenhagen Centre was founded by the Social Ministry to establish a knowledge centre on social partnerships in Denmark with the purpose of supporting and continuing international cooperation and dialogue at both company and state levels. The Copenhagen Centre was a symbolic demarcation that the Danish government intended to take a lead role in the promotion and discussion of social partnerships to meet the challenge on social exclusion not only on a Danish scale but also on a European scale, as it was set out by the European Commission on the present and future role of social partnerships across Europe[9].

The Future Challenges for the Inclusive Labour Market Strategy

Although social policy set off the agenda in the mid-1990s, there was from the outset an acknowledgement that social policy alone was unable to meet the challenges of social exclusion. To meet the social challenges, support is needed from labour market relations, educational policies, health system policies, etc. Ideally, all areas of society and across traditional divisions should be included in the action – e.g. politically divided sectors, private and public sectors and various social partners and organisations. While labour market policies in Denmark are already closely related to social and educational policies (continuous education, re-schooling, etc.), and as such create a good background for successful implementation of the inclusive labour market strategy, there are a number of fundamental difficulties, which challenge the successful outcome.

While cross-sectoral partnerships sound attractive and even necessary, they may prove troublesome entities to enact in practice. Interests, means and goals may conflict across sectors and negotiations may be tiresome and tough. Also the very integration of minorities in the workplace undoubtedly disturbs any streamlined, modern Danish organisation and slows down work processes and routines, as integration of people who do not fit the norm inherently means going beyond exiting norms. Even if the long-term goals and outcomes are favourable for the companies as well as for the social partners, certain sacrifices will be necessary in the short term. Further, the local authority bureaucracy has at times been reported as rather inflexible, which of course inhibits the process. In sum, changing practices and mindsets within a thoroughly regulated system like the Danish welfare system poses a formidable challenge since partnerships in essence have to be built on flexibility and a willingness to find new ways to solve existing problems.

While the Danish campaign on the inclusive labour market strategy is character-ised as a success, having had a large impact on social and labour market strategies in society at large and in changing the notion of social responsibility from a pe-ripheral to a mainstream issue discussed at all levels in society, the initial prob-lems which set off the campaign continue to challenge the welfare society. The number of people provided for by the Danish government is still growing. There is a widening gap between strong and weak in society, and new challenges have been posed by a growing immigration rate over the past decades.

Conspicuous Danish Institutions in Support of CSR

The Copenhagen Centre is the most conspicuous initiative from the Danish gov-ernment to support issues of CSR. Other state-supported initiatives have been taken such as The Social Index, which was initiated by the Ministry of Social Af-fairs as an instrument to support Danish companies on implementing CSR in the organisation, and The Danish Database on Corporate Ethics (Etikbasen) is an ini-tiative by the Ministry of Economics to support the debate on consumers and eth-ics. However, the new liberal-conservative government (since 2002) has not con-spicuously supported these initiatives. On the contrary, some would say. However, this year the Danish Foreign Ministry has engaged in a programme to support the United Nations Millennium Development Goals from 2000 (www.undp.dk/busi-ness). This programme "Partnering for Development" aims to establish partner-ships between the United Nations Development Programme and Danish compa-nies in their international activities. So far, three companies, SAS, Danfoss, and Aarhus United, have engaged in such partnerships. This new initiative supported by the Foreign Ministry builds on the same idea of partnerships as the initiative by the Social Ministry in the 1990s. While the Social Ministry emphasised local part-nerships across sectors, the Foreign Ministry enlarges the agenda to include inter-national partnerships across national borders.

Only very recently have the trade unions and the employers unions engaged in the debate – some would say in a non-conspicuous way. Although Danish trade un-ions have discussed the implications of CSR for their members for some years, it has not been in a pro-active mode. However, this year's annual meeting of the largest trade union, LO (Lands Organisationen), features for the first time CSR as the main issue. Also, the largest employers' organisation, the Confederation of Danish Industries (Dansk Industri), has after many years of reluctance, recently engaged in an attempt to understand the challenges of CSR to pro-actively support their member companies, which are predominantly small and medium-sized com-panies (SMEs). As such, their current approach concerns the supply-chain angle.

They also recently hosted the "Partnering for Development" initiative, which was an important symbolic statement of their support.

Simultaneously a large number of formal and informal networks have emerged in Denmark within the last 5 – 10 years with the purpose of exploring and understanding CSR and the implications for business, state and institutions. Two characteristics stand out in the formalised networks: first, the notion of partnership is vital in the networks, as they in practice embrace a broad participation from public and private organisations as well as NGOs. Second, the formal networks are initiated by NGOs or independent institutions – not companies. In Denmark there is a strong collaborative spirit amongst NGOs which for example is indicated by the establishment in 1992 of the 92-Group, which is 20 NGOs working together to promote sustainable development. It is not possible to mention all Danish networks here, but I will highlight a few of those organisations, that have managed most conspicuously to contribute to enlarge the agenda in Denmark from being a focus on the inclusive labour market strategy to also embrace other important issues of importance to the social agenda.

I have already mentioned the National Network, The Copenhagen Centre and Green Network. A few other examples are: Amnesty Business Club in Denmark, which is one of Amnesty International's national attempts to engage in a systematic partnership with private companies. 14 Danish companies participate on a frequent basis and debate human rights, and how companies may contribute to human rights. The Danish Institute for Human Rights is an independent national human rights institution with the objective to gather and develop knowledge about human rights through research, information, education and documentation relating to Danish, European and international human rights conditions. The Nordic Partnership Programme, which is an NGO initiative by WWF and embraces 16 large Nordic Companies, aims to inspire and catalyse action from governments, businesses and consumers towards sustainable production and consumption in the Nordic Region. Øresund Environment Academy is an independent organisation, which has enlarged its environmental agenda to embrace social issues. Øresund Environment Academy has the ambition to promote dissemination, innovation and commercialisation of sustainable knowledge and resources across the Swedish and Danish borders in the Øresund region. Please, see the note for website references to these organisations (www.amnesty.dk, www.humanrightsinstitute.org, www. nordicpartnership.org, www.oresund-environment.org).

Cultural Drivers and Future Challenges for CSR in Denmark

In spite of the modest expectations towards CSR in the context of the Danish welfare society, CSR debates are in practice fairly extensive in Denmark. Rather than religious or ethical heritage as argument for the high awareness and action on CSR in Denmark, I shall point to the Danish participative democracy with the state as main provider of social services, managers' openness to social initiatives and the high degree of trust characterising the Danish society as possible arguments. Precisely those same characteristics that were suggested to make CSR superfluous in the beginning of this chapter, can also be argued as excellent points of departure for further CSR engagement. Danish society seems to provide some of those cultural traits that can drive a CSR agenda forward: a general competence for dialogue and negotiation, a willingness to engage and a broad sense of trust are cultural traits sought for in the quest for increasing sensitivity towards a variety of stakeholders. The implementation of numerous partnerships across sectors and institutions is also a reflection of these traits. Theories of stakeholder relations have convincingly argued that the challenge of strategic management is about ethics and the need to create a satisfactory balance of interests among the diverse stakeholders, who contribute to or are affected by the organisation's actions (Freeman & Gilbert, 1988). It takes democratic discipline and communication skills to create a satisfactory balance between diverse interests. If corporate social responsibility is about increasing sensitivity towards stakeholders, Danish managers seem to have a good point of departure.

This does not mean that there are no challenges ahead. CSR is a moving target – also in Denmark. What was considered "good corporate behaviour" five years ago, may no longer be acceptable today. Companies need to perpetually maintain and develop their "sensory organs" towards stakeholder expectations. Although the inclusive labour market strategy still dominates the public discourse on CSR, the larger global issues on CSR are entering the Danish debate and raise the level of complexity.

One of the overall great CSR challenges in a Danish perspective seems to be the ability by private and public managers in collaboration with NGOs to pro-actively explore, integrate and manage the much broader issues of CSR, which encompass global questions on human rights, child labour, labour rights, terrorism. While many Danish companies already have encountered these global challenges, many more companies will undoubtedly have to correspond to them soon. I shall point to two issues, which currently seem to raise awareness among Danish business managers: first, CSR in the supply-chain, and second, strategic CSR communication.

A recent survey by the Confederation of Danish Industries and Oxford Research (2004) points to the supply-chain argument as the major driver of CSR for Danish companies. Although it is a major concern for many Danish companies to prove their social responsibility to large B2B customers, it is not yet an issue in the Danish public debate. The predominant part of Danish industries consists of SMEs, and a large percentage of them serves in the value chain as suppliers to larger international companies. These larger international companies are pressured from NGOs, politicians, the media and other critical associations to prove a record of social responsibility that can be traced back to their choice of suppliers: how do suppliers treat their animals in the labs? or their employees in the sweatshops? and has the supplier previously employed children as labour?, etc. Whether he likes it or not, the Danish SME manager is increasingly being exposed to the pressure from large international companies, which will force him to take action on a variety of CSR issues. According to the above-mentioned recent survey, Danish companies expect that these B2B customers' demands in terms of ethics and human rights will increase by about 70 % over the next five years (Confederation of Danish Industries & Oxford Research, 2004: 9).

While the Danish SME manager may already fulfil some or perhaps even most of the CSR initiatives required by B2B customers, he now additionally has to report on them. The strategic communication on CSR initiatives seems to be another challenge for Danish managers: how to communicate their existing and future CSR initiatives to a variety of stakeholders. While Denmark is one of the few countries in the world with mandatory requirements for environmental reporting (Olsen, 2003) and a country which has proven a broad experimentation with different forms of alternative reporting ethical, social, holistic, sustainable, etc. during the last 15 years since the first ethical accounting statement in 1989, there is still much hesitation among managers on whether and how to communicate corporate social initiatives to a large and international audience. However, there is also indication that some Danish companies after having reported on environmental initiatives for a number of years, are fit for the CSR communication challenge: the winners of the 2003 European Sustainability Reporting Awards[10] were two Danish companies: Aalborg Portland and Novo Nordisk.

Notes

[1] Former Minister of Social Affairs (1929–35), Karl Kristian Steinke implemented the comprehensive Social Reform of 1933, concerning social security for all Danish citizens.

[2] For example in 2002, Novo Nordisk's Sustainability Report was placed as the world's second best report on soft values by United Nations Environmental Programme (after Royal Dutch Shell Group).

[3] See for example Gallup International and Environics International (2002). Survey of *"Which institutions to be trusted to work for the best of society"*, in which large private and international companies are number 11 and 12 after the armed forces (= most trusted!), NGOs, United Nations, governments, religious institutions, and others. The high level of distrust and scepticism towards companies is seen to be that conspicuous in Denmark.

[4] Of the largest economies in the world, 51 are corporations; only 49 are countries, www.globalpolicy.org/socecon/tncs/countries.htm

[5] The Copenhagen Stock Exchange has since 2002 published a set of guidelines for good corporate governance, formulated by a group of Danish CEO managers.

[6] Berlingske Nyhedsmagasin, June 2004.

[7] Mette Morsing & Jonas Tue Burkhall, Research project on *"The Discourse in the Danish Business Press – a study of 9 years of reasons, themes and players"*, 2004.

[8] In 1996, the founding corporate members of the National Network were the CEOs of: Oticon, Carlsberg, Pressalit, Horsens Gummivarefabrik, Grundfos, Novo Nordisk, Ruko, DSB, Jamo, Post Danmark, Sparekassen Nordylland, Danfoss, Neckelmann, Erik Mainz, Lego and Falck. Today, the National Network has twelve members. Moreover, there is a number of Regional Networks that work locally across the country. Every year, the National Network awards a prize to a company that has made a special contribution within the field of corporate social responsibility.

[9] From its foundation in 1997 until 2003, the Copenhagen Centre worked to support an international exchange of experience in the field of social partnerships, publishing reports and organising conferences, seminars, and various international networks.

[10] The European Sustainability Reporting Awards is formed by 15 countries' accounting associations, for more information, please consult Mr Flemming Tost, ft@hlrevision.dk.

References

Berghmann, J. 1997. Can the Idea of Benchmarking be Applied to Social Protection? *Bulletin Luxembourgeois des Questions Sociales*, 4: 119–130.

Bibb, S., & Kourdi, J. 2004. *Trust Matters. For Organisational and Personal Success.* Hampshire, UK: Palgrave Macmillan.

Confederation of Danish Industries & Oxford Research. 2004. *Report: Ethics, Environment and Social Relations in the Supply-chain.* Copenhagen.

Freeman, R. E., & Gilbert, D. R. Jr. 1988. *Corporate Strategy and the Search for Ethics.* New Jersey: Prentice Hall.

Gallup International and Environics International. 2002. Survey *Which institutions to be trusted to work for the best of society.* http://www.weforum.org/pdf/AM_2003/ Survey.pdf, accessed 05.08.2004.

Giversen, J. 2003. The World's First Accounting Statement. In: M. Morsing, & C. Thyssen (Eds.), *The Case of Denmark – Corporate Values and Social Responsibility*: 36. Frederiksberg: Samfundslitteratur.

Hofstede, G. 1980. *Cultural Consequences.* London: Sage.

Hofstede, G. 1994. *Cultures and Organizations. Software of the Mind.* London: HarperCollins.

Lund, J. E. 2003. Partnerships in Practice. In: M. Morsing, & C. Thyssen (Eds.), *The Case of Denmark – Corporate Values and Social Responsibility*: 179–191. Frederiksberg: Samfundslitteratur.

Morsing, M., & Thyssen, C. (Eds.) 2003. *The Case of Denmark – Corporate Values and Social Responsibility*. Frederiksberg: Samfundslitteratur.

Olsen, L. 2003. Corporate Accountability – the Case of Denmark. In: M. Morsing, & C. Thyssen (Eds.), *The Case of Denmark – Corporate Values and Social Responsibility*: 229 – 239. Frederiksberg: Samfundslitteratur.

Smith, C. 2003 Corporate Social Responsibility. From Whether to How. *California Management Review*, (45)4.

Thyssen, C. 2003. Social Partnerships – The Role of Government in Denmark, based on an interview with Karen Jespersen. In: M. Morsing, & C. Thyssen (Eds.), *The Case of Denmark – Corporate Values and Social Responsibility*: 27. Frederiksberg: Samfundslitteratur.

Zadek, S. 2003. A Foreigner's View on The Case of Denmark. In: M. Morsing, & C. Thyssen (Eds.), *The Case of Denmark – Corporate Values and Social Responsibility*: 61 – 67. Frederiksberg: Samfundslitteratur.

3 Voluntary Partnerships as a Social Asset

Jan-Olaf Willums

Cultural Drivers and Expectation from Society

What is Norwegian society's attitude towards business and its social role, and what are the cultural drivers of CSR in Norway? This paper aims at exploring these two questions, and wants to draw some comparison with other European countries

Yale University and the World Economic Forum's annual Environmental Sustainability Index have repeatedly placed the Scandinavian countries at the forefront, and Norway tops the European list of CSR implementation in small-and medium-sized enterprises (CSR Europe, 2004). The Norwegian Government was a pioneer in acquiring carbon offsets (from Costa Rica), and together with Denmark was among the first to try out carbon emission trading systems. Norway was also the first country to insist on female quotas for company boards. And the term "compact" was already being used for partnerships between the Norwegian government and its main industry players well before the launch of the UN Global Compact.

CSR may thus appear to be firmly on the agenda both in the business community and in the field of public policy. There is, however, a multitude of various concepts related to CSR in use – and definitions on *corporate responsibility, social accountability, sustainability, corporate accountability*, to name but a few, abound. According to DNV, the Norway-based international certification entity, the Norwegian understanding is that *corporate responsibility* denotes a company's total responsibility to ensure both financially, socially and environmentally sound operations. *Sustainability* refers thus in Norway more to the environmental concerns and obligations corporations hold, whereas *social accountability* focuses more on the social element in a corporation's responsibility. *Corporate social responsibility* is the most frequently used term and is also focused on the social elements of a corporation's responsibility (Wieland, 2003).

The Roots of CSR

The social democratic tradition in Norway has clearly played a role in making the term "Stakeholder Dialogue" an easily understandable concept in Norwegian industry. Corporate Responsibility is regarded part of the political and social tradition. Authority is seen as something to continuously question and engage with. Since the industrial revolution trade unions have had a strong position: dialogue between employers, workers and government law-makers is part of the industrial tradition. It creates a "dynamic environment where problems can be raised, discussed and dealt with" (McCallin & Webb, 2004).

This tradition of dialogue contributed to the more transparent communication within society, and the negotiating framework between labour unions and employers explains the public opinion that corporations must play a double role: that of a provider of employment and that of a powerful entity in the economic and political life.

Long periods of labour government and the collective bargaining culture are major influences on Norway's present business structure and its approach to CSR.

The Norwegian Confederation of Business and Industry (NHO) underlines that "Economic measures can be motivational, but such initiatives must be carefully targeted to avoid unintentional and/or undesirable effects. Regulation and control mechanisms are therefore required to prevent dangerous and unacceptable conduct, and to ensure predictable general business conditions that promote innovation and wealth creation" (NHO, 2003).

On the other hand, both the government and industry in Norway agree that the use of legislation and regulations alone is not appropriate for promoting continuous improvement since it is hard to predict which solutions will be the most effective.

Interestingly, small and medium-sized companies in Norway rank highly when it comes to social responsibility, according to the European Commission's recent research on the topic. An estimated 95% of all Norwegian SMEs with between 50 to 249 employees are involved in social activities, making Norwegian SMEs of this size the most socially responsible in Europe (CSR Europe, 2004).

This may be somewhat misleading, as it is now mandatory to include a simple environmental report in enterprises' annual reports. But more enterprises are also using their ordinary annual reports to report on corporate social responsibility, ethics, their involvement in their local communities and matters that affect their activities abroad.

A survey of Norwegian top managers (Argument, 2003) showed that 42% had never or barely heard of CSR or knew what the concept stands for. This is a fairly high number considering that the governmental and NHO initiative, Kompakt, has been active since 1998. So how does that fit in with the fact that Norwegian companies rate above average on surveys listing the number of companies publishing other than financial reports?

Norway has a long-standing tradition of global commitments. Whether through its superior levels of development aid or facilitating peace processes in areas of conflict, Norway has worked to further sustainable development and international stability, which by Norwegian corporations is seen as a business advantage:

Human Rights have therefore been a major topic of CSR in Norway: In 1997, the Confederation of Norwegian Business and Industry launched its human rights checklist for Norwegian businesses operating in the South. The checklist, which was prepared in cooperation with Amnesty International, provides Norwegian companies with a guide to the rights that are guaranteed by the various international rights conventions that Norway has committed to. Since half of Norway's GDP comes out of international trade, Norwegian businesses have had a long history of working overseas, and often in countries where human rights violations are a concern.

In 1998, the Ministry of Foreign Affairs launched a discussion forum called Kompakt (The Consultative Body for Human Rights and Norwegian Economic Involvement Abroad), which also has produced a number of reports and guidelines for corporations. It is said to have been one reference to the Global Compact at the UN. Its task is to look further into the role of business in promoting human rights overseas. Members of this body are representatives from the business sector, trade unions, NGOs, the research community as well as government officials.

In the field of *Ethical Trade*, the Norwegian NGOs have also played a central role since the very early discussions about CSR. One group of NGOs working under the umbrella organisation, ForUM, have launched a set of human rights and environmental guidelines for Norwegian businesses working overseas. The guidelines are seen as a set of minimum standards based on the oft-cited (UN conventions on human rights and labour rights. These minimum standards are to be upheld by all businesses regardless of where they are operating.

Workforce Diversity: Compared to other countries, the Norwegian CSR history has also engaged much debate abound diversity of the work force, i.e. having a labour force consisting of individuals from different walks of life and with different capabilities. Diversity in working life is made up of individual differences, e.g. geographic location and education, in addition to factors over which individuals have no control, e.g. gender, age, racial/ethnic background, sexual orientation and mental or physical attributes.

Employers in the private and public sectors alike have been alerted to how diversity can be achieved through good procedures for recruitment, career planning and human resources development. In Norway, the public and private sectors face special challenges related to the recruitment of employees from non-Western backgrounds and the recruitment of women to executive positions and directorships.

A sponsorship scheme for immigrants: NHO co-operates with HSH (the Federation of Norwegian Commercial and Service Enterprises), LO (The Norwegian

Confederation of Trade Unions) and Aetat on a sponsorship scheme for immigrants. This involves the labour market authorities subsidising the wages of job-seekers with immigrant backgrounds. The employer undertakes to sponsor the employee by providing training and an introduction to Norwegian working life.

Through the programme "Women in Industry", NHO aspires to get more women into business and industry in general, and to augment the number of women in executive positions in particular. The organisation aims at encouraging the recruitment of a higher percentage of women at all levels of business and industry, also to directorships. To that end, NHO has drawn up a ten-point list containing practical advice for nominating committees and corporate boards.

Are There Historic Reasons for Norway's CSR Profile?

Today's cultural drivers in CSR can trace their roots back to two traditions: the part-privatisation of the social democratic welfare state, and an older tradition of socially responsible business tycoons. The most well-known examples of the latter are Throne Holst, founder of the chocolate group Freia-Marabou, and Tandberg, the early pioneer of radio and electronics. Both companies exist today – although in partly reinvented forms, but the tradition of the "concerned and responsible corporate family" remains.

This social responsibility of family-owned companies has been far more important than any religious drivers or family traditions that can be found in other countries.

CSR started in its original form at the beginning of this century, where important "start-ups" like Norsk Hydro built and ran entire local societies in remote mountain areas of Norway (where hydropower was available for fertiliser production). The company took over the full responsibility for all aspects of social life. At the same time, these companies were given more and more assignments, and became extremely important cornerstones of the local society. When many of these cornerstone enterprises had to close down and production was moved to low-cost producers abroad, the social fabric was strained.

In such situations, an enterprise's relations with its local community are often put to the test in connection with the question of reorganising or perhaps even closing down activities. As in other countries, retrenching justifies cost-cutting measures, downsizing and sometimes even the winding up of activities. This affects the local communities in question, but the impact may be substantially stronger in Norway than in most other European countries: Certain industrial locations may be completely dependent on one or two cornerstone industries, established because of easy access to hydropower or minerals. When such industrial activities are closed down or move abroad, there is often no other industry that can move into these often isolated industrial sites. The larger Norwegian enterprises have developed a tradition to explore alternatives, normally with broad participation on the part of employees as well as the local authorities and other stakeholders.

One interesting case is the closing down of Norsk Hydro's aluminium production in Northern Norway and later also in Southern Norway: In both cases the activity was largely replaced by the large-scale production of solar wafers for the future-oriented solar energy industry – giving a young Norwegian start-up company, Scanwafer, the opportunity to become the world's largest producer of solar wafers within 8 years of establishing its first factory (Willums, 2004).

There are other good examples of reorganisation processes in the wake of company closures that have led to flourishing economic development and made local communities at least as viable as previously, e.g. Kongsberg and Mo i Rana.

NHO has had a special advisory committee on ethics since 1992. As from 2000, the committee's mandate also includes efforts related to corporate social responsibility. The objective of the ethics-related efforts has been to raise ethical awareness and enhance expertise in business and industry. NHO has published a collection of case studies that shows how individual enterprises approach ethics and values, as well as a series of articles entitled "Business and Ethics". A tool has been developed for measuring and reporting how enterprises follow up their ethical values (VerdiRegnskap – ValueAccounting), and recently special guidelines were set up regarding the remuneration of business executives.

Walk the Talk: Reporting CSR in Norway

In Europe, the number of CSR or triple-bottom-line or sustainability reports shows that such reporting is gaining supporters. A number of surveys also indicates that the trend of triple-bottom-line reporting will continue in the years to come. In addition, many governments are introducing regulations and laws requiring corporations to report on their environmental and social impacts.

In Norway triple-bottom-line reporting is still uncommon and according to DNV (Munkelien & Gravlien, 2003), there are only few CSR reports. The Norwegian authorities have neither supported nor advocated triple-bottom-line reporting to any extent. Norwegian law makes it mandatory for corporations to include in their annual report issues relating to health and safety. Therefore Norwegian corporations also come out on top, only exceeded by the UK, in surveys looking at social/non-financial issues in annual reports. 81% of the Norwegian annual reports include health and safety issues, but only 29% publish separate reports (KMPG, 2002).

The Norwegian Accounting Act also requires a corporation to include in its annual report its environmental impact when this impact becomes "more than insignificant". Only 35% of the top 100 corporations, were actually fulfilling the requirements of this law in 2001 (Ruud & Larsen, 2002), the loophole being the wording "more than insignificant". The same survey was conducted in 2002, and the findings showed a decrease to 30% of the corporations (surveyed) satisfying the requirement of the Accounting Act (Ruud & Larsen, 2003). There are no requirements as to separate reports, or to include social impact outside health and safety records.

In February 2003 the Norwegian Parliament voted in majority for a new law on "the right to environmental information". The law will make it mandatory for all corporations but also all public offices to provide information on certain environmental issues that can lead to "not insignificant" effects on the environment, including foreign distribution or production, and the products being sold.

Of the 100 largest Norwegian companies, 29% issued separate non-financial (environmental (health and safety), social or sustainability) reports in 2002. At 28% this is only 1% above the average of the 11 countries surveyed (KPMG, 2002). Norway is number 7, ranging after Japan, UK, USA, The Netherlands, Germany and Finland.

Present Status and Future Developments

A recent study by the Norwegian School of Management compared the 50 largest Norwegian corporations to international counterparts. The study showed that 63% of the Norwegian companies were clearly lagging behind the internationally renowned CSR leaders, whereas 27% were roughly at a similar level, and 10% of Norwegian corporations could be seen as partly ahead of their international counterparts, especially in the finance sector (Midttun, 2004).

A more detailed comparative analysis of some of these Norwegian companies matched against similar European CSR champions, shows significant differences, mainly in the way the CSR engagement is communicated. The strong social democratic collective bargaining culture may be one explanation, where CSR activities may much more often be regulated through an agreement between government, labour union and business organisations. This means that the individual corporation may not be profiled as much as its European counterparts where an active profiling may be a commercial advantage.

In the *finance sector*, Norway has – thanks to the early efforts of Storebrand – been a pioneer, and Storebrand has had a certain impact on the rest of the Norwegian finance sector.

As in most regions, corporate responsibility as evaluated by Scandinavian investors grew out of "Negative Screening" efforts of certain investment funds. Already in 1960, Sweden's Ansvar Aktie Fond took what at the time was considered an innovative approach to investing, by boycotting companies involved with apartheid regime in South Africa (or with alcohol or tobacco). Environmental issues were added to the "exclusion criteria" during the 1970s. Norway followed with its first environmental fund that also considers social issues (Joly, 1990), and took a pioneering role in launching the first global best-in-class fund, the Storebrand "Environmental Value Fund".

Today, Storebrand encourages an active dialogue between management and stakeholders. The company also very actively involves stakeholders in the implementation of its CSR policy: in 2002, Storebrand invited representatives of various stakeholder groups to a full-day conference on CSR to identify if Storebrand was heading in the right direction. The company believes that by giving the stakeholders a better insight into its main areas of business and its procedures it can help to create better awareness about CSR issues in the finance sector in general.

An in-house survey conducted in 2002 showed that an impressive 96% of all employees were fully or partly in agreement with Storebrand's goal to be a leading player in the CSR field (Thompson, 2003). The stakeholder approach of Storebrand shows that the Norwegian companies are more likely to follow the stakeholder theory of Freeman (Freeman, 1984).

Measuring CSR performance is another challenge where Storebrand is developing new approaches well anchored in a Scandinavian tradition. The company has begun to implement a plan to assess all managers (in addition to their financial performance) in respect to their CSR action plan for which they are responsible, under a Balanced Scorecard model. Jensen (2001) argues, however, that with no way to really keep score, Balanced Scorecard theory and stakeholder theory make managers unaccountable for their action because no single value measures how they have performed. Storebrand tries to put such measures in place.

Another major player on the finance sector in Norway is Den Norske Bank (DNB), Norway's largest provider of financial services. DNB's board has among others worked out guiding principles for the company board and a code of ethics where a stakeholder dialogue has been important.

In the *consumer goods sector*, Orkla is the largest corporation in Norway. It is also a major Norwegian investor and a large player on the Oslo Stock Exchange. Corporate Governance and CSR are part of the business strategy of Orkla, but rather in a corporate philanthropy sense (Porter & Kramer, 2002). This gives, however, a certain visibility rating in the Norwegian press, but has also raised criticism that the spending for this kind of CSR work is not enough (Johannessen, 2002).

In the *oil and gas sector*, the emphasis has moved from a strong focus on environmental and human rights issues to governance. After the Statoil Iran affair in

2003/4, the issue of proper governance beyond statements and guidelines has been extensively debated. And the issue of corporate governance in the headquarter operations, and not operations in foreign countries, has become more important.

- Norsk Hydro has signed an agreement with Amnesty International in order to cooperate in this field and to strengthen its future efforts to promote human rights. Hydro makes a financial contribution to Amnesty, and Amnesty provides expertise when Hydro steps up its in-house training of managers and employees on how to deal with human rights in respect of the Hydro Group's business activities in different countries. Amnesty will also help Hydro report on specific cases.

- Statoil has also become a member of the Business Leaders Initiative on Human Rights (BLIHR). The aim is to develop tools which can help companies to systematise their human rights efforts in selected projects. Statoil represents the energy sector in this initiative, which is headed by Mary Robinson, former president of Ireland and UN high commissioner for human rights.

Prior to the Iran Corruption Scandal (the so-called Horton Affair), Statoil was regarded as an international frontrunner in sustainable development issues. Even after the Iran corruption scandal, that reduced its credibility, Statoil maintained its positions on the Dow Jones Sustainability Index World (DJSI) and the FTSE4Good index during 2003. In addition, the company was included in the Goldman Sachs Energy, Environmental and Social Index from February 2004 and ranked third among the world's oil companies after BP and Shell. FTSE4Good made a continued inclusion conditional on establishing guidelines for dealing with the rights of indigenous people affected by Statoil's operations. After submitting these, Statoil received confirmation that they meet its human rights criteria. Statoil was put under review by the DJSI following the Iran affair. As a result, its scores were reduced in such areas as corporate governance and codes of conduct/compliance/corruption/bribery. However, Statoil increased its scores in other areas, most notably for stakeholder engagement and labour practice indicators. As a result, Statoil was rated "best of industry" in all three clusters – economic, environmental and social – and the ranking improved from 2002.

The ongoing discussions about the Norwegian Petroleum Fund are linked to the petroleum sector. The dilemmas arising when investing state-owned funds became clear earlier this year when the Norwegian government was challenged to account for the investment portfolio of its Petroleum Fund. With a value of just around 550 billion Norwegian crowns, reports in the media earlier this year showed how returns were being secured by investing in, among others, companies involved in the production of landmines, ammunition, tobacco, alcohol and gambling. There are also questions about the human rights and environmental records of a number of the companies that the Petroleum Fund invests in. All of these issues collide in some way with Norway's official foreign or national policies. Based on the recommendation of a Parliamentary Committee, the Government intends now to develop clearer guidelines for the Fund, demanding active engagement in companies that align with key principles, drawn from the Global Compact.

In the Norwegian *telecom sector*, the former state-owned company Telenor is the most profiled CSR player. The company underlines its commitment to meet its corporate social responsibilities in all activities, both domestically and internationally. And its efforts are firmly anchored in its core values (dynamic, innovative and responsible). However, research studies show that many organisations do not always place their efforts in a strategic manner, especially regarding philanthropy (Brønn & Wiig, 2002).

Academic Research on CSR

CSR research in Norway has built on environmental and sustainability research. At the Norwegian School of Management, the research on environmental issues dates back some ten years, and CSR issues were only added to the scope of sustainable development research lately.

In parallel, the financial sector interest in corporate governance issues is rising in academia. Already in the late 1990s business ethics were gaining momentum, and in 2002, a Centre for Corporate Citizenship was established at the Norwegian School of Management, linking the research expertise in all these areas together in a multidisciplinary research centre.

Today, research in the CSR field in Norway is mainly linked to what specific aspects the various research institutions are already addressing. The Norwegian Institute of Technology, in Trondheim, for instance, looks more on the operational implementations of CSR as part of its earlier work on environmental management and implications of technology choices.

Similarly, the University of Oslo, with a long tradition in developing country studies, has a focus on integrating issues like sustainable development for the poor, corruption and social development issues in its CSR focus.

The Norwegian School of Management has a practical business discipline approach, looking at how corporate governance, environmental management and business ethics can address specific aspects of CSR in daily operations. After the Statoil Iran affair in 2003/4, the issue of proper governance beyond statements and guidelines has been a focus of research. For Morten Huse of the Norwegian School of Management, "governance is not only about control, incentive and ownership structure, it is also about the allocation of decisions rights, as well as normative and value-based control" (Huse, 2003).

Given the importance of the oil and gas sector in the Norwegian economy, many of these aspects are looking at the specific implications in the petroleum sector. A special focus is on the role of the Norwegian Petroleum Fund, and the social and ethical guidelines now demanded by Parliament for that fund.

Future research in Norway will most likely focus even more on the core sectors where Norwegian corporations have an international outreach, i.e. the offshore oil and gas sector. The Foundation for Business and Society is chairing an EU sponsored research programme (TRENDS) that identifies shortcomings and outlines areas of further research: they include a more formalised stakeholder process involving also countries outside the European Union. With the corruption scandals and concerns about human rights violation still fresh in memory, the CSR focus is shifting towards a more in-depth and dynamic analysis of the actual drivers in CSR development.

Summary

A central premise for CSR in Norway is that business actors taking on a commitment to CSR do so voluntarily. This separates CSR from the notion of *corporate accountability* that advocates that rather than being voluntary, working with CSR should by law be stated as a mandatory obligation for business actors.

The strong focus on the environment in Norwegian industry may have taken corporate attention away from CSR issues. Also the fact that the Norwegian government has chosen to give the Ministry of Foreign Affairs a large responsibility for CSR in Norway has led to a stronger focus on issues related to foreign policy, such as human rights.

In the finance sector, the actual transformation of CSR elements into action is seen most clearly, and the financial institutions are seen by many as the driver for both sustainability and corporate responsibility in Norway.

The petroleum sector will continue to focus on the challenges it encounters when operating in foreign countries, and human rights and anti-corruption issues will therefore remain important elements in a Norwegian CSR development.

With the growing internationalisation also of Norwegian business, we may see more individual CSR engagement by corporations in the future. The challenge for Norwegian companies in this context will be to follow up an increased communication on CSR with actual and measurable performance in this area, which goes beyond marketing and profiling.

A more modern form of CSR, where mastering the social issues are being seen as an integrated competitive advantage, has only come into the debate in very recent years when especially banks and insurance companies took the lead. The finance sector may therefore continue to be the driver of CSR in Norway.

Dialogue with NGOs and governments will continue to be an important aspect of CSR life in Norway, and has found a new expression in a rather unique new initiative called Inclusive Work (Inkluderende Arbeidsliv). Here Government and companies try to anticipate and evaluate what social challenges will develop (that can result in social stress and costly disability payments etc.), and try to cope with their root causes up front. Along with the Norwegian government and the other employers' and employees' organisations, NHO has signed a letter of intent regarding a more inclusive working life (NHO, 2002).

One special feature of the CSR approach in Norway is, as suggested by the ongoing study by the Norwegian School of Management (Middtun, 2004), a different focus on transparency compared to other countries. While it seems to be a hot topic in the UK and other European countries, especially focusing on large firms (where as a consequence, larger firms are now underlining their transparency), Norwegian society is small and thus more transparent in itself: Norwegian media are therefore used to constantly analysing potential "scandals" of not "walking the talk". Combined with the traditional egalitarian attitude of society, i.e. not admiring extremely successful individuals without scrutinising them thoroughly, the Norwegian CSR approach may already be much more transparent and up to NGO scrutiny than in other European countries.

A major challenge for the Norwegians is to balance the effects of communicating too much, with those of communicating too little, and transmit a clear and credible message continuously and consistently through the appropriate channels (Brønn & Wiig, 2002).

References

Argument. 2003. *Topplederundersøkelse om Corporate Social Responsibility (CSR)*. Oslo: Argument Gruppen.

Brønn, S. P., & Wiig, R. (Eds.) 2002. *Corporate Communication: A Strategic Approach to Building Reputation*. Oslo: Gyldendal.

CSR Europe. 2004. *Status report on CSR in Europe*. CSR Europe Website. www.csreurope.org, accessed 5.8.2004.

Freeman, R. E. 1984. *Stakeholder Management: Framework and Philosophy*. Mansfield, MA: Pitman.

Huse, M. 2003. Renewing Management and Governance. *Journal of Management and Governance*, 7: 211–221.

Jensen, M. 2001. Value Maximization, Stakeholder Theory and the Corporate Objective Functions. *Journal of Applied Corporate Finance, 14(3): 8–21*.

Johannessen, J. 2002. Social Profil for 500 millione. *Dagens Næringsliv*, April 15th.

Joly, C. 1999. *The Role of the Financial Sector*. Presentation at the UN Conference on Action for a Common Future, Bergen.

KPMG. 2002. *KPMG International Survey of Corporate Social Responsibility Reporting*. www.wimm.nl, accessed 05.08.2004.

McCallin, J., & Webb, T. Q. 2004. Corporate Responsibility progress in Scandinavia. *Ethical Corporation Magazine*, January 2004.

Midttun, A. 2004. *Comparative analysis of CSR strategy and implementation in matched pairs of Norwegian and European companies*. Working paper. Norwegian School of Management, Oslo.

Munkelien, E. B., & Gravlien, I. 2003. *Triple-bottom-line reporting in a Norwegian context*, DNV Research Report 7/03/D/7 – 03-D-2003, Høvik: DNV.

NHO. 2002. *Report on CSR*. Oslo: NHO.

Porter, M., & Kramer, M. R. 2002. The competitive advantage of Corporate Philanthropy. *Harvard Business Review*, 80(12): 56–59.

Ruud, A., & Larsen, O. M. 2002. *Miljørapportering i årsberetningen; Følger Norske bedrifter Regnskapslovens pålegg?* Rapport No. 2/02. Oslo: University of Oslo.

Ruud, A., & Larsen, O. M. 2003. Miljørapportering i større norske foretak: Fungerer Regnskapsloven etter intensjonen? Rapport No. 5/03. Oslo: University of Oslo.

Thompson, E. 2003. *Storebrand annual press briefing*. Oslo: Storebrand.

Wieland, P. 2003. *CSR Definitions in Norway*. DNV Research report. Høvik: DNV.

Willums, J. O. Presentation at CSR briefing at Bertelsmann Foundation, Berlin.

Further Internet Links

Center for Corporate Citizenship
www.bi.no

Foundation for Business and Society
www.foundation.no

Table 2. Factors motivating companies to engage in CSR as reported by CEOs

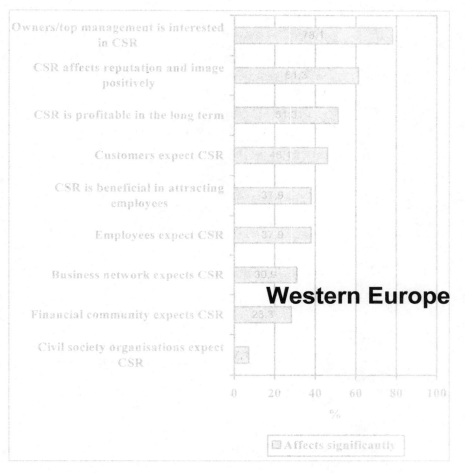

Owners/top management is interested in CSR — 78.1
CSR affects reputation and image positively — 61.3
CSR is profitable in the long term — 51.3
Customers expect CSR — 46.1
CSR is beneficial in attracting employees — 37.9
Employees expect CSR — 37.9
Business network expects CSR — 30.9
Financial community expects CSR — 28.3
Civil society organisations expect CSR — 7.1

Western Europe

0   20   40   60   80   100
%

☐ Affects significantly

Source: Keskuskauppakamari (2003)

The Role of Environmental Management in the Emergence of CSR

Two thirds of the land area of Finland is covered by forests (Kauppi, Mielikäinen & Kuusela, 1992; Korhonen, Wihersaari & Savolainen, 2001) and one third by peatlands (Selin, 1999; Savolainen, Hillebrand, Nousiainen & Sinisalo, 1994; Lappalainen & Hänninen, 1993), that is, by renewable natural resources (in case of peat, this holds if integrated over all peat areas in Finland). The vast forestry and forest industry sectors have been and continue to be the cornerstone of the Finnish economy and exports. Finnish forest, pulp and paper products are sold and consumed worldwide. For example, approximately 90 % of the main product, paper, is exported, e.g. to Germany and Central Europe.

As Finland is a relatively cold country and paper production is an energy intensive area of industrial activity, the Finnish industrial structure is natural capital intensive both in terms of raw materials and energy and fuels used. Because of this natural capital intensive nature of industrial activity, Finnish companies have been exposed both to the international and domestic public eye of environmental awareness and scrutiny. Therefore, Finnish companies have had to pay attention to sustainable management of domestic natural resources and fuel sources as well as the waste and emission flows that are the obvious outcome of material and energy intensive activities.

The annual use rate of renewable natural resources in Finland is less than their annual growth. Finland is one of the three countries in the world together with Denmark and the Netherlands that have arranged their regional energy supply systems to a large extent into coproduction of heat and power (CHP), in which waste heat is utilised for industrial steam and for district heat in an eco-efficient manner. The EU average for CHP from national electricity generation is less than 10%, while this figure amounts up to 35% in Finland (Korhonen, 2001).

With these situational factors, the availability of resources on the one hand and the pressure to produce from raw materials and in an energy intensive way on the other, Finnish industry has achieved wide international recognition in its environmental and energy technologies and management. For example, approximately 70% of the fuels used in the national forest industry are derived from domestic wood waste and 94% of the fuels used are utilised in CHP (Korhonen, Wihersaari & Savolainen, 2001; Verkasalo, 1993). In the light of the coming EU legislation for emissions trading, the international climate negotiations and conventions, and the fact that 80% of the world's energy production relies on non-renewable fossil fuels, the Finnish experience in corporate environmental management and management of energy efficiency can be determined as significant.

The development of environmental management systems in Finnish industry has influenced the emergence and development of corporate social responsibility in general. Many companies have first conducted their environmental reviews, audits, environmental reports and gathered these under environmental management systems that nowadays take the familiar forms of the EU Eco-Management and Auditing Scheme (EMAS) or the International Standardisation Organisation's ISO 14001 standard. During the last few years, companies have been linking these environmental management systems to other dimensions of CSR. For example, Fortum, Finland's largest energy company, used to publish environmental reports, until it recently included information on its environmental policies and activities into its new Corporate Citizenship report.

The findings of a recent survey of Finnish CEOs show that environmental management is viewed as one of the six central elements of responsible business conduct in conjunction with issues such as responsibility for the products and services

UNITED KINGDOM

4 An Explicit Model of Business-Society Relations

Jeremy Moon[1]

Introduction

This study presents UK CSR as part of "societal governance": the system which "provid[es] direction to society" (Peters, 1996: 51 – 52). It argues that CSR is informed by the contexts provided by government, social regulation and markets. The chapter identifies the roots of modern CSR in nineteenth century business philanthropy. CSR assumed a more implicit role during most of the twentieth century as government increased its direct responsibility for the social impacts of business and for citizenship rights. The recent rapid transformation of business-society relations from *implicit* to *explicit* CSR is explained first with reference to the crisis in societal governance in the late twentieth century and subsequently to new government regulation, social regulation and market drivers.

Roots and Traditions

The UK system of societal governance can best be described as emergent rather than the product of critical events. There were no foundation moments such as: the American war of independence, federation and declaration of rights and freedoms; the French revolution; the German post-war settlement; or the liberation of Eastern Europe. In the absence of a modern liberation or revolution, the gradual emergence of democracy and capitalism from an aristocratic order has made for a curious system. For example, civil law in England is derived from accumulated judgements of over 600 years rather than being codified in a single document. Although described as a constitutional monarchy, this is a misnomer as there is no UK constitution! The national government acts in the name of the Crown and as a result there are few limitations on its power. Citizenship rights are comparatively understated despite the UK being regarded as the home of liberalism. Ironically many of the rights enjoyed by the British derive from European Union membership.

Business, particularly the manufacturing sector, has traditionally had a relatively cooperative relationship with government.[2] But this has not been embedded in constitutional or legal requirements, rather it was borne of habits. In comparison with many continental counterparts, the UK financial sector has had a relatively powerful sway over business culture and policy. Whereas from the early 1980s this has made for a relatively dynamic business sector, in the 1960s-1970s, it was often berated for its failure to modernise.

Gradualism in political development and in business-government relations contrasts with economic and social transformations. The industrial revolution heralded a rapid shift from a largely agrarian, rural society to an industrial and urban one (Deane, 1969; Mathias, 1983). The repeal of the Corn Laws (1848) dealt the most singular and symbolic blow to the power of the aristocracy, whose power was predicated on agriculture. Legislation providing for limited liability (1855 – 6) and the 1862 Companies Act signalled the advent of a new sort of business structure which underpinned the separation of ownership and management, and the concentration of capital first in joint stock companies and later in corporations (Thompson, 1970).

The social consequences of these transformations were administered in various ways. Legislation provided a regulatory framework and inspectorates for product and labour standards (e.g. regarding child labour, working hours, trade union rights, weights and measures, hygiene). Trade unions emerged as the main vehicle for extending and protecting workers' rights and pay. Municipal government provided the major infrastructure for sewerage systems and fresh water vital to industrial society. It also provided assistance of last resort to the impoverished.

Alongside these forms of social provision grew a system of general philanthropy, often premised on religious values (from liberal Methodism to paternal Anglicanism) which addressed poverty and what were regarded as associated social malaises of, for example,

alcoholism and the neglect of children. These norms operated indirectly as a form of social regulation (e.g. against the slave trade and slavery). They also operated directly through business owners' own social responsibilities such that, aside from its transforming market roles,[3] business had a place in governance through paternalism. Certain companies provided a social infrastructure for workers and their families. This included housing (for employees and former employees); retail outlets (sometimes perniciously trading on tokens that workers earned in lieu of pay); education; baths; pubs[4]; and other recreational facilities. Companies like Rowntree's, Cadbury's, Boots and Lever Brothers became by-words for corporate philanthropy, which combined the wider values of the factory owners with their calculations about the business imperatives to maintain a loyal workforce (Cannon, 1994).

Interestingly, many of the pioneering works and standards of these philanthropic businesses set the hallmark for subsequent public sector provision (e.g. local government emulation of Rowntree's housing standards, 1910 – 1920). However, these philanthropic initiatives are often disconnected from contemporary CSR as government responsibility for society grew. In the first half of the twentieth century state provision grew where business and other forms of philanthropy had previously engaged (e.g. in public employment, sickness and old age insurance systems; education; health; the basic utilities of water, energy and communications). Although these services were often delivered by local governments or devolved national government agencies, they became increasingly creatures of central government through the latter's fiscal power. (King, 1973; Rose, 1976; Rose, 1985).

One outcome was that the direct business responsibility for society narrowed to community philanthropy, mainly in the form of charitable donations. This was often removed from a company's core business activity and was characteristically used by company chairmen to support their favourite charity. Membership of such associations as Rotary Clubs and Chambers of Commerce enabled individual business people to engage in local social issues in a philanthropic mode. Otherwise, business social responsibilities were more implicit, taking the form of obedience to the law and paying taxes but also through participation in public policy-making, particularly in industrial training, science and R&D and, periodically industrial relations and prices and incomes.

Growth of government continued on the basis of a post-war consensus. There was a shared desire among political elites to avoid the social divisions of the 1930s and to meet new electoral demands. Although Labour enacted most of the welfare reform, the Beveridge Report on which it was based was commissioned by the previous Conservative-led coalition, which also enacted the 1944 Education Act. Similarly, the 1950s public housing boom was administered by the Conservatives.

The conventional view of post-war business-government relations was of partnership in policy-making for enhancing production or for regulating commercial activity (Grant, 1993). This included: self-regulation (e.g. of the financial system); individual relations with government departments (e.g. concerning the terms of production and trade); participation of industry associations in sectoral policy-making; and participation of the Confederation of British Industry in industrial and economic policy-making (Grant, 1984; Grant & Marsh, 1977). Thus business was regarded as part of a consensual, but non-formalised, social, political and economic compact between producers and consumers (Beer, 1965).

Although the UK is often seen as illustrative of the Anglo-Saxon model of capitalism (Albert, 1991), during the first three quarters of the twentieth century its CSR was a pale reflection of the American counterpart. American business foundations provided a range of social responsibilities from poverty alleviation to medical research and higher education funding (Dowie, 2001). This was a function of: a more general habit of participation of Americans in society (Tocqueville, 1966); a predisposition to philanthropy in general (Bremner, 1988); "spaces" that US governments created for non-governmental forms of social provision to fill (King,

1973); and the incentive structure of tax expenditures to employers who provide employment and health insurance (Rein, 1982).

However, the social role of British business has changed dramatically with CSR growing and becoming more explicit in the last twenty years. This can be understood in the context of a crisis in societal governance in the 1970–1980s (Beer, 1982). The causes of this governance crisis are undoubtedly complex and vary according to style of analysis, disciplinary perspective and ideological departure points.[5] In brief, the extent of governmental social and economic commitments coupled with the number and incommensurability of societal demands prompted the perception that government was overloaded and losing legitimacy. It appeared unable to resolve such issues as industrial relations, prices and incomes policies, inflation, unemployment, economic growth, productivity, investment, and public debt.

Subsequently, Conservative and Labour governments followed a strategy of maintaining regulatory and fiscal capacity[6] whilst narrowing their responsibility for direct delivery of social goods. This is most obviously seen through the denationalisation of public utilities enacted by the Conservative governments. Although this has not necessarily led to the expansion of markets[7], it has entailed a decline in direct government responsibility for social provision as independent regulators supervise oligopolistic and monopolistic business providers. Hence business has assumed a far greater profile in social life by virtue of its "for profit" activity (e.g. in telecommunications, mass transport, water, energy).

Governments have also encouraged greater family and individual social responsibility. This is evident in the declining value of pensions and benefits; the introduction of charges for higher education; incentives for personal savings; the wider use of NGOs to deliver public services; and private finance for public projects (e.g. transport and infrastructure). These trends have been described as the "hollowing out" of government (Rhodes, 1996). One further government strategy has been the encouragement of CSR.

Thus contemporary UK CSR is part of a wider re-orientation of governance roles whereby business has not only increased its *market* mode (as a result of privatisation and contracting out) but also its *network* mode with government and non-government organisations in which the inter-dependencies of actors depend neither in authority nor market relations (Moon, 2002a).

Present Status and Debate

Although CSR was discussed during the 1970s (e.g. Beesley & Evans, 1978) the key watershed for the current explicit model of CSR was the period of high unemployment, urban decay and social unrest of the early 1980s. This specific manifestation of the governance crisis alluded to above informed key drivers (i.e. social expectations of business, recognition of social prerequisites of business success, government encouragement) for new forms of business involvement in the community or the "first wave" of CSR (Moon, 2002b).

The 1990s saw a broadening of CSR from community involvement to concern for socially responsible products and processes, and socially responsible employee relations or the second and third waves (Moon, 2002b). This arose as a result of new forms of social regulation and stakeholder engagement; governmental regulation; increased stakeholder demands for CSR and social reporting; and greater attention to the business case for CSR. Moreover, British CSR has now acquired wider global application as the trend toward the downsizing of government's role in social regulation has become more widespread and the role of global business in CSR has grown.

The Unemployment Crisis and Business Involvement in the Community

A critical juncture in the emergence of a more explicit CSR was the wave of riots in the early 1980s against a backdrop of spiralling unemployment and inner-city decay. Business re-evaluated its relations with society and was complemented by government encouragement for business to share in responding to these governance problems. (Moon & Richardson, 1985) One motivation for this re-evaluation was to protect the social licence of business to trade. As *The Economist* commented on Marks & Spencer's community work and charity, the firm was "making a sensible investment in its market place. If urban disorders become a regular fact of life, many of its 260 stores would not survive." (20.2.1982). Another motivation was offsetting threats of further regulation:

> ... companies fear that if they make no attempt to find solutions to community problems, the government may increasingly take on the responsibility itself. This might prove costly to employers both in terms of new obligations and greater intervention in the labour market. Many companies prefer to be one step ahead of government legislation or intervention, to anticipate social pressures themselves and hence be able to develop their own policies in response to them (CBI, 1981 quoted in Moon & Richardson, 1985: 137).

Notwithstanding the negative impact of government implied in this CBI quotation, the government was simultaneously encouraging business to share in resolving community problems. In an address to the Institute of Directors Secretary of State for the Environment, Michael Heseltine, stated that government could not provide all the solutions to revitalising our society, and especially that the inner cities:

> ... we (government) do not have the money. We do not have the expertise. We need the private sector again to play a role which, in Britain, it played more conspicuously a century ago than it does now. (quoted in Richardson, 1983: 1)

The Manpower Services Commission[8] prompted the Confederation of British Industry (CBI) to form the Special Programmes Unit (CBI SPU) in 1984. It consisted of secondees from individual corporations (one manifestation of CSR) who secured training and work experience opportunities in businesses (another manifestation of CSR) under the Youth Training Scheme, on which 350,000 unemployed young people participated in its first year alone.[9] The CBI SPU lobbied companies, organised conferences and acted as trouble-shooters when problems arose. The government encouraged the CBI to set up the Community Action Programme (CAP) to increase business awareness of the subsidies available for business under the Community Programme.[10] It contributed about half of the costs of Practical Action which identified business resources of equipment and expertise that could be deployed in youth employment schemes (Moon & Richardson, 1985).

Of even more long-term significance, was the government's role in convening a 1981 conference of UK and USA business leaders to discuss community involvement. This led directly to the formation of the major business umbrella group for CSR, Business in the Community (BITC) which became the largest business association for CSR (see below). Its first decade was largely spent on stimulating public-private partnerships in the form of local enterprise trusts staffed by business secondees (another manifestation of CSR). The partnerships offered diverse forms of local economic and social governance through which public and private resources were brought to bear and by which solutions to a variety of problems were brokered and managed (Moore et al. 1989). Government initiatives to articulate CSR agendas, provide and support organisational initiatives and subsidise, this first new wave of UK CSR were consonant with business re-thinking of social responsibilities.

The Socially Responsible Business Agenda

A second (socially responsible products and processes) and a third (socially responsible employee relations) waves of CSR emerged in the 1990s (Moon 2002b). They are distinguished by their greater explicitness and by a diversification in their drivers and interlocutors.

The more explicit approach to CSR is illustrated in many ways. First, there is a growth in CSR staff within companies, including designated board level responsibility. Many corporations embedded CSR in their internal systems by using codes and standards in, for example, CSR budget allocation, stakeholder relations and social reporting. Some standards are imported (e.g. from the Institute of Business Ethics, AccountAbility) and others are internal. There has been an increase in CSR reporting within annual reports, in free-standing reports and in general corporate communications (Maignon & Ralston, 2002). About 80% of the FTSE 100 companies report their CSR. Many companies entered partnerships with NGOs or governmental organisations in order to substantiate their CSR. These range from head office level partnerships with peak non-government organisations, to branch level partnerships with community organizations.

The emergence and growth of CSR umbrella associations has illustrated and encouraged a more explicit CSR. Business in the Community has a membership of over 750 companies and a regional management and policy-making structure. It provides a range of CSR services to its members; identifies and articulates a range of CSR issues for British business; and works closely with the Department of Trade and Industry in CSR policy development. BITC's programmes (e.g. on race, gender, the rural sector) illustrates the broadening CSR agenda from the 1980s.

A CSR consultancy industry has also emerged. A recent study concluded that 96 % of CSR consultants had been created in the last 33 years and 62 % in the last ten years (Fernandez Young, Moon & Young, 2003). Similarly there are numerous CSR vanguard organizations, some of which are also membership and consultancy organizations which were set up to raise CSR standards (e.g. AccountAbility, Tomorrow's Company). Ethical Corporation organises CSR conferences and publishes a newsletter. Ethical Performance publishes a newsletter and hosts of CSR jobs website. Many other organisations engage with CSR even though it is not their core concern. For example the Charities Aid Foundation recently held a major conference in 2003 to bring together representatives of the community and corporate sectors.

CSR is also the subject of increasing attention outside companies and CSR organisations. Concern about CSR has now increased in the investment community with the growth of socially responsible investment funds, which constitute another driver for firms to act, and be seen to act, more responsibly (McCann, Solomon & Solomon, 2003). CSR is the subject of increasing media attention. The *Financial Times* and the *Guardian* have dedicated CSR reporters. *The Times* carries a social responsibility index in its weekly company profile. UK business education appears to have accorded CSR a more explicit profile than have other European countries, both in terms of the nomenclature of courses and their quantity (Matten & Moon, 2004).

The wider and more explicit CSR agenda reflects business reviews of its individual and collective long-term legitimacy, pressure from various non-governmental organisations, and changing demands of employees, suppliers, customers and consumers. But, as in the first wave of CSR, the role of government is conspicuous. In his first address to the Labour Party conference as Prime Minister, Tony Blair expressed an intention to expand public-private partnerships in British schools. This was echoed by the Minister for Education, David Miliband:

we cannot do this on our own. Education is a joint enterprise – between teachers and students but also between schools and the wider community. Business can sponsor Specialist Schools and Academies. Business can contribute to curriculum enhancement. Business can offer work placements and work experience. Business can offer mentoring and governor support.[11]

Blair created the position of Minister for CSR within the Department of Trade and Industry (DTI),[12] a focal point for CSR within government by encouraging research and development on CSR issues. The DTI's Society and Business website sets out different ways in which the government can support CSR:

- Help promote the business case and celebrate business achievements,

- support partnership and business participation in key priorities – including through co-funding, fiscal incentives and brokering new partnerships,

- ensure Government business services provide helpful advice and signpost other resources,

- encourage consensus on UK and international codes of practice and

- promote effective frameworks for reporting and product labelling.[13]

Examples of projects with which the DTI is associated are set out in Table 1.

Table 1. Department of trade and industry CSR projects

Project	Contribution
OECD Guidelines for Multinational Enterprises	Publicity, advice, deals with companies on issues raised
Business in the Community Excellence Awards	Subsidy, participation in judging.
Impact on Society Report	Subsidy of research, publication and website of BITC report
Partnership Fund	Subsidies to partnerships to improve productivity and improve job satisfaction

Source: http://www.societyandbusiness.gov.uk/government/index.html 31.X.2003

The DTI website also provides information about and links to a full range of policies and projects undertaken across government. Table 2 provides examples of other government departments engaged in CSR and their respective projects.

Table 2. Examples government departments engaged in CSR projects

Department	Project (Government role)
Cabinet Office	*Women Unlimited – Women and Work* (organises multi-departmental and multi-stakeholder project to enhance women's work opportunities)
Department of International Development	*Ethical Trade Initiative* (funds ETI – a business, NGO, TU alliance to improve labour standards in MNCs' supply chains)
	Business Links Asia (funds alliance of MNCs committed to ethical business practices and transference of knowledge and skills to local SMEs e.g. health and safety)
	Just Pensions (advises support to pensions industry trustees and fund managers to benefit the poor)
	Business Partners for Development *(supports strategic partnerships working for the development of communities that help create stable social and financial environments)*
Department for Environment Food and Rural Affairs	*Business Environmental Reporting* (supports annual Environmental Reporting Awards, advice to business, promotes reporting, provides guidelines)
	Working Group on Sustainability Within Companies (administrative support to Advisory Committee on Business and the Environment (ACBE), subsidy of publications)
	Make A Corporate Commitment (promotes resource efficiency and environmental improvements by encouraging organisations to set targets and report annually on progress)

Source: http://www.societyandbusiness.gov.uk/government/index.html 31.X.2003

The government supports a range of CSR organisations (e.g. Business in the Community, International Business Leaders Forum) and NGOs working with socially responsible business (e.g. Traidcraft Exchange, War on Want). It was the key player in the creation of the Ethical Trade Initiative and CSR Academy. Many of these projects (e.g. Ethical Trade Initiative, Business Environmental Reporting) encourage business to perform according to defined standards and reports according to these – a key factor in the increasingly institutionalised nature of CSR in Britain.

The government has used its regulatory power to encourage CSR.[14] A 1996 amendment to the Occupational Pensions Schemes (Investment) Regulations required pension funds to disclose how they take account of social, environmental and ethical factors in their investment decisions. This "soft" regulation does not require any particular behaviour other than to report. Thus, the requirement for transparency encourages businesses to be explicit about their CSR. Similarly, the 2002 White Paper on Company Law Reform (Cm 5553 – 1) anticipates stock exchange listed companies having to report on how they take account of the interests of such stakeholders as employees, the community and the environment. The government also introduced fiscal incentives to elicit more CSR. For example, the "Climate Levy" which came into effect in 2002 encouraged greater energy efficiency in industry. A Landfill Tax encouraged better disposal or re-use of waste. The 2002 Community Investment Tax Credit is a means of attracting private capital into disadvantaged areas.

This section has presented clear evidence that British business has adopted a very different and more explicit role in societal governance through its CSR practices. This reflects business re-evaluation of their relations with society, new business-related and social drivers for responsibility and strategic responses by successive governments to the challenge of meeting societal expectations.

Conclusion

One reason that UK CSR can be regarded as increasingly explicit is the emergence of its new institutional context. This defines the ways in which CSR contributes to new societal governance and provides a basis for the maintenance and development of a CSR capability.

CSR has been institutionalised within corporations by the appointment of board level and senior management responsibilities, the introduction of reporting systems and organisational systems for dealing with CSR issues internally. Second, CSR is institutionalised in increased external relations that businesses have engaged, through partnerships, social reporting and expanded stakeholder relations. The impetus for some of these relationships (e.g. socially responsible investment indexes) originates outside the organisations themselves. Third, the CSR vanguard organisations and consulting industry provide a base for CSR expertise and agenda-setting to which business can be expected to continue to respond. Fourth, the various peak CSR business coalitions, most significantly BITC, offer perhaps the most important aspect of institutionalisation as they are manifestations of the extent to which business has regarded CSR as a collective issue for societal governance. Fifth, CSR has been institutionalised through a host of government initiatives. These indicators of institutionalisation of CSR suggest that CSR is relatively well-embedded into UK business practice, business-government relations and business-stakeholder relations, and therefore the prospects for maintaining capability seem positive.

A number of evaluative issues arise. First, there remains a tension between the desire for plurality of CSR definitions, practices and codes on the one hand, and the interest in relatively authoritative indicators as to what constitutes acceptable and best practice on the other. The latter perspective is illustrated by the confusion and frustration that many companies express in the face of the myriad of reporting standards, indexes and codes to which they are expected to conform. Conversely, the former perspective was illustrated by the opposition of British business to the EU Green Paper on CSR on the basis that it threatened too stipulative an approach which would have compromised the discretionary element of CSR.

Second, in the absence of certain regulations a number of firms have developed their own supply chain assurance systems, often in response to or in anticipation of NGO criticism. On one hand these could be seen as an indirect and business-oriented means by which CSR can be encouraged in the wider business community. A fear facing small and medium sized companies, however, is that they face a profusion of standards demanded by their different business customers. Another is of the costs associated with meeting emerging CSR standards which could provide signals of their responsibility. A corollary here may be that large companies, which can afford such compliance, are favoured in purchasing decisions which would be at the expense of a more traditional CSR norm, supporting small local business.

Third, the tendency for UK companies to organise their CSR through marketing and communications departments raises the question as to the extent to which CSR has become simply part of corporate branding rather than reflective of new business practices. Perhaps, given CSR's concern with transparency and reputation, this tension is inevitably ongoing.

Fourthly, what are the limits to the government's readiness to legislate for new forms of business behaviour rather than rely on self-regulation? This leads directly to the fundamental question which both inspires and tempers the CSR concept, "where does the responsibility of business stop and that of government or society begin?" The relatively benign business-government and business-society relations of the last twenty years are not guaranteed to persist. The extent to which business is blamed and held accountable for public health issues related to products which reflect societal tastes and which have received long-term endorsement of government (e.g. food, drink and tobacco impacts on heart and lung disease, obesity, drug addiction and alcoholism) is a case in point. For better or for worse, these agendas could prompt either a business retreat from assumptions about social responsibility or the emergence of very different sorts of business organisation. The former would signal a limitation and even a narrowing of the range of issues for which business is held responsible. The latter would signal not only a greater range of business responsibility but would also legitimise the increased role of business in policy and societal decision-making, raising important questions of power and accountability.

References

Albert, M. 1991. *Capitalisme contre capitalism*. Paris: Le Seuil.

Beer, S. 1965. *Modern British Politics*. London: Faber & Faber.

Beer, S. 1982. *Britain Against Itself*. London: Faber & Faber.

Beesley, M., & Evans, T. 1978. *Corporate Social Responsibility*. London: Croom Helm.

Bremner, R. H. 1988. *American Philanthropy*. Chicago: Chicago University Press.

Cannon, T. 1994. *Corporate Responsibility*. Harlow, Essex: Pearson Education.

CBI. 1981. *Company Responses to Unemployment: a Report by the Social Affairs Directorate*. London: CSB.

Deane, P. 1969. *The First Industrial Revolution*. Cambridge: Cambridge University Press.

Dowie, M. 2001. *American Foundations: An investigative history*. Cambridge, Mass. & London: The MIT Press.

Fernandez Young, A., Moon, J., & Young, R. 2003. *The UK Corporate Social Responsibility Consultancy Industry: a phenomenological approach*. Nottingham: Research Paper Series of the International Centre for Corporate Social Responsibility, No.14.

Grant, W. 1984. The Business Lobby: Political Attitudes and Strategy. In: H. Berrington (Ed.), *Change in British Politics*. London: Dent.

Grant, W. 1993. *Business and Politics in the UK*. Basingstoke: Macmillan.

Grant, W., & Marsh, D. 1977. *The CBI*. London: Hodder & Stoughton.

King, A. 1973. Ideas, Institutions and the policies of Governments: A Comparative Analysis. *British Journal of Political Science*, 3: 291 – 314.

McCann, L., Solomon, A., & Solomon, J. 2003. Explaining the Growth in UK Socially Responsible Investment. *Journal of General Management*, 24: 4.

Maignon, I., & Ralston, D. 2002. Corporate Social Responsibility in Europe and the US: Insights from Businesses' Self-presentations. *Journal of International Business Studies*, 33: 3497 – 3514.

Marx, K., & Engels F. 1970. *The Communist Manifesto in Marx and Engels Selected Works.* London: Lawrence & Wishart.

Mathias, P. 1983. *The First Industrial Nation.* London: Methuen.

Matten, D., & Moon, J. 2004. Corporate Social Responsibility Education in Europe. *Journal of Business Ethics,* forthcoming.

Moon, J. 2002a. Business Social Responsibility and New Governance. *Government and Opposition,* 37: 3385 – 3408.

Moon, J. 2002b. Corporate Social Responsibility: An Overview. *International Directory of Corporate Philanthropy.* London: Europa Publications.

Moon, J., & Richardson, J. J. 1985. *Unemployment in the UK: Politics and Policies.* Aldershot, UK: Gower.

Moon, J., & Richardson, J. J. 1993. Governmental Capacity Regained?: The Challenges to and Responses of British Government in the 1980s. In: I. Marsh (Ed.), *Governing in the 1990s: Challenges, Constraints, and Opportunities.* Sydney, Australia: Longman Cheshire.

Moore, C., & Richardson, J. J., in association with Moon, J. (1989). *Local Partnership and the Unemployment Crisis in Britain.* London: Allen & Unwin.

Peters, B. G. 1996. Shouldn't Row, Can't Steer: What's a Government to Do? *Public Policy and Administration,* 12: 1.

Rein, M. 1982. The Social Policy of the Firm. *Policy Sciences,* 14: 2.

Rhodes, R. A. W. 1996. New Governance: Governing without Government. *Political Studies,* 44: 4.

Richardson, J. 1983. The Development of Corporate Responsibility in the UK. *Strathclyde Papers on Government and Politics,* No.1.

Rose, R. 1976. On the Priorities of Government: A Developmental Analysis of Public Policies. *European Journal of Political Research,* 4: 247 – 289.

Rose, R. 1985. The Programme Approach to the Growth of Government. *British Journal of Political Science,* 15: 1 – 28.

Thompson, D. 1970. *England in the Nineteenth Century.* Harmondsworth, Middx: Penguin.

Tocqueville, A. de. 1966. *Democracy in America.* New York: Anchor Books.

Vogel, D. 1986. *National Styles of Regulation: Environmental Policy in Great Britain and the United States.* Ithaca, NY & London: Cornell University Press.

Notes

[1] Thanks to the editors for their encouragement; to the reviewer for suggestions; and to Dirk Matten with whom I have thought and talked through the implicit / explicit CSR distinction.

[2] Vogel sees UK business as "more susceptible to social pressure both from government officials and from other forums to behave 'responsibly'" than US business. (1986: 50).

[3] This was famously captured by Marx and Engels: "The Subjection of Nature's forces to man, machinery, application of chemistry to industry and agriculture, steam navigation, railways, electric telegraphs, clearing of whole continents for cultivation, canalisation of rivers … what earlier century had even a presentiment that such productive forces slumbered in the lap of social labour?". (1970: 40)

[4] Though some employers, and the cooperative movement leader Robert Owen, opposed alcohol consumption. (Cannon, 1994)

[5] This section draws on Moon and Richardson (1993).

[6] Overall since 1979 the economy has become more taxed. Taxation has become less progressive as upper marginal rates have declined and the share of taxation accounted for by indirect taxes and charges has increased.

[7] Ironically, perhaps the greatest growth of markets has been in the public sector health and education systems.

[8] Successive governments had drawn business and trade unions into policy-making for training through the Industrial Training Boards (1964) and the Manpower Services Commission (1974).

[9] Whilst companies participating in the scheme did receive some benefits in the form of subsidised labour there were significant costs of undertaking new short-term trainees.

[10] This subsidised allowances for unemployed people on sponsored community improvement projects.

[11] Speech at education conference http://www.bitc.org.uk/events/event_proceedings/education_conference_2003/ed_dmspeech2003.html (19.II.2003)

[12] The current minister is Stephen Timms. His predecessors were Kim Howells and Douglas Alexander.

[13] http://www.societyandbusiness.gov.uk/government/index.html

[14] The Conservative government made one regulatory change to encourage CSR in the form of a 1986 amendment to the tax laws to allow sponsorship as a tax deduction.

Further Internet Links

Business in the Community
www.bitc.org.uk

Corporate Social Responsibility Forum
www.csrforum.com

CSR-Academy
www.csracademy.org.uk

Department of Trade and Industry CSR website
www.societyandbusiness.gov.uk

Institute for Business Ethics
www.ibe.org.uk

Institute for Social and Ethical Accountability
www.accountability.org.uk

Institute for Sustainability
www.sustainability.com

International Centre for Corporate Social Responsibility
www.nottingham.ac.uk/business/ICCSR/index.html

Prince of Wales Business Leader Forum
www.pwblf.org

[7] Mette Morsing & Jonas Tue Burkhall, Research project on *"The Discourse in the Danish Business Press – a study of 9 years of reasons, themes and players"*, 2004.

[8] In 1996, the founding corporate members of the National Network were the CEOs of: Oticon, Carlsberg, Pressalit, Horsens Gummivarefabrik, Grundfos, Novo Nordisk, Ruko, DSB, Jamo, Post Danmark, Sparekassen Nordylland, Danfoss, Neckelmann, Erik Mainz, Lego and Falck. Today, the National Network has twelve members. Moreover, there is a number of Regional Networks that work locally across the country. Every year, the National Network awards a prize to a company that has made a special contribution within the field of corporate social responsibility.

[9] From its foundation in 1997 until 2003, the Copenhagen Centre worked to support an international exchange of experience in the field of social partnerships, publishing reports and organising conferences, seminars, and various international networks.

[10] The European Sustainability Reporting Awards is formed by 15 countries' accounting associations, for more information, please consult Mr Flemming Tost, ft@hlrevision.dk.

References

Berghmann, J. 1997. Can the Idea of Benchmarking be Applied to Social Protection? *Bulletin Luxembourgeois des Questions Sociales*, 4: 119–130.

Bibb, S., & Kourdi, J. 2004. *Trust Matters. For Organisational and Personal Success.* Hampshire, UK: Palgrave Macmillan.

Confederation of Danish Industries & Oxford Research. 2004. *Report: Ethics, Environment and Social Relations in the Supply-chain.* Copenhagen.

Freeman, R.E., & Gilbert, D.R. Jr. 1988. *Corporate Strategy and the Search for Ethics.* New Jersey: Prentice Hall.

Gallup International and Environics International. 2002. Survey *Which institutions to be trusted to work for the best of society.* http://www.weforum.org/pdf/AM_2003/Survey.pdf, accessed 05.08.2004.

Giversen, J. 2003. The World's First Accounting Statement. In: M. Morsing, & C. Thyssen (Eds.), *The Case of Denmark – Corporate Values and Social Responsibility*: 36. Frederiksberg: Samfundslitteratur.

Hofstede, G. 1980. *Cultural Consequences.* London: Sage.

Hofstede, G. 1994. *Cultures and Organizations. Software of the Mind.* London: Harper-Collins.

Lund, J.E. 2003. Partnerships in Practice. In: M. Morsing, & C. Thyssen (Eds.), *The Case of Denmark – Corporate Values and Social Responsibility*: 179–191. Frederiksberg: Samfundslitteratur.

IRELAND

5 Bridging the Atlantic

Eleanor O'Higgins

Background to CSR in Ireland

What Do We Mean by CSR

Before addressing CSR in Ireland it is essential to provide a definition of CSR. The EU defines CSR as the integration by companies of "social and environmental business concerns into business operations and in their interaction with stakeholders on a voluntary basis". It is inconceivable that any organisation can be socially responsible unless it behaves ethically and correctly. It is important to understand what CSR is not. CSR is not philanthropy. Enron was very philanthropic, as was Parmalat. CSR is nothing new. Many companies over decades have behaved responsibly, honestly and respectfully toward all their stakeholders, based on an internal culture of integrity, probity and authenticity. Seen in this light, CSR is organic and not the afterthought public relations ploy it becomes all too often. Many companies which meet the criteria devised by the proliferation of assessment agencies and consultants are not really responsible in terms of their internal operations and processes, because they may cut ethical corners. Indeed, using CSR and good deeds as a cover can itself be deemed unethical.

Ireland at the "Crossroads"

Geographically, Ireland stands at the crossroads between North America and Europe. Some of the attitudes to ethics, economic activity and the role of business in society are a unique blend of American and European approaches. At the same time, Ireland is at a crossroads economically and socially. From being the "sick man of Europe" in the late 1980s, Ireland has become one of the fastest growing economies in the OECD, having been nicknamed the "Celtic Tiger". This new found prosperity has thrown up a host of ethical issues.

Certain questions have emerged from Ireland's "crossroads" status, which highlight issues of the relationship between business and society. These issues can be examined at the individual, corporate and societal levels, and at the crossroads of these three levels.

Individual Level

- Ireland has been a traditional Roman Catholic society. The Church played a strong role in regulating people's lives and behaviour, especially on sexual and socio-economic mores. This engendered an attitude where compliance with the dictate of the clergy became almost instinctive. Although the Church was a strong proponent of capitalism, it had nothing to say about standards of behaviour in business. At this level, there was a vacuum. The Church was traditionally anti-communist, anti-socialist and made every attempt to impede state assistance for underprivileged members of society, since communist countries were identified with atheism and "godlessness".

- At the same time, at the individual level, there has been a longstanding anti-establishment attitude, a vestige of the days when Ireland was a British colony. This resulted in massive tax evasion and social welfare fraud. Thus, people did not see themselves as members of a larger society whereby they had corresponding rights and obligations. Even now, eight decades after independence, there is a general failure to recognise the practical and ethical implications of wide-spread tax evasion. It is interesting that current moral outrage at some high level instances of tax evasion concentrates on the legalistic, rather than the substantive ethical implications. This invites a discourse on the ethical differences between tax avoidance and tax evasion.

- There is a high level of fraudulent insurance and injury claims, known as the "compo culture" – the compensation culture.

- Many of the wealthiest individuals in society have legally established residence in tax havens. This is a cause of some resentment.

- In the last 3–4 years, it has become apparent that there was a "golden circle" of wealthy individuals and company directors who had systematically engaged in corruption, tax fraud etc. over decades. So far, very few people have actually been brought to trial and fined or imprisoned. Despite 16 tribunals of inquiry into various breaches in different industries, for example, the beef industry, property development planning permission, etc.

Corporate Level

- In the past, Irish workplace practice was adversarial with a strong trade union presence. Nowadays, Irish business has become very market driven. Perhaps this is an outcome of deregulation, privatisation, and being so dependent on primarily American foreign direct investment. Although the prevalence of trade union membership in Ireland is among the highest in the EU, staff have minimal participation in real decision-making in the workplace.

- The banking sector has been caught out in a number of malpractices, involving complicity in tax evasion, misappropriation of funds, etc. The sector has adopted a defensive and legalistic posture, rather than a moral reflection on the behaviour of the protagonists involved and on how business is done in Ireland. There is a general tendency among business people to blame the media rather than to look at their own malpractice. In the public mind, it is also seen primarily as a legal issue. Nevertheless, retributive and punitive justice have been slow to come.

- In response to the various scandals, and in an effort to be seen to be "doing something", the government set up 14 tribunals of inquiry to investigate the different events. An Agency for Corporate Enforcement has been established to tackle white-collar crime.

- CSR is in its early stages. Although some companies are involved in philanthropy and sponsorship, a study showed that Irish companies have little interest in the establishment of a national index or "league tables" of best practice, like the FTSE4Good in the UK or the KLD Index in the US.

- The above point relates to the undeveloped state of socially responsible or ethical investment in Ireland, with only a handful of such funds. These are funds that are committed to the principle that investors must accept some responsibility for the actions of the companies from which they profit. The Irish Association of Pension Funds was unable to help with my inquiries about the availability and performance of such funds in Ireland. What demand there is for such investments tends to come from charities and religious orders.

It is suggested that one reason why there is little demand for these funds in Ireland is the perception that they lead to a reduction in investment performance. Yet, two existing ethical funds, the Friends First Stewardship Fund and the KBC Ethical Managed Fund, outperform their investment fund peers in terms of average returns over a 5-year period. These funds invest only in environmentally friendly and socially responsible companies, avoiding organisations that are involved in armaments manufacture or nuclear power, trade in oppressive regimes, cause pollution or exploit third-world economies and communities. They also avoid producers of tobacco or alcohol, along with companies that are involved in misleading advertising, or that have any links with the pornography industry.

In defence of their lack of enthusiasm for socially responsible investment, fund managers claim that there is not much difference between mainstream and ethical funds, because by-and-large, mainstream funds do not invest in companies involved in unethical behaviour. However, this is a rather passive attitude. In contrast, a new socially responsible investment fund was launched in late 2002 by Hibernian Investment Managers. It actively seeks out companies committed to sustainable development in industries of the future, such as education, water management, renewable energy, advanced communications, or traditional businesses whose management has adopted practices that contribute to sustainability. Hibernian is an Irish subsidiary of the Aviva Group. Hibernian Investment Managers works in partnership with an active London-based socially responsible fund manager, Morley Fund Management.

Irish investors who seek ethical funds are often directed to the UK where there is a good choice of funds that invest in socially responsible companies. However, there could be adverse tax implications for Irish investors in overseas funds.

Societal Level

- One of the main reasons for Ireland's economic success has been foreign direct investment, heavily dominated by American companies. These adopt a strongly unfettered capitalist approach. The American market approach is moderated by another cornerstone of Ireland's positive performance, its membership of the EU. As an EU member, Ireland has to abide by various measures that give rights to workers and adopt a more "stakeholder" approach than the strictly Anglo-Saxon model. This has been manifested in a series of social partnership agreements since the late 1980s. These agreements have involved the main employers' body, the trade unions, government, and others, such as the unemployed.

- In CSR terms consumers in Ireland have higher expectations of business with respect to economic performance and legal compliance than any social or community agenda. Lack of consumer expectation of CSR may be one of the reasons that business has not been so proactive in the CSR field.

- Despite the generation of wealth, relative levels of poverty and inequality of income in Ireland are among the highest in OECD countries, according to the UN Human Development Report.

- Ireland, for many centuries an emigrant nation, has suddenly itself become a haven for immigrants in the past couple of years. This is a new experience for the country which is finding it hard to cope. Some anti-immigrant sentiments have been apparent. This is all the more perplexing when there has been a strong awareness, over decades, of the inequities suffered by the Catholic population in Northern Ireland. As part of the Northern Ireland peace agreement, Commissions for Human Rights have been set up in both Northern Ireland and the Republic.

- There have been a series of scandals involving politicians. While this may be no different to other countries (compare Helmut Kohl), it has aroused a great deal of anger and cynicism. This has opened the way to the election of independents, as the voters shun the main political parties. A government dependent for its survival on independents will inevitably be unstable and will skew its decisions in a short-term way that may cater to local interests at the expense of the longer-term national good. This tends to distort the democratic process.

Summary of Issues Raised about the Role of Culture and Society in CSR in Ireland

This "case study" of Ireland raises a number of issues for consideration about the relationship between business and society in Ireland. While these issues are not unique to Ireland, they arise in a unique way, as influenced by cultural, historical, political and socio-economic factors, described above:

- where to find the values that underpin socially responsible business practice?
- issues of taking individual responsibility for one's conduct and outcomes,
- compliance versus commitment to ethical values and behaviour,
- how far can legalistic/imposed solutions go?
- the relationships between business, government and democracy,
- the relationships between a stakeholder society and stakeholder corporations,
- is there really a "third way"?
- the paradox of the contrast between economic prosperity and social inequity,
- the relationships among national, corporate and individual moral development.

Promoting CSR[1]

Business Incentives and Management Tools

Enterprise Ireland (Ireland's Development Agency for Indigenous Enterprise) works closely with its client companies to improve certain elements of CSR including their environmental performance. An initiative currently operating is the Environmental Management Scheme. This scheme provides financial assistance to Enterprise Ireland client companies, to support and train the company's management in the installation and running of an Environmental Management System (www.enterprise-ireland.com).

Enterprise Ireland also runs the Environmentally Superior Products Programme. This Programme was initially run as a pilot scheme from 1999 to 2001 and subsequently extended. It aims to encourage companies to reduce the environmental impact of their products. Under the Environmentally Superior Product initiative, suitable applicants may receive grant support for projects to assess the potential for the programme within their existing or new product ranges. The initiative is open to small to medium-sized enterprises (SMEs) engaged in manufacturing and that are within the remit of Enterprise Ireland, i.e. indigenous Irish manufacturing industries.

Public-Private Partnerships

- In 2001, the *National Centre for Partnership and Performance* was established by the Government to enable organisations in the private and public sector, through partnership between employers and worker, to respond to change, build capacity, and improve performance (www.ncpp.ie).

- *National and local partnerships* involving representatives from public and private sector organisations and public authorities are also increasingly being forged in response to social exclusion. One example of local partnership is *Area Development Management Ltd. (ADM)* which has responsibility for delivery of local development measures aimed at addressing the problems of social exclusion, poverty and unemployment in specific disadvantaged areas.

- In 1993 the Government established the *National Economic and Social Forum* to help develop a wider national consensus on social and economic policy initiatives, e.g. in relation to unemployment, equality and social exclusion. The Forum is composed of national and local public representatives, business, trade union and farm organisations, and community and voluntary sector organisations (www.nesf.ie).

- *Economic Regeneration / Employment Supports* – A new Social Economy Programme was launched in September 2000 which aims to support the quality of life of local disadvantaged areas by the provision of social services and the creation of enterprises and employment opportunities.

Raising Awareness

- The Irish Government supported the establishment of the business–led *Foundation for Investing in Communities* and *Business in the Community (BITC) – Ireland* with the aim to encourage businesses to make CSR and community involvement part of their mainstream business practices and encourage philanthropy.

- The first ever business-led *Conference in Ireland on Corporate Responsibility* was held in March 2003 in Dublin and was organised by BITC Ireland. CEOs from major business concerns discussed progress on Corporate Responsibility in the areas of the workplace, marketplace, community and environment, the business case for their involvement and the benefits for both the companies and the stakeholders involved.

Social/CSR Awards

- *Dublin Chamber of Commerce, Dublin City Council and Guinness Diageo*: *The Guinness Living Dublin Awards* for business in the community, working to improve the quality of life in Dublin City and Council (www.dubchamber.ie/glda/index.html).

- *IBEC: Irish Business and Employers Confederation: IBEC Environment Awards* to promote companies that develop innovative solutions to environmental problems faced by an individual industry or sector (www.ibec.ie).

- *Northside Partnership:* In October 2003 the Dublin based Northside Partnership presented *Corporate Social Responsibility Awards* and three special merit awards which acknowledged the commitment of companies to the work of the Northside Partnership and to improving the lives of people living and working in the local community.

- *BITC Corporate Social Responsibility Charter:* October 2003 Business in the Community Ireland presented *Corporate Social Responsibility Charters* to a number of its members. Under the terms of these Charters businesses undertake to promote Corporate Social Responsibility and to promote best practice in this regard.

CSR Toolkits

- *Business in the Community Ireland*: Company support tool to measure, support and improve the impact of the business on its stakeholders.

- *Business in the Community Ireland:* Workbook on employee community involvement for employers, employees and community organisations

Ensuring Transparency

Labels

Excellence through people standard, a Human Resources standard for companies who wish to have their human resources policies and practices independently verified and accredited by the Training and Employment Authority of Ireland (www.fas.ie/services_to_businesses/excellence_through_people.html).

Social Labels/Certifications

- *Fair Trade products*, sold in Ireland by OXFAM Ireland and various retail members of the Association of fair Trade Shops in Ireland.

- *Fairtrade Mark Ireland*, operated by the Irish Fair Trade Network (IFTN), member of the Fairtrade Labelling Organisations International (FLO) (www.fair-mark.org).

- *Excellence Ireland*: Q Mark recognition for quality in management and operations, for large companies and Foundation Mark for SMEs (www.excellence-ireland.ie).

- *FAS:* Irish Training and Employment Authority: Excellence through People Standard (www.fas.ie).

CSR Supportive Policies

Sustainable Development

- In January 2003, the Irish Department of Enterprise, Trade and Employment published a new *Strategy on Sustainable Development*, which sets tasks and targets relating to the impact of business in areas such as Climate Change and Competitive Sustainability. It includes a new Strategy Goal on Corporate Social Responsibility. Implementation of this Strategy has commenced and selected measures are underway to enhance the capacity of enterprises to move towards sustainable management practices.

- *Comhar* – the National Sustainable Development Partnership, was set up in 1999 to produce a set of principles on sustainable development in Ireland for policy makers and the general public. It includes representatives of the public sector, business, environmental NGOs, community NGOs, and the professional/academic Sector.

Fiscal Policies

- In the *2001 Finance Act*, a reform of the regulation of charities and charitable fundraising provided that donations to charitable organisations by the corporate sector would be treated as a trading expense.

CSR-Related Legislation

Workplace

- *Sustaining Progress* is a national Agreement which was recently ratified by Irish social partners – the government, employers, trade unions and the community and voluntary sectors. The agreement covers a wide range of issues including redundancy payments, statutory minimum pay, work/life balance programmes and workplace learning.

- *Pensions Amendment Act (2002)* provides for the introduction of a framework for Personal Retirement Savings Accounts (PRSA), a long-term retirement account designed to meet the requirements of current and future employment patterns in a flexible manner.

Community

- *NCV: The National Committee on Volunteering* was established in December 2000, following proposals in the Programme for Prosperity and Fairness and the subsequent White Paper, Supporting Voluntary Activity. Its work has to include examining and making recommendations on the development of a National Policy and Infrastructure to support the voluntary sector in Ireland.

- The report entitled *Tipping the Balance* was launched in October 2002 and includes recommendations on the development and support of Corporate Community Involvement through Employer Supported Volunteering (www.ncvireland.ie).

- The *Special Olympics Games* were held in Ireland in June 2003 and 30,000 volunteers took part. BITC (Ireland) encouraged and organised corporate volunteering for the event. In addition 99 towns all over Ireland volunteered to act as host communities for the 7,000 athletes and 3,000 coaches and official delegates.

Environment

- *Sustainable Energy Act (2002)* provides for the establishment of a Sustainable Energy Authority of Ireland to promote and assist environmentally and economically sustainable production, supply and use of energy.

- The *plastic bag levy* was introduced on 4th March 2002, under the Waste Management (Environmental Levy) (Plastic Bag) Regulations 2001. The levy applies to the supply of plastic shopping bags, with certain exemptions, by retailers to customers. The purpose of the levy (15 cent on each plastic bag supplied at the point of sale) is to change consumer behaviour and achieve a significant reduction in the use of plastic shopping bags, thereby reducing the number of plastic bags that end up as litter. Proceeds from the levy are used to fund various litter, waste management and other environmental initiatives. The cooperation and support of the general public and the business sector was crucial in introducing this initiative and ensuring its success. It is estimated that the levy has reduced the consumption of plastic bags by over 90 %.

Conclusions and Future Directions

In general, a combination of traditional anti-establishment sentiment, ethical breaches, religious right-wing nationalism and, more recently, the embrace and success of US style capitalism, have not been conducive to the development of genuine CSR in Ireland. However, solidarity with the EU is a countervailing force toward greater mutual cooperation between business and society, as is what is regarded as the "business case" for CSR. This is a weak and probably unsustainable basis for the adoption of decent and appropriate behaviour – what if the "business case" does not work out? However, possibly, if Irish enterprises adopt CSR on the basis of the business case, it may become institutionalised in the cultures of adopting organisations and come to be seen as worth doing in its own right.

Note

[1] The contribution of M. Dominique Bé of the European Commission in compiling some of the material on Irish CSR initiatives is gratefully acknowledged.

Further Internet Links

Business in the Community (BITC) Ireland
www.bitc.ie

Comhar – National Sustainable Development Partnership
www.comhar-nsdp.ie

BELGIUM

6   A Hot Topic in Contemporary Management

Aimé Heene, Suzan Langenberg, and Nikolay Dentchev

The Societal and Institutional Context of CSR in Belgium

Belgium, located in the middle of Europe, has approximately ten million (6 million Dutch-speaking, 4 million French-speaking, and about 71,000 German-speaking) inhabitants. The country is known for its early industrialisation. Belgium's earliest "mindset" for CSR was set through the emergence of the unions in the second half of the 19th century alongside a developing charitable attitude of some entrepreneurs.

Literature on the cultural and historical background of Belgium confirms that the phenomenon of collective responsibility for the people's well-being is the result of centuries of occupation (until 1830) by diverse foreign powers. Because of these occupations a typical inwardness and collective internal defence has developed. This is specifically the case for the Dutch-speaking Northern region of Flanders because this part of Belgium suffered the most under the uninterrupted domination.

Until the middle of the 20th century the heavy, large scale steel industry and the coal mining industry dominated the Belgian industrial landscape, especially in the Walloon provinces, the southern, French speaking, part of Belgium; Flanders, the Northern, Dutch speaking, part of Belgium is a typically SME-region, and is industrially more diversified than the southern part. Almost 99% of all Flemish business activity is in the hands of small and medium sized enterprises (companies with less than 500 employees). These small companies together provide more than 70% of the employment in the Belgian business environment (Delmotte et al., 2003: 9).

Recent social research shows that the Flemish civilian population primarily expects firms to create welfare and well-being (employment, competence development) in an accountable way (VEV, 2002: 16). A recent survey by GfK Worldwide (*De Tijd*, 2003: 24) shows that Belgians in general develop a high level of trust in professional groups. Managers are the most trusted professional group in the Flemish civilian population: about 59% of the Flemish civilian population trusts managers and business leaders (VEV, 2002). The same survey showed that about 80% of Flemish managers interviewed showed high trust in business life. This survey allows the conclusion that corporate scandals (such as Lernout and Hauspie) did not significantly harm trust in the business community in general. Sociological research on "social trust towards institutions" leads to more subtle conclusions: only 40% of interviewees show the highest levels of trust in business life (Elchardus & Smits, 2001). It further shows that CSR is not *explicitly* represented in public opinion.

Other research confirmed that an intense cooperation among diverse parties in the Flemish community (that can only develop under conditions of high trust in society) allowed the resolution of a satisfactory solution for major employment problems such as the one created by Renault (a lay-off of more than 2500 employees). This case ended successfully for the majority of the employees as almost 85% of the former Renault employees eventually found a new job within two years (Vandoorne, De Cuyper, Verlinden, De Witte & Kieselbach, 2003: 92).

The Origins of CSR in Belgium

It has been observed before that "Corporate social responsibility is a huge issue in Belgium" and that Belgium has done pioneering work by issuing the law of February 27, 2002, introducing "the social label" aimed to "create a label for companies to put on their products if a company adhered to criteria and standards recognised by the International Labour Organisation" (Aaronson & Reeves, 2002: 45 – 46). It should further be observed that the Belgian government has a long-standing commitment to implementing the OECD Guidelines. In addition, the Social Economic Council of Flanders (SERV – 2000) reformulated its mission into the direction of CSR topics. This declaration formed the basis for the *Treaty of Vilvoorde* (Pact van Vilvoorde – 2001). This treaty between the Flemish government and the "midfield players" lists 21 objectives to be reached by Flanders by 2010 at the latest. A number of these objectives explicitly refer to CSR.

Generally speaking, the majority of formally organised CSR initiatives emerged in the past decade, be it inspired and stimulated by public (national or supranational, i.e. European) initiatives, or be it predominantly inspired by religious or other personal values. The latter was for instance the case for the Flemish Network for Business Ethics (Vlaams Netwerk voor Zakenethiek), founded in 1994 by four secondary school teachers who started the network to create "critical mass" in the domain of business ethics.

Earlier research (Heene, Van Laere, Desmidt & Dentchev, 2002: 325 – 367) has shown that the application of CSR in practice is often inspired by very personal values, by obvious and clear business needs (such as the difficulties of finding the right workforce on the labour market), or by the fact that CSR is a "hot topic" in contemporary management.

However, one should note that recent surveys have shown that ethical values as such are not the prime drivers of CSR in Belgian *small and medium sized companies*. Here, CSR seems to be much more driven by customer satisfaction and the aim to build a better relationship with the community (VKW, s.d.).

Ethical values do however play an inherent role in the approach that Flemish and Belgian firms follow specifically towards employees and towards the environment. "Caring for the well-being of the employee" is an implicit value in many Belgian organisations, expressed by for instance the *active* presence of many union members in those organisations, even though an open communication about ethical values is quasi non-existent in either Belgian or Flemish firms.

The role that the unions traditionally play in business in Belgium can hardly be underestimated. Unions determine to a large degree the specific evolution of labour-related human relationships within companies. Belgian trade unions primarily defend the rights of workers, rather than engaging in a joint formulation of employee policy with employers. The unions are however slow in their active participation in CSR issues especially in the *explicit* commitment to CSR towards their members and their own administration. A real implementation of CSR issues in their mission and approach to labour market concerns is still missing. This is in contrast to employers' associations (UNIZO, VOKA, VBO) whose members often participate in CSR debates.

Another striking aspect of the socially responsible approach towards employees in Belgium is that companies do everything possible – long before it becomes public – to prevent dismissals in the first place by offering retraining, internal job transitions, active job rotation and other related human resources management practices. As a consequence companies may wait far too long for the active involvement of employees in the business concerns, and above all for the start of the communication processes with external parties (government, unions, advisory boards) in order to get a shared responsibility and to build on a pro-active sustainable social-economic policy. The 2003 "Ford-Genk" crisis is a very good example of the negative effects of a continuous postponement of communication.

Landmark Events Regarding CSR in Belgium

The landmark events that boosted the interest in CSR in the Belgian and Flemish business community are listed (chronologically) and described below.

The Foundation of BENSC (1997)

BENSC (Belgian Network for Social Cohesion), the Belgian national partner of EBNSC (European Business Network for Social Cohesion) was founded in 1997, and originally aimed at achieving five important objectives (all in line with the emphasis on "labour issues" that clearly characterises the Belgian situation):

- to advance the integration of the underprivileged in the labour market,

- to improve professional education,

- to prevent preclusion in the workplace,

- to create new businesses and new jobs,

- to promote solidarity with the underprivileged.

After about five years of existence, EBNSC decided to broaden its scope from social cohesion to corporate social responsibility and redefined its mission and activities and is now called *CSR Europe*. BENSC changed course as well and changed its name into *Business and Society Belgium* in 2001. The focus on matters of "social cohesion" remains however an important attribute of the organisation.

The TRIVISI Initiative (from 2000 on)

"Trivisi" is an initiative taken in 2000 by the Flemish Minister of Employment and Tourism. Trivisi is aimed at stimulating entrepreneurship and management that take the three components of the "triple bottom line" fully into account. From the employment point of view three topics get special attention: managing diversity, learning, and responsible behaviour towards all the firm's stakeholders.

A very broad spectrum of firms, NGOs, social partners, academics, and experts actively participate in Trivisi. They develop and test instruments for applying CSR, exchange best practices, and build knowledge in the application of CSR.

Trivisi distributes brochures, checklists, CD-ROMs on CSR in the Flemish business community so that the research and development efforts of the partners can be leveraged.

In June 2002 Trivisi organised a conference to present all the material that had in the meantime been prepared. About 500 companies attended the conference.

The initiative was evaluated in June 2002 and as a result the decision to continue the initiative was taken. Four new projects were launched. These projects now mainly focus on the development of course material in CSR, the integration of underprivileged groups in the labour market, the development of teaching and learning methods for adults, and the introduction of the "social label".

The Belgian Participation in the "Social Convoy and Sustainable Employment" (SOCOSE) (2000 – 2003)

This European project explores new European arrangements for outplacement, as part of the larger concept of employability. This project confirmed that Belgium is far ahead – in relation to the other participating countries Germany, The Netherlands, Italy and Spain – in legislation concerning the protection of employees (Verlinden & De Witte, 2003; SOCOSE, 2003).

The SOCOSE project adopts the normative position that "the companies themselves that dismiss employees or ask for greater flexibility should to a greater extent than in the past be considered responsible. At the same time (…) individuals should become active partners in the process of re-orientation who bring in their personal initiative" (Kieselbach & Mader, 2002).

The Flemish Employers' Association's Congress of 2001

Though many other examples of conferences and congresses could be given, we want to especially mention the 2001 congress of the Flemish Employer's Association (FEA), a dominant employers' association in Flanders.

The most interesting feature of the 2001 congress was the attempt that was undertaken to integrate different interpretations of CSR into one more integrating framework (VEV, 2001, 2002). Sustainable development, triple bottom line thinking, and stakeholder management were presented during the conference as different approaches to CSR and were combined into one umbrella framework for CSR. It is particularly interesting to observe the attention paid by the Flemish Employers' Association to stakeholder dialogue and to increasing the firm's "accountability" towards its different stakeholder groups.

It should certainly be noticed that other dominant employers' associations (UNIZO (small SME's), VKW, VBO) have recently put CSR on their agenda and as a result deploy a diversity of activities aimed at promoting CSR in Flanders.

Employers associations thus highly contribute to the wide spread of CSR in the Belgian business community mainly in order to support their members in effectively applying CSR in practice.

Corporate Social Responsibility on the European Social Policy Agenda, Conference of the Belgian Presidency of the European Union (2001)

In the summer of 2001, the European Commission published a Green Paper launching a broad consultation on the European approach to corporate social responsibility. It is in this framework that the Belgian presidency of the European Union decided to organise a first conference on the place of Corporate Social Responsibility on the European social policy agenda (Belgian Presidency of the European Union, 2001).

For the first time, a European Union Presidency organised a debate on CSR that attracted 1,000 people, coming from 42 countries, with more than 600 delegates from outside Belgium. The speakers were evenly divided among the stakeholders:

managers, social partners, consumer organisations, development and fair trade NGOs, investors and researchers. For the first time, the central theme was the "role of the public authorities", shifting the focus of discussion which has for too long been the monopoly of large companies. Moreover, this CSR conference avoided being side-tracked by the exchange of experiences, case studies and marketing efforts, but concentrated on the underlying issues.

It should be stressed that the Belgian government's interest in CSR is mainly inspired by its concern for matters of employment, labour related issues, and social cohesion. These are undoubtedly the major underlying drivers of many initiatives on CSR taken in Flanders and Belgium.

The Federal Governmental, Interdepartmental CSR Study Group (from 2002 on)

The political agenda of Belgium has been influenced positively towards CSR through the participation of the Flemish (Agalev) and the Walloon (Ecolo) green parties in the Federal Government during four years (1999 – 2003). In the Walloon provinces the Regional Government focused on the reduction of nuclear energy and in Flanders the Regional Government focused on environmental issues. This has had an impact on companies because a lot of reckless expansion was restricted and the control of companies was focused on environmental aspects (use of water, pollution of soil etc.).

In 2002 the Federal Government set up an interdepartmental study group where all the different federal departments are represented. The Green Paper of the European Commission is used as the basis for developing a Belgian federal CSR policy, one of the priorities of this initiative. The study group wants to develop a consistent, integral and integrated policy concerning CSR and is an important stimulus in the start of a broad social and national debate on the social responsibility of companies, governments and social actors in Belgium.

The (Forthcoming) Legislation on "Whistle Blowing"

The Flemish government is now preparing a decree that will provide protection for civil servants in case they want to protest against misuse, abuse and injustice in an organisation. A specific commission for "Institutional and administrative reform and administrative affairs" in 2003 has confirmed this decree (Vandekerckhove, 2002).

The bill prescribes that a civil servant who wants to blow the whistle has to first warn his chief and secondly the internal audit. When there is no response from both levels the civil servant can bring in the "Ombudsdienst" as a neutral institution. This neutral agency is authorised, after a thorough research, to declare the claim admissible. It is a remarkable fact that in comparison with other countries and regions, Flanders has the most progressive approach of whistle blower legislation.

Other CSR Stimulating Elements in Belgium

Besides these landmark events, a second element that has contributed to the wide spread of CSR is the advent and rise of "ethical investment funds" and organisations like ETHIBEL, an independent consultancy agency founded in 1992 that supports banks and investment companies in creating their offer of ethical investments, and that evaluates investment funds on their degree of "ethicalness".

As a third element, we want to mention the attention paid to corporate governance that inevitably invites firms to rethink their relationships with their environment and more specifically helps them to better understand and interpret the concept of "stakeholders" and CSR in practice.

Academic Research in Corporate Social Responsibility

All Belgian universities have research programmes in CSR. Research on CSR is carried out in disciplines such as: biological sciences, chemical sciences, engineering sciences, economic and applied economic sciences, business ethics, law, business administration (*Business & Society Belgium Magazine*, 2003).

The research is inspired by and focuses on very specific themes and topics that follow immediately from the applied disciplines themselves. There is hardly any multi-disciplinary research taking place. Only the CDO (Centre for Sustainable Development at Ghent University) makes the difference at this moment. The clear lack of incentives to develop multi-disciplinary research may serve to explain this phenomenon.

The most dominant, most active and best known players in the research field are at the Katholieke Universiteit Leuven, Ghent University and the Vlerick Leuven Ghent Management School (Dentchev, Heene & Van de Peer, 2003). Research in *business ethics* and *in sustainable development* dominate the research field in Flanders. In the Walloon provinces research is more exclusively focused on sustainability and on environmental issues. The historical evolution of the economy in both regions largely explains these differences.

Prospects for the Future

One may expect that CSR practices will further spread in the business community. Stakeholders are progressively exercising more and more influence on firms. The government is progressively involving firms in the realisation of societal objectives and as a result progressively invites (or compels) firms to take responsibilities that go beyond "making profit for shareholders". More and more consultants are offering services to implement CSR in practice, executive educational initiatives are increasingly offered to the business community, and CSR will in the future be offered as a course in the basic education. The Ghent University for instance, will for the first time offer a course in CSR in the 3rd Bachelor in Applied Economics from the academic year 2006 – 2007 onwards.

Both the Federal and the Flemish authorities recently announced their intentions to pass rules and regulations regarding the implementation of CSR in the near future. The Federal Minister of Environment, Consumer Affairs and Sustainable Development is now starting a broad consultation process on a number of measures she wants to take to promote CSR. Employers' organisations reject any further regulation of CSR by government (VKW, s.d.).

In order to stimulate the application of corporate socially responsible firm behaviour that goes beyond the mere compliance with legal rules and regulations, it is in our opinion essential to develop a clear and precise economic and strategic rationale for corporate social responsibility.

Earlier research (Heene, Vermeylen, Van Laere & Vandersickel, 2001; Heene, Van Laere, Desmidt & Dentchev, 2002) showed that such an economic and strategic rationale for corporate social responsibility is not always prominently present in the manager's mind. Not developing an economic and strategic CSR rationale risks reducing the application of corporate social responsibility to benevolence and voluntarism, and more importantly may hinder the management from taking full advantage of the application of corporate social responsibility. Developing such an economic and strategic rationale for CSR is one of the focuses in our own research.

Analysis and Conclusion

The mindset and mentality regarding CSR in Belgium was first of all driven by social concerns that emerged as a result of the early industrial history of Belgium. Nowadays the focus on social coherence is characteristic of the entire Belgian culture. The strong development of regional identities since the Second World War, distinguished focus and concern: the Walloon region worked out an economic survival through a renewal of old industries and Flanders experienced a spectacular economic growth. The Walloon region is somewhat behind in the development of a CSR climate because of its focus on profit on behalf of the economic backlog for some decades. The lack of open communication on and transparency in business policies may lead to the impression that Belgium is far behind in the development of a CSR mentality. It should be noted for instance that social reporting has hardly got started in Belgian companies. In comparison with companies in Belgium's neighbouring states one can at this moment hardly find annual reports of Belgian companies with a chapter on sustainability or another facet of CSR. In the Belgian culture, however, it is no common habit to make voluntarily taken initiatives public. Driven by the region's culture, Flemish firms have no real tradition in explicit communication on their business practices and on the drivers of these practices. Any analysis of explicit communications on CSR (as these can be found in the annual reports, in mission statements, on firm's websites) would therefore inevitably lead to a distorted view on the practices of CSR in Flemish (and Belgian) companies.

In general we can discover a real CSR mindset that however largely remains implicit, due to a basic cultural characteristic of the Belgian culture.

References

Aaronson, S. A., & Reeves, J. 2002. *The European Response to Public Demands for Global Corporate Responsibility*. s.l.: National Policy Association.

Belgian Presidency of the European Union. 2001. *Corporate Social Responsibility* on *the European Social Policy agenda.* http://www.socialresponsibility.be/reports, accessed 28.08.2004.

Business & *Society Belgium Magazine.* 2003. *Maatschappelijk verantwoord ondernemen verovert steeds meer de wereld.* November, No. 12: 23 – 25.

Delmotte, J., Vandenbempt, K., Verlinden, R., Manshoven, J., Van Gyes, G., Van Ruysse-veldt, J., & Ramioul, M. 2003. *Arbeid in de kenniseconomie.* Leuven: HIVA

Dentchev, N. A., Heene, A., & Van de Peer, S. 2003. *Expertrapport: Mainstreaming van maatschappelijk verantwoord ondernemen.* Brussel: VIONA.

De Tijd. 2003. Blakend van Vertrouwen. November 26: 24.

Elchardus, M., & Smits, W. 2001. Een wantrouwig landje. Maatschappelijk vertrouwen in Vlaanderen. In Ministerie van de Vlaamse Gemeenschap: *Vlaanderen Gepeild. De Vlaamse Overheid en Burgeronderzoek:* 43 – 71. Brussel: Administratie Planning en Statistiek.

Heene, A., Van Laere, K., Desmidt, S., & Dentchev, N. A. 2002. Sociale Cohesie. In: L. Peeters, P., Matthyssens, & L. Vereeck (Eds.), *Corporate Social Responsibility: een verkennend onderzoek. Stakeholder Synergie*: 325 – 267. Leuven-Apeldoorn: Garant.

Heene, A., Vermeylen, S., Van Laere, K., & Vandersickel, E. 2001. Who's "in" and who's "out"? Lyon: Paper presented at the EGOS conference. July 5 – 7.

Kieselbach, Th., & Mader, S. 2002. Occupational transitions and corporate responsibility in layoffs: a European research project (SOCOSE). *Journal of Business Ethics*, 39: 13 – 20

SOCOSE. 2003. *Social Convoy and Sustainable employability, Innovative strategies for Outplacement/Replacement Counselling.* SOCOSE project founded by the EC. http://www.ipg.uni-bremen.de/research/socose, accessed 28.08.2004.

Vandekerckhove, W. 2002. Het voorstel van decreet inzake klokkenluiders van Dirk Hole-mans. *Ethiek & Maatschappij,* 6(2): 87 – 103.

Vandoorne, J., De Cuyper, N., Verlinden, R., De Witte, H., & Kieselbach, T. 2003. *Bedrijven en werknemers in nood: op zoek naar innovatieve strategieën voor "outplacement" en "replacement".* Leuven: HIVA .

Verlinden, R., De Witte, H. 2003. *Dismissed, but entitled to Out- and replacement?* Leuven: HIVA.

VEV. 2001. *Duurzaam Ondernemen... focus op geld, talent en ruimte.* Antwerpen: VEV.

VEV. 2002. *Win Vertrouwen. Win Groeikracht.* Enquêteresultaten: De mening van de burgers. Antwerpen: VEV.

VKW. s.d. Verantwoord Ondernemen – Grond- of vernislaag? s.l.: VKW.

Further Internet Links

Business & Society Belgium
www.businessandsociety.be

Kauri-Network
www.kauri.be

Vlaams Network Voor Zakenethik VZW
www.ethiekenonderneming.com

7 Redefining Positions in Society

Jacqueline Cramer

Introduction

In the Netherlands the issue of corporate social responsibility has gained increasing importance since the mid-1990s. What changed then was not so much the attention paid to social and environmental issues, because this had been a tradition for many years. Rather it was the way in which companies developed their individual visions and ideals to incorporate this theme and went beyond mere compliance with regulation. In addition, companies needed to communicate more openly than before about their performance with their employees and with the diverse stakeholders.

The main driver of corporate social responsibility in the Netherlands was the clear change in positions between enterprises, government and citizens. Complementing this development was a rise in social responsibility, within the framework of the civil society. In order to underpin this explanation, a brief overview will be presented of the historical roots of corporate social responsibility. Next, it will be explained which events triggered the development of corporate social responsibility in the Netherlands and which actors are presently involved. Finally, conclusions will be drawn about the progress made in the Netherlands in the area of corporate social responsibility and the future prospects.

Historical Roots of Corporate Social Responsibility

Corporate social responsibility has a long history in the Netherlands[1]. Towards the end of the 19th century socially responsible entrepreneurship was becoming an issue among some frontrunners in industry. For instance, the entrepreneur Van Marken, founder of the biochemical industry in Delft, introduced a works council as well as other facilities for his workers. He even went as far as supporting the textile workers in the Twente region in their strike against lower wages (SER, 2001). The employers who provided social services did so voluntarily; there were scarcely any legal obligations on them to do so.

Another important factor was the rise of trade unions and the development of their ideas on social issues at the end of the 19th century. The first trade unions concentrated on representing the interests of the members in their own professions, especially over wages and working hours. They also established funds to provide assistance during illness, in old age and in the event of death. The socio-political opinions of among others, the trade unions, triggered the debate about how much influence the government should have and what social matters should be arranged collectively or privately. After the Second World War this led to the creation of public schemes and the gradual implementation of the system of social security (SER, 2001). With the introduction of public social security, the focus of socially responsible business shifted from providing social services for the company's own employees to social issues of concern beyond the walls of the company itself. The leading role of government in social engineering lasted until the 1980s. Then a new debate arose about the division of responsibilities. This led to elements of social security once more becoming the object of collective negotiations between employers' associations and unions, or being left to individuals to insure for themselves.

During the 1960s another societal concern came to the fore: the environmental pollution problem. The first people in the Netherlands who, in the late 1940s, had already begun to call attention to environmental issues, were scientists and nature conservationists. However, it took until the mid-1960s before the new environmentalism caught the attention of Dutch society. The rise of this new environmentalism coincided with a turning point in the Dutch political culture. At that time quite a number of Dutch people began to denounce the opaque and depoliticised character of political decision-making. Moreover, they began to object to the rigid social order, which had dominated Dutch society since 1945. This changing political and cultural climate in the Netherlands after the mid-1960s broadened the political field and allowed extra-parliamentary interest groups to arise. Among them were environmental groups (Cramer, 1990).

Influenced by the growing environmental concerns of the public at large, particularly in the early 1970s, the Dutch government established a special Department of Health and Environmental Hygiene in 1971. Moreover, a variety of environmental laws and regulations were enacted during this period. After having 15 years of experience with the implementation of environmental regulation, the limits to the effectiveness of regulatory instruments became obvious. In fact, regulation led to a rather defensive attitude of companies towards improving their environmental performance. In order to promote a more pro-active approach of industry, the government propagated a new philosophy called self-regulation. The essence of this philosophy was to encourage environmentally friendly behaviour among citizens, firms and administrative bodies by reminding them of their own responsibilities to help solve environmental problems. This policy fitted very well in the overall philosophy of the government in the 1980s and particularly also in the 1990s, which aimed to decrease its involvement in social engineering and stimulate industry to take the lead (Cramer, 1990).

At the same time, there was a change process going on within the environmental movement. Originally, most environmental action groups originally considered industry as their enemy and put pressure on the Dutch government to strengthen regulation. However, since the late 1980s, the tide gradually turned. Then, these organisations became less inclined to try and influence the policies set by the national government, as they used to do. Instead they began to expand their energy on calling directly upon individual companies to accept their responsibility. The latter took the shape either of direct, organised action that was intended to step up the pressure on such organisations, or of the formation of new alliances between firms and organised environmental groups. In the Netherlands, for example, cooperative agreements have been made between the Friends of the Earth Netherlands and potato producers regarding the use of hazardous pesticides; with bulb producers about ecologically produced bulbs; and (in cooperation with other non-profit organisations) with retailers about the sale of wood certified by the Forest Stewardship Council.

This shift in the attitude towards business over the last few decades has not only become visible among environmental groups, but also in society at large. The former adversarial approach of extra-parliamentary interest groups towards industry has gradually evolved into a more cooperative attitude.

The Rise of Corporate Social Responsibility

The rise of corporate social responsibility in the 1990s fell on fertile soil for several reasons.

First, the philosophy behind corporate social responsibility corresponded well with the shift in power relations between the Dutch government and industry and a stronger dependence on market forces. This has led to a corresponding change in the nature of the role played by the Dutch government as the defender of public interests. On the one hand, public authorities tended to leave a number of tasks, which they traditionally carried out themselves, to the private sector. On the other hand, they were also required to give a clearer lead by setting the frame of reference in which companies must operate. The private sector was being given an increasingly free rein, within the limits set by the government, to match supply levels as closely as possible with the level of demand. As a result, greater responsibility is being placed on the shoulders of companies.

Secondly, the Dutch people generally have a great societal consciousness and expect from industry a responsible behaviour. The number of people who are members of one of more non-governmental organisations, is relatively high (80%). The same holds for the willingness to accept relatively high government expenditures on development aid and to donate money in emergency situations. At the same time, the purchasing of environmentally and/or socially responsible products remains a niche market.

Thirdly, the political climate was favourable. The liberal/socio-democratic coalition (the so-called purple coalition) actively promoted the importance of corporate social responsibility and was willing to give financial support to initiatives in this area. And after this coalition had to resign, the new liberal/Christian-democratic coalition continued its support.

Fourthly, the process of secularisation starting in the 1960s, further evolved. As a result the traditional view on the role of business in society changed as well. In the past, corporate social responsibility was more inspired by religious norms and values and primarily focussed on business ethics. In the course of time, however, the issue gradually acquired a more strategic character, incorporating the position of business vis-à-vis society at large.

Finally, the Dutch socio-political decision-making is based on the participation of a great variety of organisations, which have to negotiate with each other in order to reach consensus. This so-called polder model already dates back far in Dutch history. Because of the peculiarities of the Dutch election system, based on proportional representation and low voting quotas for new parties, the threshold for the admittance of these new parties into parliament is rather low. As a result, the government always consisted of a coalition of two or more parties. Moreover, the employers' organisations and the trade unions were also quite willing to reach consensus. This socio-political climate also stimulated various stakeholders to become active in corporate social responsibility.

Main Triggers to Promote Corporate Social Responsibility[2]

The Catalytic Role of the Dutch Social and Economic Council

In the Netherlands a catalytic role in the debate about corporate social responsibility has been played by the Dutch Social and Economic Council (SER). This influential advisory body of the Dutch government in which employers' organisations, trade-unions and independent members participate, published the advisory report "Corporate Social Responsibility – A Dutch Approach" in December 2000 (SER, 2001). This report was written at the request of the Ministry of Economic Affairs after discussions in Dutch Parliament about the way in which the Dutch government dealt with the issue of corporate social responsibility. In its report the SER adopted a general approach to the concept of corporate social responsibility and highlighted certain potential applications in a number of policy areas. The SER states that corporate social responsibility encompasses the core business of any company. In the SER's view the "social" activities of a firm are an inseparable element of corporate policy, so that the distinction between core business and non-core business is irrelevant.

The SER feels there are two key elements that "dictate whether one can rightly refer to *socially responsible business* in this day and age:

- consciously targeting business activities towards value creation on three levels – Profit, People, Planet – and hence contributing to society's prosperity in the longer term;

- maintaining a relationship with the various stakeholders which is based on transparency and dialogue and which responds to the legitimate demands of society".

Response of the Dutch Government

In response to this SER advice the government issued in March 2001 a document under the title "Corporate Social Responsibility: the Government perspective". In this document the government endorsed the main lines of the SER advice and promised to actively support the further penetration of corporate social responsibility. For example, it agreed to the re-vitalisation of the National Contact Point for Multinational Enterprises. This inter-ministerial body had been established earlier in order to implement the OECD Guidelines for Multinational Enterprises, first issued in the 1980s. These guidelines reflect the joint expectations of the governments of the OECD member countries with respect to the social conduct of multinational corporations. To enhance a properly functioning Dutch NCP this body should provide information and advice about the OECD guidelines and also explain to industry their correct interpretation.

Next, the government proposed to set up a knowledge and information centre for corporate social responsibility, to be used by industry. And finally, the government decided to ask the Council for Annual Reporting to recommend how the reporting of companies about corporate social responsibility can be improved. This led to the revision of the guideline 400 (as part of the Guidelines for Annual Reporting) and a document to assist companies in reporting on corporate social responsibility (Council for Annual Reporting, 2003a, 2003b).

The government proposals mentioned above were approved by the Parliament and then put into practice. One issue remained unresolved: whether or not it was desirable to make reporting on corporate social responsibility compulsory. A plea was made by Members of Parliament from the Social Democratic Party and Green Left to introduce an obligatory reporting system for internationally operating companies. However, their motion did not succeed.

In response to the initiatives taken by the national government, local governments also became interested in the issue of corporate social responsibility. Both town and provincial authorities began to stimulate corporate social responsibility in industry.

Response of Industry

To monitor the progress made within industry with respect to corporate social responsibility, the Ministry of Economic Affairs carried out a study among 300 SMEs and larger companies in 2003 (Ministry of Economic Affairs, 2003). The main conclusions were the following:

- 72% of the respondents tells that they assume corporate social responsibility but only 18% meets the criteria for being socially responsible set in advance by the researchers

- About one third of the companies importing from or investing in developing countries is familiar with the OECD Guidelines

- 50% of the companies has a specific training and educational policy for their employees

- One out of five companies imposes several requirements on their suppliers

- About 44% of the larger companies reports about corporate social responsibility, while this is hardly the case for SMEs.

From these results it becomes clear that the implementation of corporate social responsibility is still in an early stage. Particularly the larger, multinational companies have started to put in place policies and measures and publish sustainability reports. The external pressure on those companies is higher than on SMEs due to their greater public exposure and the risk of reputation damage.

However, what we do see, is a growing interest of Dutch companies to join initiatives that aim to promote corporate social responsibility. For instance, companies joined organisations like the Dutch branch of CSR Europe (called Business in Society) and the Social Venture Network. Moreover, they exchange views about the issue within their sector and employers' organisations. And finally, they participate in programmes that focus on the implementation of corporate social responsibility in practice. An example of the latter is the programme "From Financial to Sustainable Profit" coordinated by the National Initiative for Sustainable Development in which 19 large companies and SMEs participated from May 2000 – December 2002. This programme aimed to encourage the participating companies to integrate corporate social responsibility into their day-to-day working practices and communication strategies (Cramer, 2003). As a follow-up of this programme a new two-year programme "Corporate Social Responsibility in an International Context" has been set up in early 2003 together with 21 other companies.

Other Influential Actors

Financial Sector

One other very influential group in enhancing corporate social responsibility in the Netherlands has been the financial sector. Particularly the banks have actively promoted corporate social responsibility through investment programmes set up specifically for this purpose. In the last ten years these so-called sustainability investment funds have rapidly grown in number and size. Every respectable bank now has at least one "sustainability fund" to meet the demands of customers for such funds.

A major catalyst in the development of "sustainability funds" was the introduction of the Green Fund System (GFS) in 1992. This joint operation between the Dutch government and the financial sector consisted of a combination of tax incentives, a specially designed framework to designate green projects, and the active involvement of the financial sector. The GFS is incorporated into the income tax system so that if private individuals participate in a GF they receive a tax exemption. The GFS is restricted to green (environmental) projects (e.g. forestry, wind energy, organic agriculture, nature conservation, etc.). The GFS offers financial advantages for entrepreneurs who initiate or own green projects. This has boosted the number of environmental projects being undertaken (Bellegem, 2001).

In the course of the 1990s awareness of socially responsible investing increased among small investors due to factors like the success of the GFS and flourishing stock markets. Moreover, the interest in this type of investing has grown among professional investors, viz. the pension funds.

Non-governmental Organisations

Non-governmental organisations (NGOs) also belong to the group of influential actors in promoting the awareness of companies for corporate social responsibility in the Netherlands. Among them are environmental, development, human rights and consumer organisations. Until recently, however, the various NGOs hardly worked together on this issue. Each of them tended to stress their own points depending on their particular strategy and focus. This pattern of "doing politics" dates back to the 1960s and 1970s, when a great number of these NGOs were established. People from a variety of political and social backgrounds became involved in new forms of political activism and set up action groups according to their own ideas and political faiths. This led to a wide range of organisations, each of which has built its own niche and contributed in its own way to helping solve specific societal problems. Stemming from a long-standing tradition of tolerance in the Netherlands, the various groups appeared to accept each others' right to exist, but at the same time clearly emphasised the importance of its own particular approach (Cramer, 1990).

As the awareness for corporate social responsibility grew in Dutch society, the various NGOs began to look for closer cooperation with one other. In 2001 the NGOs jointly issued a first manifesto, addressing the issue of responsible business behaviour by Dutch companies outside the Netherlands, followed late in 2002 by a second one. This latter manifesto was signed by 28 social organisations and compiled into a single framework the viewpoints of all organisations involved (see www.somo.nl/mvo-platform). Whether this reference document will be the beginning of a permanent cooperation among the various NGOs still remains to be seen.

In this NGO network the trade unions are also active. However, they differ from other NGOs in that, together with the employers and their representative organisations, they control their own domain, that of labour relations. They represent the employees, who constitute one of the most crucial factors in promoting corporate social responsibility.

The Contribution of Knowledge Institutes to the Debate

Since the rise of corporate social responsibility as a political issue many Dutch consultancy firms have quickly taken up the issue. They became one of the main advocates of corporate social responsibility in the public debate. In the media they reported on specific studies made on the topic, and also on their own views concerning its importance. Most of the consultancy studies carried out were company specific or had a rather applied orientation.

In order to increase the interest of the knowledge infrastructure for corporate social responsibility, especially in the universities, individual researchers from different universities took the initiative together with the National Initiative for Sustainable Development to create a network of excellence to promote research in the field of corporate social responsibility in the Netherlands. The objective was to set up a joint research programme at universities and mobilise money to finance the research. The junior minister for Economic Affairs, Mr. Ybema was willing to support this initiative and agreed a budget of 1.4 million Euro over a period of two years. The Dutch National Research Programme on Corporate Social Responsibility has started in January 2002 and is carried out by research groups of seven universities. The main disciplines involved are economy, sociology and law.

Conclusions

The above analysis shows that in recent years the issue of corporate social responsibility has gained increasing attention in Dutch society. Due to a shift in power relations between enterprises, government and civil society, which also resulted in a changing political and cultural climate, a fertile soil was gradually developing for the rise of corporate social responsibility. After the issuing of the advisory report "Corporate Social Responsibility – A Dutch Approach" by the Dutch Social and Economic Council (SER), a variety of stakeholders have become receptive to the issue and are developing specific policies. Thus the arena around industry has also gradually evolved in the direction of corporate social responsibility.

The government at national level focused on initiatives to stimulate and facilitate corporate social responsibility in industry. Local governments are busy formulating their own role in this process. Other important stakeholders promoting the issue within industry are the financial sector, the NGOs and the workers themselves (and their organisations). And finally the knowledge institutions (including consultancy firms) began to play a role in the public debate about the social responsibility of companies.

In response to all these influences Dutch industry began to integrate corporate social responsibility in their daily business practices. However, its implementation is still in an early phase. The larger, multinational corporations take the lead in putting corporate social responsibility high on the agenda, while SMEs are slowly following. The Dutch soil is fertile though for further penetration of corporate social responsibility into the business organisation. So, it is to be expected that in ten to twenty years time the issue will form an integrated part of the business strategy of most Dutch companies.

Notes

[1] This paragraph is based on the report of the Social and Economic Council (SER). 2001. *Corporate Social Responsibility – A Dutch Approach.*

[2] The following text is mainly based on Cramer, J. 2003. Learning about Corporate Social Responsibility – The Dutch Experience, Chapter 7. Amsterdam: IOS Press.

References

Beleggem, van T. 2001. The Green Fund System in the Netherlands. In: J. J. Bouma et al. (Eds.), *Sustainable Banking – The Greening of Finance*: 234–244. Sheffield, UK: Greenleaf Publishing.

Council for Annual Reporting. 2003a. *Richtlijn 400 Jaarverslag.* Deventer: Kluwer.

Council for Annual Reporting. 2003b. *Handreiking voor Maatschappelijke Verslaggeving.* Deventer: Kluwer.

Cramer, J. 1990. The Development of the New Environmentalism in the Netherlands. In: A. Jamison et al. (Eds.), *The Making of the New Environmental Consciousness – A Comparative Study of the Environmental Movements in Sweden, Denmark and the Netherlands*: 121–184. Edinburgh: Edinburgh University Press.

Cramer, J. 2003. *Learning about Corporate Social Responsibility – The Dutch Experience.* Amsterdam: IOS press.

Ministry of Economic Affairs. 2003. *Ondernemingsmonitor Winter 2002 – 2003.* The Hague: Ministry of Economic Affairs.

SER. 2001. *Corporate Social Responsibility – A Dutch Approach.* Assen: Van Gorcum.

Further Internet Links

Samenleving & Bedrijf (Dutch Partner of CSR Europe)
www.samen.nl

National Initiative for Sustainable Development
www.nido.nu

Social Venture Network
www.svneurope.com

8 Balancing Between Constructive Harassment and Virtuous Intentions

François Beaujolin and Michel Capron

CSR in France is historically rooted in the development of society at least since the 19th century; for decades large companies introduced social plans and social institutions which covered workers and their families from birth to death. These institutions were then taken over by the welfare state from the thirties. So French industrialisation has been marked by enterprise paternalism and by the growth of the strong workers' movement which expanded in three branches during the second half of the 19th century: the union movement, the political socialist movement and the mutualist and cooperative movement. This workers' movement has developed its own social values.

During the 20th century the traditionally interventionist role of the State gave to France an important social legislation, especially in employment law and social protection systems jointly managed both by employers' and employees' representatives. National Insurance was instituted in 1945, unemployment insurance in 1958, the *RMI*[1] (minimum resources allocation) in 1988, the *CMU*[2] (medical insurance for everybody) in 2000. Since 1945, the firms' social budgets have been managed by works councils in every company or organisation of more than 50 workers.

Historical and Socio-Cultural Factors

Over the last two centuries, France has been characterised by a rich and tormented social history which is specially marked by large social movements and social revolutions (1830, 1848, *Commune de Paris* in 1871, Popular Front in 1936, Liberation in 1944–45, 1968 May movement). This specific history gave French industrial relations a strongly conflictual configuration. For a long time, trade unions were inspired by a spirit of class struggle and the employers' behaviour was guided by distrust of the employees (Mouriaux, 1994; Reynaud, 1975). This explains why the workers' participation in the decision-making process was often considered by industrial leaders as a dangerous mechanism which could lead to "Soviets" and by unionists as potential class collaboration.

However the French workers' movement has historically been driven by two ideological tendencies that are found to a greater or lesser extent in the main national trade unions: an anarcho-syndicalist (or revolutionary syndicalist) tradition of Proudhonian inspiration and another one based on a Marxist grounding (Lojkine, 1996). Both of them have been divided for a century by the attitude adopted in relation to business management and more generally in relation to knowledge of management. In the 1900s, the debate was very strained: for some, the interest in economic issues and in the results of business made the protest movement's justifications more credible and thus reinforced it; for others more in favour of direct action, trade unionism burdened itself with studies of business statistics that risk running into class collaboration. The break in the 1920s, as a result of the Russian Revolution, did not help to solve this dichotomy because the Leninist thesis of worker control paradoxically reinforced supporters of employees' intervention in management and therefore requested knowledge in that field. The factories' sit-in movement after the Liberation and in May 1968 can be interpreted in some ways as a development of this tradition.

Except for the years following World War II, dominated by reconstruction requirements, mistrust was predominant until quite recently, because CGT, linked with the French CP, had a large majority among the workers. But its weakening and its evolution towards a reformist trade unionism constitute a new deal which is more favourable to social dialogue. Nevertheless this dialogue is still difficult because industrial leaders, gathered in the MEDEF (ex. CNPF), mistrust and in many cases are even hostile to unions (Brizay, 1975). For instance the whole discussion about strategic management has been considered as a dangerous intrusion in their prerogatives and in some ways like foreshadowing workers' power. Many employers used the excuse of business confidentiality to restrict the release of economic information (Capron, 2001). This explains the weakness of collective bargaining in France in comparison with other European countries, although over the last decade efforts were made to develop negotiations instead of legal regulations, especially at company level.

The industrial terrain in France is characterised by large companies (transnationals since the 1960s) and a lot of SMEs. Since the second part of the 19th century and until the 1930s, paternalism has been pre-eminent in French firms, especially with important figures such as the "iron masters": industrial leaders, who felt themselves responsible for the life of workers and their families but did not share the smallest part of their power (Ballet & de Bry, 2001). From this time, it remains in French law that the firm has a "social interest" which is distinct from the shareholders' interests and upon them, because it corresponds to the common good for all stakeholders (the going concern of the firm); so the shareholders are not the owners of a company, but the owners of shares of a company (Robé, 1999). It means particularly that the going concern of a firm does not depend only on shareholders, directors and workers, but also on public authorities. For example, when a firm meets difficulties and is in a risky situation, local authorities, creditor banks and social organisations will try to find solutions to save it or save the jobs involved. In return, civil society expects companies to create activities for developing jobs and thus support the community. The French conception of the firm is an institutionalist conception and not a contractualist conception as in Anglo-Saxon law (Bazzoli, Kirat & Villeval, 1995). It is important to be familiar with this specific concept to understand in which context corporate social responsibility is embedded in French society.

From the 1930s paternalism has declined, because State interventionism and new social institutions (social insurance, pensions, unemployment insurance, etc.) have progressively taken over the role of firms. The social institutions are generally managed by social partners (representatives of employers and trade unions) at a national level, which is called "*paritarisme*" (equal representation) and from 1945 the social budgets in firms have been managed by the works councils created at that time. After the Liberation the State became a regulator of economic activities (nationalisations, plans, industrial politics...) and started to foster development and modernisation (Rioux, 1980). It is well known that the role of the State is traditionally strong in France: in the second part of the 20th century, it has promoted important social legislation in many fields (wages, employment, hygiene and safety, etc.). But today this predominant role of the State in the society is increasingly questioned and simultaneously the extent of what business must be responsible for in society is also in debate, because a new paternalism which could manage public affairs is feared (Salmon, 2002).

In fact, as regards welfare, people in France are expecting more from public authorities than from private firms. It seems that this feeling goes back a long way to the time of absolute and centralized power of the State. But as the role of the State, in particular regarding social funding, decreased, one can recently observe, at least in the discourses, that firms are regaining social importance in society, for example in the 1990s with the notion of "corporate citizenship". Thanks to the successful growth of French firms in international markets, the image of business in society has improved in the last years, but simultaneously has been tarnished as a result of restructuring and unemployment (Berthouin Anthal & Sobczak, 2004). This does not confer on large corporations a legitimacy in intervening alone in the construction of social well-being (Boyer, 2003).

We have focused this analysis on industrial relations and the role of the State because they are the major factors for understanding CSR in France; however, there are other factors which are less important and more difficult to perceive. First of all, the role of the Catholic Church is discreet in economic activities and one can say that its influence is weak. But there is a mistrust towards business and money, the origin of which is probably religious. This attitude also explains the scepticism when good deeds are communicated to the public. "Discretion about good deeds, on the part of individuals or companies, is regarded as a proof of sincerity and disinterestedness" (Segal, 2003).

Concerning other actors, we can emphasise the role of banks which were until recently the most important source of funding for firms. The role of financial markets has shaped only recently and popular shareholding remains limited and not very well organised. Pension funds do not yet exist but the situation is going to change thanks to a new legislation and the socially responsible investment represents a very small part of savings. Moreover the consumers' movement is not dynamic, and NGOs play an important role to influence consumers' socially responsible behaviour (Capron & Quairel-Lanoizelée, 2004). France has no tradition of consumer boycotting: for example, the call for a boycott of TotalFinaElf because of the Erika oil tanker spill failed.

Finally, France has a specific situation because there is a problem of translation concerning CSR[3] for three reasons:

- *"entreprise"* (enterprise) is not equivalent to "corporation": the term covers all kinds of firms and notably independent SMEs or social economy firms,

- *"social"* has in French a more narrow meaning than in English: it usually refers to the labour relations inside a firm and is not focused on society issues,

- there is no distinction between the notion of responsibility and the legal concept of liability: the "traditional concept of responsibility presupposes an agent, a damage, and a causal link between agent and damage" (Noël, 2003),

it is obvious that these linguistic differences often lead to confusion and misunderstanding.

Recent Drivers of CSR

The topic of CSR appeared in France only four or five years ago. Several factors have contributed to this apparently late emergence compared to other European countries. The effects of "new globalisation" demonstrations, the development of some contesting movements (ATTAC) and organised opinion campaigns like *"Ethique sur l'Etiquette"* (French branch of "Clean Clothes Campaign") have made the French public more sensitive to possible damages caused by multinational firms throughout the world. There has also been major concern because of great financial scandals in which some well-known firms (Crédit Lyonnais, Elf) were involved. The pollution caused by the oil tanker and the AZF factory accident in Toulouse have also risen awareness and pointed to the direct or indirect responsibility of firms concerning environmental damages. Extreme and intense public reaction also took place after the announcement of lay-offs decided by firms in a good financial situation (Michelin, Danone).

Another series of reasons roots in the evolution of savings. There is a rise in ethical funds or socially responsible funds and though they are weak in relation to mutual funds they nevertheless open a new way for finance to apply other criteria than financial (Ferone, d'Arcimoles, Bello & Sassenou, 2001); at the same time the rating agency ARESE (later Vigeo), highly supported by the media, has largely contributed to a judgement beyond financial criteria. The issue of retirement systems, the perspective of creating "Employee Savings Funds" and the system of stockholding for workers have nourished thinking and debates within unions regarding the use of these new means to influence firms' social practices.

Actual and Future Trends

In France, the dynamic towards CSR started through pioneer firms with ideological purpose rather than "market driven" issues. Then, in 2002 and 2003, the French government worked on Sustainable Development and the implications of CSR were studied at the same time. Additional stakeholders are entering the French CSR arena: trade unions, CSR organisations, French ISO and academics.

Business Associations

For several years, pioneer enterprises have committed them to environmental protection in associations like OREE or EPE; they also act in dialogue with local authorities to implement Agenda 21 (for example in an association called *Comité 21*). Most large transnational corporations in France take part in CSR Europe and put pressure on SMEs to adopt socially responsible behaviour. Some pioneer enterprises are experimenting with "sustainability development" and CSR processes inspired by quality management systems. For example, Danone with its "Danone way" which is a CSR driver tool; it is accessible to corporation employees (100 000 in 32 countries) and it is designed to evaluate the corporate social performance.

The large distribution sector is particularly active. An initiative called "social clause" was launched in 1998 by FCD (*Fédération du Commerce et de la Distribution*) and includes most brands, such as Auchan, Carrefour, Casino, CORA, Monoprix, Système U... Inspired by SA 8000, hundreds of audits in suppliers' factories have been carried out in about ten sensitive countries concerning some main sectors: textiles, toys, general store articles etc. Nevertheless FCD is not in favour of a social label because it wants to avoid any discrimination concerning other non-labelled products.

Danone was the first transnational firm to sign a Framework Agreement with a Global Union Federation (IUF) in 1988. The next one, in 1995, Accor, was also a French firm. Since 1998, more than twenty similar agreements have been signed in the world but, among them, only one French firm: Carrefour in 2001.

The MEDEF, the main French employers' organisation, has been recently interested in the CSR issue. The position of firms in society was one of the issues discussed at the MEDEF's summer university in 2002. According to MEDEF there must be only one global reference for all the companies in the world. For the moment, it refers to OECD works, trusts the codes of conduct and pushes ISO to release a standard in this matter. The CSR issue is supported by the international department of MEDEF, but it is not really a subject of discussion within the organisation itself.

The *ORSE (Observatoire de la Responsabilité Sociétale des Entreprises)*, a thinking circle including corporations and managers of social funds and the "*Institut du Mécénat de Solidarité*" are new organisations which intend to promote the exchange of "good practices" in CSR.

Governmental Initiatives

The interest in CSR by the French public authorities is recent, probably because they thought their own legislation was at least equal to or better than that of other members of the European Union. They began to feel concerned about international pressure coming from the Anglo-Saxon standardisation on social reporting (GRI), social certification (SA 8000) or in relation to some proposals of social labelling (i.e. coming from Belgium) at the end of 2001. The first concerted works under the aegis of public authorities was undertaken on the occasion of the World Summit in Johannesburg in 2002. Former Prime Minister Lionel Jospin created a preparatory committee constituted by civil society actors and staged a workshop on CSR which provided the first large debate between public administration, firms, unions, NGOs representatives and academics. It brought together for the first time specialists on work topics and on environment topics.

At the end of 2002, the new Raffarin government set up an official National Council on Sustainable Development in order to bring together representatives of civil society to prepare a national sustainable development strategy. In April 2003 this National Council released a final report of 160 pages. It outlines six main strategical guidelines. One is called "economic activities: from firms to consumers". The philosphy appearing in this text is that social responsibility is shared by everybody without any distinction among actors.

With regard to the French concern some other proposals can be noted:

- the creation of an Institute of High Studies on sustainable development for professional training;

- the development of professional training in CSR and in dialogue with stakeholders;

- the training of chartered accountants in environmental and social audit;

- introducing sustainable development in business schools' management courses rather than specialised lectures;

- analysing the compatibility between competitiveness criteria and the principles of sustainable development on the basis of academic research;

- the constitution of platforms for European meetings of CSR tools designers;

- the promotion of an international agreement on CSR.

In June 2003, a governmental meeting for sustainable development adopted the national strategy for the next five years. The National Strategy on Sustainable Development (3 June 2004) is an 85 page programme. Three paragraphs in the first chapter (out of four pages) "health and social dimensions" are about CSR: lifelong learning, working for disabled persons and gender equality. In the 9-page chapter about economic activities, companies and consumers, 1.5 page(s) are about CSR.

The national strategy promotes CSR through three objectives in this chapter: creation of a reference system at the national level; analysis of practices; development of Socially Responsible Investment (SRI). It will set financial means to encourage companies to start sustainable development practices. In particular, the government is encouraging firms to involve themselves in voluntary sustainable development procedures in order to bring out the promotion of environmental certification.

It has to be outlined that the French Administration can rely on some instruments to promote CSR. The *Caisse des Dépôts et Consignations,* which is a large financial tool for the State, plays an important role in maintaining social cohesion (financing social housing, collective facilities and public transportation). It has created Novethic, a public website devoted to the promotion of CSR and SRI. Public or semi-public organisations, managed by the State, employers' organisations and employees' unions, work for corporate responsibility, for example in the field of the improvement of working conditions for over 25 years (*ANACT*[4]), and more recently for energy economy and environment protection (*ADEME, IFEN*[5]).

In the field of social reporting, the law about the *"bilan social"* (social statement) introduced in 1977 has to be mentioned. It is an annual, specific, standardised and compulsory statement for all companies, organisations and institutions having more than 300 employees. This document presents a wide quantity of data (about

140 indicators) concerning useful measures about workers' situations and social firm within the enterprise: employment, wages, working conditions, industrial relations. Its importance is limited because the data only concern the relationships between employers and employees. This "*bilan social*" is not published outside the workers' council of the plant or department. Although it is often criticised in France, it became a reference and has been used as a model to set up similar statements in other European countries (Belgium, Portugal). Firms do not consider the "bilan social" either as an instrument to take social decisions, or as an instrument of social dialogue. It is never consolidated at a macro-social level. Nevertheless it is the only standardised framework allowing the disclosure of social performance indicators.

A new law about "new economic regulations" was adopted in 2001. One of the Articles (n° 116) compels publicly listed companies to report on social and environmental consequences of their activities in their annual report according to a range of information (Igalens & Joras, 2002). An administrative decree of February 2002 clarified the nature of the information that should be written in this annual report. It does not include only social and environmental information, but also new information such as relations with subcontractors, the impact of the firm's activities on local development, and also the respect for human rights in subsidiaries abroad. This law has been enforced for the first time in 2003 and the quality of the report varies very much: the majority of "CAC 40" corporations have made some efforts to accomplish their duty. The quality of the reports from "SBF 120" corporations is not that good. Concerning the others (700 companies), generally medium-sized or subsidiary companies, it seems that they have not enforced the law.

Socially Responsible Investment and Trade Unions

To promote socially responsible investment, the FIR (*Forum pour l'Investissement Responsable*) is a non-profit organisation which brings together individuals and organisations interested in promoting SRI in France. It contributes to SRI public policy making, supports research initiative in the fields of SRI and promotes socially responsible and sustainable investment practices. To assist socially responsible investors, three social (or extra-financial) rating agencies are now working in France: Vigeo which bought Arese, Core Ratings[6] and Innovest.

In April 2002 four main trade unions (CGT, CFDT, CFTC and CGC) have constituted a "*Comité intersyndical de l'épargne salariale*" which awards a label to investment managers who manage or would like to manage Employee Savings Plans according to socially responsible criteria. The product-based label can be applied for by financial establishments, which must demonstrate how savings are to be invested taking into consideration social and environmental issues and also allow for employees' representation on the fund's Board of Trustees.

Social Economy Sector

The social economy organisation wants to show its specificity because it considers CSR as having always been part of its values. It begins to put this into practice in different ways, for example:

- The workers cooperative Confederation has started giving much thought to CSR since its last convention in May 2004.

- An association for responsible finance, *Finansol* is working to create a label for ethical financial supplies.

- The issue of fair trade has been dealt with by a major dialogue on the objective to establish standards for a consumers' guarantee.

- The conception and the experimentation of "bilan sociétal" which have been started in 1995.

NGOs Circles

Some NGOs work with large firms in order to promote the use of some codes of conduct, social certification or label (for example, FIDH working with Carrefour or WWF working with Lafarge) (Najim, Hofmann & Marius-Gnanou, 2003); other NGOs like Amnesty International organise meetings with firms' executives to exchange their points of view on the matter.

Teaching, Research and Experiment

The first academic network on the topic was founded in 1998 and called "Governance, Performance and Sustainable Development" bringing together almost all French researchers in management and economy working on these topics. The academics have organised many seminars and colloquiums in 2003 on CSR; in particular the first Conference of ADERSE has been held at Paris 12 University in May 2003. ADERSE (*Association pour le Développement de l'Enseignement et de la Recherche en Responsabilité Sociale d'Entreprise*) was set up in June 2002 to promote teaching and research on CSR. It is an academic organisation specialised on CSR management, considered as a transverse approach to all management disciplines. The second congress will take place in Toulouse in October 2004.

The subjects that are expected to be discussed are:

- on the teaching side: should CSR be taught in all management courses or should it be a new discipline? Courses on CSR or on sustainable development? What kind of degrees, certifications, etc.?

- on the research side: is CSR a transnational concept? What links exist between WTO and CSR? Are there different sectoral models of CSR? Are CSR criteria influenced by cultural, national, sectoral factors? What about SMEs? What is the influence of auditing, certificating, rating, etc. on the evolution of CSR?

The main aspect of academic research on CSR seems to be a fragmentation in two ways. First, the universities that are interested by the subject seem to work alone and to place their marker. Second, most of the research on CSR is still made in each discipline of management.

The main subjects dealt with are:

- managing of issues linked to the physical environment (problems of pollution, waste management, etc.);

- strategic management of firms in relation to public decision-makers;

- environmental reporting and more generally social reporting issues;

- socially responsible investment and links between financial performance and social performance; social rating;

- managing human resources and employment issues linked to reengineering and downsizing;

- theoretical basis of CSR.

Implementation of CSR, practical measures and social audit issues have also been dealt with in some organisations (Chauveau & Rosé, 2003; Dubigeon, 2002; Capron & Quairel-Lanoizelée, 2004; Stephany, 2003). *The CJDES*, a social economy young managers' association, experiments with and promotes the *bilan sociétal* which is a self-evaluation process drawn from a reference form (questionnaire); it allows enterprises to assess their behaviour with regard to social economy values. It has been already tested in about 100 organisations (companies and associations). The *CJD* (SME's young managers' association) has created a tool (*Diagnostic Performance globale*) made for SME's executives.

The *SME key* is a voluntary self-evaluation process, known in several European countries. The tests started in SMEs in the North of France with employers' organisation support (Alliances). *SD 21000 guidelines* have been launched by AFNOR (the French Standardisation Organisation); it is applied to managers and executives of enterprises of any size. It is meant to help include aspects of sustainable development in the corporate strategy conception. It proposes recommendations to adapt the management system according to the requirements of sustainable development.

Conclusion

The issue of CSR in France was preceded by a long history of mistrusted industrial relations which explains the sceptical behaviour of most of the actors (firms' executives, trade unions, NGOs…). The importance of social legislation can also explain that the voluntary approaches in CSR are far from French culture: most of the social partners still expect that social well-being will come from public authorities rather than from private firms. The present government and many other actors do not think of CSR as a specific concept and still approach it through sustainable development. Nevertheless we can observe an evolution in business and civil society which is bringing France closer to the other western European countries than a few years ago.

Notes

[1] *Revenu Minimum d'Insertion.*

[2] *Couverture Médicale Universelle.*

[3] CSR is translated in French by: "responsabilité sociale d'entreprise".

[4] Agence Nationale pour l'Amélioration des Conditions de Travail.

[5] Agence de l'Environnement et de la Maîtrise de l'Energie; Institut Français de l'Environnement.

[6] Core Ratings stopped its rating business in 2004.

References

Ballet, J., & de Bry, F. 2001. *L'entreprise et l'éthique*. Paris: Editions du Seuil.

Bazzoli, L., Kirat, T., & Villeval, M. C. 1995. Contrat et institutions dans la relation salariale: pour un renouveau institutionnaliste. *Travail et emploi*, 58: 94–110.

Berthouin Antal, A., & Sobczak, A. 2004. *Factors influencing the Development of Corporate Social Responsibility in France*. Working paper. Audencia Ecole de Management, Nantes.

Boyer, A. 2003. *L'impossible éthique des entreprises*. Paris: Ed. d'Organisation.

Brizay, B. 1975. *Le patronat*. Paris: Editions du Seuil.

Capron, M. 2001. Accounting and management in the social dialogue: the experience of fifty years of works councils in France. *Accounting, Business & Financial History*, 11(1): 43–58.

Capron, M., & Quairel-Lanoizelée, F. 2004. *Mythes et réalités de l'entreprise responsable.* Paris: Editions La Découverte.

Chauveau, A., & Rose, J. J. 2003. *L'entreprise responsable.* Paris: Ed. d'Organisation.

Dubigeon, O. 2002. *Mettre en pratique le développement durable.* Paris: Village mondial.

Ferone, G., d'Arcimoles, C.-H., Bello, P., & Sassenou, N. 2001. *Le développement durable.* Paris: Ed. d'Organisation.

Igalens, J., & Joras, M. 2002. *La responsabilité sociale de l'entreprise.* Paris: Ed. d'Organisation.

Lojkine, J. 1996. *Le tabou de la gestion: la culture syndicale entre contestation et opposition.* Paris: Editions de l'Atelier.

Mouriaux, R. 1994. *Le syndicalisme en France depuis 1945.* Paris: Editions La Découverte.

Najim, A., Hofmann, E., & Marius-Gnanou K. 2003. *Les entreprises face aux enjeux du développement durable.* Paris: Karthala.

Noël, C. 2003. *La notion de responsabilité globale de l'entreprise a-t-elle un sens?* Nantes: Paper presented at the Colloque Audencia, Ecole de Management.

Reynaud, J. D. 1975. *Les syndicats en France.* Paris: Editions du Seuil.

Rioux, J. P. 1980. *La France de la Quatrième République: L'ardeur et la nécessité, 1944–1952.* Paris: Editions du Seuil.

Robé, J. P. 1999. *L'entreprise et le droit.* Paris: Presses Universitaires de France.

Salmon, A. 2002. *Ethique et ordre économique.* Paris: CNRS Editions.

Segal, J. P. 2003. *Les cultures d'entreprise en Allemagne et en France: l'interpellation anglo-saxonne à l'heure de la mondialisation.* Nantes: Paper presented at the Colloque Audencia, Ecole de Management.

Stephany, D. 2003. *Développement durable et performance de l'entreprise.* Paris: Ed. Liaisons.

Central Europe

9 Overcoming the Heritage of Corporatism

André Habisch and Martina Wegner

Introduction

Many European neighbours perceive Germany as a "white spot" in the European CSR landscape. In this article we try to highlight the background of that phenomenon, focusing on the tradition of Corporatism. Strong trade unions and business associations, religion-based institutions, professional associations and chambers stick to their traditional roles. They join forces with a strong state which is still expected to solve the structural problems of the country. Against this background it remains difficult for committed citizens, non-institutional organisations and third-sector groups to develop participative structures, thus contributing to a new type of social order. Reflections on civil society – as expressed by the Commission of the German Parliament on "Zukunft des bürgerschaftlichen Engagements"[1] – are forced back by day-to-day problems (Enquete-Kommission des Deutschen Bundestages, 2002). One "hot spot" has been the German reunification, attracting much political attention and absorbing the country's creativity over the past 15 years. Another factor of growing importance is the aging population and the resulting challenges in fields such as social security reforms, family policy etc. However, beyond these present political debates there are historical reasons why Germany is reluctant to embrace the concept of CSR. These reasons date back to the times of industrialisation, giving German civil society a very specific shape. We will analyse these historical developments in order to better understand the presence of the quasi monopoly of the state as the omnipotent problem solver of German society. In a second step we will discover the traces of Corporatism in the emerging CSR scene in Germany.

Roles of Business and State After 1850

Compared to its British and French neighbours, industrialisation in Germany started rather late. In the 19th century young German would-be entrepreneurs went as guest workers to the UK, where at that time the technically most advanced industry was located. They learnt about production and automation in order to be able to copy and establish these processes also in their home country. Despite these early efforts, Germany continued to be an agricultural country until the time when the German Reich was formed in the second half of the 19th century. But then industrialisation gained momentum rather quickly: By the time World War I broke out Germany ranked second among the industrial nations worldwide. This rapid economic development was enabled by the state, which played a crucial role acting as a modernisation agency for the country. The Prussian bureaucracy, which was known for its efficiency and military-type organisation, provided housing, roads and other kinds of infrastructure, such as an educational system of superior quality. The German government also repressed labour movements and union action, but at the same time introduced a social security system and a pioneering old-age pension system.

In Germany social security had its roots in civil society. Pension plans were originally developed by Christian entrepreneurs who helped their staff save money to help disabled or retired workers and their families. More rapidly than in other countries, state agencies used this concept to implement social security "top-down" in order to fight Socialists and Catholics. Reichskanzler Bismarck introduced the innovative national "Rentenversicherung", thus shaping the mindsets of workers and their families: the German population became used to relying on the state as a perfectly functioning agency for the provision of public goods. In addition, business benefited from the development of social security systems, of infrastructure like railways and roads as well as housing for the fast-growing working population.

However, this strong and pronounced role of the state also brought about other specific structures which again influenced the role of business. After their abolition during the liberal reform period at the beginning of the 19th century, the powerful corporatist institutions – Chambers of Commerce and Craftmanship with obligatory membership, business associations ("*Verbände*") and a centralised bargaining process ("Tarifpartnerschaft") – were reintroduced between the two World Wars or after World War II respectively.

"Soziale Marktwirtschaft" and the Effect of Corporatist Institutions

The concept of "Soziale Marktwirtschaft" forms the core of the German model of "Rhenish capitalism". More than other business constitutions, it explicitly outlines the role of business enterprises for the provision of common goods. Professional training ("*duale Ausbildung*"), i.e. apprenticeships combining school education and on-the-job training, may serve as an example of the corporatist tradition that integrates "private" commitment into the state system. And it is typical that though provided by business, this training is perceived as a state institution by the public.

As the example of "duale Ausbildung" shows, the social market economy in Germany is characterised by certain types of engagements and commitments which do resemble Corporate Citizenship or Corporate Social Responsibility patterns. However, in their traditional form these engagements hardly stimulate innovative projects and local forms of cooperation between business and civil society. They rarely contributed to local or regional "social capital" in the sense Robert Putnam (1993) or Elinor Ostrom (2002) conceive this term, i.e. as cross-sectoral cooperative relations that combine different resources and complementary competencies (Habisch, 2004; Habisch & Moon 2004; Habisch & Schmidpeter, 2003). The structure of a corporatist society fosters interaction rather *within* the hierarchical organisations than *across* sectors. This is further reinforced by the fact that German corporatist institutions are very professionally organised and omnipresent in the country. Whether they will adapt to future challenges and actively contribute to civil society may decide about their future impact.

Presence of CSR Ideas in Society

The Problem of Confusing Terms

In a recent study (IÖW & future e.V., 2004) it was observed that there is no official CSR process in Germany (in contrast to e.g. Great Britain). The study further revealed that scientific research on CSR was restricted, that there was no pronounced public response and that print media in Germany published rather sceptical comments. One of the major reasons for this situation seemed to be the lack of distinction between CSR, corporate citizenship and the social dimension of sustainability.

This means that an overview of CSR in Germany also has to include the reaction and progress made under the headings "Corporate Citizenship" and "Sustainable Development". Many companies in Germany started to use the term "Corporate Citizenship" to emphasise the "social side"of their corporate responsibility. Also in public discussions Corporate Citizenship and CSR are often seen as synonymous. Corporate Citizenship is still an emergent issue, which can be observed in three contexts: (a) as part of business ethics, (b) as civil society commitment of companies or (c) as part of the sustainability debate (IÖW & future e.V., 2004).

Green Tradition

Since the 1970s Germany has engaged in environmental protection. During this time many "green" movements mushroomed on a local and regional level which led to the foundation of many environmental NGOs. In addition, the social-liberal government set up an environmental programme in 1971 in response to the fact that the German population has become environmentally conscious. Over the years, environmental legislation was introduced, and also Agenda 21 had a major impact in Germany. The Green Party has continually gained importance on the German political scene and today it is a well-established force making part of the present government.

It is against this environmental background that sustainable development was first perceived by the German public. Especially in 2002 when the Johannisburg Summit on Sustainable Development took place, this issue received much public attention, though it seems that today Germany has fallen behind this peak. According to a 2002 survey of the German Ministry for the Environment (BMU, 2002: 31f.) 28% of the German population was familiar with the contents of Sustainable Development and 84% of the population fully or mostly agreed to the concept of intra- and inter-generation justice as postulated by the Brundtland Report.

Since the green movement as well the public interest in environmental issues in general started to flag in the 1990s, environmental groups jumped on the bandwagon of sustainable development. Also within companies, it was in many cases the environmental departments that were now given the task to deal with the more comprehensive and more complex issue of sustainability.

Weak Consumer Response

For consumers to show interest in CSR activities – which in turn would make companies more committed to these issues – it is necessary that they are well informed and have a basic level of interest for what is going on in their country. The BMU survey (2002) showed that as to local commitment, 9% of the population contribute to neighbourhood/community activities, 47% could imagine doing so in the future, while 44% cannot imagine having such an interest or commitment at all.

A survey carried out by *imug* (a research institute of the University of Hanover[2]) in mid-2003 showed that among consumers the interest in information about the socially responsible behaviour of companies is increasing, however only slightly. In Germany two thirds of the respondents are interested in information about the social and ecological effects of business. However, they want the credibility of such information to be ensured by an independent organisation, which reflects a lack of trust in companies – and again stresses the institutional nature of German society. Its rather passive attitude is reflected by the fact that only when given the same price and the same quality, more than half of German consumers would prefer products from companies that assume social responsibility. Consumers see child labour, the development of ecological products, the economical use of resources and energy and the creation of jobs as the most important issues in which responsible behaviour is expressed. This means that only the most shocking (child labour), the most established (ecology) and the most worrying (unemployment) problems are mentioned. These problems only represent a faint relation with CSR ideas.

This may also be the reason why still today there are no CSR-specific NGOs in Germany, as exist in environmental protection and on an international level as to CSR.

Trade Unions as a Weak Driver of CSR

Trade Unions do not appear as a predominant player on the German CSR scene. Their support of issues like sustainability, CSR or CC does not go beyond their traditional interest: They want work, social and environmental standards to be improved, fight for the right to form unions and to carry out collective bargaining, and against forced labour.

A positioning paper of the Federal Mining, Chemical and Energy Union (Mersmann, 2003) on the EU Greenbook documents that the CSR initiative is welcome, if it goes along with these goals. Trade unions consider themselves as drivers of social responsibility in companies anyway, as they fought for and achieved co-determination and have hindered unfair competition by collective bargaining. The trade unions also appreciate that the European Union's CSR concept puts competitiveness in Europe and the social responsibility of business into one context.

The lacking integration and passiveness of their approach is reflected by the fact that they do not want CSR to interfere with the "Social Dialogue" between labour unions and employers' associations. They want to be included into CSR through their works council members, but do not propose active steps. In the eyes of the trade unions the proof of successful CSR is given when companies are restructured and social and ecological standards are followed in countries where German or European legislation is not applied. Therefore also the trade unions' approach towards CSR may serve as an example of corporatist Germany, where institutions pursue their individual aims without taking horizontal networks into account.

The Impact by Church Institutions and Charities

Faith-based associations like the BKU (Association of Catholic Entrepreneurs) embrace CSR or Corporate Citizenship as part of their Christian values (www.bku.de). The BKU is also engaged in European projects and made CSR / CC "Issue of the Year 2005" staging conferences and meetings throughout Germany.

Church associations (like the large welfare associations Caritas, DIAKONIE or one-world NGOs like Misereor, Brot für die Welt) do not explicity refer to CSR since they start from their societal approach without interconnecting with companies to a larger or systematic extent. However, due to lacking funds they will have to look for new opportunities also in the business arena.

Drivers of CSR in Germany

The Role and Reactions of Multinationals

The attitudes of the multinational companies towards CSR can best be studied by looking at the associations representing them, i.e. the rather powerful BDI/BDA (Federation of German Industry/Federation of German Employers), as well as econsense (www.econsense.de), which is the association of German industry dealing specifically with sustainable development.

BDI/BDA's reaction to CSR was summed up in a positioning paper on the European Commission's Greenbook of 2001 (BDI/BDA, 2001, 2002). It highlighted the following points in the attitudes of German business:

- CSR is defined as the ecological, social and ethical responsibility of companies. It goes beyond legal requirements, i.e. CSR activities are voluntary and depend on the company's individual sense of responsibility. The voluntary nature must be kept up.

- If, at all, regulations are to be set up for companies operating in emerging markets and developing countries; however these have to be promoted and organised by the relevant international organisations.

- Companies are not able to make up for the shortcomings of governments. It is the responsibility of politicians to make sure that the individual countries as well as partners adhere to ecological and social legislation. However within their spheres of influence businesses may promote social and ecological behaviour in partnership with other societal actors.

- German business does not agree to additional European regulation on CSR since this would have a negative effect on the success and increasing proliferation of voluntary activities. Pan-European frameworks and the standardisation of CSR activities would limit the creativity of companies, it is rather important to improve innovativeness and the room for manoeuvre required to develop corporate responsibility.

In March 2004, *econsense*, which is an association of 22 globally operating German companies, from Allianz to Volkswagen, dealing with the issues of sustainability, published "Corporate Social Responsibility – A Memorandum for Creativity and Innovation" (www.memorandum_0005E200.DOCeconsense.pdf). It is an attempt to combine sustainable development and Corporate Citizenship and to respond to the EU Greenbook. It gives, however, only vague and generic information and, again, stresses the need for voluntary action and the limitation of regulations.

It was outlined before that sustainability and Corporate Citizenship have to be considered when analysing CSR activities in Germany. Therefore also the UN's Global Compact, which the German Federal Chancellor promoted by asking German multinationals to join has to be mentioned as a driver of CSR through the issue of sustainable development. However, even if companies report on sustainable development, e.g. by participating in the Dow Jones Sustainability Global Index rating, action is very often rather punctual and only few companies seem to have sustainable development integrated into their business strategy. This means that CSR is not promoted through sustainability since also sustainable development issues are only embraced hesitantly.

Mittelstand (SMEs) and CSR

In the representative survey Mind-Studie 2001, as part of which owners and managing directors of small and medium-sized companies were interviewed, 58% of all respondents said that enterprises have more social responsibility than other societal groups. This means that enterprises are well aware of their role and their importance in a changing society. This was also confirmed by recent research (Spence, Habisch, Schmidpeter, 2004) which proved the social embeddedness of SMEs.

A report published recently by the European Commission (Observatory of European SMEs, 2002) showed the following position of German SMEs compared to other European countries. Throughout the 19 countries surveyed, half of the European SME is committed to corporate social responsibility to varying degrees. The situation in Germany corresponds to these figures: across all SME size categories, 54% of all German SMEs state that they are implementing some sort of CSR activities. It was also found that Germany is no exception, in that a correlation was observed between the size of the company and its commitment to CSR: the bigger the SME, the more it tends to assume its social responsibility, however no correlation was found between the industry and CSR. The focus of CSR activities is on sports, health, social and cultural issues implemented primarily in the form of donations and sponsorships. These activities are usually carried out "occasionally" and without being integrated into a business strategy. Across Europe, in 14% of the cases European SMEs have already achieved the integration of social responsibility into their business strategy; in the case of Germany 24% of the respondents claim have done so.

But also differences were found: Compared to overall Europe, the motivation of German enterprises to implement CSR activities is rooted more often in the wish to improve relationships with the community and business partners as well as to achieve a higher customer retention, and slightly less in ethical reasons. When asked about their reasons for not taking up CSR, German companies did not mention lacking resources but the attitude towards the issue, e.g. companies "have not yet thought about it" or "do not see any relation between CSR and their business activities". While the European average indicates that out of the companies already engaged in the field of CSR 73% want to keep the same level of commitment and 14% want to increase it, the figures for Germany are 84% and 8% respectively. These results lead to the assumption that German companies do not really think about their role in society when asked about CSR. In general, neither in the case of multinational corporations nor in SMEs do we find detailed information on budget or time invested or results or systematic work steps or future plans.

German Politics and CSR

The German government reacted to the UN Millennium Goals 2000 by drafting the poverty-fighting Action Programme 2015. This programme is an interdisciplinary approach which involves all the different Federal Ministries and focuses on the issues of voluntary engagement, balance of social and ecological aspects, social standards, crisis prevention, and human rights. The *Aktionsprogramm 2015* is also seen as a task which has to be tackled by the entire community, thus forging new ties between business and civil society.

The German sustainability strategy, "Perspektiven für Deutschland", launched in 2002 by the government, sets a variety of goals, one of them being to activate civil society. For this purpose more dialogue across societal groups and more integration is promoted. An update of this strategy is expected for autumn 2004 and presently the government is holding an online stakeholder dialogue to obtain a feedback. However, till today the German sustainability strategy does not provide action plans or a quantification of goals, as does e.g. the French sustainability strategy. CSR issues have not been a major factor in this strategy.

As to CSR we find individual government activities, initiated e.g. by the German Ministry for Family, Senior Citizens, Women and Youth which presented a report on Corporate Volunteering in a large number of organisations, which was published in November 2002. In its introduction clear reference is made to the changing roles of state, economy and society as well as to Corporate Citizenship as the more established term.

The Bundesarbeitsblatt 10/03 of the Federal Ministry for Economy and Labour (Bade, 2003) gave a complete overview on state incentives geared towards CSR activities in Germany. The author states that with regard to CSR in Germany there is already a dense network of regulations (e.g. as to environmental standards) so that there is little room for manoeuvre. The legislative measures taken by the government to provide an incentive for CSR activities include financial support to integrate long-term unemployed, handicapped, job starters, women and elder people into the work process *("Teamwork for Germany")* as well as initiatives to set up networks for training, co-financed by the European Social Fund. In the environmental field, projects for Green Finance or Labelling are promoted as well as environmental management in the companies.

These incentives show that government CSR activities are based on networks, stakeholder dialogue and the cooperation across various societal groups. Many of these activities are triggered by global or European polities, since they react to e.g. the millennium goals, Global Compact, the EU's Greenbook on CSR, or are financed by EU funds. One example is the Cosore initiative (www.cosore.com) which is a project that promoted CSR in SMEs and was implemented between 2001 and 2003.

However, activities of political leaders do not always seem to be well coordinated. For example Foreign Minister Joschka Fischer sponsored the New York Global Compact, while at home the discussion on CSR / CC is not encouraged. This reflects that in Germany there exist different parts of a CSR puzzle instead of a complete picture.

Examples of CSR Initiatives

Freiheit und Verantwortung

One of the most prominent activities on CSR in Germany is the Initiative "Freiheit und Verantwortung" ("Freedom and Responsibility" – www.Freiheit-und-Verantwortung.de) organised by the leading Business associations together with WirtschaftsWoche, the leading German business magazine and chaired by the Federal President. This initiative invites organisations to present their Corporate Citizenship projects in a variety of fields including education and training, culture, work-life balance, integration of minorities or an intelligent combination of ecology and economy. Once a year the Initiative awards the best Corporate Citizenship project in the three categories: small, medium and large companies. The Eichstaett-based Center for Corporate Citizenship (CCC) serves as a scientific advisor to this initiative and also publishes on these issues (see www.corporatecitizen.de; Habisch, 2003; Schmidpeter, 2003).

Aktive Bürgerschaft

Already in 1997 the platform ‚Aktive Bürgerschaft e.V.' was installed by the Bundesverband Deutscher Volks- und Raiffeisenbanken (BVR). The goal is to promote civic engagement, private foundations and Corporate Citizenship. They provide a newsletter, a CC-portal, practice-based publications and educational tools (www.aktive-buergerschaft.de).

Unternehmen – Partner der Jugend (UPJ)

This initiative is a national network of organisations, business partners and individuals to strengthen the cooperation between business partners, social organisations and the public. UPJ has built up several networks of engaged business partners (mostly SME level). They developed consulting tools for their partners and CSR handbooks (www.upj-online.de).

Startsocial

Startsocial was founded in 2001 to promote knowledge transfer between business enterprises and social projects. Under the patronage of the Federal Chancellor excellent social initiatives are supported by individual consulting advice and networks are set up between the social institution and companies (www.startsocial.de).

D21 Initiative

The Initiative D21 is Germany's largest Public-Private Partnership. It comprises almost 300 members from all spheres of business, politics and society. The objective is to help Germany develop into an information society making up for Germany's leeway in comparison with other countries. This is done in close cooperation between business, politics and societal organisations in almost 50 projects (www.initiatived21.de).

"INQA – Initiative Neue Qualität der Arbeit"

INQA is embedded in the effort of the EU to create more and better jobs, as laid down in its Social-political Agenda, and to make the EU by 2010 the most competitive and most dynamic knowledge-based economic area in the world.

As part of this initiative for a new (and better) quality of work the Federal Ministries as well as the individual Federal States (Länder), social insurance partners, trade unions and companies cooperate to combine the employees' interest in a positive, healthy and worthy working environment and the need for competitive jobs (www.inqa.de).

Deutscher Bundestag – Enquete-Kommission des bürgerschaftlichen Engagements

The Enquete Commission (1999 – 2002) wanted to promote the public discussion of corporate citizenship in Germany as well as stimulate new initiatives in this field. The Commission showed that due to globalisation and new information and communication technologies, business is changing. This change requires new forms of democratic self-control and a more intense use of civil society potential. Against this background also business enterprises have a new role.

The Legal Framework for CSR Activities

A survey on the legal situation of CSR in Germany, which the Center for Corporate Citizenship (2004) carried out for Bertelsmann Foundation, showed that the existing laws in Germany do not really present a hindrance to CSR activities. This means that if business enterprises are willing and determined to take CSR measures this is no problem as to tax and financial incentives. However, incentives are not so high that companies make CSR depend on them, which means that these activities are not explicitly promoted by the government. The situation is characterised by a climate of non-appreciation which has a negative effect on the development of CSR. A comparison with other European countries shows that reforms for CSR legislation were more profound in other countries and that Germany lags behind in this respect.

Conclusion

The historical overview has shown that political patterns in Germany are strongly shaped by the industrialisation process of the late 19th century. Rigid positions of the state and related corporatist associations still prevail today, so that there is still little understanding regarding new roles and balances of society, state and business.

The review of activities in the political and business arena has shown that in Germany CSR is difficult to separate from sustainability and Corporate Citizenship. "Pure" CSR activities are in most cases embedded in or triggered by EU measures.

Surveys and official statements of business associations indicate that companies defend themselves against potential regulation on CSR. They like to point out that they are already "doing something" for society, but there seems to be little openness towards a strategic approach. This may also be attributed to the fact that hardly any sanctions (neither public nor political) have to be expected.

Society, represented e.g. by consumers and NGOs, do not drive CSR development in Germany since they rarely make clear requirements towards companies. Also with regard to their engagement in civil society in general, consumers do not live up to an active commitment.

Some government initiatives are orientated towards stakeholder dialogue and cross-sectoral and interdisciplinary cooperation as a step towards a civil society approach. CSR activities focus primarily on job creation and work quality issues. It has to be proven whether these initiatives, which often seem vague and generic, will lead to more CSR and succeed in activating civil society.

European initiatives and cooperation can be expected to have a major impact on regulatory processes in Germany. This relates to the integration of the public in the form of stakeholder dialogue, new social partnerships, integration of business activities in important policy issues and a more intense public discussion on CSR.

Notes

[1] The Commission investigated into the future importance and role of civil society from 1999–2002.

[2] imug is one of the rare cases in Germany where CSR matters are systematically researched. In most cases academic research is restricted to the issue of business ethics.

References

Bade, V. 2003. Gesellschaftliches Engagement von Unternehmen in Deutschland. In: *Bundesarbeitsblatt*, No. 10. Berlin: BMWA.

BDI/BDA. 2001, 2002. *Positionspapier zur Mitteilung der Europäischen Kommission betreffend die soziale Verantwortung der Unternehmen: ein Unternehmensbeitrag zur Nachhaltigen Entwicklung.* Berlin: BDI, BDA.

Center for Corporate Citizenship. 2004. *Survey on the Legal Framework of CSR in Germany* (in preparation). Gütersloh: Bertelsmann Foundation.

Bundesministerium für Umwelt, Naturschutz und Reaktorsicherheit. 2002. *Umweltbewusstsein in Deutschland 2002.* Berlin. http://www.umweltbewusstsein.de.

Cosore. 2004. http://www.cosore.de, accessed 05.08.2004.

Econsense. 2004. *Corporate Social Responsibility – Ein Memorandum für Kreativität und Innovation.* http://www.econsense.de, accessed 24.03.2004.

Enquete-Kommission des Deutschen Bundestages. 2002. *Endbericht der Enquete-Kommission "Zukunft des bürgerschaftlichen Engagements".* Opladen: Leske & Budrich.

Habisch, A. 2003. *Corporate Citizenship. Gesellschaftliches Engagement von Unternehmen in Deutschland.* Heidelberg & Berlin: Springer.

Habisch, A. 2004. Social Responsibility, Social Capital and SMEs. In: L. Spence, A. Habisch, & R. Schmidpeter (Eds.), *Social Capital and Responsibility – The World of Small and Medium Sized Enterprises.* Hampshire, UK: Palgrave McMillan.

Habisch, A., & Moon, J. (forthcoming). In: Jonker, J., de Witte, M. (Eds.), *The Challenge of Organising and Implementing Corporate Social Responsibility.* Hampshire, UK: Palgrave McMillan.

Habisch, A., & Schmidpeter, R. 2003. Das Unternehmen als Bürger der Kommune. Corporate Citizenship und Initiativen regionaler Arbeitsmarkt- und Sozialpolitik. In: H. Backhaus-Maul, & H. Brühl (Eds.), *Bürgergesellschaft und Wirtschaft – zur neuen Rolle von Bürgern, Verwaltungen und Unternehmen*: 71–84. Berlin: Deutsches Institut für Urbanistik.

imug. 2003. *Themenspot Verbraucher und Corporate Social Responsibility. Ergebnisse einer bundesweiten repräsentativen Imug-Mehrthemenumfrage.* Hannover. www.imug.de, accessed 05.08.2004.

IÖW & future e.V. 2004. Paper presented at the Multistakeholder-Workshop, Berlin.

Mersmann, M. 2003. *Corporate Social Responsibility – Die Rolle der Gewerkschaften.* Paper presented at an EU conference, 25.02.2003.

Observatory of European SMEs. 2002. *European SMEs and social environmental responsibility.* Brussels: European Commission. http://europa.eu.int/comm/enterprise/enterprise_policy/analysis/doc/smes_observatory_2002_report4_en.pdf, accessed 05.08.2004.

Ostrom, E. 2002. Soziales Kapital und kollektives Handeln – Gutachten. In: Enquete-Kommission (Ed.), *Zukunft des bürgerschaftlichen Engagements – Materialien.* Opladen: Leske & Budrich.

Putnam, R. D. 1993. *Making Democracy Work: Civic Traditions in Modern Italy.* Princeton, NJ: Princeton University Press.

Schmidpeter, R. 2002: Auswertung des Wettbewerbs "Freiheit und Verantwortung". In: Braun, B., Kromminga, P. (Eds.): *Soziale Verantwortung und wirtschaftlicher Nutzen*: 83 – 88. Hamburg: UPJ.

Spence, L., Habisch, A., & Schmidpeter, R. (Eds.) 2004. *Social Capital and Responsibility – The World of Small and Medium Sized Enterprises.* Hampshire, UK: Palgrave McMillan.

10 Concerted Action Towards Sustainable Development

Alfred Strigl[1]

Introduction

The discussion of sustainable development and its economic impact started in Austria in the late 1980s and therefore has a longer tradition than that of Corporate Social Responsibility (CSR). In a similar way to the Austrian Strategy on Sustainable Development (Federal Austrian Government, 2002), the Austrian CSR activities build upon the long-lasting Austrian tradition of broad stakeholder involvement within the so called "social partnership". This is the common dialogue platform between the main social partners. In the 1990s Austrian companies learned to deal with the terms environmental and social friendliness and finally with the term "sustainability". Enterprises nowadays begin to include this visionary concept in their own goals and business philosophy. Moreover they are starting to implement the sustainability concept in their management strategies and tools and communicate this through sustainability reporting and open stakeholder dialogue.

The broader CSR discussion arose in Austria only recently. Due to the ongoing awareness process and due to many "mosaic stones" formulated during the last few years concerning corporate citizenship, corporate governance and business ethics, it was easy to introduce the CSR discussion. The time was right when the "CSR Austria Initiative" was formed by the Ministry for Economic Affairs and Labour and key industrial players in 2002. CSR Austria is therefore the private sector contribution to the Austrian Sustainability Strategy and, on a European level, a major Austrian contribution to the Lisbon Strategy and the CSR debate.

Historic Development of Corporate Sustainability in Austria

Austria has been very much aware of controversies in the ecological and environmental field. Since the 1970s we have had the highest level of organic farming within Europe with a clear position against genetically modified organisms (referendum against GMO in 1997); and a clear policy against nuclear power plants (referendum against nuclear power in Austria in 1978). One may ask: Are the Austrians more sceptical about innovations and technological development than the rest of the world? The answer may be found in another question: How should one understand "precautionary responsibility"?

In that respect Austria is the cradle of several concepts which have often been "invented" near political or administrative programmes. The economy-oriented "eco-profit" idea for instance started in the early 1990s and the "eco-social market economy" concept was presented in the late 1980s by the former Vice-Chancellor Dr. Josef Riegler (Riegler & Moser, 1996). These concepts integrated the ideas of different groups and initiatives discussing politically and economically responsible behaviour. The concept characteristics are the definition of new eco-social boundary conditions on the outside and a new pattern of behaviour inside, in the form of "fair" and not "free" market, containing not only competition but also neutralism, commensalisms and symbiosis (Moser & Riegler 2001). Many different environmental and socially friendly economic development programmes have been part of an ongoing societal transformation process in Austria during the last twenty years. Especially the UN Summits 1992 in Rio, 1997 in Kyoto and 2002 in Johannesburg activated many initiatives in Austria:

- The Austrian Institute for Sustainable Development (founded in 1995) and the Climatic Alliance Austria (since 1997) tries to foster and implement the sustainable development process on a national scale.

- The official coordination of the Austrian Strategy for Sustainable Development (2002) and its implementation is administrated by the Federal Ministry of the Environment.

- With the Austrian Business Council for Sustainable Development (ABCSD) Austrian enterprises created their own forum in the year 2000.

- The "Arbeitsgemeinschaft Entwicklungszusammenarbeit" (AGEZ) is the official working group on development cooperation (established 2001). Around 30 NGOs from environmental, societal, social and development areas participate in this platform.

- The initiative "Sozialwort" (*social word*) of all the Austrian churches began to open the sustainability debate to the public from the religious and spiritual side some years ago. In this connection the project "Pilgrim" should be mentioned – a pilgrim towards sustainability from many different groups, initiatives and institutions coordinated by the In-Service Teacher Training for Religious Education in Austria.

Some major historic roots and initiatives are shown in Fig. 1. It gives a simplified but not exhaustive overview of the different milestones in respect to the wider landscape within which CSR is embedded in Austria.

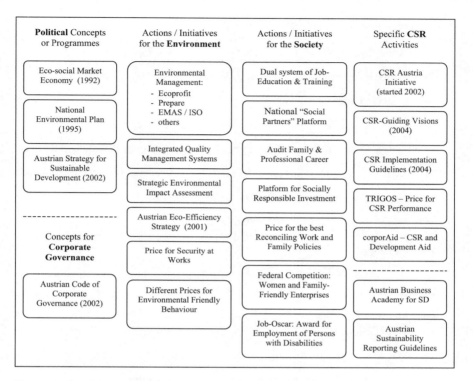

Figure 1. Corporate activities in Austria regarding sustainability and CSR

The main actors in the Austrian CSR scene are the following (the list is not exhaustive):

Austrian Federal Ministries:

- Ministry for Health and Social Affairs (BM für soziale Sicherheit und Generation)

- Ministry for Economic Affairs and Labour (BM für Wirtschaft und Arbeit)

- Ministry of Agriculture, Forestry, Environment and Water Management (BMLFUW)

- Ministry of Transport, Innovation and Technology (BMVIT)

- Ministry of Finance (BMF)

Business administrations and organisations:

- Federation of Austrian Industry (Industriellenvereinigung)

- Austrian Chamber of Commerce (Wirtschaftskammer Österreich)

- Austrian Chamber of Labour (Arbeiterkammer)

- Vienna Chamber of Commerce (Wirtschaftskammer Wien)

- Labour Union of Private Employees (Gewerkschaft der Privatangestellten)

- Federation of Austrian Trade Unions (Österreichischer Gewerkschaftsbund)

- Federal Social Welfare Office (Bundessozialamt)

- Labour Market Service (Arbeitsmarktservice)

Private organisations, Academies, NGOs

- Main Association of Social Security (Hauptverband der Sozialversicherung)

- Austrian Consortium for Rehabilitation (Österr. Arbeitsgemeinschaft für Rehabilition)

- AGEZ – Austrian working group on development cooperation

- Horizont 3000 – Austrian development cooperation organisation

- Austrian Caritas

- Austrian Institute for Sustainable Development (ÖIN)

- Austrian Business Council for Sustainable Development – ABCSD

- Austrian Business Academy for Sustainable Development – ASD

CSR in Austria – Drivers and Milestones of Success

Corporate Sustainability

Sustainable development is to be understood as a concept that ensures the integrated, well-balanced and equal treatment of the economic, social and environmental dimensions. Sustainable corporate development and, thus, social responsibility contribute to the increase of a company's value: by minimising risks, by generating innovation and by jointly shaping society. The kind of benefits derived by companies, however, depend on the approach taken. As presented in Table 2, the approach to CSR adopted by a company can be grouped into four categories.

Table 1. Types of approaches to corporate social responsibility

Category	Behaviour	Description
Passive	Problem solving	The company waits until there is pressure by the authorities and other stakeholders and then responds to their demands.
Reactive	Risk minimisation	Potential ecological and social risks are prevented that may impair the value or the reputation of the company.
Active	Innovation	The company realises that corporate social responsibility offers strategic opportunities in the market. New products, services and technologies give rise to new business fields. Internally, organisation and management develop in innovative ways.
Proactive	Responsibility to society	The company takes into account existing needs, but also shapes sustainable ways of life and business together with its stakeholders. This leads to close relations to customers, suppliers and other groups, giving the company a competitive edge.

Table 2. Core areas of sustainability management (Strigl, 2003)

Sustainable Corporate Governance	Sustainability Management Systems	Sustainable Innovation Management
Normative management Vision / mission Mission statement / strategy Code of conduct Corporate culture	Management systems for the realisation of strategies and goals (e.g. Sustainability Balanced Scorecard)	Sustainable product and service development R&D for sustainability Sustainable technology development
Capacity-Building for Sustainability	*Human Resource Building*	*Sustainability Communication*
Definition of responsibility Organisational learning Integration into all corporate divisions	Awareness raising Qualification Employee engagement	Reporting Stakeholder dialogue Media presence Image creation

There exists no universally applicable formula and strategy for sustainable corporate development. Every company has to take its own road to sustainability, and every company needs to work it out for itself. It will strongly depend on the regional, cultural, social and natural conditions of the company's operations. A company which wants to consciously orient itself to the concept of sustainability will become proactive at various levels and in various sectors. Important building blocks for a company's sustainable process are summarised in Table 2.

None of these elements exists by itself; they all interact with each other. Only the combination of all activities results in a dynamic business process towards sustainability.

Mutual Expectations of Austria and Its Businesses

Dual Apprenticeship Training System

In analogy with Germany and Switzerland Austria has an educational system which is quite unique in Europe and the world. Apprenticeships combine school education and on-the-job training, thus being called a "dual system": the apprentice is trained within an enterprise, completed by attending a part-time compulsory vocational school. Current reforms of the dual system will lead to an increased integration of economic and technological innovations. Moreover, they aim at motivating companies to invest in existing and to create new vacancies for apprentices.

The Austrian Companies and Corporate Citizenship

The overwhelming majority of Austrian companies are SMEs (small and medium-sized enterprises) with less than 250 employees. These enterprises are the backbone of the Austrian economy and therefore often the target group of specific supportive actions and programmes. According to a recent study (CSR Austria, 2003) 97% of Austrian enterprises acknowledge their responsibility as corporate citizens in relation to non-profit organisations. It results that only 17% of corporations with low public attention are actively pursuing CSR activities, whereas in the case of enterprises with high public attention this percentage rises to 47%. Publicly traded companies show a clearly higher commitment to be active corporate citizens (45% are highly active) than privately owned companies with a social engagement of only 31%. Enterprises with predominantly private customers and/or predominantly big customers show higher corporate citizenship commitment than the remaining enterprises. Altogether 81% of the small businesses, 58% of the medium enterprises and 49% of the large-scale enterprises support between one and five non-profit organisations. The ranges of topics, which most frequently find support through corporate citizenship programmes in Austria, are "health service and social mechanisms" (70%). The support ranges from money (93%) and in-kind gifts (85%) to sponsoring (68%) and volunteering programmes (58%). According to the same study (CSR Austria, 2003) 61% of the Austrian enterprises are "very satisfied" and "satisfied" with the success of their corporate citizenship activities.

Environmental Management Systems

Corporate sustainability was introduced to companies in a number of different ways. In the 1990s the Austrian government and its administration started several top-down programmes to improve and support the implementation of environmental, risk, quality, and health and safety management systems. Fig. 2 shows the number of organisations certified in accordance with EN ISO 14001 in Austria from 1995 to 2002.

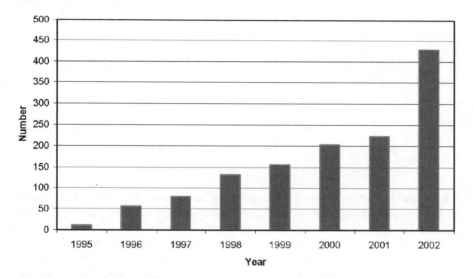

Figure 2. Increase of the number of Austrian ISO 14001 certified organisations
Source: "The ISO Survey of ISO 9000 and ISO 14001 Certificates, 12th Cycle, 2002"

CSR Activities of the "Life Ministry" (BMLFUW)

Platform for Socially Responsible Investments

The influence of the global financial markets on the economy is evident. To reach a sustainable path of development ethical, social and ecological aspects have to be taken into account when investing money. For the purpose of strengthening the market for socially responsible investments in Austria a platform for "Socially Responsible Investments" was set up in 2001 in the Austrian Society for Environment and Technology (OEGUT) with the support of the Ministry of Agriculture, Forestry, Environment and Water Management (BMLFUW). This platform constitutes a network providing information about specific activities in Austria and Europe. Within the framework of the Austrian eco-label, guidelines for the eco-label 49 "Green Funds" have been prepared for investment funds and mutual funds shares (sustainability funds, ethical funds or ethical-ecological funds, eco-funds and eco-efficiency funds as well as environmental technology funds).

CSR Activities of the "Innovation Ministry" (BMVIT)

Guidelines for Sustainability Reporting

The Austrian sustainability reporting guidelines "Reporting about sustainability" give a structured overview on how a sustainability report can be prepared. These guidelines describe in seven steps how the performance, goals and activities of a company can be presented with a perspective on sustainability. The guidelines:

- support enterprises in presenting their economic, environmental and social performance in a transparent and balanced manner,

- define the most important steps which lead to a sustainability report,

- present methods appropriate for the reporting process,

- ask questions to improve the self-assessment of companies,

- offer suggestions for stakeholder inclusion.

The guidelines are based on the evaluation of past sustainability reports produced in Austria and abroad and on practical experience gained from coaching the reporting process of two major Austrian companies. The Austrian Institute for Sustainable Development (www.oin.at) had the scientific lead in this research project. "Reporting about Sustainability" was promoted by the Austrian Federal Ministry of Transport, Innovation and Technology as part of the Austrian Programme on Technologies for Sustainable Development under the subprogramme "Factory of Tomorrow".

Austrian Programme on Technologies for Sustainable Development

The Austrian Programme on Technologies for Sustainable Development is a five-year research and technology programme (2001–2006). It has been developed by the Austrian Federal Ministry of Transport, Innovation and Technology (BMVIT). The programme initiates and supports trendsetting research and development projects and the implementation of pilot projects. The research and technology programme with its more than hundred individual projects has to be seen as a milestone in the discussion and implementation of sustainability issues in Austria and thus as a major milestone of the CSR process.

CSR Activities of the Ministry for Health and Social Affairs

Family & Career Audit

The *Family & Career Audit* is an auditing procedure trying to find the right work-life balance. "Family & Career" is guided by the "family-friendly index", an idea coming from the US and based upon insights from the Hertie Foundation. According to Badelt (1998), former Austrian representative in the European Family Observatory, the work-life balance is one of the most intensely debated issues in Austrian family policy. The *Family and Career Audit* supports companies to define and implement goals and measures for a family-oriented personnel policy (Federal Ministry for Social Security and Generations, 2004).

Federal Competition: Women and Family-Friendly Enterprises

Introduced in 1999, the federal competition "Women and family-friendly Enterprises" awards enterprises, which implement women and family friendly measures. The purpose behind this initiative is to officially and publicly acknowledge the commitment of those companies to reconcile work and family in a fruitful manner. The federal competition is based upon competitions within the Austrian states: from among the state winners and under the auspices of the federal minister, the federal winners are determined.

The Austrian Code of Corporate Governance

An Austrian Working Group for Corporate Governance made up of representatives of the Austrian Institute of Certified Public Accountants, the Austrian Association for Financial Analysis and Asset Management, listed companies, investors, the Viennese Stock Exchange and academia drew up the Austrian Code of Corporate Governance. All interest groups were integrated into the process through a broad and transparent discussion of the issues. The voluntary self-regulatory initiative was designed to reinforce the confidence of investors by improving reporting transparency, the quality of cooperation between the supervisory board, management board and shareholders, and by taking long-term value creation into account. The Code provides Austrian corporations with a framework for the management and control of enterprises. It covers the standards of good corporate management common in international business practice e.g. the OECD Principles of Corporate Governance (OECD, 2004) as well as the most important provisions of Austrian corporation law that are of relevance in this context.

The CSR Austria Initiative

A Concerted Action to Promote CSR in Austria

The main instrument of the Austrian CSR policy is the "CSR Austria Initiative", which was started in late 2002 by the Austrian Federation of Industries and the Ministry for Economic Affairs and Labour. Since May 2003 the Austrian Chamber of Commerce has been participating in CSR Austria, too, making it the main private sector contribution to the Austrian Sustainability Strategy. "CSR Austria Initiative" defines itself as a programme of the Austrian economy, which supports the great European visions – the Lisbon strategy and the concept of sustainable development. CSR Austria aims at achieving two goals: first to make evident how Austrian businesses work for the state and society; secondly to motivate entrepreneurs to intensify their efforts regarding CSR and at the same time to encourage them to communicate these efforts to a broader public.

The three main steps of the CSR Austria initiative started in June 2002 when the CSR Council Committee was founded at the Federation of Austrian Industry to prepare the CSR strategy for Austria. The first step from October 2002 to July 2003 was to initiate a broad discussion on corporate responsibility and to create a common understanding of its meaning and its benefits, as well as information and screening of international CSR initiatives for companies with regard to feasible CSR models. The survey "Corporate Societal Responsibility of Austrian Companies" (2003) concluded the first phase (CSR Austria, 2003).

The second step was the formulation of Austrian CSR-Guiding Visions building upon the Green Paper and other international texts e.g. the OECD Guidelines for Multinational Enterprises and on the special experiences, expectations and needs of Austrian companies and Austrian society at large. Following the Austrian tradition of social partnership the elaboration of the Guiding Visions involves a broad dialogue with representatives of all sectors of civil society. At the CSR Conference at the end of September 2003 around 120 members from business, NGOs, social partners, and international organisations discussed the first draft of the CSR Guiding Visions for the Austrian business community. The finalised CSR Guiding Vision "Economic Success. Responsible Action." was presented in December 2003 in Vienna. The 16 CSR principles drafted by the Austrian Industry are listed in Fig. 3.

In a third step CSR Austria is concentrating on further raising the profile of CSR and on assisting Austrian companies in their efforts to adopt and implement CSR practices. For this purpose the CSR Austria Initiative is preparing implementation tools; the following implementation activities are in the process of being introduced:

CSR Austria Guiding Vision: "Economic Success. Responsible Action."

Corporate Social responsibility means

...successful economic action:

    1.   reliable and trustworthy
    2.   long-term, value-oriented decisions
    3.   fairness in a competitive environment
    4.   playing a role model

...involving others:

    5.   employees are partners
    6.   promoting social integration
    7.   taking into account the concerns of stakeholders
    8.   helping to improve the situation in other countries

...orientation towards the environment and the future:

    9.   observing the precautionary principle
    10.   economic solutions for ecological challenges
    11.   taking consumer interests into account
    12.   encouraging sustainable development at global and regional levels

...a committed implementation effort:

    13.   adopted principles are a reference framework
    14.   transparency through information policy
    15.   cooperating in a spirit of partnership
    16.   further development of promising measures

Figure 3. CSR Austria guiding vision

TRIGOS: The Prize for Excellent CSR Performance

Trigos is a prize awarded by the association "Corporate Social Responsibility Austria" (CSR Austria) that was given for the first time in May 2004 to companies with special social responsibility. The initiators of Trigos are Caritas, Red Cross, SOS Children's Village, WWF Austria, the Federation of Austrian Industry (Industriellenvereinigung), the Austrian Chamber of Commerce and Humans World. Trigos is awarded to companies that are already attending to their social responsibility in the form of concrete projects or have implemented it in their corporate strategy.

ASD: Austrian Business Academy for Sustainable Development

In partnership with the Austrian Business Council for Sustainable Development (ABCSD) and the Austrian Institute for Sustainable Development, CSR Austria Initiative founded the Austrian Business Academy for Sustainable Development.

This institution will provide an appropriate and practical-oriented qualification programme for the business sector with respect to theory and implementation of corporate sustainability and CSR.

Building Bridges (Corporate Volunteering)

To attract more attention to the value of voluntary activities, CSR Austria is setting up a corporate volunteering programme between business leaders and non-profit organisations (NPOs) in cooperation with Caritas and Trigon. This programme is based on the experience in Germany and Switzerland and in the Austrian province Vorarlberg as well as the "Switch-Programme" from Siemens Germany.

corporAID

Initiated by the Institute for Cooperation for Development Projects (ICEP) the CSR Austria Initiative will take part as a partner in the corpoAID Initiative. The focus of this project is to support companies in carrying out projects in developing countries and to strengthen the knowledge about the needs in these countries. A second product of corporAID is the quarterly journal "coporAID magazin". The magazine reports on Austrian CSR issues in general (sustainability reporting, socially responsible investing etc.) and on global development topics like fair trade or societal and regional engagements of Austrian companies all over the globe.

The Austrian CSR Guidelines

The Austrian CSR Guidelines "Guidance for the implementation of CSR" of the Austrian Standards Institute (2004) are based on the CSR Guiding Vision "Economic Success. Responsible Action." and the guidelines "Reporting About Sustainability – 7 steps to a Successful Sustainability Report" (Kanatschnig, Resel & Strigl, 2002) which both have been produced by the CSR Austria Initiative. The guidelines on CSR principles, systems and tools were prepared by an interdisciplinary and inter-organisational working group "Corporate Social Responsibility" of the Austrian Standards Institute and are in line with international standards. In building on several initiatives focusing on the motivational aspect, the guide is designed to support the documentation, implementation, maintenance and improvement of a CSR management system. Furthermore, the CSR implementation guidance identifies possible interaction with other management systems. In general, it does not contain specifications or rules, but rather recommendations. Only references to Austrian law or the legislation of countries where the company in question is active or wants to become active are to be considered binding requirements. Even though this guide mainly addresses enterprises, other organisations, such as associations, public institutions and municipalities, are also encouraged to apply the guide.

CSR Activities of Labour Union and the "Civil Society" in Austria

CSR Positioning Paper from the "Austrian Civil Society" (2004)

A position paper titled "The social responsibility of enterprises (CSR) from a civil society perspective" (Amnesty International, AGEZ, AK, Ökobüro & ÖGB, 2003) was presented in December 2003 by the following organisations: Amnesty International; Working Group Development Co-operation (AGEZ) – the umbrella federation of 29 NGOs for social and development work; Federal Chamber of Labour (AK); Eco-bureau – the Austrian platform of environment organisations (members are e.g.: Greenpeace, WWF, GLOBAL 2000 / Friends of the Earth); and the Austrian Trade Union Federation (OEGB). The paper takes position on the CSR process in general and the CSR Austria – Initiative in detail. The organisations stress that socially responsible corporate behaviour has to go beyond the examples and principles indicated by CSR Austria and requires legal norms and norms for collective agreements.

CSR Position Paper of the Federal Chamber of Labour (2002)

The Federal Chamber of Labour (Bundesarbeiterkammer) represents the legal interests of approximately 2.7 million workers and consumers in all social, educational and economic matters. The CSR positioning paper stresses that there is reason to believe that companies need clear legal frameworks for their behaviour and strong internal and external representations of worker interests so that they can also gear their behaviour to public welfare aspects in a dependable manner. The chamber expresses the opinion that a voluntary CSR concept can only be the first step in the right direction. It needs to be followed by binding and actionable norms and clear legal incentives e.g. appropriate regulations for public procurement and competition as well as rules for promoting public enterprises.

Conclusion: CSR Perspectives for Austria

One of the biggest challenges faced by Austria in the coming years is to get actively involved in shaping the enlarged Europe (especially to the East and South) as an economic and social community. This ambitious goal hinges on two visions: On the one hand, the European economic and social model has to be further strengthened and in some respects newly designed, in order to be able to actively influence the framework conditions of globalisation. On the other hand, the integrative approach of sustainable development serves as a vision for the future. With the adoption of the Austrian Strategy for Sustainable Development in 2002 an important first step was taken to specify Austria's contribution to the sustainable quality of our work, life and the environment. The CSR initiatives in Austria – of which only the most important ones were briefly mentioned – act in synergy to the overarching vision of sustainable development for both economy and society.

Modern economy and society depend on each other: Realisation of our personal and societal goals require a well functioning economy. At the same time doing business in an economical and sustainable way requires a society free of any social tension with an emphasis on solidarity. This societal pattern produces a win-win-situation and supports an ongoing process of Corporate Social Responsibility. Therefore human and social capitals have to be strengthened to increase the competitiveness of enterprises. By accepting their social responsibility Austrian enterprises rediscover their roles within society and make a contribution on the way to a sustainable path of development.

Note

[1] I would like to thank Mag. Wilhelm Autischer, coordinator of CSR Austria, for his kind comments.

References

Amnesty International, AGEZ, AK, Ökobüro, & ÖGB. 2003. *Die soziale Verantwortung von Unternehmen (CSR) aus zivilgesellschaftlicher Perspektive*. http://www.oefse.at/download/CSR-Position%20Zivilgesellschaft%204.12.03.pdf, accessed 26.08.2004.

Austrian Standards Institute. 2004. *Corporate Social Responsibility – Guidance for the Implementation of Corporate Social Responsibility – CSR Guidelines*. Vienna: Austrian Standards Institute.

Federal Austrian Government. 2002. *Austrian Strategy for Sustainable Development*. http://www.nachhaltigkeit.at/strategie/pdf/strategie020709_en.pdf, accessed 26.08.2004.

Badelt, C. 1998. Developments in general family policy in Austria in 1996. In: J. Ditch, H. Barnes, & J. Bradshaw (Eds.), *Developments in national family policies in 1996*. Brussels: Commission of the European Communities.

CSR Austria. 2003. *Die gesellschaftliche Verantwortung österreichischer Unternehmen*. Wien: Studie im Auftrag von CSR Austria.

European Commission. 2001. *Green Paper Promoting a European framework for corporate social responsibility*. http://europa.eu.int/comm/employment_social/soc-dial/csr/greenpaper_en.pdf, accessed 26.08.2004.

Federal Chamber of Labour. 2002. *Position Paper: Communication from the Commission concerning Corporate Social Responsibility: A business contribution to Sustainable Development*. COM (2002) 347 final. http://eu.arbeiterkammer.at/www-909-IP-6257.html, accessed 26.08.2004.

Federal Ministry for Social Security and Generations (2004). *Audit for Family and Work.* http://www.bmsg.gv.at/cms/site/liste.html?channel=CH0179, accessed 26.08.2004.

ILO. 2001. *Guidelines on occupational safety and health management systems.* Geneva. http://www.ilo.org/public/english/protection/safework/cops/english/download/e000013.pdf, accessed 26.08.2004.

Kanatschnig, D., Resel, K., & Strigl, A. 2002. *Reporting about Sustainability — 7 steps to a successful sustainability report.* Vienna: Austrian Institute for Sustainable Development.

OECD. 2000. *The OECD Guidelines for Multinational Enterprises.* Revision 2000. http://www.oecd.org/dataoecd/56/36/1922428.pdf, accessed 26.08.2004.

OECD. 2004. *OECD Principles of Corporate Governance.* http://www.oecd.org/dataoecd/32/18/31557724.pdf, accessed 26.08.2004.

Moser, A., & Riegler, J. 2001. *Weisheit der Natur und Oeko-soziale Markwirtschaft.* Graz, Austria: Styria.

Riegler, J., & Moser, A. 1996. *Die Oeko-soziale Marktwirtschaft.* Graz, Austria: Stocker.

Strigl, A. 2003. *Sektorvision. Entwicklung nachhaltige Unternehmensleitbilder und -strategien, Berichte aus Energie- und Umweltforschung.* Wien.

United Nations. 2000. *The Global Compact.* http://www.unglobalcompact.org, accessed 26.08.2004.

Further Internet Links

CSR Austria
www.csr-austria.at

Austrian Business Council for Sustainable Development
www.abcsd.at

Sustainability Portal
www.nachhaltigkeit.at

11 Social Welfare Lagging Behind Economic Growth

László Fekete

The Meaning of Corporate Social Responsibility

While corporate social responsibility has become the leading doctrine of business ethics in the United States in the last few decades, its noncritical adoption causes many theoretical and practical misunderstandings in the context of European social and economic thinking. The original concept of corporate social responsibility was addressed to the large-scale publicly held business corporations of the United States, which frequently suffered from poor social reputation and even met the denouncement of the public in consequence of corporate scandals, wide-spread abuse of power, social and environmental negligence, and direct political involvement in financing autocratic regimes abroad. As a refutation of these condemned business practices, the advocates of this concept in the academic and business communities emphasise that corporations' economic, social, political and legal responsibilities towards society are equally important (Lodge, 1975). The economic argument originates from the obvious economic fact that the performance of the large-scale public corporations profoundly affects the welfare of the whole society. Accordingly, corporations should take responsibility for not only maximising the profits of their shareholders but also fostering social welfare. The advocates of corporate social responsibility also use legal arguments to support their thesis. According to the legal point of view, the large-scale public corporations cannot be regarded as a sophisticated version of business partnership based on the rights of a natural person to form, own and manage business enterprises but they are artificial creatures of the state. Since by using its sovereign power it is the government which gives the corporate entity existence, corporations in return should serve the interests of society, as well (Nader & Green, 1973).

Nowadays, the introduction of the new notion of corporate citizenship has significantly enlarged the scope of the original meaning of corporate social responsibility. Corporate citizenship seems to place corporations next to the fellow citizens as political actors in society. As if corporations were natural members of the political community and legitimate political actors in the representative democracy. Though this terminology should be considered as a serious category mistake, corporations in a few countries are entitled to a set of constitutional rights such as those enshrined under the First, Fourth, Fifth and Fourteenth Amendments to the Constitution of the United States. Thus, in 1978 the United States' Supreme Court granted First Amendment protection to the "corporate" speech of corporations. As Bradley remarks, the American "courts began to view the corporation as though it were a real person and began to afford it certain constitutional protections", especially, since the 1970s. (Bradley et al., 1999; Keeley, 1988: 237–243). The recent popularity of the notion of corporate citizenship in business and academic communities reflects not only the decline of the welfare state and its weakened economic role but also the corporate claim of the rightful and institutionalised participation in political decision-making processes. In spite of the current trend in business ethics and management literature, many critics of this new notion persistently think that the restriction on the political activity of the large-scale public corporations is constitutionally permissible and politically desirable.[1] They argue that nobody has ever conferred the legitimate authority of the political use of corporate wealth upon corporations in order to promote their own values and ideas. Consequently, corporations should play only a limited role in the political arena.

Nevertheless, the advocates of corporate social responsibility have successfully shifted the focus of the well-established academic debate and raised the question as to whether the management of the large-scale public corporations should act solely in the interests of their shareholders or whether it should take account of other constituencies as well. Briefly, the academic literature, without emphasising the wider social, economic and ethical context of contemporary business practices, tended to narrowly identify the problems of the large-scale public corporations with the side effects of widely-dispersed ownership, the separation between ownership and control, the inadequate system of corporate governance, the incomplete contracts, the improper rights arrangements, the lack of effective domestic and international regulatory environment and so forth. However, these problems cannot be explained away by using the Coasen theorem and other organisational techniques of the law and economics. The intention behind the concept of corporate social responsibility is much more ambitious, namely, to conceptualise the main social, economic and ethical issues of the operation of the large-scale public corporations and their responsibilities and obligations towards their internal and external constituencies and towards the whole society. Therefore, the concept of corporate social responsibility attempts to offer ethical guideline for the just arrangements of economic, legal, social, environmental and ethical responsibilities as well as for the reconciliation of conflicts of interest among the internal and external constituencies of the large-scale public corporations and the society as a whole. The concept of corporate social responsibility and the other mechanisms of corporate control, like the proper system of corporate governance, the legal and regulatory institutions, stakeholder dialogue and so forth, form the normative framework of fair and responsible business conduct in society.

Corporate Social Responsibility in the Hungarian Economic Context

The profound economic and social transformation that has taken place since the beginning of the 1990s has not resulted in the rise of shareholder capitalism in Hungary. There are still very few Hungarian business enterprises which can be rightly called large-scale public corporations. In other words, few domestic large-scale publicly held business corporations operate in the Hungarian economy to which the original concept of corporate social responsibility can be properly applied. The governance and ownership structure of the Hungarian enterprises mainly resemble the blockholder system of the continental Europe. Their stock market capitalisation is very low. Because they are not listed companies and their shares are not publicly traded, the coalition of a limited number of owners ("blockholders") controls them. (World Bank & International Monetary Fund, 2003). Privatisation primarily served the purposes of selling state-owned companies to strategic investors, maximising the revenues of the state, encouraging the inflows of foreign direct investment, overcoming the debt crisis, increasing productivity, downsizing, formatting a competitive market, innovation, job creation and the reorientation of labour. It did not promote the rise of shareholder capitalism. In some public offerings only a thin fraction of shares was sold in the stock market, therefore their minority holders could neither influence nor control the business activities of these large-scale public corporations. In opposition to the Polish and the Czech attempts, the Hungarian privatisation did not intend to transform the former state-owned corporations into large-scale public corporations with dispersed ownership structure. The dominant allocation mechanism was private sale to a selected group of investors and not public offerings of shares via the stock market (Biais & Perotti, 2002; Dewenter & Malatesta, 1997; Roland & Verdier, 1994).

As in the European economy, the majority of the Hungarian firms are small and medium-sized enterprises usually held in groups with complicated cross-ownership structures (VIP, 2003). This pyramid type of organisational structure raises many agency problems both for the owners and the managers of these firms (Shleifer & Vishny, 1997; Mallin & Jelic, 2000). Their managements are mainly dependent on the ultimate owners' decisions, whose intentions and long-term purposes are not particularly transparent. Since they are not public corporations they are not obliged to publish quarterly financial reports, social and environmental accountings and other public documents relating to their activities. Because of the pyramid type of economic organisations they usually do not act as distinct economic actors, therefore their responsibilities, accountabilities and business policies towards their stakeholders are difficult to identify. In this type of firm, the relationship-based system of governance is predominant in opposition to the rule-based one. Many of them are affiliates and subsidiaries of large-scale or even multinational corporations without following similar standards or being acquainted with the value statements of their owner companies. Because the pyramid type of organisational structure of firms poses extra challenges, especially for the transition economies, many authors in the management literature discuss it critically. They indicate that the dismantlement of pyramids is a preliminary condition for making fair, ethical and transparent business. Nevertheless, La Porta, Lopez-de-Silanes and Shleifer (1999) find that approximately 25% of the firms in their representative samples taken from the twenty-seven most developed countries are members of pyramids (McGee & Preobragenskaya, 2004). Other authors are much more empathetic towards the pyramid type of organisational structure. They emphasise the importance of technology-driven fragmentation and disintegration of production and distribution, which offers new opportunities to small and medium-size enterprises to integrate into the global network economy (Zysman & Schwartz, 1998). As to the ethical institutions and documents of the small and medium-size enterprises, few of them have codes of conduct, announce value statements or organise ethics training for their managements and employees. According to the representative survey of more than 400 Hungarian companies made in 1997 only 15% of the small and medium-size enterprises have codes of conduct, value or policy statements. Stakeholder management, partnership programmes, ethics officers, social and environmental reports were practically unknown institutions to them. It does not mean, of course, that the owners and the managements of the small and medium-size enterprises would be ignorant of the importance of ethical conduct in business. Their social responsibility strategies, however, are poorly documented and not particularly institutionalised. Although, the EU Green Paper (Commission of the European Communities, 2001) uses the notion of corporate social responsibility a bit loosely as it applies the term to all types of business enterprises, many survey researches show that industry, size, ownership and organisational structures, domestic, cross-border and multinational business activities play an important part in formulating and implementing ethical programmes (Spence, 1999; Jenkins & Hines, 2003).

In Hungary more than 40 of the 50 largest multinational corporations operate directly or via their affiliates and subsidiaries. Because the contributions of multinational corporations to the GDP are more than 50% and they employ 30% of the labour, the economic and social impacts of their operations on the Hungarian society and economy are enormously significant (Kaminski, 1999). Besides the positive spillover effects of the total factor productivity increase, managerial expertise, technological transfer, new organisational arrangements and foreign direct investment as well as implementation of a new corporate culture are certainly an important factors in the current transition as well.

Despite the growing influence of the new corporate culture in economic conduct the question of whether the multinational corporations foster corporate social responsibility, stakeholder management, social and environmental accounting, and other ethical institutions has not been seriously scrutinised so far in Hungary. The first difficulty is of linguistic nature. The notion of corporate social responsibility sounds a little bit mannered, even if it can be properly translated into Hungarian. Until recently it has been used in self-centred bureaucratic and managerial discourses rather than in everyday discussions. In addition, corporate citizenship is almost totally absent from the political and economic language. If a corporate speaker uses such figurative language in public discussions, he runs the risk of perplexing his audience. Of course, it does not mean that Hungarian society and the business community are unaware of the importance of fair business conduct. They simply express their views, the demands of the community and social needs in a more familiar language and not in the fashionable mode of speech of the business ethics literature. The leading daily and weekly newspapers and the economic press habitually discuss economic subjects from the ethical point of view. According to my estimation, in the last ten years the newspapers each day published at least five articles, interviews, and editorials which used moral arguments and called attention to the outstanding importance of fairness, accountability and responsibility in economic conduct. The findings of the latest survey research confirm that, 93 % of the people receive information about the social responsibility policies of the corporations from the press (Szonda Ipsos, 2003).

Interestingly enough, multinational corporations do not make great efforts to inform their clients, customers, business partners and the Hungarian public in general about their mission statements and their corporate social responsibility policies towards society. Multinational corporations usually do not take the burden of publishing and popularising their social responsibility policies, social and environmental reports in Hungarian. For instance, on Nokia's Hungarian website there is no reference at all to its ethical guideline and value statements. Nokia's *Corporate Responsibility Report 2003* and other ethical documents are available in several languages, except for Hungarian. The same practice applies to the majority of the multinational corporations, for instance, to Siemens, Electrolux, IBM and Flextronics. Multinational corporations appear to Hungarian society more like cosmopolitan sojourners than corporate citizens. Among the multinational corporations only few – Novartis, Philips, Samsung and Unilever – briefly inform Hungarian society about their business conduct and core values. These short value statements at least reveal that the vocabulary of the discourse between the corporations and society goes through some changes and is becoming partly moral and social in character.

As far as action is concerned, these value statements seem to represent the strategic incentives of the multinational corporations rather than strong commitment to comply with the ethical requirements of society towards the business community. To be sure, the motivations of the investments and operations of the large-scale multinational corporations in Hungary are purely economic. They take advantage of the cheap, disciplined and educated labour, the proximity of the Western and the Eastern markets, the economic benefits of the enlargement of the European

Union, the tax subsidies of the state and the local governments and the overall enabling environment of the country (HVG, 2004). If the original conditions change and become less favourable from the point of view of corporate profits, or if the tax subsidies of the state terminate, multinational corporations frequently choose to divest their mobile investments. Instead of following the recommendation of the EU Green Paper (Commission of the European Communities, 2001), namely "adaptation to change", many corporations – IBM Storage Production, Mannesmann, Salamander, Kenwood, Philip Morris, and others – divested in the last few years. Mission statements or corporate philanthropy do not make up for the economic and social consequences of their divestments. As I have pointed out above, the mission statements of the multinational corporations and the Hungarian public do not speak the same language. It is banal to say that a common language is a preliminary requirement for stakeholder dialogue. Due to their disregard of the local culture it is hard to find any country-specific remarks in the corporate social responsibility documents of the multinational corporations and explicit references to the geographical place where they operate in their environmental accounting. Therefore, few examples can be recalled which demonstrate that multinational corporations take a proactive stance towards the general welfare of Hungarian society. Especially, General Electric, MOL, ING Group, Levi Strauss and Richter among the multinational corporations and TVK, Pharmavit, and Architekton among the large firms show that corporate social responsibility policy is an important factor of their strategic purposes.

In spite of the above-mentioned examples the corporate social responsibility policies of the majority of multinational corporations can be characterised as mainly instrumental. For the majority of multinational corporations, corporate social responsibility merely confines to philanthropy, strategic and cause-related marketing (Melé & Garriga, 2004). They usually finance entertainments, exhibitions and shows. A few years ago the Béghin-Say sugar company financed the performance of Grimm's *Sleeping Beauty* in Budapest Circus. The old fairy tale was completely rewritten and made to serve the marketing purposes of the company. The actors made the old story into a pretext for singing songs, praising the latest candy bars of Béghin-Say. The new moral of the old story was the joy of sugar consumption. Multinational corporations are especially active in supporting schools to organise sport and artistic competitions for children in order to promote their brand names and new products and to convert children to faithful consumers. The philanthropic donations rarely contribute to the creation of new and highly original achievements in creative and performing arts but capitalise on the popularity of such pseudo-artistic happenings like "The Three Tenors" or the nostalgia concerts of the past celebrities of popular music. Sport competition is also a case in point. As sports results have lost the ideological justification of the superiority of one nation-state over the other, it is becoming more and more part of the private portfolios of the multinational corporations. As far as cause-related marketing is concerned, telecommunications companies are particularly skillful at mixing up their marketing with their corporate social responsibility policies. The donations of proprietary computer programmes of software companies, like Microsoft College Program worldwide, also raise serious debates because of the corporate influence on university curriculums and academic research projects (Cha, 2003). To sum up, the substantive accomplishment of corporate social responsibility does not appear to be an intrinsic part of their corporate agenda.

Since 1990 the Hungarian governments have not made any attempts to introduce any corporate social responsibility policies towards corporations. No governmental documents have been published since then which would have explicitly brought up this concept. The issues of corporate social responsibility are thematised by a few domestic and multinational corporations and professional organisations like Joint Venture Association or Hungarian Manager Association. Nongovernmental and civic organisations mainly focus on the protection of the social and physical environment, consumers' rights and corporate obligations towards business partners, employees, and local communities. The involvements of churches and religious organisations in promoting fair business are occasional and rather marginal.

Corporate Social Responsibility and Society

Concurring with the well-known view of a global community, Hungarian society comes to distrust domestic as well as multinational corporations. According to the latest Szonda Ipsos Survey (Szonda Ipsos, 2003) 44% of the people do not place trust in domestic corporations and 54% in multinational corporations. Business organisations have the lowest ethical index in comparison to the established institutions of the country like government, parliament, courts, law enforcement authorities, non-governmental organisations, churches, trade unions, printed and electronic media, schools, universities, hospitals and others. Corporate managers are also regarded as forming the least ethical social stratum among the professionals, for instance, doctors, lawyers, university professors, teachers, journalist, engineers, and others. The poor social reputation of corporations and their managements clearly shows that the majority of corporations has not integrated corporate social responsibility into its strategic management and daily business practices yet. Because of the priority of profit maximisation, the promotion of social welfare and the improvement of the quality of life in Hungary have lagged behind the steady economic growth and the increasing economic efficiency of the corporations since the mid-1990s (Osterman, 2000). Undoubtedly, corporations devote certain amounts of resources to local communities, public healthcare, educational institutions, sports, entertainment, and philanthropic purposes, but these contributions are only sporadic and modest supplements to social welfare. Although governments and international organisations encourage corporations to participate in such social welfare enhancing programmes as corporate social responsibility, corporations are not particularly responsive to taking the burden of promoting genuine welfare in society.

Note

[1] See Justice Renquist's dissenting opinion in *First National Bank of Boston v. Bellotti* (1978).

References

Biais, B., & Perotti, E. 2002. Machiavellian Privatization. *American Economic Review*, 92(1): 240–258.

Bradley, M. et al. 1999. The Purposes and Accountability of the Corporation in Contemporary Society: Corporate Governance at a Crossroads. *Law and Contemporary Problems*, 62(3): 24.

Cha, A. E. 2003. Microsoft's Big Role on Campus: Donations Fund Research, Build Long-Term Connections. *Washington Post*, August 25: 01.

Dewenter, K. L., & Malatesta, P. H. 1997. Public Offerings of State-Owned and Privately-Owned Enterprises: An International Comparison. *Journal of Finance*, 52(4): 1659–1679.

Commission of the European Communities. 2001. *Green Paper: Promoting a European framework for corporate social responsibility.* Brussels: EU Commission.

Jenkins, H., & Hines, F. 2003. *Shouldering the Burden of Corporate Social Responsibility: What Makes Business Get Committed?* Cardiff: Working Paper Series, No. 4, BRASS, Cardiff University.

Kaminski, B. 1999. *Hungary's Integration into European Union Markets.* Washington: Policy Research Working Paper Series. The World Bank Development Research Group Trade.

Keeley, M. 1988. *A Social-Contract Theory of Organization.* Notre Dame: University of Notre Dame Press.

La Porta, R., Lopez-de-Silanes, F., & Shearer, A. 1999. Corporate Ownership around the World. *Journal of Finance*, 54(2): 471–517.

Lodge, G. C. 1975. *The New American Ideology*, New York: Alfred A. Knopf.

McGee, R. W., & Preobragenskaya, G. G. 2004. *Corporate Governance in Transition Economies: The Theory and Practice of Corporate Governance in Eastern Europe.* Presentation at the Global Conference on Business Economics, Association for Business and Economics Research, Amsterdam.

Mallin, C., & Jelic, R. 2000. Developments in Corporate Governance in Central and Eastern Europe. *Corporate Governance: An International Review,* 8(1): 43–51.

Melé, D., & Garriga, E. 2004. Corporate Social Responsibility Theories: Mapping the Territory. *Journal of Business Ethics.* Special Issue (forthcoming).

HVG. 2004. *Milliárdos állami támogatások: Kiváltáságosok klubja.* June 19: 111 – 113.

Nader, R., & Green, M. J. 1973. The Case for Federal Charters. *Nation.* Feb. 5: 173.

Osterman, P. 2000. Work Organization in an Era of Restructuring: Trends in Diffusion and Impacts on Employee Welfare. *Industrial and Labor Relations Review,* 53: 179 – 96.

Roland, G., & Verdier, T. 1994. Privatization in Eastern Europe: Irreversibility and Critical Mass Effects. *Journal of Public Economics,* 54(2): 161 – 183.

Shleifer, A., & Vishny, R. W. 1997. A Survey of Corporate Governance. *Journal of Finance,* 52: 737 – 83.

Spence, L. J. 1999. Does size matter: The state of the art in small business ethics. *Business Ethics: A European Review,* 8(3): 163 – 174.

Szonda Ipsos. 2003. *Survey: Corporate Social Responsibility in Hungary.* Budapest: Szonda Ipsos.

VIP. 2003. European Private Company Data: AMADEUS and Business Browser Compared. December, Issue 1.

World Bank & International Monetary Fund (Eds.). 2003. *Report on the Observance of Standards and Codes, Corporate Governance Country Assessment: Hungary, 2003.* Washington, DC: World Bank & International Monetary Fund.

Zysman, J., & Schwartz, A. (Eds.) 1998. *Enlarging Europe: The Industrial Foundations of a New Political Reality.* Berkeley: University of California.

12 Discovering a New Concept of Authority

Marie Bohata

Business Practices at the Early Stage of Transformation Processes

This contribution looks at the development of business practices in the CR within the context of the country's ongoing transformation process and the emerging market economy. The findings focus on the tremendous efforts that have been made to enhance business standards and meet the growing societal demands. Examples of the improvements achieved in corporate governance are provided.

Results of a broad survey conducted in the Czech Republic in 1994 (Bohata, 1996) indicated that both the general public and companies were very critical when expressing their opinion on morals and ethics in the country. They saw the severest ethical problems in the field of legislation, jurisdiction, political life, the functioning of police, and state administration. The causes of those problems were insufficient law and jurisdiction, low support for ethics in laws, and low interest of political leaders and government in ethics. People, as well as companies, were convinced that current ethical problems would not disapear automatically with growing market experience, but would necessitate governmental action. They believed that education in families, schools and organisations, as well as new and stricter laws, greater attention of the general public, media, government and parliament could play an important role in improving the situation. The survey clearly revealed also "economic motivation"to behave ethically. Unethical practices were seen as a source of significant or substantial problems by 71 % of companies. Additional company costs due to these problems were reported by 68 % of companies. The importance of business ethics in the company strategy was stressed by 97 % of companies (76 % saw this as very important).

The severest problems at company level revealed by business people in the aforementioned surveys were:

- maintaining payments,

- maintaining quality of products and services,

- fair negotiations and bidding processes,

- adhering to verbal promises and contracts.

Another important perspective was that of consumers. It was evident that the transformation of the producer society and its pervasive lack of respect for consumers by firms and the state, established during four decades of communism, to a modern consumer society would take a long time. (We could mention various kinds of malpractice, such as sales of unsafe products which escaped effective monitoring, misleading advertising, because of underdeveloped regulation, the abuse of effective protection of privacy etc.). A decisive commitment of the government to competition policy by the government could help to ease the pains of this transformation, but the required cultural change had to grow organically within the existing society (consumer interests should become organised and new forms of business behaviour internalised).

However, the challenges to enhance ethical behaviour were seen not only in business but also in public administration. Public sector issues, due to their impact on the society as a whole, were viewed by some people as even more urgent. Two problems were considered crucial at that time:

- transparency in public procurement,

- political party funding.

There were many debates on the public service, its quality, prestige and requirements, but no special laws on public service were passed until 2000.

In the first half of the 1990s, many people in post-communist countries did not realise that a well functioning market economy required:

- particular forms of legal regulation,

- substantial levels of trust between contractors and economic agents,

- a constituted system of moral rules,

- guarantee of physical protection,

- a framework which assumes a certain level of responsible autonomy among social actors.

It stands to reason that this situation – be it caused either by ignorance or intentional negation of the mentioned principles – was reflected in business practices. When analysing the existing unethical business practices, we could see three origins: some were a heritage of the past regime and its specific way of thinking and behaviour, some represented phenomena connected specifically to the transformation period with new "opportunities" and temptations which it brought, and finally, some were new phenomena related to the market system itself (tax evasions, unfair competition, racketeering, etc.). It was assumed that most of the bad practices were of temporary character and society might get rid of them, or at least weaken them, by means of better laws and growing market experience. Several arguments supported this opinion:

- A growing attention in the Czech media was being paid to ethics in all spheres of social and economic life.

- Newly emerging foundations, associations, and other institutions endeavoured to initiate discussion about business practices and to run education and training programmes reflecting ethical concerns.

- Philanthropic activities conducted by specialised foundations, companies and individuals re-emerged, although not effectively organised.

- Activities of churches contributed to the growth of ethical awareness.

- The discipline of Business Ethics entered economic and business administration courses organised by Czech universities and Business Schools.

- First codes of conduct were formulated and introduced.

Assessment of the business climate by foreign business people is quite interesting[1]. When compared to other countries undergoing transformation, they saw the business climate in the CR as very solid. Nonetheless, they asked whether bribery and influence peddling has become a regular part of business in the CR. To answer this question we should explain why these phenomena exist and why they persisted.

Many entrepreneurs in the country sought to get rich quickly and to take advantage of new opportunities while they lasted. But the underdeveloped markets that would provide the profits also brought with them a lot of bureaucracy, antiquated laws and lack of personnel with experience in a market economy. Under these circumstances, potential fortunes might turn to frustration. To make the path smoother, many business people were willing to pay bribes (for getting a work permit, residence permit or telephone line quickly and not to wait for months). While these might be clear cases of bribery (facilitating payments), opinion about corruption varied. Judges and prosecutors stressed that they knew of countless cases, but noone was willing to come forward and testify. Others downplayed the issue, saying that corruption was no more pervasive than elsewhere.

There was a high temptation for officials, considering the enormous gap between responsibilities and salaries. Individuals earning low salaries were often in a position to approve projects where big money was at stake. For government officials every additional amount made a big difference, yet for companies those amounts were insignificant. It stands to reason that bribery was not new to the CR. Under the previous regime, petty corruption was quite widespread. After the political and economic changes, the stakes became higher. The desire for property was the main factor leading to bad business practices. What was unique about the new situation in the CR, was the time element. This sense of urgency was particularly evident in the privatisation process which was accompanied by all forms of misuse of power, including bribery.

With law enforcement slow in coming, businessmen who accepted bribery as part of doing business, and politicians who, for the most part, considered corruption a small price for a fast transition to a market economy, corruption was likely to continue. The phenomena of bribe-seeking and protection rackets were viewed by some as side effects of the implementation of capitalism into a situation of economic underdevelopment. Some people assumed that in the future, bribery and economic criminality would go down as the market economy developed. That time most foreigners did not complain about the situation and just paid. It is of interest, that the so called Corruption Perceptions Index (CPI) constructed and published by Transparency International[2], ranked the Czech Republic with the score 5.4 (on the scale 10 to 0, where 10 means no corruption) at the 25th position in the sample consisting of 54 countries. Later on we could observe worsening of these perceptions, demonstrated by the score 3.9 and 55th position among 133 countries covered in 2003. This bad assessment of the Czech business environment may have been caused by frustration that the corruption phenomenon (misuse of power and state capture) has persisted, and by decreasing social tolerance.

For largely historical reasons, Czech law is based on the continental law system, closely resembling the Austrian model. Cases are never judged according to precedent, but most attorneys conceded that the lack of case law made it difficult to know how laws would be interpreted. This was one reason discouraging clients from going to court. Moreover, it took too long to get a decision. Commercial courts were heavily overburdened, mainly due to the increase in commercial activity and because they were understaffed.

Civic society was one of the battlefields between two political views during most of the 1990s – "nothing-than-parties" concept and support of philanthropy as an engine of democracy and freedom. Civic organisations, which faced many obstacles and little support, have developed fairly thanks to international resources. Nevertheless, they have been expanding, displaying a wide range of activities. Tradition, which may be dated to the Austrian-Hungarian empire, played an important role, however, institutionalisation of philanthropy was hampered by expectations of some people that the state was there to take care of them.

The New Institutional Framework and Transformation of Power

The main institutional change was the change in ownership rights. Since private ownership serving entrepreneurial purpose was almost liquidated in the previous system, privatisation of state-owned enterprises was crucial. This change in ownership rights was accompanied by the emergence of complex contractual relationships. Freedom of choice of new economic actors to enter contractual relationships with other actors replaced the previous enforced hierarchical direction with no or very limited choice. Consequently, problems associated with the responsibility of the new actors emerged. A very vague concept of collective responsibility, which dominated in the previous totalitarian regime, did not allow the definition of concrete bearers of this responsibility. Thus, a natural feeling of individual responsibility was underdeveloped. Many of the new actors accepted their newly acquired rights and enforced their interests but did not accept responsibilities stemming from these rights.

Another unknown factor significantly co-forming the new institutional framework was information asymmetry. Instead of symmetry in a weak information access (except for the political and economic elite), information asymmetry became widespread. Insider trading emerged as a serious problem and created a lot of criticism, mainly of foreign investors. In this context, also the problem of conflict of interest and the very low sensitivity of the general public to these ethical concerns, compared to Western societies, should be understood.

Last but not least, unevenly distributed transaction costs should be stressed. While in the previous regime these costs were either unrecognised or evenly distributed among the population, in the new environment they started to play an important role and significantly influence the performance of individual economic actors and of the economy as a whole.

Economic and social reforms are centred on the transformation of power and the creation of new power relations (Bohata, 1999). This fact and its complex implications were not sufficiently stressed and explained to the general public. Thus the need for building and cultivating an appropriate legal framework as well as an informal (ethical) infrastructure of the market was underestimated and in some respects even neglected, the reason being to proceed with marketisation of the economy as quickly as possible. Moreover, the general public has been continuously educated (misled) by the dominant argumentation of reformers that market forces shall resolve everything. The source of misunderstanding was the implicit assumption of reasonable cost. Such questions as: at what cost, and who will pay this cost, have never been raised by the Czech reformers. This approach may be considered justifiable at the early stages of political and economic transition when it was necessary to generate sufficient political support, to safeguard irreversibility of democratic changes, and to lay foundations to a market economy. However, insisting on unregulated market forces in general meant misinterpreting liberal economic theory (Mlcoch, 1997). There were severe practical consequences of such an approach: lack of trust and low respect for private ownership which in some groups of population even led to discreditation of private ownership as such.

In the Czech Republic, transformation of power was accompanied by a shift in the understanding of power from a negative concept to a more positive one. While the negative concept was based on the image of one party treating the other unfairly, the positive one was associated with competence, strength, and authority. In this context, augmented by high expectations related to democracy and a free market, the underestimation of necessary checks and balances should be understood. Thus, we may argue that – supported by society at large – Czech reformers:

- overestimated the positive understanding of power ,
- left a large space to discretion,
- created only weak, if any, checks and balances.

A recognition that without these checks and balances society cannot function properly became widely shared only in the second half of the 1990s. Consequences may be observed in the Czech business environment and society in general.

To some extent, the massive decentralisation of state power found its counterpart in the sphere of civic and public life. In fact, there were two opposite views: President Havel supported the view that it was crucial for the citizens to realise that they themselves have to take on their part of individual responsibility for the sake of the whole society. Intermediary structures which would support the spontaneous initiative of citizens were needed. Opponents of this view more or less neglected the role of NGOs, stressing the role of market in the optimal allocation of resources. Nevertheless, many NGOs started to emerge. In the period of building civil society in the CR, international donors played a very important role in providing knowledge, training and also funds.

Efforts Aiming at Improvement of the Ethical Fabric of Business in the CR

In principle, we may see the challenge of improving business practices as a twofold task: first it was necessary to increase ethical awareness, and then to develop and implement appropriate ethical standards. For this purpose, such tools as ethical codes and best practices, as well as participation in various self-regulatory programmes and initiatives may be considered crucial.

At the early stage of transition, business ethics activities were driven more by academia than by business. Despite the fact that companies were aware of ethical problems and the cost they had to pay due to widespread unethical practices, almost no action was taken in the first half of the 1990s. This observation was supported by various inquiries showing no interest of top management either in consultancy in the field of business ethics or in training programmes (internal documents of Society for Ethics in Economics). Step by step the climate has changed and since the second half of the 1990s, positive signs might be observed. Not only have prestigious and professional associations started playing some role, but also some companies have already elaborated sophisticated codes of conduct or similar documents. An internal survey conducted by the Confederation of Industry and Transportation in 1998 revealed that more than 20% of some 400 responding companies in all size categories had implemented codes of conduct. However, we should not be overoptimistic about this fact: it is not clear to what extent these codes were ethically motivated and to what extent they represented a fashion or PR tools.

Philanthropic giving re-emerged quickly after political and economic changes but no policies were in place, monitoring as well as public reporting were lacking. A study elaborated by the Donors' Forum in 1996 (Donors' Forum, 1999) showed that a majority of companies did not distinguish between corporate giving and sponsoring, however, 39% of companies responding to a survey has already elaborated a long-term strategy of corporate giving or at least a set of criteria for a selection of projects to be supported. The most favoured areas at that time were social and health care, culture and sports. The PR motivation was quite common.

The situation started to improve in 1997 when a new legislation for NGOs was adopted and public incentives created. The growth of the NGO sector was quite impressive: in 1999, 108 funds, 116 foundations, 216 publicly beneficial organisations and 36 000 civic associations were registered. Another survey of the Donors' Forum conducted in 1998 (Donors' Forum, 1999) revealed that advertising was the first aim of corporate giving, followed by a feeling of social responsibility and, again, company image.

Another positive development was initiated by some enlightened companies in 1999. The Czech Institute of Directors was set up to enhance local standards of corporate governance. In cooperation with the Securities Commission and referring to the OECD Principles of Corporate Governance, a code of conduct for listed companies was elaborated and enforced in 2001. A definition of "best practice" as well as training programmes for board members are currently under preparation.

Another body, which has been operating in the country since the early 1990s, has become influential. It is the Czech affiliate of the Prince of Wales Business Leaders' Forum, which among others, acts as National Partner of CSR Europe. This initiative started with a small handful of companies in the Czech Republic aiming at creating a business culture that subscribed to responsible business practices to benefit business and society. The impulse of most companies was to focus purely on philanthropic donations. Currently, these companies are engaged in a remarkable range of activities from the protection of the environment to the promotion of equal opportunities; from building the capacity of small and medium-sized enterprises to creating business and education linkage programmes and employee engagement in the community.

Among positive developments, education should be definitely stressed. Many universities have already introduced courses in business ethics dealing with social responsibility of business into their curricula. So far these courses have been voluntary. Encouraging reports show that both students' interest and attendance are very high; however, motivation is unclear. It may well be the relative easiness of such courses compared to others that explains their apparent popularity. In any case, it may be very useful for students to conduct a deeper analysis of social and ethical aspects of phenomena which they are used to discussing almost exclusively from the perspective of a narrowly defined economic rationality. Business schools already require such courses and a majority of bodies providing management training as well.

Corporate Governance

The field of corporate governance may serve as an example to demonstrate development and improvement of business practices in the CR.

Corporate governance is a product of the environment in which companies operate. This environment is formed by several factors such as: the legal system, the culture, the ownership structure and the makeup of the financial sector. Thus, business conduct is affected by laws, regulations, and written and unwritten standards. In a corporate setting different historical and cultural experiences, customs and traditions play a significant role in setting these standards.

Privatisation methods implemented in the CR have predetermined the key players in corporate governance: investment privatisation funds, National Property Fund, banks, individual voucher investors, foreign investors and managers. These methods also co-determined the main issues in corporate governance, such as the make-up and functioning of capital markets, close relationships between banks and investment companies, and internal and external conflicts at board level.

Within the transformation design, Czech legislation created a hybrid of corporate governance having features of both the Anglo-Saxon and continental European models. This framework was quite general, providing shareholders at annual meetings with some freedom of choice. Recent empirical evidence suggested that the Anglo-Saxon model with independent directors, being not quite compatible with the existing environment and business culture, has become less favoured. Simultaneously, there was an ever increasing preference for the German model with executives serving on the board of directors and owners and other stakeholders (especially employees) serving on the supervisory board. Besides culture, geographic proximity and tight economic relationships between the Czech Republic and Germany play important roles.

Specific to the Czech model of corporate governance are in fact two roles for directors and how these conflicting roles should be interpreted: an agent and a steward. The steward position is given by statutory law. A member of the board in a steward position needs not to accept all rules stemming from the principal–agent relationship. Thus, a regulator does not affect the board of directors' duty, termed fiduciarity, which refers to directors' loyalty, accountability and compensation. The board is loyal to the company, not to shareholders. The directors are accountable for their decisions, but shareholders must accept costs resulting from bad decisions made by directors in good faith. In this respect, results of a survey conducted among board members of major companies operating in the Czech Republic in 1998 can be mentioned. Three similarly important (almost the same percentage of responses) but substantially different views were presented: (1) companies should serve the interests of managers, (2) those of shareholders, and (3) those of shareholders and simultaneously respond to the legitimate demands of other stakeholders (Bohata, 1998).

A checks-and-balances-lacking approach to transformation has caused serious shortcomings in the design of the Czech corporate governance framework: a very weak protection of small shareholders, insufficient disclosure, and concentration of ownership in the hands of irresponsible owners. This way power has become a tool for exploitation of companies (tunnelling of organisations) rather than serving as a business tool.

In the short history of corporate governance development in the CR, three stages may be identified. Their characteristics are described in the following tables.

Table 1. Stage one

Elements of the framework	1993 – 95
Legislation	Newly set up, a two-tier structure combining features of the Anglo-Saxon and continental models, unclear responsibilities of boards, dispersed ownership structure, creation of closed investment privatisation funds
Business culture	A lot of discretion, learning by doing, misusing opportunities, management dominated boards
Financial sector	Newly created Prague Stock Exchange, almost no regulation, all joint-stock companies allowed to be publicly traded

Table 2. Stage two

Elements of the framework	1996 – 99
Legislation	Securities Commission created, some protection of small shareholders introduced, responsibilities of boards partially clarified, amendments to bankruptcy law reducing the scope for owners to strip funds from a failing company before bankruptcy proceedings can be completed and giving more scope for voluntary settlement with creditors
Business culture	Concentration of ownership, more active Supervisory Boards representing mainly owners
Financial sector	Massive outlisting of companies

Table 3. Stage three

Elements of the framework	2000 –
Legislation	Opening of closed funds, amendments to the Commercial Code (plus second-round implications for other legislation particularly that relating to securities markets), improvements in related areas (ratification of the OECD Convention on Combatting Corruption of Foreign Officials, creation of a National Contact Point as an element of the OECD Guidelines for Multinationals) but no progress in law enforcement
Business culture	Increased adoption of ethical codes by companies and associations
Financial sector	Privatisation of major banks, adoption of a code by the Securities Commission based on the OECD Principles of Corporate Governance

Internal mechanisms of governance have been considerably improved since 1996, however, there is a wide scope for strengthening external mechanisms of governance, in particular by strengthening the discipline imposed by shareholders and institutional investors (creditors).

As mentioned above, good corporate governance rests, however, on more than just a sound legal framework and enforcement mechanism. Soft features, such as widespread acceptance of common standards of behaviour, codes of conduct, education and training for board members, are equally important. Major improvements in this area have been pursued by the Securities Commission. The code recommended for listed companies was elaborated in 2000 on the basis of the OECD Principles of Corporate Governance (OECD, 1999).

In conclusion of this chapter we may state that state enterprises under communism used to exercise important social functions. This was a common practice which was required. With privatisation and marketisation of the previous command economy this concept was abolished. We may argue, that under the heading of CSR, some elements are being re-introduced, however, in a modified way. The main difference is the voluntary character of these activities and their scope.

Membership of the CR in the OECD (since December 1995) has brought a commitment of the Government (Parliament) to adhere to various conventions and guidelines, such as those for multinational companies, which assume the establishment of the so-called National Contact Points, Principles of Corporate Governance, anti-bribery conventions etc.

After some hesitation, the necessary regulation was adopted and appropriate independent regulatory bodies established. The Securities Commission set up in 1998 may serve as a good example. It aims at enhancing business standards among listed companies.

The EU harmonisation process, which accelerated mainly in 2000 – 2002, has been an extremely important driving force in improving business practices in the CR and in reaching internationally accepted standards. In this respect, it should be mentioned, however, that the role of foreign investors was not only positive, as generally expected. Some of them very quickly and without any hesitation adopted lower standards of doing business (including environmental standards, lower care for employees, lobbying and corruption, etc.) and heavily profited from that situation.

Current and Future Trends in CSR

We may state that in the CR, much progress has been achieved in the area of environmental responsibility. After the Velvet Revolution, environmental awareness started to increase very quickly. This fact was demonstrated by companies' policies as well as by willingness of consumers to pay more for environmentally friendly products. There are examples of companies voluntarily entering global initiatives, such as the Responsible Care Programme, and starting reporting on their environmental activities. Motivation of companies has been increased by prestigious awards (organised by NGOs) and a growing public pressure.

In March 2004, the Securities Commission adopted a new code for listed companies (Securities Commission, 2004). This is a revised version taking into account the most recent trends in this field. Prior to the adoption of the new code, a survey was conducted among 33 listed companies. The results demonstrate some positive developments regarding the scope and quality of reporting, such as:

- 91 % of companies reports on their corporate governance structures,
- 82 % publishes information on audits,
- 48 % informs about their shareholders' rights policy,
- 39 % gives information on consumption of energy and water,
- 61 % reports on their human resources policies,
- 32 % informs about compliance with environmental standards,
- 58 % publishes information on partnerships and corporate giving.

In January 2004, the Business Leaders Forum carried out a survey on CSR, to which 111 companies, of 260 addressed, responded (Business Leaders Forum, 2004). The fact that 24 % are small (up to 49 employees) and 37 % medium-sized companies (up to 250 employees) is interesting and encouraging (Business Leaders Forum, 2004). Another positive feature may be seen in the high proportion of local ownership: 40 % of companies has a local owner (48 % is a part of a MNC and 12 % has a foreign investor). As much as 99 % of respondents agrees that besides generating profit, companies should engage for the benefit of society where they operate and 64 % is already familiar with the CSR concept. Not surprisingly, in particular small Czech companies do not know what CSR is about (60 %). Only 10 % of companies (mainly large and those belonging to a MNC) employs a CSR specialist and 80 % of those who do not have such a specialist even do not see a need to create such a position.

Respondents were asked to rank the three most important areas of CSR in their companies. The following areas were ranked on the top (answers number 1):

- care for employees (25 %),
- transparency (25 %),
- environment (17 %),
- education of employees (13 %),
- cooperation with NGOs (7 %).

The second highest ranking (answers number 2) belongs to:

- education of employees (29 %),
- care for employees (18 %),

- environment (13%),
- equal opportunities (11%),
- transparency (8%),
- cooperation with schools (5%),
- cooperation with NGOs (5%).

and the third to:

- transparency (15%),
- care for employees (13%),
- education of employees (13%),
- cooperation with schools (11%),
- relations to the state (10%),
- equal opportunities (9%),
- environment (9%).

As far as the employee care is concerned, 55% of companies offers education and training programmes. 56% is concerned with an increase in transparency (they publish information on the web, provide more information in their annual reports than required by law, their employees have access to their bookkeeping records etc.). 56% of companies taking part in the survey already cooperates with schools, mainly universities and has established a significant link to technical and economic disciplines.

44% of companies is engaged in corporate giving. Larger companies have elaborated strategies in this field, smaller companies donate on an ad hoc basis.

Motivation for CSR is mostly internal and companies do not feel preassure from outside. Company mission (93%), recruiting and retaining employees (59%), PR/marketing (55%), competitive advantage (45%) and company reputation (32%) represent the bulk of frequent answers.

According to respondents, the state does not play any role in promoting CSR. The only governmental body paying some attention to CSR is the Council for Sustainable Development. Companies would welcome communication of the CSR concept and strategies by the state to the general public, awards to socially responsible companies and information directed to consumers. Lack of CSR information is manifested in other surveys as well. For example, the STEM survey (2004) for Philip Morris conducted among Czech citizens in 2003 revealed that information about companies' CSR activities is hardly accessible. Only one fifth of the population is sufficiently informed about social, environmental and ethical aspects of corporate behaviour.

From the point of view of future developments the Business Leaders Forum survey offers an encouraging answer (Business Leaders Forum, 2004): 84% of respondents intends to extend and deepen the CSR activities.There is a need to develop tools and ways of how to trustfully inform consumers. For this purpose credible independent verification would be favoured.

It may be assumed that consumers in the Czech Republic will play an important role in the adoption of the CSR concept. This is caused not only by their ever-increasing expectations, but also by the fact that they are becoming aware of their strength. Evidence suggests that a growing pressure of consumers on corporate social responsibility may be expected. A recent public poll conducted by the Association of Advertising Companies revealed that 70% of responding consumers was willing to pay more for products and services provided by responsible companies.

CSR is seen as a viable concept in the Czech Republic. However, some important factors fostering this modern philosophy of doing business as well as an appropriate institutional framework are still lacking. Among these factors, pressure of investors and banks may be considered crucial. Socially responsible investment is not yet an option for Czech citizens. Also the role of the media should increase. Last but not least governmental incentives, mainly fiscal, but also various awards should be developed. Organisations promoting CSR should be supported.

Conclusions

Reflections on history and culture may lead us to the following characteristic of business practices in the CR. A pragmatic approach reflects the fact that there are three origins of unethical business practices: some are a heritage of the past regime; some represent phenomena connected specifically to the transformation period with the new "opportunities" and temptations which it brought, and some are new phenomena related to the market system itself. Therefore, it might be assumed that many of these problems were only of a temporary nature and would disappear when new institutions were more timely in place, market experience grew, and the country was fully incorporated into the European and global structures. Then, the business climate and business practices would meet the standards of developed market economies.

There seems to be a consensus that the first step in enhancing business standards in the emerging market economy in the CR is building a rigorous legal infrastructure. The challenge here is not only that the new laws be passed but also correctly interpreted and fully enforced. For some people, compliance with laws is sufficient and this is how they understand the responsibility of business. For others, compliance with law represents only the minimal requirement and corporate responsibility is interpreted more or less as self-regulation going beyond that.

The crucial problem, however, is to better understand the nature of the market economy, its determinants and its limitations. Obviously, this is not only a question of theoretical arguments and principles but also, and more importantly, of results of the functioning of the market. Given the circumstances, the inevitable stage of "learning by doing" has to be followed by the next step, "learning from mistakes" (whatever their reason).

With some simplification we may state that the ethics concern in the period of building a market economy was to avoid (limit) harm.The era of cultivating the already existing market economy may be characterised by demonstrating positive obligations – doing good in the social, economic and environmental spheres, at least by some enlightened companies operating in the CR. Among them, all types of companies of all sectors of the economy, be it foreign-controlled or genuine Czech companies may be found.

Notes

[1] This part is based on informal discussions and conversations of the author with business people operating in the Czech Republic and confirmed by experience of Czechinvest (support agency for FDI).

[2] Transparency International is an international non-profit organisation fighting corruption in international trade and at national levels. Currently, it has national chapters in about 80 countries all over the world. The Czech chapter – TIC – was launched in 1998.

References

Bohata, M. 1996. Some Ethical Aspects of Transition and the Revival of Entrepreneurship in the Czech Republic. In: W. Gasparski & L. Ryan (Eds.), *Human Actions in Business, Praxiology, Vol. 5*. Transactions Publishers.

Bohata, M. 1998. Some Implications of Voucher Privatization for Corporate Governance, Prague: *Economic Papers 7.*

Bohata, M. 1999. Reforming Institutions in the Czech Economy. In: M. Bohata, & F. Turnovec (Eds.), *Transtition, European Integration and Institutional Change*. Prague: Conference proceedings, CERGE-EI: 281 – 293.

Business Leaders Forum. 2004. *Spolecenska odpovednost firem* (Corporate Social Responsibility). Prague: Business Leaders Forum.

Donors' Forum. 1999. *Sponzorstvi a darcovstvi ceskych podniku* (Czech Corporate Sponsoring and Giving). Prague: Donors' Forum.

Mlcoch, L. 1997. Czech Privatization–Penalties for the Speed. A Criticism of Radical Liberalism. In: P. Koslowski (Ed.), *Business Ethics in Central and Eastern Europe*. Berlin: Springer.

OECD. 1999. *Principles of Corporate Governance*. Paris: OECD.

Securities Commission. 2004. *Code for Listed Companies*. Prague: Securities Commission.

STEM Survey. 2004. Presented at the Conference "CSR – Necessity or Luxury". Prague.

13 Business Expectations Beyond Profit

Wojciech Gasparski

Introduction

"Business Ethics" not "CSR", is the umbrella concept under which responsible behaviour in the economy is studied, taught and organised in Poland[1]. Business ethics is influenced by human action theory known as *praxiology* (Gasparski, 2002c) according to which human conduct is delimited by three dimensions or "triple E", i.e., effectiveness, efficiency and ethicality. *Effectiveness* is a dimension of the degree to which a state intended as a purpose of a given action is achieved; *efficiency* is a relation between an effect of the action and expenditure of its performance; *ethicality* is a dimension of the degree of social consent for performing the action in a given culture founded on values esteemed in the culture and on related norms of conduct. Effectiveness and efficiency are economical *sensu stricto* when one is able to measure them in monetary units. They are economical *sensu lato* when one is limited to their qualitative characteristics. *Ethicality* is qualitative by its nature. Both economical and ethical values are mutually independent when treated *analytically*, whereas in the *synthetic* sense the economical and ethical values, i.e., qualities of human actions expressed by these values, are mutually dependent formulating actions' indispensable *axiological context* (Gasparski, 2002c).

In relation to the above, corporate responsibility, as I understand[2] it, should be defined as a whole composed of four characteristics taken together:

- *accomplishing the company's goal* (increasing the company's value, delivering products and services of proper quality),

- doing it *in the long run* (harmonious permanence),

- *ensured by proper shaping of relations with the main stakeholders* (shareholders, employees, managers, clients, consumers, suppliers, local community, natural environment, etc.), and

- through conduct compatible with law and socially accepted ethical norms (on the part of all the stakeholders).

The above understanding is a consequence of a systemic (i.e. related to systems theory[3]) approach which is a precondition for integrity.

Expectations From and Attitudes Towards Business in Poland

Remnants of the past are mainly responsible for the actual situation in Polish economics and its social context. "According to surveys many Poles do not trust business people – wrote John A. Matel, an American diplomat – Poland's history partially explains this attitude. Throughout the 19th century, when free markets and free enterprise were developing in Western Europe and the United States, Poland was occupied by powers that viewed markets with varying degrees of suspicion. More recently, Communists were actively hostile to the very idea of free markets. […Nevertheless] A non-official market always existed in Poland […] but it was an inefficient, illegal, and underground shadow of a true free market. In this market, many normal business activities were, by definition, illegal: supplying goods at a market price – 'black marketeering.' Obtaining raw materials or labour from sources other than inefficient government bureaucracies – 'criminal exploitation.' […] How can it be a surprise that 'biznesmeni' [a Polish equivalent of *business people*] were perceived as crooks and confidence men. Business tended to attract marginal people. To make things work, business people were forced to rely on questionable practices, since, in the absence of market triggers and discipline of freely agreed prices, bribes and manipulations provided the only incentives to buy or sell. […] Only under free conditions can business people, or anybody else, act ethically" (Matel, 1996).

In Poland (Gasparski, 2001), like in any other country, systems of values are different for different people and different companies (Gasparski et al., 2003). Among them are people who are successful thanks to their just and fair efforts. They know sense of investment, making decisions, they use their knowledge and skills sharing them with their partners, with whom they are aiming towards not just profit but rather maximisation of owner value of their companies. Unfortunately there are also dodgers who take advantage of others' ignorance and naiveté. There are also owners who would be eager to act ethically according to moral norms, but from time to time use shortcuts that compromise ethics. There are many, too many, front page articles in Polish newspapers about misconduct of some businesses, and still too few business reactions to misconduct in the real business, and misuse of the term "businessman" mainly by the media.

The external observers of the situation in the Polish economy under transformation made the following conclusions and observations:

- [...] it is critical that reformers minimise negative consequences of reform efforts (especially severe unemployment) as much as possible.

- [...] reformers made the same mistake as did their central-planning predecessors. They assumed a degree of automatic responsiveness on the part of economic actors. Shock therapy was implemented in a spirit of "democratic euphoria" [...]. What was forgotten was that Polish workers were not automatons or robots.

- [...] economic performance is irretrievably connected to the culture, religion, politics, history, values, beliefs, and sense of "nationhood" of the people. Economic transformation cannot be separated from any of these intercepts.

- [...] the process of transformation will be difficult, socially wrenching, confusing, and oftentimes misunderstood. Essentially, however, the process will work.

- [...] the political landscape still remains a veritable minefield. Politics is fraught, with decision, disunity, shifting alliances, new configurations, old grudges being replayed, and so forth. However, this is the quintessential Poland! (Hunter & Ryan, 1998: 196–197).

The quoted scholars trying to answer the question "What economic and social challenges confront society as Poland enters its third millennium?" formulated several suggestions, putting in front of them the following imperative: "Attention must be refocused on the *development of human capital* by improving declining educational and health care systems, by encouraging basic scientific research, and by increasing the emphasis on management and entrepreneurial training. Institutions must be developed to improve the long-neglected natural environment and to encourage responsible consumerism, cultural traditions, societal tolerance, and diversity" (Hunter & Ryan, 1998: 198).

Cultural Drivers and Opinions of CSR in Poland

Let me start from the religion position, for religion, especially because of the Pope's teaching, takes special position in the country of his origin, his priesthood, and academic activity as a Professor of Ethics at the Lublin Catholic University. His addresses, especially directed to business leaders, are quoted and used as memento. As an example let me quote of what has been said by John Paul II in his address to the Presidents of the European Industrial Confederations delivered on December 6th, 1990: "[...] no model of progress that does not take into account the ethical and moral dimensions of economic activity will succeed in winning the hearts of Europe's people" (John Paul II., 1996).

Recently the Polish Academy of Sciences' Committee of Sociology published a special *Report on Moral Condition of the Polish Society* (Marianski, 2002). The Editor of the *Report*, a Professor of the Lublin Catholic University, in his contribution (Marianski, 2002: 481 – 504) refers to the Social Opinion Research Centre (CBOS) survey of December 2000 according to which: 21.9% respondents accepted the view that moral principles of Catholicism are the best and sufficient morality; 27.4% declared that all Catholic principles are right but because of life's complexity they should be supplemented with some other rules; although 43.8% considered the majority of catholic moral principles as right, they did not accept all of them or considered them insufficient; for 3.8% respondents the principles are strange; and 1.0% had no opinion about the issue. In conclusion of his contribution Marianski points out the so-called critical state of morality founded on the church's ethical system. The post-modern morality, according to which freedom to act turns to be lawlessness, emerges out of uncertainty, vagueness and ambivalence. For many people autonomy is becoming ultimate and the last resort for itself.

Some other contributors to the *Report* discuss different issues, e.g., erosion of ethical standards in Polish business (A. Dylus op. cit., 271 – 304), corruption in relation to the moral consciousness of Poles (A. Kojder op. cit., 233 – 252), moral orientation of Polish society (K. Kicinski op. cit., 369 – 404) and many others. Overviewing the moral orientation Kicinski characterises the following elements: (i) marginalisation of moral categories, (ii) hidden mental structures of a "moral system", (iii) low level of moral reflection, (iv) moral autonomy, (v) moderation in moral assessment of others, (vi) situational ethics dominating over principalism, (vi) acceptance of people who make different ethical choices, (vii) projecting attitude towards personal patterns[4].

Recent surveys by Polish researchers were focused on: (i) managers' opinion about business responsibility (Rok, Stolorz & Stanny, 2003); (ii) consumer attitudes and leaders' opinion on CSR (Foundation of Social Communication, 2003); (iii) in the final stage of preparation is a report of *"The Public's Views of Business in Poland Survey 2003"*, a project carried out for the Institute of Public Affairs by leading research company CBOS.

According to the first Report 57% of managers (out of a list of the 500 biggest companies[5] operating in Poland published by a newspaper *Rzeczpospolita* (The Republic)) consider it very important, and 42% important, that a company follows ethical principles. They point out two types of benefits from CSR: (i) internal benefits like: development of organisation culture 57.1%, encouragement of the best personnel 40.0%, higher motivation of managers and other employees 36.5%, improvement of managerial quality 32.9%, growth of sale 28.8%, compliance 27.1%, lower costs 17.6%, and (ii) external benefits like: improvement of image and reputation 78.2%, increased loyalty of clients 37.1%, greater chance for long-term success of a company 31.2%, easier access to the media 30.0%, better conditions to run a business 29.4%, sustainability 18.2%. On the other hand only 23% of managers work in firms with a written code of ethics and 34% declares that their firms have an unsolicited collection of rules (a "virtual code").

As far as the CSR concept is concerned: 24% of managers are familiar with it, 48% have some knowledge, 28% know nothing or almost nothing about it. The respondents define CSR as: to act according to ethical norms 56%, adequate and paid in time wages 55%, transparency 46%, environmental protection 37%, cooperation with all stakeholders 32%, compliance 33%, taking care of those who are in need 16%, creating positive perception of a firm 14%. The following motives of business social involvement are declared: image and brand creation 72.9%, better relations with the local community 46.5%, to be a good citizen 34.7%, it pays in the long run 30.0%, willingly 25.9%, public opinion pressure 11.8%, other firms do the same 9.4%, to conquer a new market 8.2%, others 1.2%.

As many as 81% of respondents believe that state policy may encourage a firm to get involved in CSR (39%-yes, 43%-rather yes), 78% believe in NGO support of CSR (26%-yes, 52%-rather yes). The role of stakeholders is pointed out by 62% – clients, 81% – local communities, it is considered as very important or important that all employees should have equal opportunities (99%).

The following form of CSR activities of the companies are mentioned: financial support 75.3%, material support 64.7%, rendering of facilities 38.2%, mutual projects with NGOs 27.1%, voluntary activities 10.6%. Degree of CSR involvement: below 1% of the year profit (yp)- 62% firms, 1 – 3% yp-32% firms, 3 – 5% yp-6% firms, above 5% yp-1% firms. The degree of the importance of publishing reports is presented in *Table 1*.

Authors of the Report conclude it with comments that there is a growing interest in CSR, and a kind of "political correctness" in declaring the involvement is noticed. Lack of relevant knowledge of debates in EU countries about CSR causes a passive attitude of the companies operating in Poland, and neither the government

Table 1. Is it important for a company to publish reports

Type of report	Very important	Important	Not so important	Unimportant	Don't know
Financial	38%	47%	10%	3%	2%
Environment protection	23%	43%	16%	15%	3%
CSR	18%	35%	24%	10%	14%

nor NGOs offer an effective framework that might encourage companies to get involved in CSR initiatives to a higher degree.

The second Report is an outcome of the survey done in December 2002 on a sample of 1000 persons (aged 18+) interested in CSR (statistical error 3.6%). The investigation was supplemented in March-April 2003 with 21 individual interviews with business, political, and media leaders. The following factors influence respondent opinion of a firm: quality of products/services 68%, how employees and suppliers are treated 63%, quality of client service 50%, CSR 30% (7% the most important, 23% as important as other factors), ethical conduct 29%, open and clear information about products/services 24%, reaction to complaints 21%, reputation 21%, environment protection 21%, charity 21%. As many as 53% of respondents believe that big companies should act for profit, pay taxes and offer lawful employment, 14% that they should introduce higher ethical norms, and be engaged in social betterment to all stakeholders, and 30% suggest something in between the two extremes. A company, to be considered socially responsible, should: treat employees with respect 23%, be honest 15%, offer employment 11%, take care of the common good 10%, offer higher wages 9%, not exploit personnel 6%, pay taxes according to the law 5%, take care of personnel health 5%, offer charity donations 5%; as many as 20% of respondents have no idea about any factors of a company's social responsibility.

It is interesting to learn how far institutions are really trusted to act for the common good, *Table 2*. In addition to that, respondents declared they most trusted the reports about companies' behaviour elaborated by independent organizations

Table 2. Institutions and common good

Institutions	Trusted in full	Trusted to a certain degree	Rather not trusted	Not trusted	Don't know
Universities and academic institutions	24%	53%	13%	3%	7%
Media	12%	61%	19%	7%	1%
Ecological organisations and groups	14%	57%	18%	4%	7%
NGOs and charity foundations	18%	53%	18%	7%	4%
EU	7%	44%	26%	17%	6%
Big Polish companies	4%	46%	31&	11%	8%
Polish Government	5%	43%	32%	20%	-
Multinationals	3%	36%	33%	19%	9%

(30% trusted in full, 48% rather trusted) or state organs and inquiries by interest groups and journalists. Companies' own reports are trusted the least, 43% (4% trusted in full, 39% rather trusted).

According to the respondents, commercial firms are involved in CSR because of: promotion 93%, to create a positive image among consumers 94%, to create a positive image among personnel 89%, to create positive relations with society 89%, they do not ignore social affairs 83% (7% fully agree, 49% agree to a certain degree, 27 rather agree).

The authors of the Report offer two answers to the following question "Why despite actual knowledge about CSR, is the idea not a live issue?": (i) consumer knowledge is not sufficient, for consumers are mostly interested in product/services quality and their prices; their knowledge about firms comes from friends, independent journalist enquiries, and the media; (ii) companies are considered not to be serious in declaring their engagement in CSR; communication for CSR. In the light of that it is paradoxical that 79.9% respondents declare they would prefer to buy products from socially responsible firms if they knew about that, and 67.3% is ready to pay more if a product is environmentally friendly. It proves the lack of relevant communication on CSR aspects of companies' operation.

The third Report is not available yet, therefore the following results are only a part of the survey conducted among a representative sample of 1003 Polish adults (aged 18+) across the whole country. In the opinion of 66% of respondents, the market economy in Poland works badly. More than 54% think that after 1989 private enterprises were created mostly by people having strong connections with the former communist regime. Almost 61% strongly believe that the incomes of the richest should be legally limited. Furthermore, only 6.5% of respondents would like to work for private companies, and more than 41% prefer to work for state-owned companies. Almost 60% of the public think that private employers do not care about the well-being of their employees. On the other side, however, the public in Poland feels that the activity of private enterprises has a major influence (i) on economic development in Poland (81.4%), (ii) on the level of employment (79.8%) and (iii) they are involved in community partnership (64.5%). The majority (70.6%) recognises that the management system is more effective in private enterprises. An individual entrepreneur is a good example for others (51.9%), well educated (53.2%), honest (27.1%), thrifty (63%) but also trying to avoid paying taxes (65.6%). As many as 52.3% of respondents believe that it pays to be ethical in doing business, especially long-term, while 37.7% don't think so. But the most important factors for commercial success are: money (58.7%), good idea (45.6%) and a proper education (40.1%). Only 6.3% of the public believe that honesty is such a crucial factor.

Past, Present, and Future Trends of Business Ethics and CSR in Poland

Although the name of "corporate social responsibility" is relatively new in Poland the issue is not a new one. Some of today's supporters of this approach refer to the words related to moral aspects of economic activity of Adam Krzyzanowski (1935), a Jagiellonian University Professor, expressed in the nineteen thirties. Others, for whom it is a lip-service, consider CSR as just *public relations* going by a different name.

If one would like to identify the exact birth dates of business ethics and CSR in contemporary Poland he or she should consider 1994 as the year in which the first nation-wide conference on business ethics was organised by the Learned Society of Praxiology (LSP) together with the Entrepreneurship Education Foundation[6]. Since the same year, special seminar ("round table") sessions on "Business, Management, Economics and Ethics" are organised once a month at the Polish Academy of Sciences (PAS). The seminar is co-organised now by the LSP and Business Ethics Centre (established in 1999), a joint unit of the Institute of Philosophy and Sociology (PAS) and Leon Kozminski Academy of Entrepreneurship and Management. In 2002 two NGOs promoting business ethics and CSR were established in the country, the Forum of Responsible Business (related to the CSR Europe) and the Polish Business Ethics Association (EBEN Poland).

Participants in the above and other conferences and seminars as well as members of the NGOs represent academia (more) and businesses (less). During debates, theoreticians of management argue with ideologues over the "stakeholder theory", which the former consider a management theory and the latter – a "doctrine". Experts on system theory approach the issue calmly and without emotion, pointing to the context of all activity realised in the complex cooperation of people, something that praxiologists keep pointing out with the determination of Sisyphus (Gasparski, 2002a).

It is worthy to add that people in contemporary Poland expect more from businesses than just the profit. Since business plays the most important role nowadays – to some extent the role played by the government in the previous regime – people expect business to be more *socially* responsible in terms of fulfilling societal needs to a greater degree, and blame it for not doing that in a straightforward and immediate way. On the other hand business people are mainly profit-oriented, although gradually they declare the importance of ethical conduct. Therefore one may notice that it is a melting-pot in which the new standards of business conduct are created out of tradition (religion, morals, ethical theories, human action theory, i.e., praxiology, etc.) and modern approaches (management science, entrepreneurship, psychology, sociology, etc.) plus some ingredients extracted from experience, misconduct and best practices.

The *axio-normative system*, as Piotr Sztompka, a world-famous Polish sociologist and President of the International Sociological Association, calls it after Florian Znaniecki, forms "the central segment of culture, in which the social rules of human activity are contained". Each of the domains of social life identified for their important social functions "has rules characteristic for it" that are (in the sociological sense) an institution. A company is one such institution, and according to Sztompka it is characterised by the fact that it is not "a group of workers in a factory building, but a set of rules specific for economic activity. Hence, [it is a set of] such values as effectiveness, success, promotion, quality, profit, earnings, retirement, the company's honour, professional pride, or such norms as professional duties and powers, work discipline, punctuality, reliability, responsibility etc." (Sztompka, 2000).

The responsibility – with the adjective "social" or without – of an organisation (enterprise, company, partnership, corporation, firm, etc.) does not involve selecting one of the above-mentioned values and norms and treating it as the only one, but means identifying and accounting for the intricacy of connections (systemic nature) of all the values and norms making up a business institution in the social and natural environment within which it functions, and without which it would be unable to function. "The actual producer is not any element on its own, but the industrial enterprise as a whole", writes Joseph Maria Bochenski (1985). A comprehensive approach is the condition of integrity, and for corporations that do not have the pseudo-problem of whether to choose "business ethics" or "corporate social responsibility", integrity means a combination of the two (Gasparski, 2003a).

There were different triggers and starting points of business ethics and CSR on different levels of business operation in Poland. On the micro level ethics is related to issues of exchange made by acting individuals aiming at fulfilling their intentions (purposes) for which exchange is a means. An exchange is for instance: to proffer services, buying and selling of goods, employing and working as an employee, offering credit, advising, helping etc. All kinds of exchange are always risk-connected. The smaller the risk, the higher is the degree of trust, which depends on positive experiences of the actors' partnership, i.e. the chain of exchange processes performed over a longer period of time. The longer the period is the higher is the positive experience and therefore also trust. This experience forms norms of the so-called merchant's fairness. These norms are: to consider people as subjects, to keep one's word, to comply with law and duties, truthfulness, justice, integrity. These norms applied to all processes of exchange are the norms of business ethics on the micro level. Let us mention as an example that these norms were introduced into the *Code of Ethics of the Polish Dealers Association Volkswagen-Audi* which was presented at the 2nd World Congress of Economics, Business and Ethics (Sao Paulo 2000) as a Polish contribution to the European track (Gasparski, 2002b).

On the macro level it was Poland where the UN Secretary General's initiative named the *Global Compact* was launched for Europe in spring 2001. It was followed by the establishing of a GC Steering Committee and a special conference to enhance social dialogue on business ethics and CSR was co-organised by the Business Ethics Centre and the Office of the UN Resident Co-ordinator in Poland with the presence of Professor Marek Belka, then Deputy Prime Minister and Minister of Finance, now the Prime Minister of the Republic of Poland. The conference adopted a special *Appeal for Polish Business* to develop ethical programmes and its engagement in responsible behaviour.

On the mezzo level the Warsaw Stock Exchange introduced in 2002 a *Code of Best Practices* addressed to the listed companies. It contains rules governing the conduct of general meetings, supervisory and management boards, and relations with third parties. The implement concept of the Code is based on a comply-or-explain rule for the practices recommended by it. "When implementing and evaluating the corporate governance implementation process, it should be remembered – the authors of the Code warn – that running a business in line with these guidelines increases the transparency of the management process and its effectiveness, and in turn affects the assessment of a company by investors and its market valuation" (Warsaw Stock Exchange, 2002: 3). Earlier the Polish Bank Association adopted the *Principles of Best Practices* and set the Ethical Commission as well as a position of bank ombudsman to mediate in cases submitted by clients and consumers.

Further codes of best practices are now in a process of elaboration and acceptance. For instance the State Office for Competition and Consumer Protection is going to establish in Poland a foundation similar to the Warentest Foundation operating successfully in Germany. The Polish Consumer Federation, as well as the Association of Polish Consumers and some other organisations are in a process of fostering principles of best practices. The office of Prime Minister enacted the Code of Best Practices in public service, while at the initiative of the Polish Ombudsman Office the European Code of Best Practice in Administration (elaborated by Jacob Söderman, the EU Ombudsman, in 2001) was translated into Polish and published as a pattern to be followed by administrative organisations operating in the country.

Conclusion

Let me conclude this short review of the Polish attitude to business ethics and CSR with what I said at the "CSR European Marathon" Conference organised by the Forum of Responsible Business in co-operation with World Bank Poland, Warsaw, October 2003:

The Polish saying "to take something as a good coin" means to take somebody's words as their face value, i.e., to consider it honest and not false, therefore to trust it. One says also "to pay somebody in his own coin". It is worthy to realise that each coin has two faces: one shows the nominal value defined by the bank of issue, the other shows the emblem of a state, effigy of a state head or picture of a country element. The first face of a coin or a note may be called "economic", for it states the economic value, the second face is "social", for it symbolises one of the highest values of the society in a given country. Both faces are inseparable: it is impossible to use the "economic" face leaving the "social" face in a wallet. This inseparability is the best illustration of indissolubleness of two sides of business activity: its economic side and its social side. The activity – if run in a good manner – increases the economic value of a company, and doing that enriches social values, which in the course of nature influences further growth of the economic value, which again gives rise to the social value. If, however, business activity does not increase economic values, the social values are reduced, which influences negatively economic value. In other words one side of business activity "pays back the other in its own coin".

Conducting business with responsibility is the *sine qua non* condition of growth of the economic values (immanent aims), which subserves to the growth of social values (transcendent aims), which creates better conditions for subsequent growth of economic values and furthers the social values and so on. They create a double helix, a business DNA of its kind; the healthier it is genetically, the fuller is its – the business's – actual responsibility (Gasparski, 2003b).

Notes

[1] This is characteristic not only for Poland but also for other regions in Europe. According to the "Survey of Teaching and Research in Europe on CSR" elaborated by Matten, D., Moon, J., Barlow, C., & Alvis Lo, K. Y. of the Nottingham University Business School's International Centre for CSR presented at the EABiS Colloquium, Copenhagen, September 2003, "Business Ethics" is the most popular module label at European universities in Nordic Countries, Central and Southern Europe.

[2] I am very much in favour of the CSR explanation offered by A.B. Carroll in earlier editions of the book republished recently: Carroll, A.B., & Buchholtz, A.K. 2003. *Business and Society: Ethics and Stakeholder Management.* 5th Edition. Mason, Ohio: Southwestern. See also: Schwartz, M.S., & Carroll, A.B. 2003. Corporate Social Responsibility: A Three-Domain Approach. *Business Ethics Quarterly,* 13(4): 503–530.

[3] "A good stakeholder theory defines a 'stakeholder' in a broad manner: first, as someone who benefits from (or is harmed by) a particular social situation in the present (the usual definition); and second, someone who can throw new light on 'insider' understandings. The sweeping in of 'outsider' perspectives creates new relationships, meaning that a stakeholder comes to be defined as someone who is, or ought to be, involved in or affected by a social situation in the present or the ideal future" (Midgley, 2000: 149).

[4] One may also refer to outcomes of culture-theoretical studies done by Michael Fleischer of the Willy Brandt Zentrum at the Wroclaw University. He studied semantic representation in words of reality/actuality (Realität/Wirklichkeit) perceived by users of a language in some Polish cities. One of the results of the research is a comparative list of collective symbols (i.e., functional units of strong positive or negative distinctive feature and cultural meaning transgressing lexical meaning, the understanding of which is a precondition to become a member of a given culture) characteristic for Poland, Germany and Russia (Fleischer, 2002).

[5] In 24% of them foreign capital dominates, the same percentage of firms is with Polish capital domination, 23% are with state capital domination, 30% are private in full (19% Polish and 11% foreign). Present condition of the firms is: good 54%, fair 23%, very good 20%, bad 2%, very bad 1%. Out of them 39% have not noticed any change in the recent period, 35% some improvement, 13% great improvement, 11% some decrease, 2% substantial decrease.

[6] For the proceedings see: Dietl, J., & Gasparski, W. W. (Eds.) 1997. *Business Ethics* (in Polish). Warsaw: PWN.

References

Bochenski, J. M. 1985. *Zur Philosophie der industriellen Unternehmung.* Lecture delivered at the Hofmann Bank AG, Zürich.

Carroll, A. B., & Buchholtz, A. K. 2003 *Business and Society: Ethics and Stakeholder Management.* 5th Edition. Mason, Ohio: Southwestern.

Dietl, J., & Gasparski, W. W. (Eds.) 1997. *Business Ethics* (in Polish). Warsaw: PWN.

Fleischer, M. 2002. *Construction of Reality* (in Polish). Wroclaw: Wroclaw University Press.

Foundation of Social Communication. 2003. *Communication for CSR: A Research Report* (in Polish). Warsaw: Foundation of Social Communication.

Gasparski, W. W., & Ryan, L. V. (Eds.). 1996. *Human Action in Business: Praxiological and Ethical Dimensions.* New Brunswick, USA & London, UK: Transaction Publishers.

Gasparski, W. W. 2001. Business Ethics in Poland. In: R. Lang (Ed.), *Wirtschaftsethik in Mittel- und Osteuropa:* 59–68. München & Mering: Rainer Hampp Verlag.

Gasparski, W. W. 2002a. Business Ethics on the Way to Integrated Europe: As Seen from the Polish Perspective. In: N. Vasiljeviene, & R. Jeurissen (Eds.), *Business Ethics: From Theory to Practice:* 153–171. Vilnius: Vilnius University Business Ethics Centre.

Gasparski, W. W. 2002b. Codes of Ethics, their Design, Introduction and Implementation. In: H. von Weltzien Hoivik (Ed.), *Moral Leadership in Action: Building and Sustaining Moral Competence in European Organisations:* 142–158. Cheltenham, UK & Northampton, USA: Edward Elgar.

Gasparski, W. W. 2002c. Effectiveness, Efficiency, and Ethicality in Business and Management. In: L. Zsolnai, & W. W. Gasparski (Eds.), *Ethics and the Future of Capitalism*: 117 – 136. New Brunswick, USA & London, UK: Transaction Publishers.

Gasparski, W. W. 2003a. *Corporate Social Responsibility – Two Types of Argumentation: Cons and Pros*. Paper presented at the 2nd Colloquium on CSR organised by the Academy of Business in Society, Copenhagen.

Gasparski, W. W. 2003b. *The Story on Business and Its Responsibility*. Paper presented at the CSR European Marathon Conference, Warsaw.

Gasparski, W. W. et al. (Eds.). 2003. *European Standards of Business Ethics and Social Responsibility* (in Polish). Warsaw: L. Kozminski Academy of Entrepreneurship and Management Press.

Hunter, R. J. Jr., & Ryan, L. V. 1998. *From Autarchy to Market: Polish Economics and Politics 1945 – 1995*. Westport, USA & London, UK: Praeger.

John Paul II. 1996. Adressess to Managers, Business People, and General Audiences. In: W. W. Gasparski, & L. V. Ryan (Eds.), *Human Action in Business: Praxiological and Ethical Dimension*s: 119 – 154. New Brunswick, USA & London, UK: Transaction Publishers.

Krzyzanowski, A. 1935. *Contemporary Morality* (in Polish). Cracow: Economic Society in Cracow.

Marianski, J. 2002. *Moral Condition of the Polish Society* (in Polish). Cracow: WAM Publishers.

Matel, J. A. 1996. Ethical Leadership in a Free Society. In: W. W. Gasparski, & L. V. Ryan (Eds.), *Human Action in Business: Praxiological and Ethical Dimension*s: 245 – 266. New Brunswick, USA & London, UK: Transaction Publishers.

Matten, D., Moon, J., Barlow, C., & Alvis Lo, K. Y. 2003. *Survey of Teaching and Research in Europe on CSR*. Presented at the EABiS Colloquium, Copenhagen.

Midgley, G. 2000. *Systemic Intervention: Philosophy, Methodology, and Practice*. New York: Kluwer Academic.

Rok, B., Stolorz, S., & Stanny, D. 2003. *Managers 500 and Responsible Business: Knowledge, Attitudes, Practice: A Research Report* (in Polish). Warsaw: Forum of Responsible Business.

Schwartz, M. S., & Carroll, A. B. 2003. Corporate Social Responsibility: A Three-Domain Approach. *Business Ethics Quarterly,* 13(4): 503 – 530.

Sztompka, P. 2000. *Sociology* (in Polish). Cracow: Znak Publishers.

Warsaw Stock Exchange. 2002. *Best Practices in Public Companies in 2002.* Warsaw: Warsaw Stock Exchange Press.

Further Internet Links

Business Ethics Centre
www.cebi.pl

Responsible Business Forum
www.responsiblebusiness.pl

Foundation for Social Communication
www.fks.dobrestrony.pl

Academy of Development of Philanthropy in Poland
www.filantropia.org.pl

Environment Partnership Foundation
www.epce.org.pl

Eastern Europe

14 The Roadmap: From Confrontation to Consensus

Nijole Vasiljeviene and Aleksandr Vasiljev

Introduction

Lithuania is a new participant in the European community. Many social economic processes, which are peculiar to most Western countries, are just evolving here. Though private business, a free market and all features of modern enterprises testify to the progress of Lithuania, many global initiatives and advanced social innovations are rather late in arriving here. The idea of corporate social responsibility (CSR) has not emerged in Lithuanian public discourse yet. It is still a new paradigm of social economical development. In the country where the civic society has not fully formed, there is no clear comprehension of the idea of business social responsibility and most companies do not actively express readiness to meet the expectations of society. On the other hand, the expectations of various social groups towards business are just forming and are not properly articulated. The community's expectations of business enterprises are often reduced to the creation of new workplaces. In turn, companies regard all social problems (unemployment, social security, healthcare etc.) as entirely a concern and responsibility only of the Ministry of Social Security and Labour. Their understanding of responsibility is bound to the creation of jobs for the community and tax payment to the state. In many cases philanthropy is emphasised as the essence of CSR. Some elements of CSR can be traced in management practices of certain companies. However, CSR issues are not officially put on the public agenda in all their completeness. Ethical issues and social consequences of companies' downsizing, hiring and dismissal practices, career planning are still not considered. Though certain forms of discrimination (e.g. on the basis of sex, age, ethnic origin, etc.) are discussed in the public arena, they are not reflected in companies' policies and the necessity to reflect these issues has not reached them yet.

Taken as a definite quality option of business activity, CSR constitutes a process of "achieving commercial success in ways that honour ethical values and respect people, communities, and the natural environment" (www.bsr.org). To a great extent CSR can be regarded as a substantial parameter of business performance and an efficient means for economics humanisation and sustainable development. It can be practically realised through the tools provided by business ethics (ethics programmes, codes of conduct, ethics officers, ethics committees/commissions, social audits, round tables, "hotlines", etc.). Its constructive, rational and goal-oriented options in aggregate with enhanced moral competence and ethical sensitivity enable companies to implement CSR principles and establish them as an indispensable and advanced remedy for performance improvement, as an essential contribution to sustainable development.

Determinants of CSR Development

Analysis of the reasons why CSR is rather an expectation and outlook than a reality in Lithuania and what determines such a situation cannot be properly accomplished without taking into account Lithuania's historical and socio-cultural development. The given analysis is also based on the results of continuous situation monitoring made by the Centre for Business Ethics. It holds an insider's position and possesses findings of extensive qualitative research obtained by using methods of case analysis, content analysis, public discourse analysis, focus groups, interviewing. These findings as well as theoretical presuppositions and hypotheses about ethical context in Lithuania have also been confirmed and complemented by quantitative research.

Lithuania was a colony of the Russian empire from the 18th century till the beginning of the 20th century. Up until the declaration of independence in 1918 it was a society with an incomplete social structure. Lithuanians were mainly engaged in agriculture. Trade, industry, banking were underdeveloped and mostly controlled by other ethnic groups and aliens. In spite of rapid development of the country's economics at the beginning of the century, private business could not form deep traditions, as two decades of free economy were displaced by the subsequent 50 years of socialist planned economy. After the forcible incorporation into the USSR in 1940 the development of economic infrastructure of the former Lithuanian Soviet Socialist Republic was purely aimed at the metropolis' needs. The collapse of the former Soviet Union and regained independence of Lithuania changed its social economic system and created favourable conditions for private business. However issues of social responsibility in the activity of many newly created private companies were out of the question. Many local enterprises of that period constituted typical examples of "take and run" business for which the very idea of social responsibility was alien. Foreign companies, which entered Lithuania in this transition period, did not raise the question of social responsibility in their activity either, and just adapted themselves to the existing business environment. So the CSR initiatives as such could not be born in the milieu of immature business. A more likely absence of business subject's responsibility to the community correlates with the previous social economic system of the ex-USSR and its nomenclature-based management traditions.

An insufficient level of economic development in Lithuania is worthy to be marked out as the most important factor that still prevents local business from investments into CSR programmes. In other words, the economic state of many enterprises impedes them from assuming social responsibility since it would lead to the loss of competitiveness or even bankruptcy. Yet increasing competition makes companies change their approach to profit as the only aim of business. This tendency is gradually becoming apparent in Lithuania where competition with local and foreign rivals forces firms to fight for every consumer. CSR cannot be formed by somebody's subjective will even if it stems from really noble and sincere intentions.

Another important factor influencing CSR formation in Lithuania is determined by recurrences of communist ideology in the mass consciousness. Many ethical issues and dilemmas in business practice are often caused by stereotypes of moral consciousness and behaviour models inherited from the communist past along with local customs and traditions.

After the regaining of independence in 1990 private business evolved under conditions of total deficiency of consumer goods, foodstuff and services. The saying "one shouldn't look a gift horse in the mouth" could best describe the relations between business and consumers of that time. Most people in Lithuania did not have adequate knowledge about the market system or about the progress of business practice in the developed countries. In public discourse of that time there was little information that a modern market rests on orientation towards consumers' expectations and needs that business in principle can have some social obligations. Affected by communist ideology for more than 50 years, people regarded private business, capitalism and free market from a Marxist perspective. Business was regarded as a morally suspicious and deceitful game without rules and the relations between workers and employers as a cruel and relentless fight between the exploited and the exploiters.

These attitudes were especially strengthened by the first instances of the new economic activities followed by numerous concussions (crashes of finance pyramids, bankruptcy of banks, small and big enterprises, investment companies, holdings, etc.). They criminalised society and dealt much damage to the state economy. The irresponsibility of business was generally understood as normal. The saying "business is business" was used as an argument to justify one's own or others' widespread irresponsibility, moral nihilism, infringements, lack of integrity, indecency, etc. To some extent, the community itself provoked such behaviour, as it would accept the role of a helpless, sceptic and pessimistic actor. This experience of "fast profit" companies only confirmed the attitude that companies act as exploiters, who should be fought against. Thus, even today the very terms of *private business or free market* still carry a negative connotation among common people in Lithuania.

A stereotypically established contradiction (according to Marxism dogmas) in the consciousness of common people between *work* and *capital* also precludes the formation of adequate CSR understanding and implementation of its principles in Lithuania's business. The treatment of employment relations from the perspective of "poor workers" and "exploiting employers", subordinates and supervisors, determines performance inefficiency, extra costs for control and increases the risk of losing competitiveness. Since this factor significantly influences the acceptance of the new paradigm of business development, it demands greater explanation.

The aforementioned social confrontation is obviously reflected by polemics in Lithuania's public discourse. For example, a round table discussion "Employer, employee, trade unions: the three in a rocking boat" in the journal "Manager's world" (Zinkeviciene, 2001) tackled the visions of more harmonious co-existence among these three opposing yet inseparable social partners. According to the polemics results, the state is the one to be blamed most, though the employer turns out to be the most threatening party as he "uses unemployment flood, strives to become a slaveholder and is rowing towards slavery", and the employee "is ready to agree to everything and wants nothing else but work" (Zinkeviciene, 2001), even not asking trade unions to defend his/her rights.

However, socially responsible business leaves no place for the noted social contradiction. As social development issues are mostly solved by soft management techniques, human resource-centred programmes and business ethics systems inside organisations, the role of workers' struggle for their rights has lost its significance. A management system that is based on social dialogue and partnership can self-regulate, model and organise a propitious, employee-friendly environment in a company. That eliminates the need for threats, class struggle and erection of barricades. In other words, ethical management techniques shift the emphasis from the ideas of class struggle to those of social dialogue.

Yet, the mentioned discussion, like many others, has shown that relations among trade unions, employers and employees are still perceived as antagonistic. People view employers and business owners with suspicion. This confrontation is deepened by "blind, total defence of employees" (Zinkeviciene, 2001), disregarding objective criteria for business performance results, legitimacy of the demands, etc. Moreover, the discussion demonstrated that all parties had no notion about CSR, all the more they were obviously unaware of the achievements of social sciences in transforming public mentality, instrumental construction of social partnership. Lack of modern knowledge about replacement of the social struggle paradigm by the one of social consensus was cogently demonstrated by a categorical statement of the Lithuanian trade union leader and MP that "the world has not invented anything better than class struggle" (Zinkeviciene, 2001).

The fact that the discussion was moderated not among common people, but among the members of the Lithuanian parliament, CEOs of big companies, trade union leaders and journalists witnesses that general unawareness of the modern paradigms of *social order* was obvious. The discussion indicates that neither the possibilities offered by social sciences to build a social dialogue, nor the conceptions of CSR and stakeholders came into the field of vision of business people and politicians. Later on we still find the same reflections in the mass media. It was especially evident during the political crisis of late 2003 / early 2004, when the President of Lithuania was dismissed. The period was noted by further increase of social confrontation.

This status quo is maintained by a widespread model of authoritarian relations both on the macro and meso level of social life. For example, a survey of Lithuanian residents conducted by the centre of public opinion and market research "Vilmorus" in 2001 revealed that an authoritarian communist regime was approved by 55% of the respondents. Positive evaluations of the communist economic system are expressed by 73% of the population and the figure has not been considerably changing since 1993, though renewal of the regime is desired only by 14% of the Lithuanian population (*Veidas*, 2002). A need for authoritarian control in organisations is often reasoned by the conviction that otherwise it breeds chaos (Lenčiauskas, 2001).

The model presupposes a lack of social partnership inside companies, between employers and employees. As the economic situation and employment possibilities in Lithuania are complicated, employees do not dare to declare their needs and expectations to the employers, who feel psychologically and socially right by exploiting people, violating human rights and dignity and fairness principles. They justify their irresponsible behaviour and disregard of CSR standards by financial profit. Though labour laws have been passed, they are not efficient since many of them do not correlate with ethics norms and have no moral enforcement mechanism in business organisation. Companies would rather pay fines for breaches of labour laws than correct the situation. In Lithuanian society this makes for a situation where such behaviour is regarded as a natural order of economic life, capitalism, market system.

Consequently, the predominance of authoritarian social relations hampers adequate awareness of public interest (and CSR is a subject and manifestation of public interest). Trade unions or labour councils (the substitute of trade unions in some organisations of Lithuania) in many cases just perform formal functions, keeping a passive position instead of negotiating for the workers' interests, explaining their rights and settling conflicts that arise between workers and managers. The content analyses of the mass media show that journalists who engage into representation and defence of the public interest often limit their journalistic research to the identification of a state official's political beliefs, but do not tackle a conflict of interest, its reasons and social consequences in their forums, interviews and publicistic TV shows. When judging personal or organisational behaviour (the latter is still quite rare) ethical criteria are still not applied, the company responsibility towards stakeholders not considered. When companies decide to reduce the number of their employees, society just sighs that this is the way business is carried out. There are not many morally concerned people who would dare to demand that their rights should be considered when decisions affecting their welfare are made.

A survey of the ethical standards of employees and firms that was conducted by Vilnius University in 2001 reflects that out of 940 respondents a majority gives priority to profit over social responsibility in business. Only 17% of the survey respondents think that ethical behaviour is reasonable in business. The others tend to believe that when faced with the dilemma "profit/benefit or morals" a Lithuanian business person always chooses profit/benefit. Lithuanians seldom relate economic success with the implementation of social responsibility/ethics standards in the organisation because they are concerned about survival in the market. Such an economic situation still sustains the orientation of Lithuanian business towards a quarterly balance but not sustainable development.

An adequate comprehension and realisation of public interest could be promoted by the activity of nongovernmental organisations (NGOs). However, in Lithuania, business people, manufacturers, or industry representatives still do not experience any organised pressure from NGOs concerning social responsibility and the accountability of business. We can trace back the origins of CSR to the activities of environmentalists ("Greens") as well as the movements for human rights, including consumers' rights. They tackle separate aspects of these complex phenomena that constitute the ideology, policy and practice of CSR today. NGOs take steps to defend consumers' rights, the natural environment, cultural heritage, etc. However they act inefficiently, fragmentarily, and mainly resort to single actions. That is why they are still unable to carry out organised joint activities regarding business.

Some attempts to introduce the idea of business (corporate) social responsibility have been made by Lithuanian NGOs. For example, the NGO "The Centre for Social Responsibility" indicates social responsibility as one of its priorities and sets its mission "to be the intermediary between private companies and NGOs to promote their mutual collaboration and responsible companies' activity through allocating some part of their incomes for the public good" (www.sacentras.lt). Despite a wide range of assumed activities, this NGO focuses exclusively on social work, provides social services, social advertising and propagates the ideas of philanthropy. This example is not the only one and it definitely indicates that many NGOs equate business social responsibility with social work.

The most articulated aspect of CSR in Lithuania is philanthropy, which is often understood as its kernel. It is the focus of many NGOs activities, and some research and surveys undertaken both by the state institutions (Department of Statistics) and NGOs (Lithuanian Free Market Institute, Non-governmental organizations information and support centre etc). However, the findings of these institutions reveal another problem: "the existing law base and fiscal policy undermine economic incentives for many prospective philanthropists to undertake acts of charity giving" (http://www.labdara-parama.lt/docs/Filantropija_verslo_lyder_akim.doc). It partly confirms that even in such a narrow comprehension CSR is not on the state policy agenda.

In spite of the widespread practice of business charity in Lithuania, it is mainly a non-official, anonymous activity. Many business people regard it as a sort of "scheduled" loss. At best it is a form of moral satisfaction for the company CEOs. Moreover, the philanthropy practice in Lithuania sometimes takes deviant forms. There are paradoxes when some company or business people are rewarded by a local municipality or governmental institutions for charity and philanthropy, though at the same time their employees are underpaid, endure intolerable working conditions, and their management is publicly known as arbitrary. In the worst cases the rewarded companies or persons appear to have problems with the labour inspectorate and law-enforcement institutions.

Little is spoken about the CSR standards like SA8000, AA1000, Global Reporting, or ILO conventions in Lithuanian public discourse. Though they come into Lithuania by the EU integration process, very few organisations fully implement them in practice. It is obvious from the workplace conditions in many organisations. Due to the archaic (authoritarian) relations between employers and employees, individuals often experience spiritual discomfort, psychological violence, mobbing in the workplace. Even though an individual's feelings of fairness and justice are offended and organisational performance is impeded, workers (especially in underdeveloped regions) reconcile themselves to the dysfunctions. This situation is rather typical not only for Lithuania and it was indicated in surveys of scholars from the other post-communist countries (Bakshtanovsky & Sogomonov, 2002; Gasparski, 2001; Seilius, 1999; Ungvári-Zrínyi, 2001).

Besides, the same authoritarian model is extrapolated to the treatment of CSR standards. Quite often they are viewed as a dictate from the EU. Furthermore, business people envisage another danger for their business arising from the incoming standards, i.e. they are regarded as efforts of the EU authorities to place external constraints on local business and decrease its competitiveness. Even representatives of the Lithuanian Industrialists Confederation express the opinion that standards are just hidden obstacles to hamper national production. The state institutions, especially in the spheres of social policy, do not duly regard the ideas, proposals and opinions of local and foreign scholars concerning implementation methods of modern European social standards. Instead much attention and resources are invested into the creation of an attractive image of the state and society (for the EU experts), while a real situation, which could objectively determine the development of the desired social properties of a state, is not (re)constructed. As a result, the standards are viewed with hostility and stipulate covert disobedience to them. As disobedience is actually not possible, companies resort to their imitation. The gap between formal and real implementation of the standards is usually regarded as a norm of social life.

The distinction between declarations and personal determination to act is obvious in the answers received from the above survey conducted by the Centre for Business Ethics. The responses about ethical duty to reveal a co-worker's abuse of an upheld position reflect scepticism and indifference to the breaches of workplace ethics and regulations. When asked about the reasons for refusal to disclose unethical behaviour, the respondents expressed positions of a passive social actor: they did not want to interfere (36%), destroy old and useful relationships (21%), did not expect any changes from this act (26%). The participants presented various projections of possible consequences of the disclosure of unethical behaviour. Only 19% welcomed the action, 18% were afraid of revenge or gossip, 21% did not express their attitude. Thus, the projections manifest a contradictory variety of attitudes towards a principled stand against disobedience to norms, standards, rules, laws, which allows us to state that standards of socially responsible behaviour are just being formed.

Furthermore, the research has shown that the imperfect legal system, strained economic circumstances and imperfect governance of the firm and/or the country most often justify ethical breaches. Only 39% of 940 respondents demonstrated readiness to comply with the law without questioning it. That is largely due to the fact that in Lithuania social order is often determined by the will of individual actors, authorities and their power, but not by universalised rules.

Though the empirical data hint at the legislation elements to be corrected, CSR is absent at the state level as a long-term policy. The government policy, which could be an important aspect of CSR promotion, is insufficient. Despite the fact that sometimes the state officials mention it as a formal phrase, their further interpretations demonstrate complete unawareness of the CSR paradigm and the contents of the concept. Up to now no laws granting some advantage for socially responsible behaviour to companies have been passed by the parliament. The issues of business social responsibility are often narrowed to a necessity to improve the social security system and doles to maintain social stability.

In practice, the role of Lithuanian politicians in CSR promotion is more negative than positive. The latest political crisis (impeachment and removal of the president of Lithuania) in the country and preceding political scandals have demonstrated the extreme level of politicians' irresponsibility and disrespect for laws and ethics norms. Some higher state officials (e.g. a minister, the head of department, or a member of parliament), who were dismissed from their posts for abuse of power or corruption, still dare to appeal to the law for rehabilitation and often manage to return to their previous posts. It indicates that there is still no correlation between legal norms and the social standards or ethics codes in political and governmental structures. Such circumstances have a strong influence upon the business community and business environment that impedes the formation of socially responsible business conduct on all levels. The most obvious example of this kind is the document named "Long-term economic development strategy of Lithuania until 2015", adopted by the Lithuanian Ministry of Economics (2002). In this document business (corporate) social responsibility is reduced to the relocation of money from business to the state social programmes.

The educational system facilitates a deepening comprehension of the CSR concept and promotes some of its aspects. However, many teachers and students still perceive the concept as some utopia borrowed from European educational programmes and business practice. In addition, there is a lack of professional business ethics teachers and experts in CSR related issues in Lithuania. Quite often, those engaged in ethics teaching resort to the analysis of psychological portraits of the character or moralising on a prescriptive level, in the manner of the metaphysical school of thought. Combined with the prevailing notion of traditional – idealistic – morality in society, such programmes determine a situation in which values promoted by the concept of CSR are understood in isolation from real practices.

CSR Promotion Prospective

Overwhelming negative evaluations of the current situation with regard to CSR in Lithuania are diminished by the fact that an *ethics infrastructure* has been implemented at the state level. The Governmental Commission for Ethics of State Officials was established in 1997, the Commission for Ethics and Procedures in Lithuanian parliament in 1999. Also, in 1997 the Law on the conflict of public and private interest was passed. Though these first germs have not become a system yet, nevertheless there are definite indications that Lithuanian society has become less tolerant to socially (economically, politically) irresponsible decision-making of both governmental structures and the business activities of local companies and multinational corporations. Positive changes can be traced even among students: two years ago they would often declare that corruption has positive effects while today such attitudes are rare. Though the spread of bribery, corruption and nepotism has not been significantly reduced, yet today nobody publicly regards them as a merit. Also, nobody declares that abuse of power is human and justifiable.

In addition, the situation has been gradually changed for the better by the ever-growing influence of socially *responsible partners from foreign countries.* They are rather exigent to the local partners and their moral reputation, and require observance of EU workplace standards and ethics codes from Lithuanian companies. In this way, they accelerate the growth of morally concerned local companies. Though it should be admitted that quite often ethics codes are just copied from foreign patterns, treated as a fad and not used as guidelines for responsible business practice, they at least deepen understanding of ethics issues, and make Lithuanian organisations think again about ethics and social responsibility issues.

Still another optimistic sign is the growing number of business and professional associations, NGOs, interest groups and their impact upon companies and appropriate governmental policy. The analysis of the current situation shows that the promotion of CSR in separate companies is especially difficult. So business associations and partly the Chambers of Commerce, which formally promote business self-government, could be a good tribune and forum for the dissemination of CSR ideas. The practice of Lithuania shows that business associations are the most successful mediators in establishing dialogues and bridging business, authorities and NGOs. For example, the confederation of Lithuanian Industrialists (www.lpk.lt), the most influential non-governmental organisation in Lithuania, has an ad-hoc coordination council for social polity. It used to act like a short-term crisis management team ("fire fighters"), especially when solving social ethical problems, resulting from violations of labour legislation and industrial safety/health norms. However, it has recently adopted a thorough and progressive code of ethics and honour that emphasises business commitment to the community. Another instance is the Business Leaders' Club of Lithuania, which consolidates prominent representatives of the business community in all regions of Lithuania. It attaches great significance to CSR in its recently adopted Charter as well (www.klubai.lt).

An increasing interest of professionals and business people in modern knowledge and management innovations, including programmes on value management, business ethics, social responsibility and human resource management, and their rapid introduction through various educational institutions, enables real involvement of

Resuming the above mentioned, we can maintain that in order to promote CSR in Lithuania, ethics teaching along with implementation of modern social standards is needed to increase the sensitivity of separate companies and the whole business community to these issues. We believe that social responsibility can be taught through ethics programmes during which sensitivity to certain socio-cultural aspects is developed, rationalisation of the process of implementing social responsibility standards, value management is provided; skills to use business ethics tools in daily activities are improved.

It is very important to note that methodically and theoretically reasonable ethics training is essential in post-socialist countries where social behaviour dysfunctions are rather frequent. Socially detrimental phenomena obstruct positive transformation of the society and objectively determine a need to implement social responsibility standards into practical activity. At the same time, pure moralising and mere imperatives without adequate reasoning of the need to implement value management and proper enforcement mechanisms are usually met with scepticism and automatically rejected. To diminish cynical attitudes towards CSR, attention should be primarily focused on the aspects of socially responsible employment practices. The improvement of workplace standards, maintenance of ethically sound labour relations by fair payment, safety and health standards, a CSR monitoring system, professionally and impartially conducted social ethical auditing in organisations, systematic evaluation of practising standards would promote the values of compliance and integrity and, consequently, the realisation of CSR in Lithuanian organisations.

References

Bakshtanovsky, V., & Sogomonov, Y. 2002. Ethics of Russian Entrepreneurship: the Dialogue of Theory and Practice. In: N. Vasiljevienė, & R. J. M. Jeurissen (Eds.), *Business Ethics: From Theory To Practice.* Vilnius: Vilnius University.

Gasparski, W. W. 2001. Business ethics in Poland – a New Look. In: Vasiljevienė, N. (Ed.), *Business Ethics: World Tendencies and Actualities in Post-socialist Countries.* Vilnus: Vilnius University.

Lenčiauskas, J. 2001. Nedarysiu! Pavesiu pavaldiniui. (I won't do it. I will tell a subordinate to do it.) *Kauno diena*, February 22.

Lithuanian Ministry of Economics. 2002. *Long-term economic development strategy of Lithuania until 2015.* Vilnius: Lithuanian Ministry of Economics.

Seilius, A. 1999. Collective management: theory and practice. *Organizacijų vadyba: sisteminiai tyrimai.* Kaunas: VDU, 12: 189–211.

Ungvári-Zrínyi, I. U. 2001. Tendencies of Moral Culture in Post-Communist Societies. In: Vasiljevienė, N. (Ed.) *Business Ethics: World Tendencies and Actualities in Post-socialist Countries.* Vilnius: Vilnius University.

Veidas. 2002. Daugiau nei trečdalis lietuvių nori būti valdomi diktatoriaus. (More than a third of the Lithuanian population want to be ruled by a dictator). March 7th.

Zinkevicienė, V. 2001. Employer, employee, trade unions: the three in a rocking boat. *Vadovo pasaulis* (Manager's World), No. 7–8.

15 Incubating Radical Political and Economic Change

Mari Kooskora

Introduction

For Estonian people ethical and corporate social responsibility issues are relatively new, because only 15 years ago, they made the first shy attempts to start their own private businesses and create their own careers as entrepreneurs after 50 years of Soviet occupation. In this building and starting up process, political and business leaders as well as society were neither ready to think about the issues of ethical business or corporate social responsibility, nor did they consider the importance of these topics in their action.

It is true that over the last 10 to 13 years, after restoring the country's independence, Estonia's development has been relatively successful compared to other transition countries. But at the same time it seems that we have forgotten ethics and ethical behaviour, caring for others and taking responsibility, which is creating many problems on personal, organisational and societal levels.

Today, more and more people in Estonia realise that in order to be recognised as an equal partner and competitor in the globalising world, we need to make important strategic decisions and changes, which will guarantee us a strong society, conscious citizens, administrative responsibility, defined national interests, protection of these interests and local high-level competence in the key areas, etc. The pressure from society and the media for discussing these issues is perceptible and it is quite obvious that corporate social responsibility is gaining importance also in Estonia.

As business ethics and CSR are relatively new concepts in Estonia and companies are only starting to implement the ethical and CSR processes, there is not much research being done in the field. Some research focuses on ethical decision-making and ethical leadership and other related topics revealing how the attitudes towards ethics and CSR have changed and how the businesses and organisations see their responsibilities towards society and the environment today.

Society's Attitude Towards Business, the Roles of Economy, State and Society

The main factors when talking about today's situation in Estonia are the steady growth of GDP and foreign investments as well as remarkable economic and political success. The new concepts characterising Estonia today are related to IT and new technologies – E-business, e-banking, e-government, E-stonia. We can also name positive privatisation practice, much of the present success is due to young and energetic leaders. Estonia can be called an "incubator", able to make radical changes and make them fast. At the same time we cannot deny that these changes have been too fast, which has led to difficulties, problems and even conflicts on social, organisational and personal levels. Today we witness a lack of trust and responsibility among our politicians, business leaders and in the community; we see that our people long for true values, they expect higher ethical and moral values and increasing responsibility and reliability from politics and business leaders.

Today, we realise more directly than ever before that the current development model does not guarantee us sustainable development. Our success has turned out to be too expensive. The power of money and market is going to turn us down in the long run and if we do not want to stay at the periphery of the global market, we have to change our strategy (Kaevats, 2003).

For centuries before the first Estonian Republic was founded people were not self-determined and the last occupation has made them used to blaming others for mistakes and bad living conditions. And as we now have back our so-long dreamed of independence, there are people who feel disappointed and cheated by our own government and authorities.

Today, most of our present business and political leaders belong to the generation which was born and grew up in the Soviet totalitarian society; they went through Soviet education and lived through the system of great restrictions and limitations. On the one hand the state took care of people, their housing, health, education and security, while on the other hand it kept the quality of life, products and services relatively low. Today's leaders remember the time when managers used to be autocratic, mainly directing, giving orders and controlling, when people in the organisations did not often have the right to participate in decision-making or their opinions were not considered important.

During the last 15 years Estonia has experienced different business eras and practices. We have witnessed and seen typical cowboy capitalism or so-called shark capitalism, which is oriented to legal norms. Or in other words, those things which are not forbidden or limited by law, are allowed. This kind of business society is known by decision-making and making choices, in which processes, ethics or moral values are not considered important, even lacking ethical and moral dimensions. Therefore fast profits, efficiency and consumerism have forced backward concepts such as long-term planning, environmentally friendly and human and value centred business practices.

Today – at the end of 2003 / beginning of 2004 – the situation has somehow changed. We witness voluntary initiatives by successful businesses and business leaders, making an effort and helping children, nursery and primary schools and elderly people. Initiatives, such as paying for medicines, vaccines, high-cost operations, smaller school classes, buying clothes, food, materials and books for orphanages and children's hospitals have become important and even popular.

Reasons for these kinds of initiatives are the maturing of our society, stabilisation of the economic and political situation, increased security, positive changes in the value orientations of our people and current leaders. In addition, integration into EU structures and international interactions have been influencing these activities. Today business enterprises have a higher respect for laws and being legal in (business) activities is considered important (http://www.koda.ee/e_index_en.html). Various activities are evaluated following not only the criterion of economic efficiency, but significantly also with regard to moral and ethical aspects.

Brief Historic and Cultural Overview

Estonian culture is that of a nation of one and half million people. Along with the language, this culture is the main vehicle for the Estonian identity, hence the respect which Estonians feel for it. On a global scale, Estonia's history is not a particularly long one — around 10 000 years — but its people have throughout this time retained a relatively stable ethnic homogeneity; Estonians can therefore be regarded as one of Europe's oldest nations (http://www.einst.ee/publications/cult_history/).

At various times and under different reigns Estonian people have had various attitudes and expectations towards businesses. A succession of Danish, German, Swedish and Russian invaders occupied the country and governed it until Estonian nationalists succeeded in defeating the soviet army in 1920. Estonia was free for 22 years and then Soviet troops occupied the country again for 50 years. The culture, religion and values of Estonian people have been traditionally influenced by all these foreign authorities who have governed the country.

For centuries until 1920, Estonian agriculture consisted of native peasants working large feudal-type estates held by ethnic German landlords. Historically and culturally most Estonians have roots in the countryside and were used to grow their own food and make their own products in smaller communities; for centuries most of the people were rural. At the same time most of these small communities had to take care of their weaker members and help those who needed help. It was a normal thing and nobody questioned these activities.

In the years 1920 to 1930, Estonia underwent a number of economic, social, and political reforms necessary to come to terms with its new status as a sovereign state (http://www.nationmaster.com/encyclopedia/History-of-Estonia). Working hard, being honest, reliable, respected and loyal were important values. Caring, helping the weak and less fortunate, giving better education to poor people and charitable activities were widely practised, especially by the wives of politicians and business leaders. People felt loyal towards the state, and dignity and good reputation were important issues. Businesses and business people were respected and they saw their role in helping society. The state was young and weak, but politicians and government leaders were trusted and respected.

However, all these developments came to an abrupt end when World War II brought Estonia once again under Russian occupation. The Soviet occupation lasted half a century (interrupted from 1941–44 by German occupation) and resulted in immeasurable damages and suffering. Most of the business people and people who had reached well-being by working hard either escaped to the West or were killed or sent to Siberia.

The population of Estonia dropped from 88.2% Estonian in 1934 to 61.5% by 1989. Farms collapsed due to collectivisation, businesses and private houses (homes) were nationalised. In those times private enterprises, businesses and private ownership were forbidden, and people were not officially allowed to attend church services or talk about religion.

During that period, business was considered something unethical, dirty, cheating and not moral at all and was totally forbidden by the authorities. Yet, it was generally known that the authorities were corrupt and taking bribes. The totalitarian system created people who could not trust each other and people had to learn how to lie, hide and not reveal their real ideas and thoughts. Unfortunately all these things have left very strong traces in our people's attitudes, habits and minds and it is not easy to become free from these.

Building up the Economy and Businesses, Drivers of CSR

In those circumstances and with such attitudes common in society, Estonia gained back its independence in 1991 and our businesses started to form the market economy. Not only did they have to learn ways of surviving in the conditions of a market economy, they also had to learn how to operate a business in order to give a successful output. Material wealth at any cost was most valued. Things that were not forbidden were considered allowed, and ethics and corporate social responsibility seemed to be the last things business could think of.

However, studies carried out in recent years show that the level of dissatisfaction in our society is increasing rapidly. Every day the media reveals new cases of un-ethical and thoughtless decisions and actions taken by prominent business people resulting in even greater disaffection throughout our society. The rapid develop-ment has left people disillusioned in their hopes for a brighter future. The reasons for that are the ethical scandals among government and business leaders, where millions of kroons disappear and nobody takes responsibility. Expressive exam-ples here are the cases of privatisation scandals (Kooskora, 2003).

Today we can see a perceptible social pressure for finding, creating or discovering new values and higher morality. There has been the rise and popularity of a new political party, Res Publica, which promised to put much effort into ethics and higher values, and was the most successful during last year's parliamentary elec-tion. People were hoping to see changes in behaviour and more responsible action.

At present there are many endeavours in that direction. We see it in several differ-ent initiatives by our government, president, business leaders, environmentalists, social scientists and others. Unfortunately Estonian people are very individualistic and it is difficult for them to find common ground and start working together on CSR goals.

To introduce the principles of sustainable development and create possibilities for implementation of sustainable development, a joint project of the Ministry of the Environment, Ministry of Economy and UNDP *Estonia 21* was initiated in 1997. As part of this project, a collection of articles under the name of *Estonia in the 21st Century. Strategies for Development. Visions. Options.* has been published. The book aims at the opening of public discussion for the selection of alternative development routes for Estonia in the 21st century, the setting of national devel-opment priorities in the light of social consent, and wide introduction of the ideas of sustainable development (http://www.agenda21.ee).

SE 21 is a fully innovative development analysing and joining together three dif-ferent development models (a sustainable scenario, conservative development and partnership development) that gives us a sense of direction for the future (http://www.envir.ee/saastev/06.pdf). Although it is not a miracle, bringing an immediate and complete solution, it does help bring clarity to daily decisions and presents them in the light of a vision of the future and that is what we really need today. The agenda highlights the need for emphasising such new concepts as a national state and the sustainability of the nation. These values should not be con-nected in any way to changes in the political parties that hold government – they should be sustainable, given first priority and comprehensible. Estonia needs a new, ethical attitude towards its people. This agenda stresses the need for broad-minded individuals with a good education; an ability to learn; and an interest in life-long learning, training and special educational programmes. Only with these people who have sufficient knowledge and skills can we secure success in economic and social life. Ability to learn is the criterion of survival and sustainability in the post-information society. Favouring such self-development would create the preconditions for completing the catching-up process.

In 1996 an expert commission for elaborating single questions of the *Programme for Sustainable Development* was established at the Government by a governmental decision (Riigi Teataja Lisa, 1996). The Commission advises the Government concerning issues of sustainable development. Its functions include the following:

- the consideration of information provided by different working groups of the sustainable development programme concerning the implementation of the national policy in the area of sustainable development, and delivery of opinions and comments,

- analysis of the national policy in the area of sustainable development and delivery of opinions concerning different sectors (energy, agriculture, utilisation of resources, etc.),

- submission of proposals for solving questions regarding sustainable development to the national and local governments,

- submission of proposals for drafting legal acts regarding sustainable development.

The Commission on Sustainable Development is chaired by the Prime Minister, the co-chairs are held by the Minister of the Environment and the Minister of Economy. According to the areas of activity, 23 experts in the field of sustainable development representing different institutions have been elected members of the Commission on Sustainable Development (Riigi Teataja Lisa, 1999).

Estonian Success 2014 is a development programme which helps to achieve higher living standards and better living quality for Estonian people. It helps to provide sustainable and people-centred social-economic development through competitive economy and a knowledge-based society. This programme unites purposed future vision and coherently links executive authorities to government roles in political planning in order to create an integrated programme and guarantee its implementation (http://www.lepe.ee/orb.aw/class=file/action=preview/id=3299/Eesti_Edu_2014.doc).

On 20 February 2003, representatives of different political parties, employers and employees, universities and third sector organisations signed the *Memorandum of Public Understanding*. In that memorandum the 39 parties who signed the agreement promised to prepare and enter into a cooperative contract. In order to conclude this contract the Estonian President made an initiative to establish the *Public*

Understanding Foundation, which was registered on 10 April 2003. The mission of this foundation is to start and enhance the process of social participation and cohesion in society, which enables different societal parties to come to a negotiated agreement on common values, the priority development areas and necessary activities in Estonia (http://www.lepe.ee).

In 2003 the newly elected parliamentary members and coalition partners prepared and signed a *Coalition Agreement*, which stressed values like freedom, caring, knowledge, tolerance, openness, well-being, contriving, creativity and entrepreneurial ability and responsibility and promised to govern Estonia according to these values during the years 2003 – 2007 (http://www.riik.ee/et/valitsus/r3koalitsioon.htm). The purpose of this *Coalition Agreement* is to strengthen independent statehood and Estonian vital capacity, offer support for those who need it, and create more and better self-realisation opportunities for people.

All these projects have almost the same purpose, to guarantee Estonian sustainability as an independent country, to enhance economic growth and social stability, to offer better opportunities to those who have entrepreneurial spirit and give support to those who are in need. Some programmes put more stress on environmental issues, others on sustainable development.

There are people, academics, researchers, environment specialists, who are concerned about common values and social responsibility, but it seems to be that everybody is trying to make their own effort to achieve some results in this area. Corporations see their responsibility mainly in an economic and legal sense, and towards their owners and clients. Sponsorship is mainly considered as a corporate social responsibility activity (Kooskora & Rikkinen, 2004). Even today it is too soon to say that companies feel responsible towards stakeholders, it might be written in the texts or told to the people, but very often the reality tells us a different story.

The Attitude of Estonian Business Towards CSR

The Estonian Business School started CSR research in 1996 and 1997 including a comparative study of values among present and future managers (Kooskora & Türnpuu, 1999; Ennulo & Türnpuu, 2001; Aaltio, Türnpuu & Kooskora, 2002) as well as a study of conflicts in Estonian organisations (Virovere, Kooskora & Valler 2002; Kooskora, 2003).

In the study of values the respondents were asked to evaluate items as to their impact on managerial success. These items were divided into 10 different value categories and were ranked by Estonian respondents (Aaltio, Türnpuu & Kooskora, 2002) on a ranking scale between 1 and 10:

Table 1. Value orientations of Estonian business students (1989 – 2001, n = ca. 900)

Business ideological values	1
Ethical values	8
Leadership ideological values	5
Social values	7
Personal values	2
Cultural values	6
Organisational-legal values	3
Professional values	10
Values related to the way of life	9
Speciality-related values	4

The collection of real conflict cases provided detailed information on business situations and attitudes of people. The conflicts of ethical decision-making in Estonia today are caused by many factors, the biggest problems being fraud by officials and politicians, personal interest dominating over public interest, and our authorities abusing their powers as well as gaps in our legislation (Suits, 2000; Kooskora, 2001). As a result we found that in almost all cases power was more important for managers than solving the conflict, and a win-win outcome was almost never achieved. Since the conflicts were approached from the viewpoint of personal interest and power, the interests of society and companies were almost fully ignored.

A great number of conflicts that have arisen in our organisations and society and the value judgements made by the people of Estonia show that there are great problems with ethics in Estonia. It is very common in decision-making that ethical criteria are not considered (Kooskora, 2001; Virovere & Kooskora, 2002). Bad and unethical decisions have caused severe consequences: conflicts, damaged relationships, failed businesses and bankruptcies. But the lack or weakness of education in the area of ethics and CSR does not allow people to foresee the consequences of their actions. Unethical decisions mostly do harm to the general development of Estonia. This can be seen from the outcome of the privatisation process (Kooskora, 2003), carried out in a rushed manner and without sufficient consideration of the ethical issues. Research has indicated that very often in order to achieve short-term success or material wealth the interests of citizens are neglected and public officials give priority to their own personal interests (Virovere & Kooskora, 2000a, 2000b; Virovere & Kure, 2001). In most cases public officials act as private businessmen bearing in mind success and gaining profit.

Other recent studies conducted in Estonia give a clear picture that we lack ethical thinking and knowledge and if we do not change something fast the overall situation is getting worse every day (Fontes, 2001; Praxis, 2003).

In order to get a better and clearer picture of Estonian companies' CSR activities, three different surveys were made at the Estonian Business School in Spring 2004. The first two researches were made under the supervision of the author of the current article.

Stakeholder Research

As part of one survey interviewing 24 managers / executives and specialists in well-known Estonian organisations (Rikkinen, 2004) the participants were asked to make their own priority list choosing between ten different stakeholders (reputation of the organisation, owners/shareholders, peers, customers, competitors, market, environment, society, participant him/herself, family); there was also an option to add an object not included in the priority list.

There were some differences in the answers of men and women, managers and specialists and even participants with or without Business Administration education. The male participants gave priority to reputation of the organisation, clients, and owners, which outweighed peers, and female participants signified peers, organisation, and themselves; for them clients had less importance. Managers considered more significantly organisation, peers, and clients, and specialists attached more importance to themselves, organisation, and clients, which outweighed peers. Participants having education in Business Administration signified organisation, peers, and clients and attached importance to themselves as well. Participants without education in Business Administration gave more importance to organisation, clients, themselves; for them peers had less importance.

According to the results all participants showed a similar trend – organisation, clients, peers were considered more important than competitors, environment, and society, because practically nobody put these in the first half of rankings.

Another interesting aspect was revealed in this survey: females and participants having education in Business Administration acted more ethically compared to the other groups being studied during the research.

CSR Situation in Leading Estonian Companies

The second survey was carried out through research among six of the biggest Estonian companies, some of them being quoted on the Tallinn and Helsinki Stock Exchange (Omair, 2004). The selected companies were among the leading companies in their business field and also the leading companies in Estonia in the field of corporate governance and implementing new business models. Therefore it can be said that the overall situation of CSR in these companies reflects the situation in Estonia as a whole.

The research involved information collection of news and articles from media, local newspapers and economic magazines. The second stage involved collecting the annual reports, business and other reports containing relevant information of the participating companies. Third, the author visited the participating companies to carry out interviews with various personnel from various levels of the company.

To analyse the situation of the organisations, Dr Rodger Spiller's ethical scorecard (Spiller, 1997, 2000), which considers business and society issues from a stakeholder perspective, was used. The scorecard aims to enhance the financial performance by building quality relationships and developing increased commitment towards community, environment, employees, customers, suppliers and shareholders.

The results of the research showed that companies do not have a very clear concept of CSR in the company, or they are not implementing it. Even if a company finds CSR activities to be important and they are set in a corporate mission and values, yet the companies lack the knowledge and know-how of what activities to concentrate on. CSR seems to be a matter of sponsorship to many of the participants and this shows that they are lacking in CSR competence.

Participating companies did not have a systematic approach to CSR and implemented just a few activities. They saw simple sponsorship as synonomous to CSR.

One very important thing that companies were not doing was reporting on social and environmental activities. This showed that these activities are not included in a company's strategy and are not systematically managed. Participants following some kind of standardisation processes did measure some of their activities, yet the reports were not made public.

It became quite clear that the participating companies do not hold a systematic approach towards corporate social responsibility and that it is not a part of business strategy. However, it does not mean that they are not searching for means to implement ethical activities.

In a recent study of understanding and implementing CSR principles in their activities 30 Estonian companies from different fields and regions were under closer investigation (Pitkänen, 2004). The organisations involved in the research were divided into three groups: small, medium-sized and large companies; from each group ten well-known enterprises were studied. The information was gathered through personal interviews mainly with the companies' CEOs, sometimes also PR and marketing executives.

The results of the research showed that Estonian companies deal with social responsibility, but they all understand the topic in a different way. Depending on the company's size and opportunities, the enterprises are returning some of their profit to the community.

Companies' social responsibility is divided into internal and external. The internal social responsibility includes mainly the employees of a company and the correlating problems like human capital, health, safety, and changes which derive from management. The solving of environmental problems should be given special attention. The external social responsibility includes everything outside the company, such as the relationship between the owners and the community. This includes the environment and all the business partners, clients, and different organisations that represent the local community.

When putting together these recent researches and taking a closer look at the different groups of companies, some common aspects can be brought out:

CSR in small companies: The level of awareness of CSR among the small companies is relatively low, the common view is that when a company offers jobs to people, it has already fulfilled its responsibilities towards society. Obeying the laws is important to avoid sanctions, but going beyond these regulations is still rare. Most of the managers of small companies are afraid of new and strict European Union regulations and feel threatened.

CSR in middle-sized companies: The awareness of CSR issues among the medium-sized companies was much higher. They realised that a company is a part of society and the environment, and they felt that they have responsibilities towards society and they have to consider the consequences of their activities. These companies consider relevant both internal and external responsibilities, want to take better care of their employees and help society. But at the same time, some of these companies' managers considered sponsorship as the main CSR activity and stressed their operations in these areas. Even more worrying is the fact that managers think that companies can perform successfully without any CSR activities and that when this CSR fad is over, companies can turn back to their main and most important goal – to profit earning.

CSR in large companies: The large organisations' top executives stressed that their activities are in general socially responsible. They play a big role in their industries and without them society cannot function. These companies pay much attention to their employees, but they make a quite perceptible distinction between different hierarchical levels. Top executives, managers and top specialists get better training, sporting opportunities, compensation packages and special events, etc. whereas the same kind of favours are not for the lower levels. Companies realise the importance of supporting society, much is done to help children, but quite often these events are organised in order to gain a better reputation or earn benefits. The common view is that CSR activities have to be beneficial for the organisation.

When looking at the comparison of the two most well-known models of CSR, the Continental European and the US models (Hoivik, 2003), we can see that the Estonian companies' social responsibility pattern shares characteristics of both models. The similarity with the US model is mainly because the emphasis is on society, and environmental problems have been untouched. The main impacts are from the European Union and the Estonian favourable tax system for Scandinavian companies, who might install their headquarters in Estonia. Adhesion to the European Union brings with it regulations and directives. Scandinavian enterprises again will bring along their own culture and understandings, which can have effects on the Estonian companies' social responsibility model. Therefore it is quite probable, that the Estonian model will move towards the European model.

Conclusion

Corporate Social Responsibility can best be understood in terms of the changing relationship between business and society. Many people believe it is no longer enough for a company to say that their only concern is to make profits for their shareholders, when they are undertaking operations that can fundamentally affect (both negatively and positively) the lives of communities in countries throughout the world.

Although CSR has been a widely discussed and debated topic in most developed countries of the world in the past twenty years, it is still a relatively new concept in Estonia. The long history of foreign rule and especially the 50 years of soviet occupation have left traces in our people's morality and attitudes. During the first years after regaining our indepencence, Estonian people and businesses had to fight hard in order to survive and remain free. Therefore for years most businessmen preferred financial success over ethics and CSR seemed to be something irrelevant and unimportant. And today even if the businessmen are aware of the concept and find it important, they are lacking the knowledge to implement it in their companies.

Recently, Estonia has seen a few changes taking place in the companies. We see it in several different initiatives by Estonia's government, president, business leaders, environmentalists, social scientists and others. We can say that the awareness is rising; now companies need to take actions. There are a few good examples of corporate social responsibility in Estonia, many are implementing some areas of CSR but there is no company that has a systematic programme of CSR as a part of its business strategy.

As the awareness of companies rises and CSR gains more importance in the coming future, the number of stakeholders and issues which companies consider strategically important will presumably increase and CSR will come to mean balancing the interests of a wider group of stakeholders and also strategically managing the social, environmental and business activities for companies in Estonia.

References

Aaltio, I., Türnpuu, L., & Kooskora, M. 2002. From Social Movements to Identify Transformation: Comparison of Estonian and Finnish Management Students' Values. In: M. Kelemen, & M. Kostera (Eds.), *Critical Management Research in Eastern Europe. Managing the Transition.* Hampshire, UK: Palgrave Macmillan: 65 – 79.

Ennulo, J., & Türnpuu, L. 2001. An Intercultural Comparison of Management Values among Business School Students and Teachers. *Trames*, 5(4): 336 – 344.

Fontes. 2001. *Study of Estonian Top Managers.* Tallinn.

Hoivik, von Weltzien, H. 2003. *Corporate Social and Moral Responsibility?* Presentation at EBS. December 5th, Tallinn.

Kaevats, Ü. 2003. *Arengukiirendus või ääremaastumine.* 27.06.2003.

Kooskora, M. 2001. *Ethical Aspects of Decision Making.* Master Thesis. EBS, Tallinn.

Kooskora, M. 2003. *Privatisation in Estonia.* Presentation at EBEN Research Conference, Oslo.

Kooskora, M., Rikkinen, E. 2004. *Study of Morality of Estonian Business Leaders.* Unpublished paper. EBS, Tallinn.

Kooskora, M., & Türnpuu. 1999. *Estonians' Consciousness is Changing More European, Problems of European Integration in EBS.* Paper presented at the Scientific Conference, Tallinn.

Omair, K. A. 2004. *Social Accountability.* Master thesis. EBS, Tallinn.

Pitkänen, T. 2004. *Social Responsibility as a Part of Corporate Strategy in Estonia: the current situation and future trends.* Bachelor thesis. EBS, Tallinn.

Praxis. 2003. *Pilot-study of Estonians' mental health.* Tallinn.

Riigi Teataja Lisa. 1996. *Official Journal* (in Estonian): RT I, 82, 1463. http://www.riigiteataja.ee, accessed 5.8.2004.

Riigi Teataja Lisa. 1999. *Official Journal* (in Estonian), 137, 1922. http://www.riigiteataja.ee, accessed 5.8.2004.

Rikkinen, E. 2004. *The Role of Ethics in Conflict Management.* Bachelor thesis. EBS, Tallinn.

Spiller, R. 1997. *Business Ethics, Investment and Socially Responsible Business*: *A New Paradigm Business Perspective*. Doctoral Thesis. University of Auckland.

Spiller, R. 2000. Ethical Business and Investment: A Model for Business and Society. *Journal of Business Ethics* 27:149 – 160.

Suits, A. 2000. *Towards Ethical Decision-making in Estonian Society*. Bachelor thesis. EBS, Tallinn.

Virovere, A., & Kooskora, M. 2002. Conflicts in Estonian Companies. In: N. Vasiljevne (Ed.), *Business Ethics: world tendencies and actualities in post-socialist countries:* 270 – 279. Kaunas: Vilnius University.

Virovere, A., & Kooskora, M. 2000a. Personal Resources and Ethics in Public Service. *EBS Review*, No 11.

Virovere, A., & Kooskora, M. 2000b. *Ethical analyses of business leadership in action – Conflicts in Estonian Companies*. Paper presented at the 5th Annual conference of European Council for Business Education – Ethics in Business. Geneva, Switzerland.

Virovere, A., Kooskora, M., & Valler, M. 2002. Conflict as a Tool for Measuring Ethics at Workplace. *Journal of Business Ethics*, 39(1 – 2): 75 – 81.

Virovere, A., & Kure, K. 2001. Ethical Problems in Post-Soviet Countries. In: *Construction of Ethics in Multicultural Societies*. Japan: Chiba University International Conference.

16 The Thin Line Between Small Business and Big Politics

Konstantin Kostjuk

General Description of Business Development in Russia

Development and forms of corporate social responsibility depend in each country, first of all, on the role private business plays in the social life of a country, on how much the basic principles of the market economy are acknowledged, i.e. private property, competition, economy growth. In this respect the situation in Russia is quite a specific case and has a number of peculiarities (Andrianov, 1995; Akhieser, 1997; Radaev, 1998) which will be outlined in the following.

- In the recent decade social and economic systems have been radically reformed. Most of the state-planned economy has become private and transformed into a market economy. There have appeared a lot of new institutions whose establishment was accompanied by resistance of traditional principles and values. Traditional institutions such as the state had to radically change their goals and actions (Zudin, 1998; Shikhirev, 1999, 2000). In addition, the state can no longer dispose of the resources of economic units. As a result, enterprises that used to provide financing for the social infrastructure of whole cities, have given up such responsibilities and left the country's social sphere unprotected. Many social entities were found abandoned.

- Private business and the market economy in Russia are a still developing, totally new historic phenomenon. It cannot refer to CSR traditions. The private property institution does not inspire so much trust in people. Business and society interaction patterns are only being developed, quite often in the form of experiment. This is the reason for its loose connection with society, discrepancy of expectations and reality. For example, up to 40 – 50 % of the economy is shadow; the percentage of tax evasion, smuggling and corruption is rather high (Klyamkin & Timofeev, 1996; Igoshin, 2003; Yavlinsky, 2003).

- Provision of government financing via taxation of enterprises is practically a new historical phenomenon which businessmen and society do not take for granted so far. The same can be said about charity and sponsorship of private enterprises. The ratio of state budget to gross domestic product is about $10-12\%$ (in highly-developed economies, $30-40\%$), charitable contributions are extremely small. Therefore, it is pretty naive to discuss the question of business social responsibility, at least for small-scale business. Business is more often than not parasitic to society and state, however, they in their turn try to have the same parasitic attitude to business, making use of its resources.

- On the other hand, the success of this reformation and the solidity the new institutions are developing cannot be doubted. Leading companies try their hardest to meet the world standards. Economic stabilisation influences the stabilisation of relations between business, society and government. Not long ago a problem of wide-spread private business control by criminal structures ("shelters") was topical, though now this practice is localised, as in common world practice, to criminal business, or seems to have been exhausted. In Russia there have appeared companies which are big on a world scale: these are companies involved, first of all, in the extractive and power industries as well as transport companies and metals producers. Private business management is young and energetic, quick to study and to follow new directions of world development. Young managers are willing to adopt CSR practice, showing responsibility for the role it plays in society.

- The specific character of corporate responsibility in Russia is explained by the fact that Russian companies have experience of socialism under which companies were responsible and financed social institutions: kindergartens, schools, institutions of public charity (Leikind, 2001). Traditional social expectations also concern new economic entities. The social responsibility of a Russian company was too much for it from the very beginning. This overloading is not acceptable for it, thus private business has tried to get completely rid of any social responsibility in an opportunist manner. Meanwhile the pressure and expectations of society are rather great, therefore it is not an easy thing to do. The result of these two tendencies specifies the CSR scale which can be fixed in Russia today.

- The fact that civil society institutions are not solid neither contributes much to CSR development. Therefore private business looking for dialogue with external forces finds only one partner for dialogue – the authorities. There are no social counteragents who could take up CSR impulses and transform them into social initiatives. As a result, private business initiatives are interpreted as intervention in politics. Indeed, the absence of social control over its social initiatives prompts private business to attach advertising character to its commitment. For example, it is expressed by the fact that sponsoring has become a wide-spread phenomenon; while charity and philanthropy are not typical of Russian businessmen.

The unstable, fragile balance between business, society and the state initiates new models of their interaction. The liberal euphoria of the early 1990s concerning private property and the market, which made society harmonious and prosperous was accompanied by limitless confidence in businessmen as effective social managers. So, a number of big businessmen had good positions (big businessmen – B. Beresovsky and V. Potanin were ministers; big managers of state entities – V. Chernomyrdin, V. Kadannikov, A.Chubais were prime ministers and vice-prime ministers; many big businessmen, including notorious ones, were governors (B. Abramovich, V. Khloponin, D. Zelenin), presidential candidates, deputies). The beginning of the 21st century is noted rather for gradually decreasing confidence in businessmen, which is aggravated by the results of unjust privatisation. This period is characterised by a significant desire to establish distance between businessmen and the authorities. All these facts give rise to active social discussion of business social responsibility, which is held by associations of businessmen and representatives of big business.

Sociological Research

The monitoring of the modern CSR state made it possible to realise a sociological investigation carried out by "Association of Russian managers" in 2003, supported by Philippe Morris International: "Corporate social responsibility: public expectations" (Litovchenko & Korsakov, 2003). This comprehensive investigation is even more valuable because it is a comparative investigation: it was carried out simultaneously in several countries of Eastern Europe, including Hungary, Poland, Czech Republic, Ukraine.

The issue to be explored was the attitude of different social groups to corporate social responsibility: on the one hand, the common people including a *socially active* group of the population and on the other hand, *"leaders of public opinion"* including leading businessmen, politicians and mass media representatives. They interviewed 1200 people from the biggest cities of Russia, 300 representatives of big and medium-sized businesses, and conducted twenty in-depth interviews with experts.

The aim of the survey declared by the organisers was to reveal the public attitude towards big and medium-sized businesses as social institutions, to help businessmen recognise the criteria according to which their activities are considered, and take them into account in future. Much attention was paid to the channels through which information about the social activity of business is distributed as well as to the priorities society sets. It should be noted that questions of the investigation revealed interest for large-scale business, particularly for international corporations. The interest for national CSR features was not so obvious. The questions were set as if the survey was carried out in Western Europe, in countries with stable economies. Therefore, the picture was principally close to these countries. However, insufficient attention was paid to those normative layers which cause violations and instability of institutions. For example the problems of small-scale business which is closer to society but far from world standards should have been considered as well.

Nonetheless, the results are very interesting and instructive. In general they testify to more progress than could be expected. People have quite certain ideas of business responsibility and present them to companies. Two thirds of interviewees are sure that a company's aim is not limited to production, creation of work places and gaining profit, but should cover more: to support social programs, set high standards of behaviour and promote social development. Most of the respondents are convinced that social responsibility demonstration is favourable for business (86%), and the most prosperous companies are the most socially responsible (67%). 64% of respondents would not buy the products of socially irresponsible companies. Yet, the social role of companies in society is estimated to be low: the majority (87%) does not believe that companies' declarations about social responsibility are serious enough. In this respect 46% of interviewees, that is half of them, do not trust home companies, and 36% do not trust international companies. Among all social institutions, including the Government and mass media, companies are the least trusted.

The survey revealed problems in obtaining information about the social activity of companies. 86% of interviewees think that it is impossible for them to find out if a company is socially responsible. The overwhelming part of this information is obtained via mass media (88%) and via communication with other people. Here it should be underlined that only 3% absolutely trust it, 40% said they absolutely distrust it. Information coming from companies hardly reaches its aim. Two thirds of the population lack this information. Most of them hope that they can get it from companies under the system of companies' social reporting. Only 16% think it unnecessary.

It is an interesting fact that business people consider companies' role and achievements in CSR to be great.

The investigation also revealed the areas of concern. First of all, the very concept of business social responsibility is not clear. Experts and business people admitted it. In the investigation it showed up in the fact that the basic criteria of social responsibility were the parameters which characterise business as business, e.g. its basic functions – production and services quality (48%), taking care of workers (15%), contribution to economy via tax payments. On the contrary, the role of charity, the environment, relations with business partners and the company's behaviour in society turned out to be estimated as quite low (1–4%). Thus, signs of "bad" social behaviour were the poor quality of products and services and high

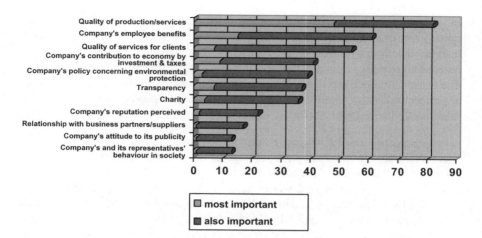

Figure 1. CSR features as perceived by the public

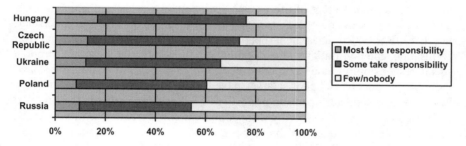

Figure 2. CSR in eastern and central European countries

prices for them. This testifies to the fact that people do not make a clear difference between internal and functional aims of a company and the responsibilities a company takes in view of its social engagement, in addition to its business tasks. This aroused discussion in the expert committee. Some people thought that relating product quality to social requirements was right, some of them did not.[1]

Besides, both common people and businessmen do not have a clear idea of whether socialistic forms of social activity, for example, city building companies supporting city social infrastructure, could be considered forms of corporate civic consciousness as well. Along with that, the list of social responsibility indicators include such terms as openness and transparency of companies, rendering assistance in the case of natural disasters, reliability and honesty, non-participation in corruption, protection of Russia's interests, support of education, assistance in reducing the number of human rights violations, respect for national culture, etc.

In comparison with Eastern Europe, the requirements for companies' social responsibility and the concern it arouses in Russia are generally somewhat lower than in other countries. At the same time business in Russia is less trusted than in other countries. But in general there are more common points than dividing ones. The basic difference is that a much greater percentage of people expect companies to perform their key functions – to produce products of good quality, to pay good salaries. All the rest seems to be luxury.

The investigation results will not be understood completely if some specific Russian conditions are not taken into account. In Russia two economic worlds have been formed: the world of economic prosperity and the world of economic decline (Igoshin, 2003: 79). The first world consists of enclaves of big companies and modern cities. The second world is the world of small-scale business and state officials, the provincial world which is hardly integrated into national economic life, the remains of the Soviet economy which has not been reformed. The first world is civilisation; the second is its periphery. More than 20% of the population – first of all, representatives of the second world – live in extremely poor conditions. The peculiar feature of life in such "two bottom worlds" is the double standards which make sociological investigations less effective. There is understanding that life is better somewhere. People *understand* what they can demand from civilisation, and civilisation in their opinion is expressed in the form of "corporate social responsibility" and "corporate civic consciousness." On the other hand, these people get "black" poor salaries, have bad social infrastructure, do not have insurance or satisfactory pension protection. *They require nothing.* They react to their own reality in one way: by disappointment and distrust. Two thirds of the population think that business should be responsible, but the same people are convinced that it is not. That's the question for business to answer.

YUKOS Case: Deoligarchization of Russian Politics?

Speaking about CSR development in Russia, it is impossible not to take into account the events of 2003 taking place around the oil producing company "YUKOS", which presented a most significant milestone and tendency of CSR development for the near future.[2] The YUKOS case has already been called by journalists as "antioligarchic revolution" (Pribylovsky, 2004). We can agree with this interpretation, for these events really influence the very basis of the social and political forces constellation and the political preferences which the powerful elite exercises. For two years the third "oligarch" has been outside the law.[3] This time we are talking about "oligarch number one" – not just the richest man in Russia,[4] but also the businessman who in many respects was an example, oriented towards civilised, European methods of running business. He entered international stock markets, therefore, tried to achieve business transparency, realised social and charity programmes on a national scale, showed his independence from the authorities and represented a new generation of young and energetic businessmen. Even if this businessman has "evident" sins – absurd political ambitions or violations during privatization, the scale of what is happening still far exceeds the history of "one oligarch's fall".

The monopolistic structure of Russian capital was inherited by Russia as a Soviet heritage. About 50 of the biggest companies account for about 50% of the Russian gross domestic product. Privatisation could not avoid this peculiarity of the Soviet economy and was destined to "give birth" to the system of "oligarchism" (Kostjuk, 2003). Among its inherited features was a mixture of politics and economics, in new terms – "a combination of power and business". In conditions of economic crisis in the 1990s and total corruption, the power of big money, "business power over power" represented a real threat to society. The political class of Russia found this situation quite acceptable as long as it concerned only state government corruption. However, when private business became an independent political actor, entrepreneur of "political performances", it was quite painful. B. Beresovsky, minister in one of the governments, was accused of political intrigues, Gusinsky representing independent media policy, aimed at discrediting the authorities. Both "oligarchs" have something in common: both of them were media magnates and they were actively pursued until they were deprived of their media assets. M. Khodorkovsky crossed "the red line" when he began positioning himself politically, supporting institutions of education and political analytics, threatening to "buy" deputies and go into politics. Formally, all three oligarchs were accused of financial intrigues against the state.

Autumn 2003 was the beginning of a new historic epoch in Russia. The agreement on which the partnership between business and state is based – not to reconsider privatisation results – is not so much trusted if not disavowed. Unshakable private property began to shake. Some people thought the combination of business and politics was broken. Whatever the hidden motive of this very story would be – a wish to "bring down" the ambitions of "an oligarch who's gone too far", the unwillingness to give a company to foreign proprietors, personal dislike, a sincere wish to teach business a lesson in relation to tax discipline – I would like to draw your attention to the consequences of these events rather than to their reasons.

They represent new boundaries and forms which the system of corporate social responsibilities can have in this national culture. This boundary is fixed not only by political power – V. Putin's actions concerning oligarchs are supported by most of the Russian population.

Probably in other countries, for example, in Italy, Khodorkovsky would not have problems creating an image of a business-enlightened social leader. It is impossible in Russia: there is a taboo against private business being active in "big politics". At the same time one cannot deny that CSR has a problem in itself. Active social and political engagement of business – whether it is intended or not – may serve as a channel for private interest promotion which is typical of private property from the very beginning. The established cultures of highly-developed countries have developed here more subtle mechanisms of not allowing the use of the idea of charity and sponsorship in such a manner. In Russia this boundary is seen to be quite clear and distinct for all. It is evident that big business will become more careful and dependent in its political projects. Probably, from now on it will be more passive in charity and in CSR. Nevertheless, it has become evident for everybody that the cultural line between undesirable political engagement of a businessman and neutral CSR is where it is drawn as a result of the "antioligarchic campaign". The aim for society and businessmen is to explore this field which society and culture allow for CSR.

It is of interest that M. Khodorkovsky admitted indirectly that these limits are objective, having published in March 2004 a letter that found a great social response. In this letter he admitted the collapse of politics and liberal ideas of the 1990s (with A. Chubais at head), which did not take into account common interests and made politics serve the interests of the business community. Underlining that not only the social responsibility of business (which in his opinion Khodorkovsky tried to take up) but the social responsibility of politics is necessary, the author of the letter drew attention to how difficult it is to harmonise the interests of market economics, institutions development, and the interests and ideas of other social forces. "Crash" on business in his opinion was just a reverse side of distrust of liberals, expressed by the population at State Dume elections in 2003.

Organizations Promoting CSR

CSR initiatives are too chaotic and spontaneous to call them a social movement. Nevertheless, at present in Russia there are many organisations which realise CSR ideas to some extent. There is, first of all, the absolute leader of this movement, "Association of managers of Russia" (www.amr.ru), supporting quite a number of CSR programmes: "Social strategy of Russian business"; "Social responsibility and Russian business reputation"; "Social programme of Russian business"; "Management of company's social programmes"; "Social investment: business and state interaction"; "Social portrait of Russian company"; "Corporate social report: fashion or company's reputation?". It is this association that is called a pioneer and its activities are the most systematic in this field.

Other business associations such as "OPORA" ("Business support", small enterprises, www.opora.ru), "Business Russia" (medium enterprises, www.deloros.ru), "Russian PR association" (RASO) (www.raso.ru) and the most famous "Business support", Russian Union of Manufacturers and Businessmen (big enterprises, www.rsppr.biz) share CSR ideas. In spite of the fact that for RSPP, representing big business, it is typical to put the stress on communication problems of business and authorities as well as problems of intercorporate communication, recently RSPP has put forward quite a number of CSR initiatives, which provide system support of social projects of enterprises. Social initiatives in the CSR manner are realised by some companies (e.g. "Philippe Morris International" JSC, "Aeroflot – Russian airlines", JSC GMK "Norilsk nickel", "Sual Holding", JSC "Gazprom") and public state organisations (e.g. Federal Committee for Securities, National Programme "Russian Business Culture", Academy "Civil Society" (Lerman & Kostjuk, 2003) and others). Representatives of foreign civil and business organisations also put forward their initiatives, particularly, the British charity foundation CAF (magazine "Money and charity", www.cafrussia.ru), IBLF, Amnesty International, the German Konrad Adenauer Foundation (www.adenauer.ru), Moscow representative office of Eurasia Foundation (www.eurasia.msk.ru), the Internet magazine Maecenas (www.maecenas.ru) and Sponsoring-Site Sponsoring (www.sponsoring.ru).

Notes

[1] Since data in other countries were similar, it can be concluded that the definition of CSR poses a general methodological problem typical of not only developing and transforming markets.

[2] Here we speak about the charge of the Russian Prosecutor against YUKOS proprietors (M. Khodorkovsky, L. Platonov, L. Nevzlin, etc) according to a number of articles concerning economic crimes.

[3] Official persona non grata in 2001 – 2003 were declared B. Beresovsky, main shareholder of telecompany "ORT-1 Channel", and V.Gusinsky, telecompany NTV proprietor.

[4] According to *FOBOS* M. Khodorkovsky with a fortune of 7 billion US dollars was the richest man in Russia in 2003.

References

Akhieser, A. C. 1997. *Russia: critics of historical experience.* Vol. 3. Novosibirsk, Russia.

Andrianov, V. D. 1995. *Russia in the world economy.* Moscow, Russia.

Igoshin, I. N. 2003. *Institutional distortions in Russian society.* Moscow, Russia.

Klyamkin, I. M., & Timofeev, L. M. 1996. S*hadow mode of life. Sociological self-portrait of post Soviet society.* Moscow, Russia.

Leikind, O. (Ed.) 2001. *Charity in Russia.* S. Petersburg, Russia.

Litovchenko, S., & Korsakov, M. (Eds.) 2003. *Corporate social responsibility: public expectations.* Moscow, Russia.

Kostjuk, K. 2003. *Will oligarchic system be dismantled in Russia?* Material of the Internet Conference: Institutional Russian Economics organized by the Moscow Public Scientific Foundation and Higher School of Economics, Moscow.

Lerman, E., & Kostjuk, K. (Eds.) 2003. *Corporate Ethics and Value Management.* Moscow, Russia.

Pribylovsky, V. 2004. *The genuine Oligarchs are politicians.* http://rspp.biz/articles?fid=3& aid=505, accessed 05.08.2004.

Radaev, V. 1998. *Formation of new Russian markets: transactional costs, forms of control and business ethics.* Paper presented at the 14th World Congress of Sociology, Montreal.

Shikhirev, P. N. 1999. *Ethic principles of running business in Russia.* Moscow, Russia.

Shikhirev, P. N. 2000. *Introduction to Russian business culture.* Moscow, Russia.

Yavlinsky, G. 2003. *Provincial capitalism.* Moscow, Russia.

Zudin, A. 1998. *Image of businessman in new Russia.* Moscow, Russia.

17 In Search of National Identity

Volodja Vorobey

Introduction

The concept of Corporate Social Responsibility (CSR) is yet to be introduced to Ukraine in the diversity of methodological and practical approaches developed during the last 10 years in other countries. However, Ukrainian companies have followed certain practices that are now attributed to CSR for years.

In this paper I argue that Ukraine has a number of factors, both historical and cultural, that could lead to the introduction of a CSR concept in the Ukrainian corporate environment, different from those developed in other European countries.

Ukraine has not experienced an institutionalisation of the CSR movement. In fact there is no CSR movement as such but rather the existence of socially conscious managers. A national framework for corporate citizenship has not been developed and no business or multi-stakeholder fora on the topic have been established.

Rather than focusing on an assessment of CSR as an institutionalised approach, this paper endeavours to provide a background and to highlight factors, which arguably will be crucial for the inception of CSR in Ukraine.

Place of Business in Ukrainian Society

For a long period of time Ukraine was divided between different empires including the Russian, Austro-Hungarian and Ottoman Empires. Such division has clearly left its marks on the attitude of the general population towards entrepreneurship and business. There have been no large Ukrainian-owned enterprises in any part of the country, with the majority of enterprises being either affiliates of national companies in their respective states or foreign-owned interests on Ukrainian territory.

Up until the middle of the twentieth century agriculture played a dominant role in the economy. The attitude of landowners towards field workers and seasonal workers has varied significantly from close integration of landowners' families into the local community to blatant denial of any social rights. This had an impact on the attitude of the population towards landowners and their enterprises, in some places providing a fertile ground for the future emergence of the anarchist movement (Zaporizhya region).

In Central and Eastern Ukraine, landowners, mainly aristocrats, had started to play a more active role in developing the social infrastructure of the region in the second half of the 19th century. Medical, educational and social institutions were set up with direct support from industrialists.

Industrialists turned philanthropists played a key role in supporting the revival of the Ukrainian national movement in that period. The activities of Mykola Tereshchenko, Lev Brodskiy, Mykhajlo Degterev, Bogdan Khanenko, Baron Steingel and others, included not only support for new hospitals, churches and museums but also investments into public educational institutions. An interesting example is provided by a Movenpick figure of Evgen Chikalenko, wealthy farmer and trader from Southern Ukraine, who gradually transferred his profitable agricultural know-how free of charge to common farmers, his previous employees. He also gradually sold his land to nearby small farmers, established the first Russian land mortgage bank in Odessa and dedicated his time and wealth to the promotion of an idea for an independent Ukraine.

Small and medium-sized businesses were a basis of economic development in Western Ukraine, although there was a large industry present in the (then) oil-rich Carpathian Mountains. There were examples of large companies created around the idea of catering for small Ukrainian mostly family-run businesses, e.g. the Ukrainian cooperative bank Dnister.

The turmoil at the beginning of the 20th century has shown what an impact social engagement of owners could have had on the acceptance of business practices among its employees (workers). While the staff of some enterprises was fully supportive of the 1917 revolution's goals, with workers taking management of enterprises in their hands, staff at other plants stayed loyal to their managers for months and even years from the beginning of revolution.

During the period of Soviet command economy, the mere notion of "business" was equated to "speculation" with negative popular connotation attached to it and all but outlawed. Companies [enterprises] could not and should not bring profit in the capitalist economic sense. Large collective enterprises were present in all sectors of the economy from farming and trade to heavy engineering. With such a system in place, development of management skills, entrepreneurship and innovation were limited. Environmental concerns, the social impact of development on local communities, and other long-term considerations were not taken into account as decisions were taken far away from the location of facilities/enterprises, usually in ministries in Moscow. This created a highly inefficient resource-dependent economic system. However, with enterprises driven not by generation of profit, the Soviet planned economy favoured the creation and support of social infrastructure by enterprise (youth camps, kindergartens, entertainment centres, etc.). Such a model of employees' benefits is deeply rooted in Ukrainian society. Companies that have emerged as profitable businesses through the transformation period are looking back to introduce these kinds of social facilities for their employees.

After the collapse of the Soviet Union the Ukrainian population started gradually adjusting to the notion of *business* in its modern meaning. In many cases companies (especially small ones) were considered as results of *speculation* and thus illegal. True *companies* were equal to *enterprises* in popular thinking. Such an understanding was not helped by the legal system, which lagged behind the realities of the economy. In addition, lack of transparency in the privatisation process in the 1990s did not add trust to the corporate sector. Management teams from Soviet times often privatised profitable enterprises just to become the eventual owner of the enterprises without any investment commitment[1]. Not always transparent and efficient privatisation did not contribute to the creation of trust towards new companies.

During the last fifteen years the Ukrainian legal system has been gradually shaped, and often business interests have been a driving force in this process. With a lack of civil society engagement and resources invested into lobbying efforts, companies and especially leading business groups were better positioned to create laws favouring specific business interests. There are examples showing how particular business groups' interests often drove changes in Ukrainian law in the 1990s. In Europe, debate on CSR often evolves around CSR as a way for companies to do more for society than demanded by the law. Aforementioned particularities of the Ukrainian legal environment make such debate ambiguous if applied in Ukraine. The concept itself often raises issues not addressed or inadequately addressed by law.

Factors Defining CSR Inception

CSR as a concept is mostly unknown in the country. Ukraine is situated at the transition point from unrestrained capitalism to a modern market economy, with many markets already matured and with identified market leaders. Strong economic growth in recent years and sound economic policies of the last governments have provided an enabling environment for corporate growth and the structural development of the economy, although a lot is still to be done. However, there are no formal strategies with regard to corporate citizenship and corporate champions of the concept are yet to emerge in Ukraine.

Multiple factors are at work, which arguably could lead to the inception of CSR into Ukrainian companies. The table below attempts to summarise such factors.

Table 1. Factors defining CSR inception

	Factor	Factor manifestation	Impact on CSR policies and CSR inception
Economic factors	Increased industrial output	Increased resource utilisation and waste generation, increased demands for quality of services and products, competition for highly skilled labour; ecological problems are increasingly drawing attention of local officials and local peer groups.	Need to distinguish from competitors (esp. in the areas of reputation management and recruitment); forces companies to accept better management practices;
	Corporate concentration	Industrial groups at national and regional level are being formed, some are expanding internationally.	Need to gain access to capital putting pressure on companies for disclosure of information; formalisation of corporate governance standards, social and environmental policies.
	Labour migration, shadow economy	Lack of skilled and qualified work force in many regions with almost 7m Ukrainians working abroad; problems with level of required salaries (high level of shadow economy incomes in comparison with officially declared ones).	Brain drain and illegal labour migration are becoming social and economic problems putting pressure on companies to retain workforce; differences between levels of official and shadow economy incomes are a distorting factor for foreign investors.
	Level of SMEs development	In the regions with a relatively high level of SMEs development social and environmental problems are less tense; reliance on large industrial complexes in Eastern Ukraine created many environmental problems with people dependant on work provided by the complexes.	Western Ukraine and Kyiv capital area have better environment for stakeholder dialogue inception.
	Changes in law and legal system	First attempts to incorporate requirements for corporate governance, ecological and social standards, with low penalties however; increasing activity of local authorities; environment highly favourable for corruption (rapid and frequent changes in law); low level and selective law enforcement.	Situation creates highly political environment for up-take of CSR-companies taking active stance on issues are vulnerable for political accusations; low law enforcement makes justification of CSR business case very hard.
	Low though increasing foreign investments	Transfer of management skills and technologies; increased competition creates social problems; negative perception towards ownership of Ukrainian assets by foreign interests among large part of population.	Improved environmental policies and working conditions, need to adjust to local realities, e.g. taking into consideration cultural needs and realities.

Table 1 (continued)

Socio-economic factors	Corruption	Companies are under constant pressure to find ways to adjust to corruption in their policies and strategies; existence of ethical problems, esp. in relations to foreign partners and investors.	Greater openness of the economy will lead to companies taking active stance on changing attitude towards corruption and better law enforcement.
	Industrial infrastructure and processes heritage of Soviet economy	Large infrastructure utilised non-efficiently or abandoned in 1990s; multiple environmental and social problems linked to the closure of complexes; biggest capital investment and international assistance projects' target throughout 1991 – 2003.	Social and environmental problems linked to the adjustment of processes and systems have stimulated the most debate on role of business in society;
	Mass media openness, freedom of speech	Diverse levels of freedom of speech across regions, national mass media linked to political and economical blocks; critical reports are rare in Ukrainian mass media and are often politically motivated; internet media are popular with young population and mostly free of censorship.	Close links between economics and politics makes it hard to communicate case for CSR (critical publications linked with political motives, no trust in mass media); internet is yet to be discovered as a means for promoting corporate citizenship.
	State of health and social services	Reliance on free social and health services provided by state; high recognition of the decrepit state of both; increase in private sector's importance in these sectors of the economy; Ukraine has one of Europe's highest level of work-related traumatism (UNDP, 2002).	Stimulates companies to provide more medical and other social services to employees; increasing importance of corporate pension plans among leading Ukrainian companies; potential defining factor of CSR inception.
	Re-integration of deported population	Lack of integration between Crimean Tatars and local Slavic population; social problems of returnees in housing, employment, social protection, access to education, etc. (Drohobycky, 1995).	Issue of re-integration of Crimean Tatar population in Crimea will become important with the rapid economic development of Republic of Krym, esp. for industries like agriculture and tourism.
	Chernobyl after-affect	Highly recognised social issue with over 10 % of working population affected; special social insurance plan and special system of medical institutions for people affected exist; corrupt and inefficient systems addressing the issue, lack of credibility towards state-run programmes; awareness among population of effects of the catastrophe on health.	Prompted companies to address health issues in product development, social marketing etc.

Table 1 (continued)

Social Factors	Civil society development	Different levels of participation in civil society organisations: high among young population and low among 35+ age group; significant and rising number of Non-Governmental Organisations (NGOs); relatively low level of impact of NGOs on decision-makers at all levels in society; political sensitiveness of NGO funding[2]; NGOs are the drivers of engaging corporate sector into social dialogue (Counterpart Creative Centre, 2000).	Lack of prominent NGOs for engaging in dialogue; population is mostly not associating companies' engagement with NGOs as a corporate citizenship; NGOs already engaged in collaboration with corporate sector might become champions of CSR inception in Ukrainian companies.
	Poverty	Stratification of population; gap between working and non-working or those with dependants[3]; geographical gap; taboo on addressing poverty as a social problem among companies; level of salaries for low-paid positions is not defined by unions (de jure) but by employers (de facto).	Issue largely not addressed directly by companies except through ad hoc philanthropic activities; could have a long-lasting effect for companies, which address the issue in a coherent way.
	Level of education and educational needs	Companies' interaction with state-run educational system; rising importance of private sector in education, especially higher; gap between importance of training and qualification of younger employees and training/continuing education of employees of 35+ age group;	Competition, recruitment and retention of qualified workforce is intensifying, esp. between local companies and companies with foreign investments; companies are keen to adopt new approaches to address the issue.
	Receptiveness towards foreign influence	Restrained and often negative attitude of a big part of population, mostly elderly, towards foreign ownership, management practices, etc.; gap in managerial practices between Ukrainian-owned and foreign-owned companies;	Creates psychological barrier for CSR inception as an imposed model; accelerates the need for localisation and integration of foreign models and practices; environment for bottom-up inception of CSR.

There are examples confirming the inception of CSR, albeit often by chance and driven by the demands of business strategy.

In 2001 the leader of the Ukrainian beer market, JSC Obolon (www.obolon.ua), made a decision to significantly expand its soft drinks line. After extensive research Obolon decided to address health concerns of the post-Chernobyl population by introducing an apple-flavour soft drink with the extract of Echinacea, a herb used to improve the immune system. *Zhvyvchyk* brand name was chosen despite a market trend for Western-like brands. The new drink became instantly a brand of choice among different groups of the population. Appealing to health concerns of the nation and with a true Ukrainian name, *Zhyvchyk* has gained a 12% market share and became second only to Coca-Cola on the Ukrainian market. By introducing *Zhyvchyk*, Obolon has created a whole market for healthy carbonated drinks.

Another example is provided by the Industrial Union of Donbas (Industrialnyj Sojuz Donbasu, ISD – www.isd.com.ua), a large Ukrainian conglomerate active in the metal industry. With sales topping EUR1.5 billion in 2003, the company was formed through the murky privatisation of the early 1990s and is controlled by Rinat Akhmetov, a Ukrainian tycoon. Until recently, both Rinat Akhmetov and ISD were avoiding media attention. Almost no disclosure of financial information was taking place and the company paid limited attention to its stakeholders. By 2002, ISD became one of the largest companies in Ukraine.

Dependent on the industrial heritage of the Soviet Union and export revenues, the company needed investments to stay competitive in international markets. Shortly after forging a strategic alliance with the Swiss metal trading company Duferco, which became a major investor in ISD, the company made public announcements about large-scale investments in new technologies, improvements of working conditions and large donations to local charities (*Halytski Kontrakty*, 2004). In 2003 ISD, in partnership with Duferco, won the privatisation auction for the Hungarian steelworks Dunaferr. In 2003 – 2004 ISD is involved in bidding wars for the Polish steelworks Huta Czestochowa. Exposure to international markets (need for a strategic partner, access to cheap capital, recognition as a stable and reliable business partner for privatised complexes) has pushed the company towards more disclosure of information and more active community involvement.

The German automotive supplier, LEONI (www.leoni.de), became the largest investor in Western Ukraine in 2002 with its over 5,000 staff plant in Stryi, Lviv region (*Halytski Kontrakty*, 2003). Despite the high official unemployment rate and average monthly salary of EUR 50 in the region, the company faced a problem of retention and high turnover of personnel. Apparently the region chosen by the company has one the highest level of illegal immigration to EU countries as well as a high level of shadow economy. Remittances and incomes from non-taxable small business activities provided the local population with income, significantly higher than that provided by the company. By increasing salaries, investing in training and education activities and improving employees' relationships, the company has largely reversed the trend. LEONI is committed to building a new factory in Ukraine in 2004 taking into consideration its experience in Sryi and paying closer attention to local communities' needs.

Historical and Cultural Identity Factors

Ukraine is a large country that is still forming its national identity. Different regions of the country have their own historical heritage and cultural identities that put unique imprints on the inception of CSR. To name a few of them:

- Linguistic and cultural differences between the predominantly Ukrainian-speaking West and Russian-speaking East;

- The Autonomous Republic of Krym (Crimea) has a large population of Crimean Tatars who are Muslim and non-Slavic;

- Heavily industrialised, the Eastern Ukrainian Donbas region's economy is based on large industrial conglomerates as opposed to SMEs. It has developed a strong "Soviet" culture and identity;

- There is a large number of SMEs in Western Ukraine. To some extent, it could be explained by the historical heritage of the Austro-Hungarian and Polish rule in the region which was less oppressive than that of the Russian Empire in the rest of Ukraine;

- Existence of three Orthodox Churches and a Greek-Catholic Church. Division of church property was a highly contentious issue at the beginning of the 1990s.

Companies that emerged or extended their operations to Ukraine in the 1990s had to cope with these and other historical and cultural factors. Corporate strategies have been playing an important role in creating a Ukrainian identity as opposed to a Soviet one, mostly through marketing strategies.

The Soviet period in modern Ukrainian history is of particular importance to the inception of CSR. But formally adhering to the Soviet model would probably require companies to take into consideration other factors. If companies could refer to Soviet traditions in their marketing strategies in Southern and Eastern Ukraine, the population of Western Ukraine could react negatively to this.

The welfare system inherited from the Soviet Union is also an important historical factor for the inception of CSR. While education, medicine and social systems suffer from underinvestment and underfunding by the government, mostly relying on the infrastructure and systems from Soviet times, there are many political discussions regarding the social responsibility of government. In such conditions, many companies are taking active steps in providing medical, educational and other social services to their employees, retired employees and their families, which arguably distorts the notion of social equality. Ukrainian companies as well as the State are yet to clarify relations between the state-funded welfare system and corporate social programmes.

Common with Other CEE Countries and Ukrainian-Specific Factors

A number of factors defining the up-take of CSR in Ukraine are similar to those in other Central and Eastern European countries:

- Heritage of the welfare economy – Generous social benefits were in place during socialism in all countries across the CEE region. Apart from low incentives for companies to be involved in the social dimension of CSR, such a heritage creates many incentives for tax avoidance practices.

- Economic dependencies – All countries in the region have strong economic dependencies on different factors with at least one as a dominant. Ukraine is strongly reliant on its metal export and transit of Russian oil and gas. Thus, the up-take of CSR in the whole economy depends primarily on the response of companies working in these two sectors of the economy.

- Environmental, economic and societal legacy of socialism – During the period of planning economy, industrial output was defined by the plan, which often did not take into account the actual needs of the population. This created multiple inefficiencies in resources allocation (over- or undercapacity).

- A psychological border between past and present – The rapid political changes in the beginning of the 1990s supported by a vast majority of the population created a strong distinction between "bad communism" [bad past] and "good capitalism" [good future] among the economically active population. It imposes difficulties in many cases, e.g. identification of trade unions with the *bad past*, practical denial of efficient enterprises' existence in *bad past* leading to sometimes inefficient privatisation, stratification of the labour force based on the age principle with the older generation in a disadvantaged situation.

- The rise of nationalistic feelings and national identities – Business in CEE has a much stronger national identity than elsewhere in Europe and is also expected to play an important role in national revival.

There are factors that distinguish Ukraine from other CEE countries:

- Ukraine is not an EU accession country – This provides fewer incentives for business to reach EU standards in environment and consumer protection etc.

- Large social infrastructure inherited by all industrial enterprises – Ukrainian industrial complexes are mostly older than in other post-Soviet and CEE countries. Less efficient and with a larger social infrastructure, such enterprises are struggling to balance social concerns with economic and environmental efficiencies.

- Legal system and traditions of state – Ukraine has not been independent for over four centuries: there is no tradition of state building; the legal framework is in a state of construction. The balance between the interests of business, state and society is still being defined, making it easier for Ukrainian large industrial groups to interfere in the law-making process.

Recognised vs. Hidden Factors

Some factors that define the role of business in Ukrainian society are finding regular coverage in the media and often involve the corporate sector in related dialogue. Although not sufficient and regular, cross-sectoral conferences (often including both the corporate sector and government), round tables and discussions take place regarding the following issues:

- Corruption,

- Freedom of speech,

- Civil society development,

- Level of education and educational needs,

- Chernobyl post-effect.

However, a number of factors remain largely ignored by the corporate sector. It is evident in the low involvement of companies in activities related to these social issues:

- Poverty

- Re-integration of deported population, namely Crimean Tatars

- State of health and social support systems

Apart from those, the alarming level of HIV/AIDS spread in some regions should become an important issue for companies.

Players

Taking into consideration the stage at which CSR development is in Ukraine, it is important to identify organisations able to pursue the concept within the Ukrainian corporate environment and to define the positioning and communication channels for this concept to enable its wide up-take.

In many cases Ukrainian companies are already investing their resources in addressing particular aspects of CSR. For instance, almost all leading industrial enterprises and companies have restructured their processes to drastically decrease the negative impact of their activities on the environment. Partly this was supported by new governmental regulations in place, the availability of cheap financial resources from international organisations and increased prices of commodities used as inputs in the industrial process (such as water, electricity and land). However a major factor affecting corporate decisions was the heritage of a Soviet management system and obvious inefficiencies stemming from this. Thus, to a large extent corporate decisions were retrospective rather than proactive and linked primarily with the environmental efficiency of production-oriented enterprises.

Another important aspect of CSR that is increasingly drawing the attention of corporate managers in Ukraine is corporate governance. International financial institutions have been operating in Ukraine since its independence. The World Bank, International Finance Corporation (IFC) and European Bank for Reconstruction and Development (EBRD) have been consistently trying to improve corporate governance standards in Ukraine. The Ukrainian Corporate Governance project of the IFC has already resulted in National Standards on Corporate Governance being approved by the Securities and Stock Market State Commission in December 2003 (Pryntsypy Korporatyvnogo Upravlinnia Ukrainy, 2004).

Thus, the international funding community (both private investors and international financial institutions) could play an important role in the inception of CSR through accommodating it into requirements for private projects funded in Ukraine. International funding agencies could move one step ahead from addressing issues of governance, involvement of civil society and protection of environment to urging companies to assess their CSR policies. Better cooperation in this area with private foreign investors could be an advantage. Potential players/organisations that could be involved in dialogue regarding up-take of CSR in Ukraine include:

- Companies actively working with foreign investors and financial institutions,

- Companies transforming into regional players,

- Affiliates of transnational corporations (TNCs), especially those with defined CSR strategies,

- Export-oriented companies that constitute part of supply chains (esp. in forestry, garment industry, heavy engineering and metallurgy).

Other important players in Ukraine include certification agencies, the Ukrainian Quality Association and business schools, e.g. Kyiv Mohyla Business School. These organisations do not have a defined approach towards communication on CSR but are actively integrating social concerns into their activities aimed at the business community.

Forecast for CSR Development in Ukraine

There is a clear need to create a Ukrainian understanding of Corporate Social Responsibility to utilise the momentum of transition and to avoid any mistakes made by other Central and Eastern European countries. Ukraine holds a unique position between the European Union market and Russian business interests with a handful of rapidly growing Ukrainian companies actively transforming into regional players. Unlike other CIS countries, Ukraine does not have natural resources of international importance that could make major international players out of Ukrainian natural monopolies, and no backing from the European Commission to ensure external funding for the state like its EU member neighbours to the West. Combined, it makes it a unique business environment with a need to define local pathways for economic and social development. Not linked to or nurtured by Western interests, home-grown solutions are required to enable the new generation of self-confident Ukrainian businesses to create their own understanding of business in society.

Many companies do have policies regarding employees, environmental standards etc. Many other companies are developing such policies. However, these policies are stand-alone and not linked with each other in a coherent manner. Gradually companies will need to create a consistent set of policies regarding different stakeholder groups, causing them to look beyond philanthropy and legal obligations, stimulating the appearance of national corporate champions in the area of CSR (Cherp, 2003).

It could be expected that hidden factors of CSR's inception in Ukraine could become much more visible for companies during the coming years. Either social processes, political events or economic consequences could bring such issues forward and trigger corporate response.

With the development of civil society, cooperation between NGOs and the corporate sector will increase. In many cases, NGOs could play an important educational role in raising awareness about CSR among Ukrainian companies. However, there are two potential threats. Firstly, NGOs might present CSR as a philanthropy and thus confuse managers with the concept. Secondly, NGOs might have a conflict of interests trying not to lose financial support from companies (often philanthropical). Companies supporting NGOs might re-assess their programmes and channel their funding to other NGOs or other areas while introducing CSR policies.

At this particular stage, communication and awareness-raising play a crucial role. Not only TNCs, international funding institutions but also formal and informal networks of business leaders could be used as channels promoting the concept. Further development of CSR in Ukraine largely depends on how efficient such communication will be.

Notes

[1] Ukraine opted for a *voucher* privatisation where all eligible citizens obtained *vouchers* (coupons) entitling participation in privatisation auctions. Management teams of enterprises intended for privatisation often bought vouchers from the population for negligible amounts to buy profitable enterprises they managed.

[2] In March 2004 in the Verkhovna Rada [Parliament], the Communist Party of Ukraine has accused NGOs at large of being funded by anti-Ukrainian governments.

[3] Elderly, children, unemployed spouses, other.

References

Cherp, A. 2003. *Corporate Sustainability Reporting in Eastern Europe: First Experience and lessons learned.* Brussels: CEU, Department of Environmental Sciences and Policy. http://www.ceu.hu/envsci/, accessed 05.08.2004.

Counterpart Creative Centre. 2000. *Social Partnership as the Future of the Third Sector* (in Ukrainian). Kyiv: Counterpart Creative Centre.

Drohobycky, M. 1995. Ukraine and its Ethnic Minorities: An Overview. In: M. Drohobycki (Ed.), *Managing Ethnic Tensions in the Post-Soviet Space: The Examples of Kazakhstan and Ukraine.* Washington: American Association for the Advancement of Science.

Halytski Kontrakty. 2003. Leoni zbilshuje prysutnist v Ukraini. No. 45. http://www.kontrakty. com.ua/show/ukr/article/8/4520031167.html, accessed 20.03.2004.

Halytski Kontrakty. 2004. ISD pidbyla pisumky 2003 roku. No. 06. http://www.kontrakty. com.ua/show/ukr/article/1/0620041803.html, accessed 20.03.2004.

Pryntsypy Korporatyvnogo Upravlinnia Ukrainy. 2004. *Derzhavna Komisia z Tsinnyh Paperiv ta Fondovogo Rynku.* http://www2.ifc.org/ukraine/ucdp/materials/Principy.pdf, accessed 20.03.2004.

UNDP. 2002. *The Power of Participation. Ukraine Human Development Report 2001.* http://www.un.kiev.ua, accessed 20.05.2004.

Further Internet Links

Trust for Civil Society in Central & Eastern Europe
http://www.ceetrust.org

Ukrainian Association of Quality
http://www.uaq.org.ua/

Kyiv Mohyla Business School
http://www.kmbs.kiev.ua

18 Confronting a Leadership Vacuum

Alpar Losoncz

Introduction

In the last few years many new inquiries have taken place in the "collective", in-stitutional parts of economic dynamics and several tentative findings suggest that the concept of CSR can be used as the analytic for the assessment of dimensions of corporative social performances. The idea of CSR presupposes some forms of *bounded social world* within which the allocation, the distribution of economic resources and the determination of the scale of corporate business activities come into existence. According to this, the corporative context is partly non-functional and resorts to the intrinsic motivation of the agents and to the responsibility of people who manage the corporations (McWilliams & Siegel, 2001; Barclay & Smith, 2003; Birch, 2003; Greenfield, 2004; Manokha, 2004).

It is to be mentioned that some theoreticians are sceptical about CSR as the blan-ket term and corporation-as-person theory. The CSR advocates argue that on the basis of managing social and environmental issues, companies will perform better financially with less risk in the long run. As the recent corporations-related melt-down events have demonstrated, the management systems, *per se,* offer no assur-ance of improved ethical performance. It is necessary to articulate the aspects of CSR in the light of the common ground of the existing market society. When cor-porations praise the free market, they often (too often, actually) mean freedom from having to subordinate the use of property to external value. The market power of the corporations serves as a means of escaping from market's freedom of entry condition; consequently, market power of corporations is the means to un-make the entry to market on the basis of industrial protection and intellectual pov-erty (Kingston, 2000).

Many firms have adopted some of the relevant CSR management techniques, but there is a lack of information on whether or not social and environmental perform-ance has, in reality, been altered. CSR gets relevance only through a systematic approach defining the changes needed to make business responsible and sustain-able. The CSR discourse is legitimised if it proves to be an impetus for the re-thinking of the structure of the contemporary market society and the massive rents of corporations, i.e. the structural tendencies of the non-responsible property rights in the context of the "race to the bottom".

One potential path of interpretation is to differentiate the features of responsibility in connection to the diverse components (economic, legal, ethical, and discretionary or philanthropic). Also, there is corporate social responsibility, at the institutional, organisational, and individual levels. At the organisational level, CSR addresses *public responsibility* in that businesses are responsible for outcomes related to their embeddedness within society. In addition, at the individual level, the principle of *managerial discretion* states that managers are moral actors. Within every field of corporate social responsibility, they are obliged to exercise such discretion as is available to them, toward socially responsible outcomes. This principle is not limited to corporate philanthropy or community involvement, but covers the entire area of managerial actions. It is very important to accentuate this principle in the case of Serbia, in fact, in Serbian corporate law the manager is a leader in the strong sense. In addition, this position of manager is in line with the earlier tradition. Without any exaggeration we could say that his/her discretion power and impact on the corporation practice is enormous. Accordingly, any reflection on the corporate responsibility in Serbia should begin with the elucidation of the manager's responsibility in relation to the social embeddedness of the corporation.

In order to avoid the empty normativity it is always indispensable to interpret the apparent contextual dimensions of CSR that are to be detected as the starting point of further reconsideration. Above all my interpretation stresses the ambiguous character of the meaning of CSR in Serbia. This article covers matters as diverse as law and government, corruption-practices, war, and so on. Some trends are simply ignored and others dealt with rather summarily. The purpose is to shed light on the complex social processes in and through which specific institutional orders and their broader social preconditions are structured in Serbia.

The Socio-Economic Context of CSR

The case of Serbia *does not fit into the continuum* of the Central and East European countries. In the 1990s it was exposed to the war, war-like situations, even to bombing by the NATO alliance. Due to its war politics Serbia was strongly sanctioned by the economical and political measures of the UN (Yugoslav Federal Government, 1995). Even more decisive was that the "uncreative destruction" of the regime formed an unprecedented economic disorder, financial chaos with hyperinflation, inflationary financing of the economy, disinvestments as the main forms of economising, subordination of the business criteria to the political cycles, spontaneous insider privatisation governed by crude force, and widespread political rent-seeking activities. The economic hardship and the tendencies of impoverishment are connected to the deep cynicism and insecurity in the field of personal economic interests. The sources of public authority are eroded. The war as the domain for robbery and production of capital maintained the state of diffusion of violence (Bolcic, 1999a, 1999b; Lazic, 1999; Pusic et al., 2001).

In response to the absence of stable formal rules, individuals in Serbia have invoked in their business practices certain informal[1] networks: paying bribes that break rules, creating informal social networks to compensate for organisational failure. It is clear that this practice has clear ethical connotation; actually, it produced forms of "business" that made ethical norms redundant, and has minimised the demand for responsible practice. Furthermore, business is treated as sheer survival in the system that makes public morality extremely fragile. The significance of this moment is far-reaching; it concerns the fundamental dimensions of the perception of business in Serbia. Recalling and paraphrasing Hirschmann's well-known scheme, business was interpreted as the *exit* option from formal employment, and formal law-based rules. In fact, formal employment was conjured up as insurance on the minimal level of existence and business appeared to be something radically informal and overembedded in corruption as the form of life (Rose-Ackermann, 1999; Vukotic et al., 2000; Colombatto, 2003). Besides, the constellation opened the door for low-level equilibrium between a distorted market and failed authoritarian democracy.

To sum up shortly the key consequences:

- Serbia had the legacy of the most liberalised ex-communist country, namely, the legacy of Yugoslavia and different experiences from the other countries of transition. At this point, however, it is important to note that the citizens of Serbia have been involved in the repeatedly failing transformation to the market-like economy. One may contrast the legacy of distinctiveness in Serbia to Hirschman's treatment of disappointment as a central element of human experience.

- The war-like situations have led to the perception of business as the collective exit option from formal networks. The informal business world[2] is not to be equated with the illegal economy. At the border of the illegal and legal economy there are multifaceted forms of economising, non-market transactions, *coincident forms* of mutuality, corruption, and trusts that make opportunity for informal practice.

- Noncriminal exit forms in relation to business have had a stabilising effect on individuals in the short term.

- The case of Serbia has demonstrated the coexistence of exit and voice-options. The degree of this interdependence between the exit and voice-options is to be depicted.

- There was a negative social return due to the spreading of the informal networks. The economic and moral crisis did not accelerate the collapse of social capital, but it contributed to the reorganisation of social capital in accordance with the different trust-entities which emerged. The origin of this trust could be located in the field between the people who are interconnected, and bound by the inclusion into the economic grievances (Knack & Keefer, 1999; Paldam & Svendsen, 2002).

After the political breakthrough in 2000 a complex task emerged: to provide both the ethical basis and the stability of the community. The pursuit of reform generated many demands. The orientation toward the future required the ethical overcoming of the legacy of the past loaded with unethical aspects. There were connections between the criminalised economic activities and the moral crisis of society. In addition there are still real obstacles owing to the unequal distribution of resources held by war-makers and the uneven incidence of opportunities for collective action (for the long-term unemployed, small businessmen etc.). There are various factors that serve to limit the reform agenda and define certain issues as lying beyond the scope of government action and democratic accountability. The strategy of the government was committed to the pragmatic legitimising of the speed of structural adjustments in Serbia and it neglected and subordinated the need for ethical reflection on the past.

The context of business in Serbia is constantly loaded with two features: the perpetuation of high *uncertainty* and *weak institutions*. The weaker the institution, the greater the diversity of possible response and the higher the uncertainty with regard to expected outcomes. The problem of Serbia and its business agents is that there are still institutions and practice of odd transitions. The newly introduced market mechanisms are weak. Institutional weaknesses lead to (oligopolistic) competitions between a few producers of institutions and could not prevent organised fraud and bribery. The forms of social capital which proved to be successful for business as an exit during the previous period appear to be the hindrance for the completion of reforms. Hence, we encounter conflict between formal and informal institutions, e.g. formal rules that intend to prescribe rule-bound practice, and informal rules that prohibit doing so and instead prescribe to protect wrongdoers.

It is essential to observe the social profile of the entrepreneurs. In accordance with the results of a research (Bolcic, 1999b) there is a strong continuity with the beginning of the 1990s. The people turned out to be the entrepreneurs in line with their deprofessionalisation. They are in fact forced to be entrepreneurs due to unemployment, so they are forced-entrepreneurs. In addition, the qualification structure of entrepreneurs is lower than in other countries of transition.

At this point, we cannot avoid the short recourse to the often mentioned problem of corruption. To summarise the current dimensions of corruption:

- After the political turning point the new government set in motion anti-corruption measures, but it is not to be ignored that overembeddedness in earlier corruption has generated negative social learning.

- There is a recurrent contradiction between the publicly expressed negative evaluation of corruption and the willingness to take part in the corruption. Many people accept merit-based distribution of income and view education as a legitimate basis for social differentiation. However, they accept the corruption-like practices as the device for the solution of their problems.

- The "overadaptation" (actually, adaptation deficits) to the practice in the previous regime led to the change of the informal rules of the game, and generalised the unsuitable practice. The above-mentioned answers demonstrated that the transition from high corruption to low corruption is sometimes very costly for individuals, and the path-dependences are at work, which means that the interconnection between the demand and supply of bribe/corruption produces a vicious circle.

At the end of this part let us examine, what is expected from the business, taking into account the contextual dimensions and the business-narratives during the 1990s.

The answer to this question has to be *ambiguous*. *On the one hand* business is confirmed as an enabling practice that contributes to the enhancement of the capabilities of people. In so far business opens the door to "normal life", economic freedom and interest-led particular enterprises. In accordance with the research, some entrepreneurs can be endorsed as leaders of reforms (Pusic et. al., 2001). In this way, business serves as a tool for overcoming the loaded and embarrassing past and it entails the potentialities for changing life. *On the other hand* there is doubt concerning certain forms of business that casts shadows on business in general. We should not neglect the scepticism that business people take action in the *social sphere* operationally defined as performing for the common good. It is unfeasible, for instance, to ignore the experiences in the nineties when most national company leaders were deeply involved in the corruption-led political regime and practiced irresponsible codes. Having in mind that there is a continuity in the personnel structures of such an important field as financial business, the caution amongst people is understandable.

The Potentialities of Societal Drivers of CSR

Government in the Framework of CSR

When the government launched market reform, it needed to legitimise reform policies among the agents of the state and to intervene to create the institutional framework of the economy. The main reason is that trust in economic exchange could not be sustained without the availability of third-party and impartial enforcement by the state. Hence, trust among anonymous individuals should be a function of the *moral predispositions of citizens* and their social experiences as expression of their trust in government institutions.

However, the burden of government in Serbia is manifold. The people whom the state relied upon to serve in the implementation of reform policies were regularly the source of the state's difficulties. Many operational units were involved deeply in pursuit of private gain by drawing on their positions in networks that gave them privileged access to both public and private resources. Actually, government officials have few incentives to provide efficient third-party enforcement, if they remain members of the previous networks preserved for the purpose of rent-seeking.

Despite the efforts of the new government agencies the previous business-like arrangements and networks may play the role of a protective club in relation to the new entrants. The government did not succeed in enacting the anti-monopoly law for securing a relatively predictable business environment. It is subordinated to the predatory strategies of the powerful oligarchic groups and this faces us with the standard question of the post-communist countries as to how to liberate the state captured by different groups (Hellman et al., 2000; Bruszt, 2002).

The government is overembedded in the informal social capital from the previous regime that reduces the capacity of government to enact the formal rule-bound practice of business. The weak government compensates its deficiencies by concrete interventions at the cost of its qualitative aspects; therefore, the previous forms of informal social capital have been transformed, but in order to make themselves fit into the new, changed business surroundings (Dasgupta & Serageldin, 1999; Schneider & Enste, 2000; Glaeser, Laibson & Sacerdote, 2002).

Quite clearly, there is a legitimate role for government in the area of urging the thinking on CSR (Rothstein, 1998; Nelson & Zadek, 1999; Nee, 2000; Roddick, 2000). However, the government agencies dealing with the accomplishment of privatisation in Serbia have largely abdicated from this sphere. The government has implemented the so-called council for the detecting of the corruption-related problems that occupies scientists, lawyers and other reputable people. But, there is a frequent discussion on the competences of this council and a lot of confusion of consequences of its reporting on the subject. One possible future path is to discuss these reports widely and to conceptualise it as the momentum for a broadened discussion on CSR. There is a widespread belief in the public concerning the lack of incentives of government officials to rely on formal institutions which would facilitate the emergence of extended trust in formal networks and public officials. The earlier trust within informal networks contributes to the sluggishness of the stabilising of formal networks and impersonal rule-bound practice. Actually, the earlier trusts within informal networks are going to be weak ties.

NGOs and Other Institutions

There is little doubt that civil engagement has not taken deep root in Serbia and the weak interest-groups failed to articulate their interests. Also, the authoritarian patterns abate the readiness for civil engagement and the absence of mediating agencies makes it difficult to translate social capital into collective action.

Nowadays, the number of NGOs is increasing; however they are not as active in the business ethics area. Throughout the nineties the reigning political elites put their executors and beneficiaries in civil society to gain international support, and to expand the discursive power of the regime. The parties were the channels of transfer from the NGO-elite to the government elite. For example, one of the influential political parties (the so called G-17) arose from the earlier NGO and established an institute with scientific and think-thank ambitions at the same time. It demonstrated a certain interest in the promotion of business ethics and CSR. Namely, last year in collaboration with the Belgrade Chamber of Economy it arranged a roundtable on the social responsibility of firms in Serbia calling for a rapid implementation of the ethical codes in firms. The ethical codes in the light of social responsibility are mentioned as the main condition for attracting the investors. This rhetoric could be described as a departure from the interpretative practice in Serbia, since we can report on the articulation of corporative governance, but without the aspiration to explain the ethical dimensions of it. Also, there have been intensive discussions recently on the ethics in media that consider CSR in this sphere (Ekonomist, 2004: 49). In addition, there are certain signs of orientation towards clarifying the conditions of social dialogue amongst workers, trade unions and firms with reference to the social responsibility of economic agents (Mihajlovic, 2002; European Movement Serbia and Center for Economic Development, 2003).

Firms

It is necessary to regard the dialectics of endogenous and exogenous dimensions (Falcetti, Sanfey & Taci, 2003). To do so, we could consider the difference between the corporate transnational firms in Serbia such as British Tobacco, Henkel-Merima, Raiffeisen Bank, or Lafarge and the small and medium sized Serbian firms. It seems that the public rhetoric of the transnationals and the public corporations bring into light the need to meet social demands. For example, the already mentioned Lafarge as the bearer of the most successful privatisation process (Ekonomist, 2003) pointed out the importance of its own ecological investment that is not based on profit. This type of rhetoric is quite missing in national companies. But this evidence is too fragile to conclude that the multinationals take the "leaders game" concerning CSR.

The national firms practice communicative silence on social demands and it is very hard to get insight into the form of their embeddedness in broader society. If we accept this line of reasoning it is obvious that transnational corporations have great responsibility for universalising some ethical issues and initialising the learning process of ethical arrangements. In terms of corporate responsibility, common issues such as labour integration, social investment strategies, lifelong learning for the workforce, gender and ethnic minority representation and participation in decision-making face all industries and sectors in varying degrees.

Taking into account *the strong position of managers in the Serbian corporation law* and during the ongoing privatisation there are valuable views on the management's arrangement in light of its relationships towards workers. In reality there is a current consideration of the preparedness of managements to learn from the different traditions and on their competencies to employees as potential stakeholders.

Religion

It is to be mentioned that the religious institutions demonstrate communicative silence on moral values in business and it is very problematic to speculate upon their readiness to take part in articulating CSR. Naturally, we should bear in mind that there are different religions and traditions in Serbia with diverse, often conflicting historical narratives, and that the cultural context could not be regarded as a single-channel, or as a homogeneous entity, but as a complex entity. This is not the only root of the mentioned silence; more significant is the undefined and contradictory relationship of the major church ("pravoslav") towards the values and bounded social norms of the modern market society. It recognises the loosening societal bonds, the lack of the cohesive ties, but is not preoccupied with the modernisation processes and the repositioning of business. For this reason, it is very difficult to refer to the tradition as the source of business values; it is very likely that there is a *tension* between the meanings of tradition and the readiness to articulate CSR.

Academy

One academic field that is of indirect relevance for the CSR research is sociology of work that is highly developed in Serbia. The reason for its significance lies in the fact that this discipline treats problems that are often hidden for the business experts, for instance, those regarding the relevant knowledge on determinants of work, the global system, culture and technology. There is a very weak discipline of business ethics that is not represented in the academic sphere but appears as fragmented in the education sphere invented by certain NGOs dealing with the problems of the engagement of women in business or of the chances of small and medium sized business for the employment structure. I observe some opportunities in the field of private universities, since some privatised universities have introduced this subject into their curriculum. The state-owned universities up to this moment are sceptical towards new, alternative thoughts in business and remain in the context of the exclusive profit-centered view. As a result there are quite few articles on the subject of business ethics and CSR.

Conclusion

At this moment CSR is to be located within the *unfinished transition* process. There is a lack of stable rule-based context for the sophisticated and far-reaching interpretation of CSR. Consistent with the fact of the postponed transition and sticky institutions in Serbia it is of importance to situate CSR in the perspective of forming and completing the socio-economic transformation. Instead of speculating on the speed and the ideal type of privatisation we should concentrate on the development of an appropriate institutional framework, and well-enforced rule. Fundamental changes by altering norms were the most important source of institutional change, which subsequently created incentives to construct more efficient institutions. To summarise: *this means that the dynamics of CSR in Europe could make a great impact on the interpretation practice in Serbia.* This leads to the conclusion that CSR sensitiveness is intermingled with endogenous and exogenous tendencies.

In Serbia we can report on the prevalence of informal bonding social capital over bridging formal social capital. There are negative impacts of social capital manifested in powerful social groups, which are not accountable to citizens at large. The case of Serbia demonstrated that the decline of trust and the weak norms of civic cooperation are demanding in countries with the lack of formal institutions that effectively protect property and contract rights.

Most businesses in Serbia are focused primarily on avoiding short-term reputation-related risks, making very small expenditures as an extension of their traditional corporate philanthropy, or merely re-branding good business practices (e.g. engaged and sensitive human resources management). These practices should be welcomed, since they can and do make a difference to people's lives and might support overall good business performance. Thus, the "business case" cannot be expected to deliver when the short-term demands of the stock market provide perverse incentives for not addressing sustainability. *This means that corporate responsibility in relation to the situation in Serbia is in the phase of the so-called first generation of social responsibility.* CSR in the "strong" sense goes beyond this low-level business case to the "second generation" of corporate responsibility. For these companies, corporate responsibility is becoming more closely integrated into key aspects of their business strategy and practice.

The real assessment is that Serbia is exposed to the *leadership vacuum* in relation to the cultural drive of CSR. Some initiatives could come from the EU and the subsequent measures of the European Commission and from international organisations (such as European Foundation for the Improvement of Living and Working Conditions), particularly from the United Nations with its measures in developing an increasing support for CSR.

Notes

[1] Using the notion of informality I accept the definition that informal institutions produce at the same time constraints and opportunities.

[2] During 2003 the government has organised a meeting with the most influential business-men in the country dealing, for example, with the privatisation processes. It was very symp-tomatic that a lot of agents who took part in this meeting were powerful in the collapsed Miloshevich regime. *Given the reality of these imperfections it is very difficult to recognise the national bearers of CSR, and it is unnecessary to mitigate the extreme intricacy of the implementation of adjustment in relation to this issue.*

References

Barclay, J., & Smith, K. 2003. Business Ethics and the Transitional Economy: A Tale of Two Modernities. *Journal of Business Ethics,* 47: 315–325.

Birch, D. 2003. Corporate Social Responsibility: Some Key Theoretical Issues and Con-cepts for New Ways of Doing Business. *Journal of New Business Ideas and Trends,* 1(1):1–19.

Bolcic, S. 1999a. O univerzalnosti i kulturalnim posebnostima poslovnih strategija i struk-tura savremenih preduzeća (On Universalism and Cultural Specificity of Strategies and Structures of Contemporary Enterprises). *Balkan Forum,* 2: 221–240.

Bolcic, S. 1999b. Civil Performance in a Pauperized Society. In: D. Skenderovic Cuk, & M. Podunavac (Eds.), *Civil Society in the Countries in Transition*: 197–215. Subotica: Center-Agency of Local Democracy.

Bruszt, L. 2002. Market Making as State Making: Constitutions and Economic Develop-ment in Post-communist Eastern Europe. *Constitutional Political Economy,* 13: 53–72.

Dasgupta, P., & Serageldin, I. (Eds.). 1999. *Social Capital: A Multifaceted Perspective.* Washington, DC: World Bank.

Colombatto, E. 2003. Why is Corruption Tolerated? *The Review of Austrian Economics,* 16: 363–379.

EBRD. 2001. *Transition report update.* London.

EBRD. 2002. *Transition Report 2002.* London.

Ekonomist. 2003. Dobre promene (Good Changes). July 7: 22–23.

Ekonomist. 2004. Etika u medijima (Ethics in the Media). March 8: 49–57.

European Movement Serbia and Center for Economic Development. 2003. *Towards Stabil-ity and Prosperity, Social Dialogue in Serbia and Bulgaria: Comparative Experiences of Two Southeast-European Countries.* Unpublished report: http://www.emins.org. ac-cessed 28.08.2004.

Falcetti, E., Sanfey, P., & Taci, A. 2003. *Bridging the gaps? Private sector development, capital flows and the investment climate in south-eastern Europe.* EBRD Working Paper, No. 80.

Glaeser, E. L., Laibson, D., & Sacerdote, B. 2002. An Economic Approach to Social Capital. *The Economic Journal*, 112: 437 – 58.

Greenfield, W. 2004. In the name of corporate social responsibility. *Business Horizons* 47(1): 19 – 28.

Hellman, J. I., et al. 2000. *Measuring governance and state capture: the role of bureaucrats and firms in shaping the business environment. Results of a Firm-level study across 20 transition economies.* EBRD Working Paper, No. 51.

Kingston, W. 2000. A Spectre is Haunting the World – The Spectre of Global Capitalism. *Journal of Evolutionary Economics,* 10: 83 – 108.

Knack, S., & Keefer, P. 1997. Does social capital have an economic payoff? A cross-country investigation. *The Quarterly Journal of Economics,* 112: 1253 – 1288.

Lazic, M. 1999. Social presumption for the Development of civil society in F. R.Yugoslavia. In: N. Skenderovic Cuk & M. Podunavac (Eds.), *Civil Society in the Countries in Transition*: 171 – 195. Subotica: Center-Agency of Local Democracy

McWilliams, A., & Siegel, D. 2001. Corporate Social Responsibility: A Theory of the Firm Perspective. *Academy of Management Review*, 1: 117 – 127.

Manokha, I. 2004. Corporate Social Responsibility: A New Signifier? An Analysis of Business Ethics and Good Business Practice. *Politics*, 24(1): 56 – 64.

Mihajlovic, S. 2002. *Gradani u susret institucijama tranzicije* (The Citizens and the institutions of transition). Belgrade: Center for Policy Alternatives Working paper.

Nee V. 2000. The Role of the State in making a Market Economy. *Journal of Institutional and Theoretical Economics,* 156: 64 – 88.

Nelson, J., & Zadek, S. 1999. *Partnership Alchemy: New Social Partnerships in Europe.* Copenhagen: The Copenhagen Centre.

Paldam, M., & Svendsen, G. T. 2002. *Trust, Social Capital and Economic Growth: An International Comparison.* Cheltenham, UK: Edward Elgar.

Pusic, Lj. et al. 2001. *Preduzetnici i grad* (Entrepreneurs and the City). Novi Sad: SAS & Centar za socioloska istrazivanja.

Roddick, A. 2000. *Business as Usual.* London: Thorsons.

Rose-Ackerman, S.1999. *Corruption and Government – Causes, Consequences, and Reform.* Cambridge: Cambridge University Press.

Rothstein, B. 1998. *Just Institutions Matter: The Moral and Political Logic of the Universal Welfare State*. Cambridge: Cambridge University Press.

Schneider, F., & Enste, D. H. 2000. Shadow Economies: Size, Causes, and Consequences. *Journal of Economic Literature,* 38: 77 – 114.

Skenderovic Cuk, N., & Podunavac, M. (Eds.). 1999. *Civil Society in the Countries in Transition,* Subotica: Center-Agency of Local Democracy.

Yugoslav Federal Government. 1995. Causes of Black Economy and Factors Promoting its Expansion. *Yugoslav Survey*, 1: 85 – 94.

Vukotic, V. et al. 2000. *Sistem i korupcija* (System and corruption). Beograd: IDN.

Southern Europe

19 Social Responsibility in a State-Dependent Business System

Melsa Ararat

Introduction

This contribution summarises the roles of economy, state and society in Turkey with respect to society's attitude toward business and attempts to explore how cultural characteristics of society may have an impact on CSR. We argue that the cultural characteristics combined with the economic fundamentals of Turkey do not encourage socially responsible behaviour of corporations beyond legal requirements and only to the extent that they are enforced. We conclude that the drivers for Corporate Social Responsibility in Turkey will be exogenous and institutional rather than endogenous and cultural.

Background

Turkey is frequently described as a country of conflicts or a country of dualities. Economic and historical factors combined with its unique geography cause duality and diversity in economic, social and cultural dimensions. This duality manifests itself in business with the existence of two segments with different behavioural patterns as we will explain later in this paper.

After the establishment of the Turkish Republic in 1923, especially from the early 1930s onwards, a strong emphasis has been placed on the role of the state in economic development. Until 1945, the state was the major economic player and subsidised the development of the private sector. Although state involvement in the economy continued throughout the history of Turkey, the fledgling private sector eventually came of age and market economy institutions acquired a new dynamism due to a new wave of pro-market policies in the 1980s – which started with the liberalisation reforms (Ararat & Ugur, 2003).

Turkey's declared foreign policy focus since the mid-1980s has been the achievement of full EU membership. In its long march for integration with Europe, following decades of chronic inflation and economic crises, Turkey made substantial improvements during the past 5 years to achieve macroeconomic stability by restructuring the financial industry, implementing a tight fiscal policy, dramatically reducing its inflation, deregulating the monopolised sectors and generally reducing the role of the state in the economy. Despite the improvements, Turkey needs accelerated entry of foreign capital to reach its potential growth rate of 7–8% to close the gap with EU in income levels. In their Turkey update of 25th June 2002, Morgan Stanley estimates that EU membership may enable the Turkish economy to attract annual FDI flows of over US$ 10 billion by 2015. This estimate is based on a conservative assumption of attracting net FDI flows of 2.2% of GDP (Morgan Stanley Web-site, www.morganstanley.com).

According to UNCTAD's 2001 World Investment Report (UNCTAD, 2001) Turkey has an inward FDI index of lower than 1, indicating that its ability to attract investors is below the level implied by its "economic fundamentals". This historical and remarkable underperformance is closely related to investor and analyst *perceptions* of Turkey's governance framework as well as its wider political environment. The most important legal and judicial constraints relate to insufficient clarity and respect for the rule of law. Part of the explanation for this underperformance can be seen in a report by PriceWaterhouseCoopers (2001), which ranks Turkey as the fourth least transparent country in the world. Their estimate of the impact of opacity in terms of lost FDI is $1.8 billion per year. Again, a research on 188 companies places Turkey at the bottom of the ranking with respect to board oversight and transparency and second from the bottom with respect to shareholder rights (McKinsey Global Institute, 2003). *Perception* issues of a similar nature are reflected in Transparency International's Corruption Perception Index (Transparency International, 2001, 2002). Turkey ranks 54th among 91 countries in 2001 and a worse 64th among 102 countries in 2002 in transparency. Turkey is perceived to be more corrupt than Chile, Malaysia, Poland and Morocco, and better than Argentina, India, Russia and Indonesia. Whether the perceptions reflect the comparative reality or not, opacity and corruption are related to the role of the Turkish state in the economy and the way it interacts with business. Turkey has been typified as an example of a state dependent business system (Whitley, 1994).

The Role of the State

According to Ararat and Ugur (2003), "the state's heavy involvement in the economy has led to two undesirable consequences. On the one hand, it fostered a political culture in which the legitimacy of the state is a function of the "rents" that the government could distribute rather than its ability to provide "public goods" such as a stable macroeconomic environment, a transparent regulatory system, and social conflict resolution mechanisms, etc. On the other hand, the state's heavy involvement increased "private risks". Therefore, it induced private economic agents to pressure the government of the day to compensate at least part of their risks – irrespective of whether or not such risks have been due to government action or the private actors' own actions. This second tendency combined with the first led to persistent favouritism, corruption practices, opacity, etc. – all of which have their own path dependencies" (Ugur, 1999: chapter 3). In 2003 the Ankara Chamber of Commerce and Industry estimated that bribery adds 15% to contract prices in Turkey. Similarly the World Bank estimates that lack of transparency in public procurement costs 16% of GDP to Turkey. Resistance to let go of the private benefits driven from this opacity slows the deregulation/privatisation process. Corrupt practices exacerbate the difficulties in tax collection, slow down the fight against bribery to circumvent regulations, and nurture the informal sector, which is estimated to be as large as the formal. One of the multipliers of this problem is the existence of a powerful and highly monopolised media with strong political and commercial affiliations.

The Role of Business

Perhaps because of the special circumstances behind the development of the private sector in Turkey, entrepreneurs have always been almost apologetic about their wealth and felt unconfident about the legitimacy of their ventures (Bugra, 1994). This psychology materialises in a strong discourse of social purpose and value of private enterprise. Hence shareholder value is a weakly emphasised concept for Turkey. Highly concentrated family ownership does not help to mitigate the timidity about shareholder value. As one of the strongest business organisations in Europe, the Turkish Businessmen and Industrialists Association (TUSIAD), follows suit with a mission not to protect the interests of its member companies but to establish the social role of Turkish private enterprise. Consequentially corporate philanthropy is strong in Turkey; most companies that are organised in business groups (diversified conglomerates) have provisions in their by-laws to donate a percentage of their net profits to foundations set up by their founding families. The drivers behind this phenomenon can be related to the need for gaining legitimacy and social acceptance for relatively new wealth, in a country where duality in income levels is disturbing. Yet there is no evidence that Turkish companies or society at large appreciate corporate social responsibility. The fact that Turkish companies do not incorporate any dimensions of CSR into their operations may be attributed to this attitude. We will try to explore later the possible impact of cultural characteristics of Turkey on corporate behaviour.

Turkey is going through a major transformation. Despite initial scepticism due to its Islamic roots, the ruling party is establishing its legitimacy based on both the economic recovery Turkey is enjoying as the outcome of an IMF backed restructuring programme, and its carefully formulated discourse on participative democracy, anti-corruption, human rights, the importance of NGOs etc. In a nutshell, the state's (including the military's) dominant role in economic and political scene is being gradually balanced with that of the private sector and civil society, a process driven primarily by the desire to meet the Copenhagen criteria that Turkey must meet before accession negotiations can start with the European Union.

The Role of Society

Corporate behaviour is eventually based on decisions made by management (leadership) whose judgments are influenced by the values driven from the societal and the organisational culture. In a global study conducted in 2001 by Environics International (www.environics.com), it is found that Turkish consumers value business ethics, labour practices, environmental impacts and demonstrated social responsibility much less than brand quality when forming an impression of a company. The same study also found that in low to mid income level countries, companies are considered socially responsible based on reasons which are not CSR-related. The study notes that although the level of education has an influence on the public's expectations of corporations; society predominantly expects economic performance (jobs) from the business in those countries and, consistent with the findings, in Turkey.

After experiencing three military coup d'etats in 20 years (1960, 1970 and 1980), Turkey has been deprived of strong civil society initiatives. This had a negative effect on the development of civic involvement initiatives. Most of the 750,000 civil society organisations have been distanced from their purpose and serve as social clubs. On the other hand it is important to note the differences between civil society organisations headquartered in Istanbul and those in Anatolia. Most of the surviving organisations in Istanbul are funded by big businesses and there is an upsurge in organisations focusing on economic and environmental issues in Istanbul. Anatolian organisations seem to have a more political orientation, but they lack experience and funding. Considering this imbalance, the Civil Society Development Programme funded by EC (www.stgp.org) aims to support NGOs located outside Istanbul. Despite all the vitality observed in the NGO movement in the recent past, the current legislative system reflects the authoritarian character of the state and imposes many limitations on civil society organisations. It has been common practice for the state to prosecute board members of Civil Society Organisations for "threatening the indivisible integrity of the state and the nation" arguably evidenced by their speeches or press releases.

Limitations imposed upon civil society organisations coupled with a highly monopolised media and the tradition of opacity exacerbate the information asymmetry between society on the one hand and the state and the private sector on the other.

Cultural Drivers of CSR and Their Importance

The cultural drivers for CSR (or any behavioural aspect of corporations) can be explored from institutional or cultural perspectives. Some cross cultural researchers describe culture as the collective mental programming of the people. Culture underpinned by values has a broad influence on organisational behaviour and action (Hofstede, 1980). On the other hand, organisations with their own values and beliefs also represent collectives leading to behavioural patterns, while globalisation perpetuates universalism of leadership behaviour and leads to standardisation of management practices (House, Wright & Aditya, 1997). Therefore understanding the effect of culture on corporate behaviour requires an understanding of societal culture, organisational culture which would be influenced by societal culture, and the degree of influence of globalisation in inducing universal values.

In his renowned attempt to cluster the countries, Hofstede (1983) identified four dimensions that distinguish societal cultures such as power distance, uncertainty avoidance, individualism/collectivism, and masculinity. Additionally, value dimensions such as paternalism, abstractive versus associative thinking are proposed by various scholars and furthermore, developed and developing countries are differentiated (Adler & Boyacigiller, 1995).

Turkey represents large power distance, low individualism, strong uncertainty avoidance and low masculinity (Hofstede, 1980). According to Schwartz (1994) Turkey ranked above average in values of conservatism, hierarchy, egalitarian commitment and harmony. A recent study on the Turkish culture was conducted as a part of GLOBE study which revealed in–group collectivism and power distance as two predominant characteristics of Turkey among 62 cultures surveyed (Kabasakal & Bodur, 1998). Turkey ranks below average on gender egalitarianism (56th), uncertainty avoidance (49th), performance orientation (45th), societal collectivism (42nd), humane orientation (37th), and future orientation (36th), whereas it ranks higher in terms of in-group collectivism (4th), power distance (10th) and assertiveness (12th).

Kabasakal and Dastmalchian (2001), based on their study of Middle Eastern countries for Project GLOBE, note the similarities in positioning of Turkey to that of Iran, Kuwait and Qatar but also draw attention to the role of the Turkish state's secular construction to possibly account for the differences. Future orientation which is tested as a cultural variable in the study is related to having long-term perspectives in society and hence to the commitment of society to sustainability. All four countries scored below the world average in future orientation. Kabasakal and Dalmachian explain this low score with the concept of "fate" in Islam and note that it is a factor negatively influencing future orientation of societies and demonstrating itself as acceptance of all conduct as coming from God. On the other hand the Koran also explains the importance of a human being's responsibility and choice. Therefore one may argue that chronic economic instability and associated unpredictability may be the reasons behind a low score for future orientation.

Kabasakal and Bodur (1998) also found Turkish organisations to be significantly more future-oriented than Turkish society at large. They argued that this may be due to the necessities of the task and higher education levels. Although society is not future-oriented, leaders are expected to be "visionaries" and demonstrate future orientation according to the same study.

Undoubtedly leadership behaviour is one of the determinants of corporate behaviour. Paternalism is considered to be a distinctively common attribute of leadership in developing countries by many scholars. Dilber (1967) describes Turkish industrial leaders as authoritarian paternal rather than benevolent paternal, where authoritarian paternalism includes emphasis on duty and lacks generosity on the part of the superior, and benevolent paternalism emphasises loyalty to the superior and the superior's generosity for the subordinates. This may be changing however; recently, Fikret-Pasa found that culture-specific behaviours of "granted authority" and "sharing the responsibility" of the followers in Turkey were more dominant relative to the universal influence behaviours of rationalising, legitimising, pressure-control and exchange indicating some move towards benevolent paternal behaviour (Fikret-Pasa, Kabasakal & Bodur, 2001).

Among the studies of culture-specific leader attributes, "consultation" and "participation" require further attention as they are related to the democratic traditions. Pasa, Kabasakal and Bodur (2001) found that leaders in Turkey use participation to induce feelings of belonging to the group rather than to get consensus or improve the quality of the decisions. Islam may play a role in this aspect of leadership since Ozen (1998) found that consultation emerges as a dominant leader attribute in a Turkish organisation which is known to have Islamic values. Abdalla and Al-Hamoud (2001) note the importance of consultation in Islamic tribal societies as it is strongly recommended by the Koran. This is evidenced by the ruling Justice and Development Party's demonstrated willingness to consult with important stakeholders to reach a consensus in important policy matters, which may partially be associated with the Islamic values they hold.

Overall, several studies on societal culture point out that the most dominant characteristic of Turkish societal culture is in-group collectivism. Fikret-Pasa, Kabasakal and Bodur (2001) conclude that a leader in the Turkish context emerges as a parent who takes care of the followers' feelings of belonging to the family. One manifestation of this is the "regionalism" fed by local businesses in Turkey. Local businesses seek competitive advantage and legitimacy by being involved in and financing community activities (e.g. funding the local soccer team). Regionalism on the other hand can also feed the relationship of oligopolistic collusion between political power and business, negatively affecting corporate accountability.

Drivers of CSR

What is the effect of all this on CSR? I would argue that it is not positive. Low future orientation, low societal collectivism and low humane orientation combined with the authoritarian orientation of the leaders are difficult to relate to CSR. This is demonstrated in low ethical and legal social responsibility performance of the corporations in Turkey. This is not a contradiction to the existence of strong philanthropy, as philanthropy usually strips social responsibility from its organisational context and frequently disassociates it from corporate strategy. All these factors suggest that in the short term the real drivers for CSR would be institutional and exogenous.

Ascigil (2004), in her unpublished survey conducted for TESEV explored management attitudes towards CSR in Turkey. Using Caroll's (1979) and Aupperle's (1984) contextualised questionnaires, Ascigil found that 75 % of the managers included in the survey give priority to economic criteria when making decisions whereas 19.1 % give priority to ethical criteria and only 6 % to legal criteria. Ascigil notes that Turkish managers do not differentiate between legal and ethical responsibilities as evidenced by the structural analysis of the responses. Furthermore, the study shows that customers are considered to be the most important stakeholders by 75.8 % of the managers, employees being the second by 50.8 % and the society at large by only 24.3 %. According to the same survey, 53.5 % of the managers would not give priority to ethical considerations if these would negatively impact economic performance. "Quality" and "Customers" are the most frequently used concepts in companies' mission statements by 61.5 %. "Society" is mentioned in only 22.1 % of the statements whereas "Profitability" is mentioned only in 3.3 %. This may be related to the timidity about wealth and concerns about legitimacy of business. Ascigil notes that the mere existence of a mission statement positively affects the management attitudes towards CSR and that awareness of CSR increases with post-graduate education and with the increased share of foreign capital. She further notes that 49.7 % of the managers consider themselves as reactive with respect to CSR issues, 13.6 % totally ignore the concept and 33.5 % believe that they handle CSR as a strategic matter. She concludes that CSR in Turkey has not moved beyond a Public Relations matter in Turkish companies.

Considering the fact that most of the institutional driving forces for CSR, including the legal framework and market mechanisms, are not sufficiently developed, and variables for non-market institutions such as NGO activity and academic research and teaching are not yet mature enough, we may conclude that the role of international drivers is becoming more important.

Improvements in laws and regulations and their enforcement in an attempt to harmonise with international developments, introduction of better practices, if not best, by global companies, pressures from global NGOs and multilateral organisations and initiatives driven by rational choices are currently driving CSR in Turkey.

In fact, a survey conducted by the Turkish Ethical Values Centre (TEDMER) reveals that 35% of the sample group observed unethical behaviour at work. Most respondents considered fraud, tax avoidance, bribing and discriminations as important ethical issues whereas disclosure quality in informing the public, protecting the environment, valuing diverse opinions and keeping legal records and reports were less important. 57% of the respondents thought that organisations face unfair competition because of being ethical. 92.6% of the respondents believed that a reconstruction of state and government would be necessary for ethics to be settled. This is comparable to 92.3% who believe economic development would be the necessary precondition. 67.9% of the respondents considered the increased existence of international firms as a very important factor in improving ethics in Turkey (www.tedmer.org).

The decision to commit to an ethical code or rules of business conduct can be understood as an irreversible investment decision under uncertainty in which the firm chooses to give up on certain future options. For a profit-maximising firm, these costs must be offset against benefits and costs committed in case of non-compliance (Thomsen, 2001). It will be in the interest of the profit-maximising firm to signal commitment to principles and values which are not associated with economic benefits directly, only if the signalling costs are small and ethical appearance is perceived to have a positive financial effect (Harrington, 1989). We argue that achieving economic and political stability may activate the drivers for CSR and induce socially responsible behaviour beyond philanthropy. Indeed, with the lowest inflation for more than three decades and a government apparently committed to macro-economic stability, companies are becoming more confident about the future as evidenced by the recent press releases about adaptation of a Code of Ethics by Turkish companies.

The current restructuring programme, recent improvements in the financial audit and accounting standards, the government's promise to focus on eliminating the unregistered economy next year, the establishment of a banking regulatory agency which improved monitoring capacity substantially, and any potential improvements in enforcement mechanisms including a technical infrastructure to monitor and detect capital markets fraud, will be the real drivers of change.

Quality Movement

An important organisational variable which may be exploited as a driver of CSR in Turkey is quality. Turkey has a strong quality tradition thanks to the long established efforts of the Turkish Quality Association as evidenced by the word "quality" being the most frequently appearing concept in mission statements of Turkish companies (Ascigil, 2004). The total quality concept is based on ethics. The growing attention to ethics fits very well in the evolution of thinking on quality. The new EFQM (European Federation of Quality Management) standards include a CSR framework that uses the existing EFQM Excellence Model addressing all stakeholders and the three dimensions of CSR. Many Turkish companies comply with EFQM standards and executives of Turkish companies frequently sit on the board of EFQM. This interest in quality culture may be exploited if triggered by institutional drivers to induce commitment to CSR.

History of CSR and Future Trends

Excluding philanthropic activities, the very first manifestations of CSR were observed in the business conduct of multinational/global companies in Turkey. What constitutes CSR is context dependent. Where laws and regulations are not enforced either by the state or by social pressure, compliance with the law can be reduced to a matter of cost and benefit analysis. Hence, prudent governance which is based on respect for law and regulations is the first step in responsible business conduct, and defining CSR as "voluntary behaviour beyond the requirements of law" would be too simplistic in the context of developing economies. Multinational corporations, due to the obligations to comply with the standards of their home country, tend to obey the laws and set an example for local companies.

Since compliance is associated with costs, ignorance of laws creates illegitimate sources of margins for traditional companies. In fact McKinsey's Productivity Survey for Turkey (2003) finds that the economy functions in two separate tracks in most industries. On the modern track, businesses have adopted global best practices and new technologies, boosting productivity to 62% of best-practice levels. On the other track, however, small-scale, traditional businesses operate at productivity rates that are 24% of average best practice and well below one half of the rates achieved by small business counterparts in other countries. The main reason for this discrepancy is that traditional businesses have little or no incentive to improve. They often circumvent tax or labour laws to save money and can thus manage to sustain themselves without being productive.

The triggers in creating awareness in CSR were related to observance of the business conduct of multinational companies and campaigns of international organisations. Notable among these are BP's social and environmental impact analysis regarding their major Bakus-Ceyhan pipeline installation projects and various activities of the International Business Leaders' Forum (IBLF) in cooperation with the Turkish Economic and Social Studies Foundation (TESEV), UNDP, the British Council and British companies operating in Turkey. Anecdotal evidence suggests that BP's CSR policies had a profound effect on Botas, the state-owned petroleum Pipeline Company who contracted BP for the Baku-Ceyhun Pipeline project. IBLF has organised a series of CSR events in co-operation with TESEV which included seminars, talks, workshops – as well as a conference that aimed at improving labour standards in the ready-made clothing sector supply chain sponsored by Marks and Spencer (http://www.iblf.org/csr). Greenpeace activists demonstrated against hazardous waste and toxic discharges from industrial plants and vessels which resulted in improved practices in most cases (www.greenpeace.org). Global Response (www.globalresponse.org) and the Friends of the Earth (www.foe.co.uk) led the campaign against Eurogold, a mining company extracting gold using toxic cyanide in Bergama.

The author believes that the real challenge for triggering or improving corporate accountability/social responsibility is related to investor attitudes. In fact the opening of EU accession discussions would encourage both foreign direct investments and portfolio investments in Turkey. Persuading mainstream investors of the long-term business case for responsible behaviour is difficult. This is one of the findings in the report "Values by Value" published in January 2003 by the World Economic Forum and the International Business Leaders' Forum. Based on surveys of top executives, the Report reveals that investors rarely ask companies about their social and environmental policies. These issues never come up unless there is a direct and explicit financial risk or short-term exposure. Despite the growing size of funds managed under Socially Responsible Investment schemes and their arguably better performance over long periods, big investors do not take social responsibility seriously. When this is combined with the speculative and short-term nature of most equity investments in developing countries, the situation gets even worse as per the impact of investors' expectations of companies in emerging markets. Institutional investments are largely based on financial models; hence in the absence of adequate information and of standard reporting on social and environmental performance, these parameters are unlikely to be included in value analysis. The efforts of the Global Reporting Initiative and also some of the cutting edge regulations requesting investors to consider the social responsibility of the companies they invest in and encourage long-term investments would be effective only if CSR can be incorporated in financial modelling.

Major Documents, Milestones and Institutions in the Development of CSR

In addition to research and surveys cited in this paper, the most notable document in the development of CSR is the Principles of Corporate Governance (a voluntary code of corporate governance) issued by the Capital Markets Board of Turkey in July 2003 with a special section on stakeholders (www.spk.org). As of 2004, publicly listed companies are obliged to comply with the principles or explain why they do not in their annual reports.

The Corporate Governance Forum of Turkey hosted by Sabanci University conducts research, runs regular courses for Corporate Boards and organises seminars and workshops to promote corporate accountability.

In summary, CSR is not yet a topic by itself but is brought to the fore by related matters such as corruption, public governance reform, transparency, corporate governance, environmental concerns etc.

The real milestone in CSR would be the restructuring and reforming of public sector governance, reducing the size of the informal sector and the declared focus of the Turkish government on economic and political stability in the near future.

Conclusion

By reviewing the research regarding the cultural characteristics of Turkey and the limited number of surveys and research on ethical values and corruption in Turkey, we conclude that the observed poverty of CSR in Turkey may be partially attributed to cultural characteristics. Given also the weaknesses in the institutional framework, the cultural characteristics of business organisations and leadership behaviour in Turkey, we argue that the drivers for CSR may be exogenous (CSR practices of multinational companies, laws and regulations imposed upon Turkey by international agreements, international NGO activism, rational choices driven by the desire to join EU, academic research and management education etc.). We note that the quality culture in Turkish organisations may be exploited as a driver of CSR.

We consider Corporate Governance and Corporate Social Responsibility as mutually reinforcing concepts and as such, draw attention to the potential impact of a change in investors' attitudes toward CSR and the need for innovation in the area of financial modelling to incorporate CSR.

References

Adler, N. J., & Boyacigiller, N. 1995. Going beyond traditional HRM scholarship. In: R. N. Kanunga (Ed.), *New approaches to employee management*, Vol. 3. *Employee management in developing countries*: 1 – 13. Greenwich, CT: JAI press.

Abdalla, I., & Al Homoud, M. 2001. Exploring the Implicit Leadership Theory in the Arabian Gulf States. *Applied Psychology: An International Review*, 50(4): 506 – 32.

Ararat, M., & Ugur, M. 2003. Corporate Governance in Turkey: An Overview and Some Policy Recommendations. *Corporate Governance, International Journal of Business in Society, 3(1): 58 – 75.*

Ascigil, S. 2004. *TESEV research on CSR,* unpublished.

Aupperle, K. E. 1984. An empirical measure of corporate social orientation. *Research in Corporate Social Performance and Policy*, 6: 27 – 54.

Bugra A. 1994. *State and business in modern Turkey: A comparative study.* New York, NY: State University of New York Press.

Caroll, A. B. 1979. A three dimensional conceptual model of corporate performance. *Academy of Management Review,* 28(2): 446 – 443.

Dilber, M. 1967. *Management in the Turkish Private Sector Industry.* Ann Arbor, Michigan: University Microfilms Inc.

Fikret-Pasa, S., Kabasakal, H., & Bodur, M. 2001. Society, Organisations, and Leadership in Turkey. *Applied Psychology: An International Review,* 50(4): 559 – 589.

Harrington, J. E. 1989. If Homo Oeconomicus Could Choose His Own Utility Function, Would He want One with a Conscience? Comment. *The American Economic Review,* 79: 588 – 593.

Hofstede, G. 1980. *Culture's consequences: International differences in work-related values.* Thousand Oaks, CA: Sage.

Hofstede, G. 1983. The Cultural relativity of organisational practices and theories. *Journal of International Business Studies,* 14(2): 75 – 89.

House, R., Wright, N. S., Aditya R. N. 1997. Cross-cultural research on organisational leadership. A critical analysis and a proposal theory. In: P. C. Early, & M. Erz (Eds.), *New Perspectives on international industrial/organizational psychology.* San Francisco, CA: Lexington Press.

Kabasakal, H., & Bodur, M. 1998. *Leadership, values and Institutions: The Case of Turkey.* Research Paper. Bogazici University, Istanbul.

Kabasakal, H., & Dalmachian, A. 2001. Introduction to the Special Issues on Leadership and Culture in the Middle East. *Applied Psychology: An International Review,* 50(4): 479 – 89.

McKinsey Global Institute. 2003. *Türkiye, Verimlilik ve Büyüme Atılımının Gerçekleştirilmesi.* Istanbul: McKinsey and Company.

Ozen, R. 1998. *Mentoring, gender and ideological perspectives: A case study.* Doctoral dissertation. Bogazici University, Istanbul.

PriceWaterhouseCoopers. 2001. *Opacity Index.* http://www.opacityindex.com, accessed 05.08.2004.

Schwartz, S. H. 1994. Cultural Dimensions of Values: Towards and understanding national differences. In: U. Kim, H. Triandis, C. Kagitcibasi, S.-C. Choi, & G. Yoon (Eds.), *Individualism and collectivism, Theoretical and methodological issues*: 85 – 119. Thousand Oaks, CS: Sage.

Thomsen S. 2001. Business Ethics as Corporate Governance. *European Journal of Law and Economics,* 11(2): 153 – 164.

Transparency International. 2001. *Corruption Perceptions Index Report 2001*. Paris. http://www.transparency.org/cpi, accessed 05.08.2004.

Transparency International. 2002. *Corruption Perceptions Index Report 2002*. Paris. http://www.transparency.org/cpi, accessed 05.08.2004.

Ugur, M. 1999. *The European Union and Turkey: An Anchor/Credibility Dilemma.* Aldershot: Ashgate Publishers.

UNCTAD. 2001. *World Investment Report 2001.* New York & Geneva: UN Publications.

Whitley, R. 1994. Dominant forms of economic organisation in market economies. *Organization Studies*, 15(2): 153 – 182.

20 The Experiment of Market Extension

Betty Tsakarestou

Introduction

Corporate Social Responsibility (CSR) is being recognised internationally, and also in Greece, as a significant political attitude advancing sustainable development, cross-sector dialogue and cooperation and experimentation with new models and competing ideas of citizenship such as welfare, social, civil, European, and privatised citizenship. Since the 1980s, citizenship theories have predominated in academic literature and "two types of experiments with citizenship are emerging: those concerned with the extension of the market, that is the re-expression of market freedoms as integral to, rather than in conflict with, citizenship; and those concerned with trying to transcend formal political patterns with more social and participative approaches" (Crouch, Eder & Tambini, 2001: 8). In the context of these theoretical debates and more specifically, adhering to the theoretical strand of the experimentation with "market extension", we define corporate citizenship as a political commitment undertaken by corporations towards the global society and local and international stakeholders in order to address pressing social and environmental issues.

We regard CSR as a major driver of corporate culture change, in an era where corporate reputation, competitiveness, leadership and risk management are increasingly embedded in corporate social and environmental performance. The notion of CSR is also directly linked with the concepts of civil society and stakeholder capitalism (Kelly, Kelly & Gamble, 1997; Kay, 1997; Hutton, 1999) since it establishes a new business model for the 21st century, the Corporate Citizen (McIntosh, Leipziger, Jones & Coleman, 1998; Janoski, 1998).

In Greece CSR is a new concept, almost a neologism, that has gained impetus over the past three years amongst business leaders, opinion makers, media professionals and government. Academic research on the issue is taking its first steps, focusing on the changing role of business in society (Lipovetski, 1992; Bovens, 1998) and the new model of "citizen brands" that integrate corporate citizenship, core values and branding (Willmott, 2001: 5). Other areas of research include ethical consumption, stakeholder theory and cross-sector partnerships, the impact of CSR policies and communication on corporate reputation, and the media's CSR. Public opinion surveys map the changing perceptions and social expectations, fostering our hypothesis that the CSR movement can also be a driver of social change in its own right. On the other hand, our political tradition favours conflict and social confrontation and rarely does it value structured dialogue, cooperation or partnership building among social partners and stakeholders. Nevertheless, during the elections of 8th March 2004, the concepts of "dialogue", "transparency", "responsibility", "participatory democracy", and "cooperation" were introduced into our mainstream political agenda, signalling the eve of a new era where the concept of corporate social responsibility can be embedded in the emergent socio-political values.

Economy, State, and Society as a Context for CSR

The Greek State, over the last fifty years, has acquired an extensive control over social, economic and cultural spheres, especially in the formation of ideas, national-identity and religious perceptions. Sociologist C. Tsoukalas (1986: 55–65) analyses the expansion of the role of the state in postwar Greece in order to interpret citizens' direct or indirect dependence on the public sector for securing jobs as civil servants and a respected social standing. A reinforced culture of political clientalism has been the norm till now. At the ideological level, the state becomes an icon of a national collective identity. The public and private spheres are symbolically separated and mutually exclusive. The public sphere represents the epitome of goodness while the private sphere, the evil. As a consequence, the pursuit of corporate or individual profit was somewhat ostracised as ethically inferior. The anti-globalisation movement, the recent Enron-type corporate scandals, corruption, and economic recession, all these interrelated aspects of contemporary economic and political life have intensified anti-corporate sentiments, suspicion and cynicism among citizens.

Only in the last few years has the Greek Government, endorsing deregulation policies, started withdrawing from economic activities, though maintaining its hold on social and cultural domains. The most important challenge for the Greek economy for the coming years is to become more competitive in attracting foreign investments, to be more innovative and more knowledge-based. A serious impediment in achieving this strategic goal, and consequently a real barrier in the adoption of CSR, is the extensive corruption in Greece. According to Transparency International (2004: 193, 284–286), in the Corruption Perceptions Index 2003, Greece scores 4.3 (50th out of 133 countries). The Transparency International report on Greece summarises the current situation: "Greece has been pursuing an accelerated economic development programme over the past few years, due to approval of the third EU funding package and its hosting of the Olympic Games

2004, which has increased the need for public works. The two programmes have multiplied opportunities for bribe taking and raised concerns about the authorities' ability to monitor such large procurements for maximum transparency and optimal growth" (Transparency International, 2004: 194). The adoption of corporate governance principles and accounting standards for the public companies are becoming topical for the Greek government and the business community. Facing the problem, the newly elected government is preparing to pass a new legislation to combat corruption in October 2004. The new laws will regulate among others, the financing of political parties and political candidates during elections and the operation of public administration bodies, providing stricter penalties for corrupt civil servants. The ratification of a law that forbids a principal media shareholder to participate in public works contracts because of his influence on public opinion and politicians will be the most critical issue (Kathimerini, 2004b).

The Social and Economic Committee of Greece (SEC) issued an "Opinion on CSR" (2003). According to the authors of the "Opinion", the Greek law makes special provisions regarding labour rights (e.g. health and safety) and the protection of the environment (e.g. water pollution) that meet the standards of a CSR-informed legal framework. Nevertheless, in Greece, business and public officials, and even private citizens are accustomed to operate at the periphery of the law (e.g. tax avoidance, illegal labour, bribery, favouritism). Apart from the enforcement of new laws, it is equally important to ensure compliance with the existing ones.

The SEC has already pinpointed a series of obstacles for implementing CSR in Greece. First, 90% of all companies are small and medium-sized enterprises (SMEs) which are not run by professional managers. Most of the SMEs are family-owned and rely on the owners' entrepreneurial skills. They lack the scale and the managerial staff and tools to take advantage of new business opportunities. Usually, they focus exclusively on the pursuit of short-term profit as they strive to survive in a highly competitive local and international market. These firms are not ready or willing to follow a CSR mindset because of cost implications and the structural deficiencies mentioned above.

Second, the public sector is the biggest employer in Greece, providing social services such as the national health system, education, transportation, social security, water, and energy. On the issue of environmental protection, the public sector adopts contradictory practices, risking its own credibility. On the one hand, the parliament has ratified strict environmental laws while on the other hand, the state and public sectors are under national media scrutiny for violating these very laws. Greece is going through a transition period where state-owned monopolies are transformed into competitive public and privately owned enterprises. Public administration can play a critical role for the diffusion of CSR but it is important to stress that CSR cannot be a substitute for state policies on environmental and consumer protection.

Third, the agricultural sector, structured around small producers, operates to the lowest labour, environmental and social standards, although agriculture is considered to have a heavier impact than any other economic activity on the environment (e.g. greenhouse effect, water pollution by chemicals).

Fourth, the multinational industrial companies operating in Greece and a few local ones are the more active organisations in implementing CSR policies. Some of them have published annually social and environmental reports since the early 1980s. Greece could also develop a reliable CSR rating system to monitor triple-bottom line (TBL) performance, following the Global Reporting Initiative guidelines. According to *PriceWaterhouseCoopers's Management Barometer* survey (2002) "two-thirds of multinationals in Europe and 41% in U.S. consider 'triple bottom line' in corporate reporting in order to influence stakeholders and the global capital markets". Misser, Global and U.S. Leader of PwC Sustainability practice, comments: "With the current breakdown of confidence in financial reporting, large companies are facing increasing demands and expectations from stakeholders and are being held more accountable for their performance and actions. The TBL approach is a proactive step in providing shareholders with increased transparency and a broader framework for decision making".

Fifth, the services and commercial sectors manifested a robust economic development over the past few years in Greece. As a consequence, service and commercial firms invested mainly in arts and sports sponsorship programmes supported by intensive advertising campaigns. Currently, emphasis is put on human resources development, and sporadically on community relations programmes. Multinationals which implement their international CSR initiatives locally are more CSR-oriented.

The SEC makes a special case of the construction sector, which is of high importance to the development of the Greek economy. Here, the fierce competitive practices among companies in undertaking state-financed projects (e.g. infrastructure works associated with the Olympic Games) do not allow enough room for CSR initiatives. Cost-effectiveness and profit maximisation prevail at the expense of any social or environmental sensitivity. A noteworthy exception is the TITAN cement company that since 2002 has been the first Greek company member in the UN Global Compact, followed by S&B Industrial Minerals.

Finally, the SEC "Opinion on CSR" proposes some policy directions that can promote the CSR concept in Greece as it has already happened on European level. The Greek Stock Exchange could follow in the footsteps of European Stock Exchanges and launch an index of socially responsible investments like FTSE4Good. The aim would be to attract Greek and ethical foreign investors. Partnership building, cross-sector dialogue and responsible products labelling are also considered as crucial initiatives for the development of CSR. In that case, the Hellenic Network for CSR, business, Greek government and NGOs could benefit from the experience made by CSR Europe or U.N. Global Compact in these fields.

Cultural Drivers of CSR

A recent European Social Survey on "Society-Politics-Values" (Jowell et al., 2003; Voulgaris, 2003), conducted in 23 countries reveals several contradictory findings concerning the evolution of public morals and values in Greece. According to the survey, on an average, Greek people have these values: family (9.7/10), friends (8.6/10), leisure time (7.7/10), work (8.7/10), religion (8.4/10), good citizenship (8.4/10), and respect for the law (8.7/10).

But one can question the adherence of the population to these values as they come out of the survey, since the same survey reveals some discrepancies between social values and social practices. Xenophobia emerges as a disturbing social characteristic during the last decade. Greece is a country where many economic immigrants are choosing to live. A high percentage of the respondents (59.5%) believe that just a few immigrants should be allowed to live in the country and they should be expelled if they commit any crime (52.5%). The respondents consider economic immigrants as a threat to their jobs. This is an unsubstantiated public perception that contradicts Greek economic reality. The immigrants' positive role in the economic development of Greece during the last years is well documented by eminent economic analysts. A noteworthy example is the case of the Greek-international SME Coco-Mat. Coco-Mat is a leading company in sustainable development and winner of several international awards and prizes, such as the first prize in EFQM awards 2003, and the Ethical Value prize from Cambridge University. The company employs mainly economic immigrants and disabled persons in first line and managerial positions alike, connecting convincingly profitability with sustainability and diversity of the workforce (Kathimerini, 2004a).

Social connectivity seems under threat as Greeks are not only suspicious towards the immigrants but they also mistrust each other. According to the European Social Survey, the majority (62.5%) believes that their fellow citizens are ready to take advantage of each other. This climate of wide-spread suspicion, mistrust and cynicism among Greek citizens is socially and politically alarming. Another striking finding is that Greeks have lost their interest in politics during the last four years. Today, those interested in politics account for only 31.4% of the population compared to citizens' continued high interest in politics (60%) during the years from 1988 to 1999. Greek citizens do not trust politicians. They believe them to be indifferent to people's problems and motivated only by self-interest. They are just above the average satisfied with the way democracy is functioning. Greeks are presented as dissatisfied with their lives, insecure and deeply religious. The extended corruption and economic recession might have contributed substantially to this growing social anger and anxiety in all critical aspects of people's lives.

In their leisure time 38% are watching more than three hour's television per day. Television is the most influential medium of information on all aspects of economic, social and cultural life in Greece, according to all media or social surveys, conducted year after year.

Another issue of concern is the slow development of civil society in Greece. Here we have a quite interesting situation. On the institutional level, the Ministry of Foreign Affairs has gathered data on 32.453 "non-governmental subjects" that are operating in the area of its responsibility. There are also 3.500 voluntary, social-sector NGOs operating. It seems that there is some ferment in the field. On the other hand, the presidents of three well-known NGOs admit that Greek citizens are not interested in participating in such civil, non-party organisations. According to them, when people are invited to participate in NGOs they are very cautious and they ask "What's in it for us?" And they conclude: "The citizens don't believe that they have the power to change the world" (informal interview with three leading Greek NGO presidents).

We traced the same detached attitude by the citizens in another national survey, conducted in 2001, which explored the environmental consciousness of Greek citizens (Focus Research Company, 2001). The findings revealed that Greeks are strongly worried about the environmental risks. A majority of 90.2% rated the pollution of the environment as the most pressing global problem, and they admitted (57.8%) that Greeks are not acting in an "environmentally friendly" manner. Although the majority trusts environmental NGOs for the effectiveness of their actions (84.3%) in contrast to only a small fraction (17.8%) that trusts the state or the companies (12.8%) for adopting "green" policies, they expect mainly the state to resolve all the problems (75.3%). Regarding their own role as citizens and individuals, the respondents stated that they feel "powerless" and cannot resolve any problem alone (68.1%). Only a small minority (5%) is participating actively in environmental NGOs. Adolescents and young adults (aged 13–24) are starting to adopt a quite different stance from the older generations, and they are disapproving of the "powerless" and socially passive approach towards issues that are critical for their future and their well-being (55%). Some results can be compared – and thus further supported – to those of the European Opinion Research Group survey conducted in 2002 on a similar subject (*Eurobarometer*, 2002). From the comparison it appears that "Greece always – that is for all the environmental issues – emerges as the most "worried" country. It is also generally true that on the "more worried" side there are a number of Southern European Countries (Italy, Portugal), while on the "less worried" side are northern countries (Netherlands, Sweden, and Finland)". In the same survey it appears that Greek citizens stated that "the environment is an issue beyond their control as individuals" (56 in averages). The French (58), Italians (50) and British (58) are adopting the same pessimistic attitude. In contrast, northern countries such as Finland (66), Sweden (63) "have more confidence in their ability to take action and make a real difference to the environment" (*Eurobarometer*, 2002).

The Greek survey and Eurobarometer findings are indicative of some structural characteristics of the evolution of the Greek State and society. The citizens, due to the hegemony of state and party politics have not developed a sense that they are responsible for their own lives. Political clientalism prevails.

Socially responsible consumption and consumer activism is internationally one of the driving forces of CSR. In Greece, the consumer's rights are protected by the General Secretariat of Consumers founded in 1997 by the Ministry of Development, and by several NGOs such as the Institute of Consumers, whose mission is to inform the public on corporate malpractice and to call them to action. Although these consumers' organisations are trying to mobilise active consumerist awareness in Greek citizens, e.g. organising boycotts, it seems that as a society we have a long way to go to develop such a participatory and activist ethos regarding consumption practices.

The Development of CSR in Greece

The corporate sector in Greece participates in the European Union's CSR Marathon for social and economic cohesion through the creation and activation of voluntary business networks for Corporate Social Responsibility. For the Greek Government, CSR represents a new opportunity to stress its pro-European orientation, supporting actively the European Union's strategic goals for a competitive and inclusive Europe. Furthermore, government officials are well aware of the changing public expectations of companies, of state, and of politics. The Lisbon Summit in March 2000 was a turning point. Anna Diamandopoulou, former European Commissioner for Employment and Social Affairs has been a strong proponent of CSR since then. She said "CSR and reporting thereof is a win-win opportunity not just for companies and financial investors but more importantly for European citizens across the EU" (Rienstra, 2000: 11). The publication of a Green Paper further reinforced the government's political will to facilitate CSR initiatives. In this vein, the government promotes the concept of Business Excellency in the domains of CSR, environmental protection and innovation and more specifically in technological research and development, in the energy and tourist sectors, taking also advantage of the funding opportunities of the third FP in the above-mentioned fields. All these governmental environmental initiatives are coming at a moment when the national media report extensively on the lack of transparency and ineffective state environmental policies.

In June 2000 the Hellenic Network for CSR was established, setting as its primary goal to inform and raise awareness within the Greek Business community on the importance of CSR in the strategic evolution and operation of modern business in the new, internationalised environment of the market. Today sixty multinational and Greek companies are members of the Hellenic Network. Most of them belong to the industrial sector and the rest mainly to the services sector. According to Analytis, chair of the Hellenic Network for CSR "Greek companies, and especially the SMEs, need guidance and more importantly, corporate culture change in order to adopt and implement CSR. Although the Hellenic Network is taking some initiatives to promote CSR concept and best practice, it has not yet gained a wide awareness among business" (Kathimerini, 2003). The structural and managerial problems that face the SMEs, and which are mentioned in the first part of the paper support this view. There is also confusion around CSR notion and practices. For example, many managers cannot distinguish between sponsorship, corporate philanthropy and CSR.

In 2002 the Greek Advertisers Association (GAA) launched the "Social Excellence Awards" in order to reward the best advertisers for their contribution to the domains of society, environment, and culture. It is worth noting that GAA launched the Award independently of the newly established Hellenic Network for CSR. This is quite indicative of the prevailing competition among institutions, organisations, companies and individuals in attempting to benefit from a new trend. CSR is the new arena of power redistribution amongst business networks and federations; cooperation and synergy as strategies to make a strong and convincing case for CSR in Greek society and economy is not a priority. Consultants and PR agencies also compete for new business opportunities in the field of responsibility programmes, challenging each other's expertise on CSR.

The Athens Chamber of Commerce, founding member of The Hellenic Network for CSR has also awarded prizes to companies exhibiting commendable social and environmental responsibility since 2000.

www.responsibility.gr is the first Greek portal promoting sustainable business, focusing on labelling socially responsible SMEs of the North Aegean region in Greece, through the support of innovative actions. The University of the Aegean in cooperation with Lesvos Chamber of Commerce set up this initiative that runs a pilot phase in 2003 – 2004. The EU Department of Regional Policy funds the whole project (known with the acronym NAIAS). This is an important initiative that can help correlate enhanced competitiveness with social responsibility of SMEs.

The Greek CSR Survey: Main Findings

In 2001, Panteion University in collaboration with Research International conducted a qualitative survey on the role and the responsibilities of corporations in contemporary societies with focus on Greece, on behalf of the Hellenic Network for CSR (Tsakarestou, 2001, 2003).

In the context of this first national survey the researchers adopted the term "citizen-consumer" instead of the term "public opinion" in order to emphasise the political dimension of the consumerist act in contemporary democratic societies.

Corporations, State, Society, and Citizen-Consumers

Citizen-consumers, public opinion leaders and corporate representatives who participated in the survey, believe that poverty, terrorism, violation of human rights as well as the destruction of the environment, are the most serious problems that global society faces. Domestic problems that demand solutions include the unsustainable management of the environment, economic recession, unemployment, inclusion of economic immigrants, increasing racism, drugs and poor education.

Responsibilities are primarily requested of the State. Nevertheless, its role as the exclusive social regulator is not recognised any more, since bureaucracy and partisanship have shaken the public's trust in it. The contribution of the State to the resolution of societal problems is still considered to be crucial, especially by individual citizens, yet it has to seek for the cooperation with other social parties as well as the private sector (this remark has been consistently made by opinion leaders and business representatives).

Responsibilities for the generation of societal problems are also being attributed to corporations (seeking exclusively short-term profits), the mass media (for disorienting people and not fulfilling their educative role), the passive citizen-consumers as well as to the catalytic influence of technology in all areas of social and economic life.

Citizen-consumers are not ready to accept that corporations have the honest intention to contribute to the solution, given the fact that they themselves do cause serious problems.

As far as their participation in the public issues is concerned, the researchers traced three typologies of citizen-consumers: a. the "detached" citizen-consumer, b. the "sensitive" citizen-consumer and c. the "active" citizen-consumer.

The first two types are dominant, showing that consumerist practices do not always reflect the social and political perceptions of respondents.

The recognition of corporate social responsibility practices in the conscience of the citizen-consumer will increase under the following three conditions:

- If the company or the brand that wants to be linked with the promotion of a social cause are of undoubted reliability and quality.

- If the cost of the social performance of the products is not transferred to the end prices.

- If the social reporting of corporations is communicated to the entire society.

The Socially Responsible Corporation

Nowadays, the Greek citizen-consumers recognise that corporations can display socially responsible practices. They also accept that there exist some reliable brands that they trust. However, the corporations' socially responsible actions do not automatically acclaim them as such in the citizen-consumers' perception. The profit as sole motive overshadows the impact of the corporate social contribution or even reduces it to a marketing "trick", especially when it is combined with an intense publicity programme. In that case, the publicity of the social activity is not perceived as information but as "advertising".

Opinion leaders and business representatives define as socially responsible a corporation which, beyond its business practices, implements such activities that do not aim directly at profit but rather contribute to the solution of major societal issues, giving back to society part of its profits. Respecting the laws of the State is not enough to characterise a corporation as socially responsible. However, opinion leaders insist that obeying the law is a prerequisite for the application of corporate social responsibility strategies.

It is expected that corporations should undertake more initiatives for the sustainable management of the environment. They are also invited to invest in social areas that have been neglected until today: health, education, social minorities, disadvantaged people and good working conditions.

CSR and Companies' Typologies

We distinguished five types of companies, based on how they perceive and implement as social responsibility programmes:

1. The "non-socially sensitive" company obeys the law but does not recognise willingly its social responsibilities.

2. The "philanthropist" company's acts are based on the moral values and choices of its founder.

3. The "random sponsor" aims at forming a good corporate reputation through its sponsorships, without any further connection to its broader strategy.

4. The "consistent sponsor" selects projects that are linked with the corporate strategy and involves its employees.

5. The active "corporate citizen" places CSR into the heart of the corporate philosophy, and the decision-making process in order to serve it.

Most of the companies in our sample belong to the first four typologies. The active corporate citizen as well as the active citizen-consumer remain a challenge for our society.

Conclusion

With certain reservations, Greece welcomes the new perspective according to which corporations have the ability and are entitled to play an important role in social development and progress. It is a process of social transformation that will result in considerable changes in the social structure and the way we think and act.

The notion of corporate social responsibility today functions as an emblem, that the companies themselves raise towards a consensual social "revolution" that will eventually benefit all the stakeholders of our society.

Until today, the parties involved have not formulated a cooperation framework. We may see the need for the establishment of an independent body that will develop evaluation criteria, accepted by all the parties involved, and will achieve the blending of all the views regarding the content of corporate social responsibility.

Greece is on the move. State, economy, society and its citizens are trying to adapt to a changing world, each one at a different pace. It seems that, at this moment, the state and economic actors are more confident about the future than the citizens. In Greece, corporate social responsibility is strongly supported by the corporate sector, and some academic institutions. The state is following, taking some steps. I believe that CSR will be embedded gradually in Greek society. The Hellenic Network for CSR, CEOs of several companies, business federations, the academic community and the Greek government are taking several steps – anti-corruption laws, conferences, research projects, CSR programmes and awards – in order to raise business and public awareness on the issue and make it a political and business priority. CSR should not end as a fancy marketing or PR tool. It is about social transformation, about change management, about pursuing a meaningful life as individuals and citizens; it has the potential to trigger some social changes in Greece. The social anxiety shows that what Greece needs mostly is a novel model of governance.

References

Bovens, M. 1998. *The Quest for Responsibility. Accountability and Citizenship in Complex Organizations.* Cambridge: Cambridge University Press.

Crouch, C., Eder, K., & Tambini, D. (Eds.). 2001. *Citizenship, Markets and the State.* Oxford: Oxford University Press.

Eurobarometer. 2002. The Attitudes of Europeans towards Environment. Brussels: The European Opinion Survey Group.

Focus Research Company. 2001. *The Environmental Consciousness of Greek Citizens.* Athens, Greece: Focus Research Company.

Hutton, W. 1999. *The Stakeholding Society*. Cambridge: Polity Press.

Janoski, T. 1998. *Citizenship and Civil Society*. Cambridge: Cambridge University Press.

Jowell, R. et al. 2003. *European Social Survey 2002/2003*: *Technical Report*. London: Centre for Comparative Social Surveys. City University. http://www.ess.nsd.uib.no, accessed 27.08.2004.

Kathimerini. 2003. Interview with Nikos Analytis, Chair of the Hellenic Network for CSR. November 16: 17.

Kathimerini. 2004a. Interview with Pavlos Evmorfidis, CEO Coco-Mat Company. March 21: 14.

Kathimerini. 2004b. New laws against corruption. May 30: 6

Kay, J. 1997. The Stakeholder Company. In: G. Kelly, D. Kelly, & A. Gamble (Eds.), *Stakeholder Capitalism*: 125 – 141. London: Macmillan Press.

Kelly, G., Kelly, D., & Gamble, A. (Eds.). 1997. *Stakeholder Capitalism*. London: Macmillan Press.

Lipovetsky, G. 1992. *Le Crepuscule du Devoir*. Paris: Editions Gallimard.

Makridemitris, A. 2002. *State and Civil Society (in Greek)*. Athens, Greece: Metamesonikties Editions.

McIntosh, M., Leipziger, D., Jones, K., & Coleman, G. (Eds.). 1998. *Corporate Citizenship*. London: Financial Times Pitman Publishing.

Misser, S. 2002. *New Era of Transparency: Two-Thirds Of Multinationals In Europe, 41% In U.S. Consider "Triple Bottom Line" In Corporate Reporting*. Pricewaterhouse-Cooper's Management Barometer. http://www.barometersurveys.com, posted 26.09.2002.

PriceWaterhouseCoopers's Management Barometer. 2002. http://www.barometersurveys.com, accessed 27.07.2004.

Rienstra, D. 2000. *The Challenges of Corporate Social Responsibility*. Brussels & Paris: The Philip Morris Institute and the OECD LEED Programme.

The Social and Economic Committee of Greece. 2003. *The Corporate Social Responsibility*. Opinion of S.E.C. No. 95. Athens, Greece.

Transparency International. 2004. *Global Corruption Report 2004*. London: Pluto Press.

Tsakarestou, B. 2001. *Corporate Social Responsibility in Greece. Issues and Prospects. Executive summary*. Athens, Greece: Hellenic Network for Corporate Social Responsibility.

Tsakarestou, B. 2003. Citizen-Brands and Citizen-Consumers: The emergence of CSR. In: T. Doulkeri (Ed.), *The Sociology of Advertising*: 235 – 264. Athens, Greece: Papazisis Editions.

Tsoukalas, C.1986. *State, Society and Labor in Postwar Greece* (Greek version). Athens, Greece.

Voulgaris, Y. 2003. *European Social Survey Technical Report*. Athens: National Centre for Social Research. http://www.ekke.gr/ess, accessed 27.07.2004.

Willmott, M. 2001. *Citizen Brands*. West Sussex, England: John Wiley & Sons.

Further Internet Links

The Hellenic Network in CSR
www.csrhellas.gr

Economic and Social Committee of Greece
www.oke.gr

Institute of Communication
www.instofcom.gr

21 Mapping a New Business Landscape

Gheula Canarutto and Claudio Nidasio

Introduction

In Italy the social responsibility of firms has roots dating from long before the emergence of the Corporate Social Responsibility (CSR) movement during the 1990s. Industrial districts and small firms have often engaged in sustainable forms of conducting business through the convergence of employees, management and local community interests (Confindustria, 2002). Also in academia the concept of the social role of business was pioneered during the 1950s: "Profit doesn't represent the final end of the firm, but is instrumental for satisfying the needs of shareholders and workers" (Masini, 1979).

In order to understand the social and economic context in which a first phase of socially responsible initiatives emerged – especially in the post-war period – and to better contextualize the more systematic and widespread current CSR approach, a historical background of Italy's socio-economic situation is provided.

After the Second World War Italy found itself in a dramatic situation: the country had to recover from war destruction and start living within a new political context, thus passing from monarchy to democracy. At the beginning of the 1950s Italy was still an underdeveloped country, mostly agricultural. 36% of labour forces were employed in agricultural sectors; industrial sectors employed another 32%. In 2003, according to Istat[1] data, 4.8% of labour forces were employed in the agricultural sector, 31.8% were employed in the industrial sector and 63.8% in the services sectors and others. On one side this shift in employment percentage (from a higher employment in the agricultural sector to service and industrial sectors) shows that Italy, during the last sixty years, has undertaken a major economic development. On the other side, the high rate of development has affected more northern areas than southern ones. The higher percentage of Italian family income is still concentrated in the northern regions (53%), while 26% of family income can be found in southern areas and 21% in the central areas.

Italy is a country characterised by a huge gap between North and South since the beginning of the previous century. This gap has historical roots which can be found in the southern agricultural frame where wide properties were concentrated among a small amount of owners; an underdeveloped agricultural commerce where very few products reached external markets and most products were produced for internal demand. This situation was very different from northern Italy, whose development was tied to northern European countries. Being close to these important markets gave the opportunity for rapidly growing trade and wealth accumulation. The income gap associated with wider job opportunities, caused more than four million people to emigrate from southern Italy to North Italy between 1951 and 1974. According to Istat (2003) data, the emigration flow, which had slightly diminished during the first years of the 1990s, started again between 1994 and 2000. 30% of Italian families transferred from the southern regions to the North-Eastern areas and Central Italy.

Cultural and Societal Characteristics of CSR

Culture and Business

Cultural expectations of companies' behaviour need to be related to regional differences. Cultural traits differ a lot between North and South: the northern part is much more managerially oriented and influenced by all continental European development. Ethical values represent another feature of diversity between North and South. In some parts of the South the informal domain of illegal associations is still reigning. This has a deep influence on trade transactions and initiatives and has prevented many businesses from being developed in the south. Somewhere a sort of Second State can be found, with its own laws and requirements. Northern Italy is the core site of all economic activities. The Italian stock exchange site (Piazza Affari) is located in Milan. Italy's main business exhibitions are located in Northern Italy too, thus confirming the central position of the north in business and financial activities. Firms' attitudes and behaviour differ according to their geographical position. The major economic development is happening in Northern Italy, while the South is still trying to overcome its backwardness; southern companies are involved in core activities and hardly find time or resources to invest in socially responsible activities. A research promoted by the Milan Chamber of Commerce shows that the attention of northern Italy towards the environment and care for social issues is much deeper than in southern Italy. Elements such as energy and water consumption, waste recycling and the existence of environmental firms were taken into account. Results also showed that the northern part is paying higher attention to waste recycling and other environmental issues (Chamber of Commerce of Milan, 2002).

Society's Attitude Towards Business

In Italy the constitution (Article 41) – promulgated the 1st of January 1948 – provides a strong basis for affirming the social responsibility of private corporations. Besides introducing that "private economic initiative is free" it underlines how "[economic activity] cannot be undertaken in contrast with social usefulness or in any way that it brings any form of damage to human security, freedom and dignity". Furthermore "law determines suitable programmes and controls such as the economic activity could be addressed and coordinated towards social purposes". In this context CSR can be viewed as substantial innovation in terms of corporations' real interest in building trust relationships with society (Zamagni, 2003).

Organised societal movements looking into corporate practices have been almost absent until the 1980s when the increase of not-for-profit and voluntary activities, the birth of consumers' associations and the increasing role of the media have been conducive to a higher degree of monitoring business practices. In such respects CSR can be linked to the birth of sustainable and cooperative consumption initiatives (Zamagni, 2003); recent research shows that 84% of Italian consumers believe CSR to be an important factor of corporate reputation (Italia Lavoro & Censis, 2003). The role assumed by citizens' groups – such as for example Cittadinanza attiva – together with boycott campaigns led by NGOs, contributed to create a more critical analysis of corporate practices. Moreover the unions played a role in promoting and negotiating labour rights and conditions. Societal involvement towards corporate behaviour is usually locally undertaken, due to the Italian industrial sector being predominantly characterised by small and medium enterprises. In more recent years restructuring of major Italian firms – e.g. FIAT or Alitalia – and major financial scandals – e.g. Parmalat and Cirio – involved thousands of employees and citizens; the effect, also through television debates and newspapers' thorough investigation, has been a higher degree of public attention. Nowadays the debate on corporate social responsibility and ethics of management is highly present at academic, media and business levels.

Roles of Economy, State, and Society

After the post-war period the Italian cultural and political environments have been characterised by the contrast of Catholicism and Marxism, i.e. by substantially opposite visions towards the market economy. After the fall of the Berlin wall, the creation of PDS (Democratic Party of the left) in 1990 represented the end of a major communist party and the constitution of a leftwing side accepting the principles and dynamics of the market economy. The public sector played a major role in the economy through state-controlled companies which represented a significant proportion of the economy. For years the State has been characterised by a pre-eminent role of "assistentialism" often resulting in the provision of financial resources to private firms in difficulty without driving management and organisations towards reforms. Since the 1980s this role has progressively diminished due to a substantial privatisation process (mainly in the transport, utilities and tele-communications sectors). This has caused a change in Italian industrial composition linked to a more limited role of the State in the economy. The increasing integration in the EU has strongly diminished the possibilities of "assistentialism" practices providing space for increased competitiveness within the private sector. Though there has been a decrease of its influence in the business environment, the State still has a strong role in society providing a relevant quota of social, education and healthcare services through one of the highest European tax rates. Considering the role of the State towards CSR, recently the Italian government has taken a step towards the promotion of CSR practices (CSR-SC project of the Ministry of Welfare) aiming at promoting a standard on CSR reporting (CSR-level) and sustaining the constitution of a Social Fund in order to finance socially beneficial activities and rewarding CSR practices of firms (SC-level). Until the recent past, the role of the economy – with particular attention to major corporations – was primarily viewed as creation of wealth for shareholders. In 1999 Franco Modigliani – Italian Economics Nobel Prize winner – introduced a textbook on corporate finance (Brealey & Mayers, 1999) for Italian students emphasising that "the role of managers is to serve the interest of all shareholders, essentially through the maximisation of the firm's market value. At present this doesn't seem to be the main driver for Italian managers[2], but in the coming years through the opening towards Europe and the world, this approach will be more wide-spread also in Italy". As discussed below Italian corporate leaders seem to have evolved towards a wider vision of the role of business in society. The role of society is more present in the north of Italy, characterised by a high presence of not-for-profit and volunteer organisations, rather than in the South of Italy where the culture of the *clan* still appears dominating. In some northern regions *horizontal subsidiarity* – involving civil society organisations in providing public services – is being widely practised. This area of investigation has profound linkages with cultural aspects of CSR, which are more deeply described in the next chapter.

CSR Cultural Drivers

There are many cultural aspects which have influenced, implicitly or explicitly, the Italian attitude towards social responsibility commitment. A recent research (Donati & Colozzi, 1997) highlights the core values that are driving the young Italian generation compared to adult values. The research considers adult values and compares them to the young generation ones. Adults ranked values in the following scale: Family at the first position, Work at the second one, Friendship as third one, Religion fourth one, Politics fifth one, Social Commitment sixth one, Leisure Time seventh one. Though there is great importance accorded to family as a value, families receive little help, due to the uncertain nature of targeted policies which too often fail to provide them with sufficient economic or social support.

The marked decrease in the birth rate that has been afflicting the Italian population for many years is beginning to have a negative effect on society.

The younger generation has shifted values, according lower importance to family and changing other items. Friendship is ranked as the most important value while Family shifts to the second position, Work to the third, Leisure Time fourth, Social Commitment fifth, Religion sixth, Politics seventh. As far as the influence of these values on CSR is concerned, interesting data can be found in the increasing importance accorded to Social Commitment by the younger generation. The research highlights the higher weight given to social relationships and volunteer activities. It can be inferred that the next Italian trend in values will have an influence on organisational behaviour too, thus pushing firms towards social initiatives. The authors of the research summarise three main conclusions about the cultural traits of Italian actual generation:

- Catholic culture represents the major influencing source, thus inspiring ethical and moral values. It represents even one of the major pushes towards social activism,

- 1968 movements have still an impact with its transgression waves towards politics and religion,

- A new frame of values is arising and it can be defined as a mixture of the previous two.

These sorts of values are pushing towards social activism and solidarity programmes that combine religious and social values in new forms of commitment. There are some other cultural elements that can be analysed in a CSR framework; Italian sensibility towards voluntary work and not-for-profit activities, which show a deep care about social topics. According to Istat data, not-for-profit institutions increased from 61,000 in 1991 to 235,000 units in 2003; there was a 283% increase. Culture, sport and recreation represent the main sectors where not-for-profit activities developed. Social care (8.8%), education and research (4.8%) and health care (2.6%) follow. Voluntary work is seen as a structural component of the Italian social picture (Istat, 2003). 8% of the Italian population are involved in activities that are not paid or in voluntary groups. In Northern Italy, especially Northern East Italy, there is a higher rate of people involved; 21% of total Italian volunteers are involved in Trentino Alto Adige area, followed by Veneto (14.3%), Friuli Venezia Giulia (10.4%), Lombardia (10%) and Emilia Romagna (9.7%). South Italy has the lowest rates (Fondazione Nord Est, 2003).

Italy is a country where attention to social topics and needs is quite high. The difference that can be found in people's rate of involvement between North and South recalls a distinctive feature of the Italian picture. The presence, on Italian territory, of the Vatican State can be seen as another element driving social commitment influenced by religious values. The role of the Catholic Church on Italian people and government has been always very strong. According to various Church statements, work has a "social" dimension through its intimate relationship not only to the family, but also to the common good, since "it may truly be said that it is only by the labour of working-men that States create wealth" (Ioannes Paulus PP. II, 1981). Catholic Church social doctrine directly intervenes in defining social corporate ends. The Church requires the establishment of effective instruments of solidarity, which drive an economic growth linked to social development and ethical values. Catholic-inspired institutions and individuals made a contribution in establishing producers', consumers' and credit cooperatives, in promoting general education and professional training, in experimenting with various forms of participation in the life of the work-place and in the life of society in general. Regarding corporate values that drive CSR, the above-mentioned research promoted by ISVI (Institute for business values) (ISVI, 2003) shows the following results. Firms have been asked to rank the values that drive them towards CSR topics.

- Ethical reasons were ranked as first cause,

- Relationship with workers was ranked as second cause,

- Customer loyalty was ranked as third,

- Community relationship was ranked as fourth,

- Economic results was ranked as fifth.

While most of the enterprises understand the importance of social responsibility issues, there are some cultural aspects that prevent Italian firms from adopting these strategies. Firstly, many firms admit that they do not undertake any social responsible activity because of time constraint. Secondly, many others consider the CSR topics too complex and hard to implement (due to scarce knowledge of the legal framework). Thirdly, the impact on corporate costs due to CSR policy adoption is considered another obstacle.

The typical instruments adopted for CSR should be modified according to small and medium enterprises' needs. Entrepreneurial associations and public institutions should try their best to contribute through the creation of an enabling environment (e.g. funds, fiscal incentives, endorsement) for CSR implementation. The development of not-for-profit institutions, voluntary activities that involve more and more people, and religious background can be seen as significant drivers of social responsibility involvement.

CSR in Italy: Characteristics, Development, and Trends

Studies on business ethics and associations dealing with ethical finance have at least 20 years of life. In fact in Italy a first wave of CSR began in the mid 1990s, in 1995 the constitution of Sodalitas[3] represented a pioneer event in the Italian landscape of CSR and some researchers and students studied systematically the implications of social responsibility on corporate competitive advantage. A second wave can be referred to the European Commission Green Paper which fostered and helped several initiatives to emerge. Due to the differences in the Italian business landscape it seems necessary to differentiate the analysis considering the birth of CSR in big firms and in SMEs. Afterwards the roles of the public sector and not-for-profit sectors will be considered as – in some circumstances – they contributed to the expansion of CSR practices.

Analysis by Business Sectors

CSR in SMEs

Italy is the country with the highest number of enterprises (3.9 million in a European total of 19.4); microenterprises are dominant with an average size of 4 employees. The Italian industrial system is characterised by a large majority of SMEs; they account approximately for about 80 % in weight of Italian Gross Domestic Product (Confindustria, 2002). Among SMEs two main types of firms can be identified with respect to CSR: 1) firms where the ownership is oriented towards increasing margins of profitability 2) firms with a higher degree of linkages to the economic and social context where they operate in terms of relations with different stakeholders (employees, local communities, not-for-profit sector). Typically the second type of SMEs have a higher perception of socially responsible behaviours and, even without the CSR label, acted responsibly especially in terms of strong attention to employees' satisfaction, creation of financial supporting conditions for relocation of employees, attention to the environment. In such respect the country's smaller businesses have had a strong tradition of regionally clustering around certain products (referred as "distretti industriali"). As a result, communities are often bound together through cooperatives that produce specific ceramics, machine tools or textiles. Such close ties within their local communities have meant that many of these family-based businesses have long been engaging with and involving their stakeholders as a matter of business survival and success. It may therefore be said that they have indeed been practising what is now known as "corporate social responsibility" for years. As far as it concerns the majority of SMEs, the limited degree of commitment on "formalised" CSR actions can be explained by a number of reasons (Unioncamere, 2003):

- the interventions in favour of co-workers and the community, often carried out by persons in charge of these enterprises, are usually executed on a personal basis and in an unstructured way, thus making an objective observation impossible,

- all life expressions of these enterprises are characterised by a low degree of formalisation: the corporate culture does not entail any sophisticated use, which is immediately perceived as bureaucratic thus representing an obstacle for the management,

- financial resources that can be invested in CSR activities are limited, therefore the range of noticeable actions is reduced,

- the impossibility of assigning staff with specific expertise and the shortage of time of people carrying out control privileges, taken up by operational management, do not enable a due consideration of CSR topics,

- in the event the channel of trade is made up of few companies for which a sub-supplier activity is carried out, initiatives devoted to the promotion of corporate image are not so relevant.

CSR in Big Firms

As concerns big firms, accounting approximately for the 20% of Italian GDP, two major examples can be made: 1) Public Companies (such as ENI – National Firm of Idrocarbures – and IRI – Institute for Industrial Reconstruction) represented an instrument for the development of the south of Italy (not always successful) and on the other side promoted throughout Italy the development of managerial competencies 2) Major private firms which viewed CSR essentially as the respect of law. In the post-war period the presence of CSR practices among big firms has been almost absent; well-known exceptions are Olivetti and Merloni. In such cases the main drivers towards adopting social policies for employees were mainly determined by personal mission and values of the management (often in the person of the President or Chief Executive Officer) rather than systematic evaluation of the financial and economic impact of socially responsible practices. In recent years, though, many big firms have engaged in CSR plans; most of the major companies of the country create an annual social balance sheet and participate in different national and international networks dedicated to CSR (e.g. UN Global Compact, CSR Europe, Sodalitas). Recently the Parmalat case (7th largest firm in Italy), characterised by false billing and transactions – totalling 14b Euro – and false financial gains gave further evidence of the links between ethics and business in Italy. The shock had an even bigger impact considering that the Parmalat top management was viewed by the majority as example of corporate leadership and social responsibility.

Development of CSR in Italy

The development of CSR in Italy can be seen from three inter-related perspectives:

- The first deals with academia, research centres and other organisations (business, not-for-profit) that investigated and promoted CSR,

- The second involves public policies for sustaining CSR both at central and local government levels,

- The third provides evidence of the increasing CSR culture and widespread adoption of related management tools by firms.

Without pretending to be exhaustive major research, mainly based on Italy's CSR context, is reported below.

The Italian Union of Chambers of Commerce research on models for Corporate Social Responsibility underlined that business size deeply influences companies' stance towards social responsibility. Medium-sized and large enterprises have a high propensity to CSR; whereas, in very small and small enterprises the commitment to CSR issues is still limited. Geographical implications are also presented where the centre-north firms present a higher level of social commitment rather than southern ones.

The proposal of the Ministry of Welfare for a CSR-SC standard was preliminarily based on an investigation by Bocconi University which resulted in an integrated frame for reporting on CSR; the research analysed all the major international reporting tools identifying a set of indicators coherent with the stakeholder approach proposed by the European Commission.

The REBUS (RElationship between BUsiness and Society) Project funded by the European Commission and conducted by ISTUD (*Istituto Studi Direzionali SpA – Milan*) explored CSR among large Italian corporations and SMEs emphasising that CSR is a structured process of development in different stages: experimentation, rationalisation and organisational learning, consolidation.

ISVI (Institute for business values) prepared the first annual report on CSR which should be followed by a yearly update. The research includes an overall analysis of CSR in Italy focusing on four dimensions: the main actors offering CSR services (certification bodies, rating agencies, public administrations, etc.), the development of CSR in SMEs, the social responsibility of financial institutions and a review of social reporting experiences (ISVI, 2003).

The Q-RES Project, promoted by the Centre for Ethics, Law and Economics of Castellanza University (CELE) identifies a management model addressing the social and ethical responsibility of corporations within an integrated tool. Within this model CSR is viewed as "enlarged governance" (Sacconi, 2003) based on which the management of the firm has obligations to comply both towards propriety and in general with respect of all stakeholders.

Finally the Sodalitas Social Award is to be mentioned, which sustains and promotes CSR through public recognition of excellence projects within five categories: internal CSR processes, partnership with the community, social marketing campaigns, socially responsible finance and CSR of SMEs. The 2004 edition has seen a large participation of companies (84) which competed for the award.

Public policies in Italy have been widely adopted in the attempt to promote and sustain Corporate Social Responsibility. Most policies at central, regional and local government levels focus on SMEs.

Regional and local governments have been actively involved in promoting CSR; they understood that CSR – sometimes referred to as "public role of private enterprise" – in order to be effective needs to be confronted with public sector strategies. As such the promotion of CSR standard and reporting systems and the search for public private partnerships have emerged.

Regional and local governments have worked towards the promotion of SA 8000 certification especially among SMEs: Toscana Region's Fabrica Ethica project involves supporting training and allocation of funds to companies and is interrelated with CSR criteria for public procurement, while the Region of Umbria created a regional Register of SA 8000-certified companies.

Furthermore the search for integrated CSR management and reporting systems has seen the active involvement of public authorities: Region of Umbria promoted "measures for the certification of quality, environmental, safety and ethical systems of Umbrian companies", Region Emilia Romagna is creating a Label of Social Quality, Region of Abruzzo has proposed the introduction of quality certification systems on the environment and corporate social responsibility for the administrative procedures of the Region of Abruzzo, local territorial bodies and other public bodies working in the Region". On the local government level the Province of Lecce and Province of Novara have promoted systems for ethical and social certification.

A third area of public sector involvement concerns long term strategic planning programmes of local authorities sustaining public private partnerships in the area of CSR. The Management Committee of the strategic plan of Reggio Emilia[4] included two strategic lines dealing with sustainable development and social projects including CSR; the strategic plan of Verona includes projects focused on reenforcing partnerships on CSR with local firms, the University and the local civil society.

At the Central Government level the Ministry of Welfare has predominantly led the agenda of Corporate Social Responsibility in Italy. In December 2002 a first proposal about a CSR-SC standard and reporting tool was publicly presented; following a consultation process in December 2003 the Ministry presented a final proposal during a European conference held in Venice entitled "The role of Public Policies in promoting CSR". CSR was also one of the main themes during the Italian Presidency of the European Union during the second semester of 2003. The aim of the project is to disseminate the culture of CSR and best practices among enterprises while developing commonly agreed guidelines and criteria of CSR self-assessment, measurement, reporting and assurance (CSR level) which result in the preparation of a Social Statement. The SC Level calls for enterprises to finance social projects and to benefit from tax allowances and facilitate access to the financial markets through the "ethical funds". The implementation of the project is nowadays characterised by a three-fold strategy:

- based on the European experience, in May 2004 an Italian CSR Multistakeholder Forum was established to discuss the CSR agenda; the Forum will meet up in several sub-committees; it is headed by the Ministry of Welfare and includes around 45 institutional, social and economic actors,

- within the Ministry of Welfare a CSR dedicated organisational unit has been created in order to monitor and guide the implementation phases of the project,

- a protocol agreement has been signed with Unioncamere[5] and Confapi[6] in order to develop operative supporting units (Sportello CSR-SC) through the territorial network of the chambers of commerce and to jointly promote the project with specific attention to SMEs.

CSR culture and adoption by Italian corporations has undoubtedly increased during the last few years. Various management and reporting tools provide enterprises with the opportunity of learning and implementing CSR. The introduction and spread of social reports in Italy has strongly increased in recent years: many private and public institutions create a social report in order to provide evidence to the general public of their social commitment, values and initiatives. According to a recent investigation by the Ministry of Welfare there are more than two hundred bodies (companies, not-for-profit organisations, etc.) that publish social reports or environmental reports while there are almost twenty companies that publish sustainability/social-environmental reports, in line with the triple-bottom-line approach. Among these a large number of private firms (banks, manufacturing and telecom firms especially), federation of industries (e.g Assolombarda[7]), not-for-profit organisations (NGOs, social cooperatives, foundations) and public institutions (city councils, special bodies for social services, healthcare local organisations) have already created some sort of integrated report on social and environmental practices. Some have done it in 2002 for the first time, while others have reached several editions. In Italy CSR has been also fostered by a relatively large (the largest so far in the EU) adoption of the SA 8000 certification; environmental certifications have also increased steadily[8]. On the financial side ethical finance experiences are growing: in September 2003 1.5 billion Euro were managed through ethical funds (Ministry of Welfare, 2003). In 1998 the first Ethical Bank – Banca Popolare Etica – was constituted. It primarily provides financing to not-for-profit organisations based on both social and economic analysis. Finally it has to be mentioned that Cause-Related Marketing accounts for 0.3% of the entire advertisement sector. In order to provide evidence on the integration of CSR into traditional management accounting practices, since 1995, "social accounting" has become a category of an award (Oscar di Bilancio) traditionally given to best practices in financial accounting. The 2003 edition of the Oscar has been granted to ENI as the social report reflects the adoption of a coherent and significant CSR strategy. Main elements being represented by:

- Adoption and implementation of the ethical code,

- The constitution of a risk management committee,

- The introduction of an environmental management system,

- A detailed analysis of the triple-bottom-line approach using suitable indicators evaluating impacts on stakeholders,

- External independent qualitative survey on stakeholders' evaluation of ENI's social responsibility.

Conclusion

According to Censis (Italia Lavoro & Censis, 2003) analysis, Italian firms are moving towards CSR because of the following assertion. "The idea that profit cannot be achieved without paying attention to social results, has driven the rise of a new managerial and institutional ratio which relates to the firm as a subject able to increase social welfare. Profit must be achieved balancing economic, environmental and social dimensions. Italian companies are moving towards a social responsibility commitment because of the rising globalisation phenomena and the reduction of manufacturing components in the production process. Social costs and negative externalities are becoming clearer to external parties: environmental disasters, juvenile work, scarce attention to work safety policies and speculation activities on financial markets".

In order to address future trends on CSR development in Italy it has to be said that scarce evidence is available on positive and long-term correlation between CSR adoption and increased economic and competitive advantage based on financial return and market penetration.

Notes

[1] Istat is Italy's national statistical institute. It has been operating for more than 75 years and it is the main producer of the country's official statistics, representing, in a way, its quantitative memory (*www.istat.it).*

[2] Italian managers in fact are intended to be primarily focused on self-interest rather than shareholders interest.

[3] Sodalitas, Association for the Development of Entrepreneurship in the Social Economy, is an intermediary organisation established in 1995 by Assolombarda, the largest employer federation in Italy, in association with some of its leading corporate members. Sodalitas is the Italian representative of CSR Europe – the business-to-business network for Corporate Social Responsibility in Europe. Among various initiatives aimed at promoting CSR in Italy, Sodalitas established a Social Award which in 2004 reached its 2nd edition.

[4] The Committee is composed of the Province of Reggio Emilia, the municipality of Reggio Emilia and the Chamber of Commerce

[5] Italian Union of Chambers of Commerce

[6] Italian Union of small enterprises

[7] Federation of Industries for Milan area.

[8] There are 52 companies with a Social Accountability 8000 (SA 8000) certification, out of 285 global certifications. In the last few years, there has been a remarkable increase in: ISO certifications 14001 (more than 2.400), OHSAS 18001 certifications, EMAS registrations (146), quality certifications and environmental certifications – Eco-Label (issued for more than 60 groups of products), biological certifications (+23% of sales in 2002 in modern retail), social labels (Transfair), other environmental labels (Forest Stewardship Council – FSC) (Ministry of Welfare, 2003).

References

Brealey, R. A., & Mayers, S. C. 1999. *Principi di finanza aziendale.* Milan: Mc-Graw Hill.

Chamber of Commerce of Milan. 2002. *Research of Chamber of Commerce of Milan: Environmental issues.* Milan: Chamber of Commerce of Milan.

Confindustria. 2002. *Confindustria investigation on CSR trends and evolution.* Rome: Collana Studi e Ricerche Confindustria.

Donati, P., & Colozzi, I. 1997. *Giovani e generazioni,* Bologna: Il Mulino Ed.

Fondazione Nord Est. 2003. *Social responsibility and social conscience. The case of Padua and North East entrepreneurs.* Venice: Fondazione Nord Est.

Ioannes Paulus PP. II. 1981. *Laborem Exercens.* Vatican City: Libreria Editrice Vaticana.

Istat. 2003. *Annual Report.* Rome: Istat.

ISVI. 2003. *CSR annual report.* Milan: ISVI.

Italia Lavoro, & Censis. 2003. *Research of Italia Lavoro and Censis on corporate social responsibility.* Rome: Italia Lavoro & Censis.

Masini, C. 1979. *Lavoro e risparmio.* 2nd Edition.Turin: UTET.

Ministry of Welfare. 2003. *Research by the Ministry of Welfare on a proposal for a CSR standard.* Rome: Ministry of Welfare.

Sacconi, L. 2003. *Standard, autoregolazione e vantaggio comparato dell'impresa cooperativa.* Florence: Il Ponte Editore.

Unioncamere. 2003. *Research of Unioncamere: Models of CSR.* Rome: Unioncamere.

Zamagni, S. 2003. *La responsabilità sociale dell'impresa: Presupposti etici e ragioni economiche.* Florence: Il Ponte Editore.

Further Internet Links

Gruppo di Studio per il Bilancio Sociale
www.gruppobilanciosociale.org

Forum per la Finanza Sostenibile
www.finanzasostenibile.it

ISVI – Istituto per i Valori di Impresa
www.isvi.org

Sodalitas
www.sodalitas.it

Impronta Etica
www.improntaetica.org

Cittadinza Attiva – Gruppo di Frascati
www.cittadinanzattiva.it

22 From a Paternalistic Past to Sustainable Companies

José Luis Fernández Fernández and Domènec Melé

Introduction

During the last seventy-five years in Spain there have been great and sometimes spectacular changes in what the country expects of companies, and these changes include the way of doing business, the corporate role in society and the constantly evolving profile of directors and managers in charge of business organisations.

At the beginning of the 20th century, Spanish business enterprises generally understood that their responsibility was to make profits and to comply with the law, especially where penalties were effectively applied. Apart from this, some companies also assumed a certain paternalism towards their workers in matters such as housing, food, grants for children's studies, etc.

After the Spanish civil war (1936–1939), Spain was under General Franco's authoritarian regime up to 1975. Democracy arrived with a new Constitution in 1978, which established a parliamentary monarchy system. In the post-war era, an autarchic economic system came into play, which was liberalised from 1959, opening the Spanish economy to external markets. In the sixties, sensible economic development began. During Franco's time many regulations protecting workers from dismissal were promulgated and a wide social security system was developed. However, as in many other countries, there were scarce regulations in matters such as consumerism, the environment and fair competition. The hidden economy and tax evasion were relatively pervasive. Lack of democracy was frequently offered as a pretext for tax evasion, but the cause was probably more complex, since this problem has persisted up to now, although currently an efficient monitoring and a relatively rigid inspection system has been introduced, and tax fraud has reduced considerably.

Since the 1940s Spain has had numerous nationalised companies and seen many regulations and state interventions in the economy. A mixed economy persisted after economic liberalisation. A new boost to the Spanish economy took place in 1986, when Spain became a member of the European Economic Community. In the 1980s and above all in the 1990s, most state companies were privatised, as happened in other West European economies. A great number of big companies is now operating in Spain as a consequence of these privatisations, as well as of mergers and acquisitions and the establishment or consolidation of well-known transnational companies.

Since the 1990s a great number of Spanish companies have expanded their business to Latin America and, significantly less commonly, other industries have set up business in Morocco, Eastern Europe and elsewhere. Now large companies of financial services, energy and telecommunications are well-established in Latin America.

Throughout the 20th century many business, especially the largest, assumed their responsibilities to some extent, implementing policies and practices related to this topic. In Spain, as in other countries, two waves can be distinguished regarding Corporate Social Responsibility (CSR). The first, which was rather weak, was in the 1970s, and the second at the beginning of the 21st century[1]. Since then a renewed interest in CSR has arisen in Europe and worldwide (Fernández, 2004).

With respect to business directors and managers, we might generally affirm that Spain has definitely developed a better image of them, along with ample social acceptance, instead of a certain mistrust and even rejection in the past.

Spanish capitalism has thus stopped being oligarchic and has advanced towards a popular form of it. As proof we may look at Spain's growing number of stockholders and the increasing importance of the Spanish stock exchanges in the last eight or ten years. Still, a lot remains to be done in the areas of corporate governance and the exercise of power in the large corporations. Like their counterparts in the developed world, Spanish companies have on their agenda the challenge of Corporate Social Responsibility and what it means for management, internal structuring and interaction with society.

Up to now, there have not been many studies on the situation of CSR in Spain. An exception is the work of de la Cuesta and Valor (2003), who, among other things, present measurement systems and some observations on the development of CSR in Spain. In addition, some limited surveys on CSR in Spain have been carried out by Forética (2002) including 398 companies and PriceWaterhouseCoopers (2003) including 43 companies (most of them quite sensible with sustainability and CSR). Also worthy of note is the annual report on activities related to CSR in Spain which the Fundación Ecología y Desarrollo began to publish a few years ago.

All of these works can be considered as exploratory studies, while a research in depth on CSR in Spain is still to be made; something that this paper will not attempt. Its purpose is only to give an overview of the current situation of CSR in Spain, paying particular attention to the cultural factors and driving forces for

CSR and major documents, milestones and institutions in its development. A summary of the current situation in academia and in business, and future trends, will also be provided.

Socio-cultural Factors

Generally speaking, Spanish society is concerned about social issues related to labour, such as temporary labour contracts, work conditions of immigrants, safety in the workplace, redundancy and unemployment. According to national surveys carried out by CIS (www.cis.es), a governmental centre for sociological statistics, unemployment frequently takes one of the first places in the ranking of preoccupations of the Spaniards. However, in the last two decades other concerns have also been increasing about other issues related to CSR, such as consumerism, the natural environment, quality of life in the workplace, work and family life, involvement of business in the community, and globalisation problems.

Spanish society is probably more tolerant than other non-Latin countries with themes such as tax evasion, lack of compliance with the law, and in developing certain underground economies in certain industries. However, there appears to be a tendency, perhaps still gaining momentum, to overhaul these attitudes.

Corruption became a focus by the end of the 1980s and at the beginning of the 1990s when some notorious cases came to light regarding bribes to politicians. Fortunately, these have decreased in the last few years, as the TI Corruption Perceptions Index for Spain shows. It jumped from 4.31 in 1996 to 7.1 points in 2002 and its corresponding position in the ranking of countries went from 32nd place to 20th (Transparency International, 1996, 2002). Fortunately the waters seem to have calmed insofar as people appear to have more good sense in questions of ethical values, the *raison d'être* of the economy and the role of business companies. This suggested background explains the present concern of companies concerning their impact on social reality and their supposed responsibility or obligation to go further than just obeying the laws on the books.

Spain is a traditionally Catholic country. Even now, about 80% of the Spanish population profess to be Roman Catholic, although a strong process of secularisation has taken place in recent decades and consistency between Catholic faith and the actual behaviour of many is often lacking. With democracy certain values relating to individual freedom, such as tolerance, autonomy, awareness of one's own rights and those of others, have increased, while a sense of solidarity, friendship and loyalty has probably diminished.

Probably, the Catholic Church as an institution has lost influence in the field of social and moral issues related to business, but its teachings can still have a real influence through citizens involved in business who are trying to live according to their faith. This leads them to defend aspects related to human dignity and rights, environment, and to promote the common good.

After several years of a welfare state, Spanish civil society is still relatively under-developed in social initiatives, and the degree of association with, and member-ship of political parties and unions is lower than in other countries which are Spain's geographical neighbours. However, there is a growing interest in volun-tary service, and the number of NGOs is increasing, although they are not as ac-tive in the business area as in other Western countries.

Studies of the Spaniards' values (Orizo, 1996; Megías, 2000) show that the Span-ish have a high sense of the importance of family, tolerance and solidarity in sup-porting certain social issues, acceptance of competition but balanced with egalitar-ian measures, personal safety and respect for the individual and for individual freedom.

As has been mentioned in the introduction, the framework for social responsibili-ties of business has been the law, with many regulations in labour and other issues. But now, this is changing. Some business people ask for less regulation, especially in labour matters, and rules which are not so rigid, because there is awareness that a lack of flexibility in labour contracts and dismissal is detrimental to employ-ment. This leads to decreasing state interventionism and a more active role for civil society, which means civil organisations and citizens' demands that busi-nesses assume more social responsibility toward employees, consumers, the envi-ronment, etc. In practice, however, the pleas to business from Spanish civil society have not been excessively strong thus far. They are not at all comparable with those in the USA, the UK or Germany.

Demands of Spanish civil society include protection of the environment, promot-ing safety in the workplace, bettering job conditions, harmonisation of work and family life, fairness in restructuring and lay-offs, corporate transparency, respect-ing the rights of consumers, minority shareholders, etc. Avoiding discrimination (women, immigrants), sexual harassment, mobbing, conflicts of interests in corpo-rate governance and certain complaints regarding globalisation are other specific concerns.

Driving Forces for CSR

Respect for individual rights and a certain sense of solidarity are potential cultural factors which can foster CSR. Apart from this, other elements have prepared the land for an increasing awareness and even for the implementation of CSR in Spain.

One of them is the movement of business ethics, which in Spain began in the middle of the 1980s and underwent a considerable development in the 1990s, mainly in academia, but also in some companies. Business Ethics in Spain, in spite of some troubles and ambiguities in the past, is moving forward (Argandoña, 1999). A good number of Spanish companies, especially the largest, have introduced ethical business policies (Melé, Garriga & Guillén, 2000), and there is a tendency toward an increase in corporate ethical practices (Fontrodona, Mele & Santos, 2003). Related to business ethics, Catholic social teaching should also be mentioned. Several scholars, most of them involved in AEDOS (association for promoting the study of the Catholic social teaching), have been working in this field in matters related to economics and business ethics. In addition, a book with a collection of addresses of Pope John Paul II to business people and economists was published (Melé, 1992). Recently, an ethical investment fund has been created by Santander Central Hispano, one of the leading banks in Spain, with statutes following Catholic social teaching, written by faculty members of the *Instituto Social León XIII* (Fundación Pablo VI) in Madrid.

Some driving forces for CSR come from Europe and worldwide. By the end of the 1990s and since the beginning of this new century, with globalisation and its critics, and concern for a sustainable world, corporate social responsibilities have received a new impulse worldwide.

The European Union is now promoting CSR in all its member countries, and Spain, up to a certain point, has come under this influence. In 2001, the European Commission published a Green Paper (Commission of the European Communities, 2001) in order to initiate a debate over the nature and contents of CSR. This debate brought about 250 responses from business, employer federations, trade unions, NGOs, and academics. Despite mutual differences, a strong consensus emerged from respondents that CSR is becoming a vital component of companies' core business, and a determinant of future competitiveness. Respondents considered CSR a global issue, and an integral part of world efforts toward sustainable development. Consequently, in 2002, the European Commission published a communication on CSR (Commission of the European Communities, 2002), encouraging companies, including small and medium-sized businesses, to voluntarily assume CSR that went beyond their legal obligations. In 2003, the European Union Council published a resolution (European Union Council, 2003) regarding the social responsibility of business, urging the member states to undertake initiatives in this field. In addition, some European governments, such as those of France and the United Kingdom, have promulgated laws regarding matters such as sustainable development, CSR, ethical investments, social audits and social balances.

Another source of influence has been a number of well-known international initiatives, which have promoted CSR in the last few years. Among others, the World

Business Council for Sustainable Development, the International Chamber of Commerce, CSR Europe, the European Academy of Business in Society, the International Labour Organisation (ILO), the United Nations Global Compact, the OECD Guidelines for Multinational Enterprises, and the World Business Council for Sustainable Development (WBCSD). It is also worth mentioning the interest of the Global Reporting Initiative (GRI) for social and environmental reporting, and various social accountability systems, such as the SA8000 and AA1000 proposed respectively by Social Accountability International (SAI) and the Institute of Social and Ethical AccountAbility (AA).

Finally, a certain influence on sustainability and CSR in Spain can be attributed to the low but increasing popularity of special indexes for listed companies regarding CSR or sustainability, such as the Dow Jones Sustainability Indexes, which track the financial performance of the leading sustainability-driven companies worldwide, and the FTSE4Good indices series which have been designed to measure the performance of companies that meet globally recognised corporate responsibility standards, and to facilitate investment in those companies.

All of these initiatives and the cultural factors mentioned have probably had a real influence on CSR assumed by companies, but when business executives are asked about the driving forces for CSR, they mention as the three major reasons: improving reputation, obtaining a competitive advantage and tendencies of industry; though the demands of various stakeholders are also important. Up to now, pressure from NGOs is still not too important in Spain (PriceWaterhouseCoopers, 2003).

Many countries have a long tradition in Socially Responsible Investments (SRI), and this seems to be an important driving force for promoting CSR. It is not yet so in Spain, since these types of investments started only recently and the amount of funds attracted is low, although, according to experts, it will be increased in future years (IPES, 2002).

For many people, Business Ethics and CSR have a close relationship. Business ethics provides foundations and gives moral legitimacy to CSR. At the same time, business ethics is an objective reference to distinguish legitimate social demands for CSR from others which do not have any ethical support.

Business Associations and Fora for CSR

Some businesses, especially large corporations, are active players in implementing CSR through associations and fora. The latter, generally receive technical support from academic or consulting organisations. One of these fora is the "Forum on Business and Sustainable Development" (www.foroempresasostenible.org), which was launched by the IESE Business School in 1999 after beginning to work in sustainable development four years before. This forum, which involves CEOs of large Spanish companies, proposed a "Code of Governance for Sustainable Business" in 2002 with the cooperation of PriceWaterhouseCoopers and the "Fundación Entorno". It meets once a year to discuss topics related to corporate sustainability and sustainable development.

In 2002 four big Spanish companies (Telefónica, BBVA, Repsol-YPF and Grupo Agbar) launched the "Forum de Reputación Corporativa" (*Corporate Reputation Forum*). The goal of this forum (www.reputacioncorporativa.org) is to provide a meeting place to analyse and spread tendencies, tools, and models of corporate reputation in management. It has an active website and publishes an annual report on corporate reputation. Afterwards, other large Spanish companies joined the forum, which has the technical support of the "Instituto de Empresa", a business school based in Madrid.

That same year, a group of important Spanish companies, including Alstom, Amena, BASF, BSH Electrodomésticos, Cemex España, Cepsa, Holcim (Spain), Iberdrola, MRW, Port Aventura, RENFE, Siemens, Telefónica Móviles, Tetra Pak España, Unión FENOSA and Vodafone, established the "Club of Excellence in Sustainability" (www.clubsostenibilidad.org) with the aim of promoting a sustainable growth in economic, social and environmental fields. It tries to offer a forum for stakeholder dialogue and to foster benchmarking in sustainable development.

Another important network for promoting CSR is the "Mesa Cuadrada" (*square table*), which is the Spanish chapter (www.pactomundial.org) of the UN *Global Compact,* the well-known set of principles on human rights, labour rights and environmental issues proposed by the United Nations' Secretary-General Kofi Annan in 1999, and operative since 2000. Mesa Cuadrada involves public institutions, academic institutions, companies, charities, large NGOs and foundations. All participants around the table have equal rights and obligations, and they contribute with a membership fee that covers the annual budget.

Finally, the Asociación Española de Contabilidad y Administración de Empresas (AECA) — www.aeca.es — (*Spanish Association for Accounting and Business Administration*), which includes academics and practitioners, has recently created a commission of experts to work on CSR.

Non-Governmental Organisations and Mass Media in Promoting CSR

Several NGOs and the mass media are also contributing to foster the implementation of CSR from different perspectives. Many of them have adopted the legal form of a "fundación" (*foundation*). We will consider the most relevant.

In 1992 a group of professionals created the "Fundación Ecología y Desarrollo" (ECODES – www.ecodes.org), *Ecology and Development Foundation,* to promote sustainable development. Now it is the Spanish partner of the Sustainable Investment Research International Group (SiRi Group) and of the Ethical Investment Research Service (EiRiS), organisations whose principal function is the evaluation of CSR. They are carrying out a number of activities which include, among others, the publication of an annual report on CSR in Spain.

In 1995 another organisation related to the environment was created: the "Fundación Entorno" (*Environment Foundation* – www.fundacion-entorno.org), with the mission of harmonising economic development with environmental protection and helping companies to improve their commitment to the environment.

The "Fundación Empresa y Sociedad" (*Business and Society Foundation* – www.empresaysociedad.com) was created in 1995. Its main goal is to promote the involvement of Spanish companies in the community as a natural part of their strategy. It is trying to improve business involvement in the community, the corresponding strategy and a proper communication of these strategies to society.

In 1999, several companies and other partners created "Forética" (www.foretica.es) a non-profit organisation which tries to apply key concepts of quality management to corporate ethics management. Since 2002 Forética has offered a Corporate Ethical Management System (*Sistema para la Gestión Ética de la Empresa,* SGE).

The "Fundación Economistas sin Fronteras" (*Economists Without Frontiers Foundation* -www.ecosfron.org), an NGO oriented towards needy people both in developing and industrialised countries, is also active in promoting CSR. Right now this foundation is working on developing an "Observatory of CSR" to communicate to society the performance of large companies in meeting their social responsibilities.

The mass media also has an influence, which may be important in promoting CSR. Presenting relevant opinions, best corporate practices, rankings, tendencies and so on, contributing to fostering managerial opinion and designing managerial agenda. In Spain, the media has given an increasing importance to CSR, mainly since 2001, when some international initiatives were made public and since then public opinion has been more and more sensitive to corporate scandals. There have been some topics related to CSR which are presented frequently in the economic or general media, such as safety and health in the workplace, lay-offs and the delocalisation of plants, environmental issues, contracting immigrants, labour conflicts, fraud and financial and accounting scandals and corruption.

Governmental Initiatives

Most people agree that CSR is wider than compliance with legal rules, but this compliance already covers many requirements of social responsibility for business. In this sense, Spanish legislation, as with most countries, has numerous aspects, regarding work conditions, contracts, job safety, handicapped workers, dismissals, family issues, consumerism, environment, etc. that many people could consider implicit CSR or minimum CSR.

In the field of responsibilities in corporate governance, some governmental actions are worthy of note. By the end of the 1990s, the Spanish Government had entrusted to a special commission of experts chaired by Prof. Manuel Olivencia, the preparation of a report on an ethical code for boards of directors, which was published in December 1998. The "Olivencia Report" presented 23 specific recommendations for good practice in corporate governance (Olivencia, 1998). These rules were of a voluntary nature, but companies were told that they should inform the market about their acceptance or rejection. It was expected that the market would compensate companies that had adopted the "Olivencia Code", and sanction those that had not. In practice there is not any evidence that this has been so.

In July 2002, the Spanish Government created another special commission, chaired by the businessman Enrique Aldama, to prepare a report to promote the transparency in the stock market of listed companies. The "Aldama Report", published on 8th January 2003, was focused on the duties and responsibilities of directors and proposed legal changes in order to improve transparency in corporate governance. In July of this year, a law was promulgated which included several recommendations of the "Aldama Report". In this way, a step was taken to introduce a sense of social responsibility in boards of directors, although limited to a few specific issues.

On the other hand, the Spanish government gives support to the OECD Guidelines for Multinational Companies. These guidelines, which involve the 30 country members of the OECD as well as Argentina, Brazil and Chile, are addressed to multinational companies in order to promote their responsible behaviour, a favourable climate for international investment and to increase positive contributions of multinational companies in the economic, social and environmental fields. For the effectiveness of these guidelines, the National Contact Points are crucial. They are responsible for encouraging observance of the guidelines in a national context and for ensuring that the guidelines are well-known and understood by the national business community and by other interested parties. Companies assume voluntarily the OECD guidelines and should then apply them in every country in which they are operating. It is expected that the National Contact Point (NCP) will gather information on national experiences with the Guidelines, handle enquiries, discuss matters related to the *Guidelines* and assist in solving problems that may arise in this connection and generally help to implement the *Guidelines*. In Spain, the National Contact Point of the guidelines is contained within the Spanish Ministry of Economy. However, as far as can be told, this National Contact Point is not yet sufficiently active in promoting the OECD Guidelines.

Thus far, the Spanish government has not proposed any law focused on ethical investments, social audits and social balances, similar to those already existent in France, Germany and the United Kingdom for managing investment funds. Neither are there any financial incentives or tax compensation to foster CSR in state and/or regional governments. An exception is the regional government of Aragon (Northeast of Spain) which is giving some economic compensation to small and medium-sized companies which implement some CSR practices (Lafuente, Viñuales, Pueyo & Laria, 2003: 63).

It should be added that the Spanish Governmental Agency for Standardisation (AENOR) is working to produce a standard on Ethical and Social Corporate Management System (PNE 165010), but after several months no result has been brought about.

To summarise, up to now, the Spanish government has taken very few initiatives to foster CSR, preferring initiatives on CSR exclusively from business. Some NGOs expect more governmental actions, while companies insist on the voluntary character of CSR. What many Spanish companies would like is a general framework on CSR from the EU – 31.3% in Forética survey (Forética, 2002: 43) – but not compulsory duties or governmental interventionism. However, both the conservative party (Partido Popular) and the socialist party (PSOE), the two major Spanish political parties, consider that some legislation and political action should be undertaken to foster CSR, although with different approaches (Corres, 2004; Jáuregui, 2004).

Teaching and Research

By the 1970s, some business schools and business administration degrees in Spain already had courses on corporate social responsibility. In 1980, Prof. M. A. Gallo (IESE Business School) published a book on corporate social responsibility as a product of the courses he had taught on this topic at IESE Business School, University of Navarra.

In the 1980s and 1990s many courses were aimed at both undergraduate and graduate students. More recently, courses on CSR or business in society have been taught in several universities. Additionally, this topic has been included in syllabuses as a part of other academic subjects.

Now, most private universities have compulsory or optional courses on business ethics, CSR and so on, and they are even trying to introduce an ethical and social approach in every academic discipline. In some public universities there are elective courses on CSR, but these are rarely compulsory.

In the University of Barcelona there is a Master programme of 300 hours on Corporate Social Responsibility, Social Accounting and Auditing. For its part, the University of Navarra offers another Master and a Doctorate degree on culture and governance of organisations.

Furthermore, several research centres and academic chairs devoted or related to CSR have been set up in Spain, mainly in the last decade, including "Instituto Empresa y Humanismo" (*Enterprise and Humanism Institute* – www.unav.es/empresayhumanismo), the Department of Business Ethics and the Chair on "Economy and Ethics" (www.iese.edu) and the Centre for Business in Society (www.iese.edu/en/RCC/CBS/Home/CBSHome.asp) at IESE Business School, University of Navarra; the "Instituto Persona, Empresa y Sociedad" (IPES, *Institute for Person, Business and Society*, http://www.esade.es/institution/institutos/ipes/index.php), ESADE Business School, University Ramon Llull; the Foundation ÉTNOR (www.etnor.org) in Valencia and Castellón, the chair on "Business Ethics and Social Responsibility" (http://alumni.ie.edu/usr/catedra_etica.asp) at the "Instituto de Empresa", a business school based in Madrid, the UNESCO Chair in Technology, Sustainable Development, Imbalances and Global Change (http://www.catunesco.upc.es/esp/fpre.htm) at the Polytechnic University of Catalonia in Terrassa, Barcelona; the Javier Benjumea Chair of Ethics for Economics and Business (http://www.upco.es/webcorporativo/Centros/catedras.asp) at the University of Comillas, Madrid.

Current Situation and Trends in CSR in Spanish Companies

Many Spanish companies have introduced practices related to CSR. A considerable number of companies include some initiatives related to CSR in their corporate statements on mission and/or corporate values, and/or present a certain public commitment to assuming CSR, although some do not mention the maximisation of stakeholder value as their main or exclusive mission. However, it can be deduced that even these latter companies accept some CSR at least as a constraint, because a vast majority present a commitment to respecting the natural environment and to having a code of ethics. In addition, practically every company also has a code of good practice for corporate governance, which is encouraged by current legislation.

Most companies have some community involvement but only a small proportion present themselves as family-friendly companies, and very few say that they are maintaining a dialogue with stakeholders.

Most companies also present an annual social and/or environmental report in addition to the financial. Generally speaking, these reports are not too extensive, neither do they follow specific standards. In fact, it appears that they are only focused on extolling the positive actions that the companies have carried out. However, a limited number of significant Spanish companies have adopted the Global Reporting Initiative (GRI) to prepare sustainability reports. In this way they are considering the "triple bottom line" by presenting financial, social and environmental reports. In addition, a few Spanish companies have adopted the SA8000, a social accountability system which provides workplace standards and a verification system.

The international proposal most successfully adopted in Spain is the UN Global Compact. The "Mesa cuadrada" mentioned above was established in January 2003, and since then the number of companies that have adopted it has increased dramatically. By the end of 2003 almost 200 Spanish companies had joined this network.

A few Spanish companies have a strategic approach towards CSR while others are re-labelling old concepts or are talking about CSR only for reasons of public relations. Some companies have implemented methods for managing CSR and/or for improving corporate reputation. Many of them have created specific departments or managerial positions for dealing with these issues.

Among companies in Spain with a relatively outstanding implementation of CSR, one could mention: BBVA in banking; Endesa, Iderdrola, Unión Fenosa and Gas Natural in energy; Inditex and Mango in dressmaking and fashion; NH Hoteles in tourism; Novartis in pharmaceuticals; Telefónica, Vodafone and Siemens in telecom; Corporación Mondragón, BSH Electrodomésticos and Tetra Pak in manufacturing; and MRW in logistics, among others.

Conclusion

Spanish companies are considering corporate reputation, competitive advantages and the current tendencies of the industry as the major driving forces for CSR. But these elements are closely related to some cultural, social and political influences which have been referred to above.

Some initiatives coming from the EU, such as the Green Papers and subsequent measures of the European Commission, and from international organisations, particularly from the United Nations with its Global Compact are fostering CSR. Associations and fora where leaders of the major corporations are involved, leading business schools and other academic institutions, NGOs and media are also actively promoting CSR in Spain.

Although the degree of implementation of CSR is still moderate, now large and admired business corporations are sensitive to CSR initiatives and implement them in an effective way. This leads one to think that a promising development and implementation of CSR will soon take place in Spain.

Note

[1] Actually, CSR is an old topic which first emerged among practitioners in the 1920s and has been a subject of lengthy debate among academics, at least since the middle of the 1950s when H. R. Bowen (1953) wrote the seminal book *Social Responsibilities of the Businessman* (see recent revisions on the main theories of Carroll, 1999; Windsor, 2001; Garriga & Melé, 2004). Throughout the 20th century many businesses, especially the largest, assumed their responsibilities to some extent, implementing policies and practices related to this topic.

References

Argandoña, A. 1999. Business Ethics in Spain. *Journal of Business Ethics,* 22(3): 155 – 173.

Bowen, H. R. 1953. *Social Responsibilities of the Businessman.* New York: Harper & Row.

Carroll, A. B. 1999. Corporate Social Responsibility – Evolution of a Definitional Construct. *Business & Society,* 38(3): 268 – 295.

Commission of the European Communities. 2001. *Promoting a European framework for corporate social responsibility. Green Paper.* Brussels: EU Commission. http://www.jus-semper.org/Resources/Corporate %20Activity/Resources/greenpaper_en.pdf, accessed 17.02.2004.

Commission of the European Communities. 2002. *Communication from the Commission concerning corporate social responsibility: A business contribution to sustainable development.* Brussels: EU Commission.

Corres, P. 2004. Regulación y voluntariedad en la RSC. In: M. de la Cuesta & L. R. Duplá (Eds.), *Responsabilidad Social Corporativa:* 117 – 131. Salamanca: Publicaciones de la Universidad Pontificia de Salamanca.

de la Cuesta, M., & Valor, C. 2003. Responsabilidad Social de la empresa. Concepto, medición y desarrollo en España. *Boletín Económico del ICE – Madrid,* 2755: 7 – 19.

European Council. 2003. Council Resolution of 6 February 2003 on corporate social responsibility. *Official Journal of the European Union,* 18.2.2003. C 39/3:2003/C 39/02.

Fernández, J. L. 2004. La Responsabilidad Social: Una nueva forma de gestión empresarial. In: M. de la Cuesta, & L. R. Duplá (Eds.), *Responsabilidad Social Corporativa:* 189 – 201. Salamanca: Publicaciones de la Universidad Pontificia de Salamanca.

Fontrodona, J., Melé, D., & Santos, J. 2003. *Ethical Practices in Large Spanish Corporations: Current Status and Perspectives.* Copenhagen: Paper presented at the 2nd Colloquium for the European Academy of Business in Society (EABiS) hosted by the Copenhagen Business School.

Forética. 2002. *Responsabilidad Social Empresarial. Informe Forética 2002. Situación en España.* Madrid: Foretica.

Garriga, E., & Melé, D. 2004. Corporate Social Responsibility Theories: Mapping the Territory. *Journal of Business Ethics:* forthcoming.

IPES. 2002. *Observatorio de los fondos de inversión éticos, ecológicos y solidarios de España.* Barcelona: Instituto Persona, Empresa y Sociedad, Esade.

Jáuregui, R. 2004. La responsabilidad social de las empresas. In: M. de la Cuesta, & L. R. Duplá (Eds.), *Responsabilidad Social Corporativa:* 132–145. Salamanca: Publicaciones de la Universidad Pontificia de Salamanca.

Lafuente, A., Viñuales,V., Pueyo, R., & Llaría, J. 2003. *Responsabilidad Social Corporativa y Políticas Públicas.* Documento de trabajo 3/2003. http://www.ecodes.org/documento-secores/ecodes_fa_RSC_politicas_publicas.pdf, accessed 17.02.2004.

Megías, E. (Ed.) 2000. *Los valores de la sociedad española y su relación con las drogas.* Barcelona: Fundación "la Caixa".

Melé, D., Garriga, E., & Guillén, M. 2000. *Corporate Ethics Policies in the 500 Largest Spanish Companies.* Barcelona: Working Paper No 00/4, IESE Business School.

Melé, D. 1992. *Economía y empresa al servicio del hombre. Mensajes de Juan Pablo II a los empresarios y directivos económicos*: Pamplona: Eunsa.

Olivencia, I. 1998. *El buen gobierno de las sociedades.* http://www.etnor.org/html/pdf/pub_olivencia.pdf, accessed 17.02.2004.

Orizo, F. A.. 1996. *Sistemas de valores en la España de los 90.* Madrid: CIS.

PriceWaterhouseCoopers. 2003. *Responsabilidad Social Corporativa: Tendencias empresariales en España.* http://www.pwcglobal.com/es/esp/ins-sol/spec-int/pwc_rsc.pdf, accessed 17.02.2004.

Transparency Internacional. 1996. *TI Corruption Perceptions Index.* http://www.transparency.org/cpi/1996/cpi1996.pdf, accessed 16.05.2003.

Transparency International. 2002. *TI Corruption Perceptions Index.* http://www.transparency.org/pressreleases_archive/2002/2002.08.28.cpi.en.html, accessed 16.05.2003.

Windsor, D. 2001. The Future of Corporate Social Responsibility. *International Journal of Organizational Analysis,* 9(3): 225–256.

23 Traditional Values and the Pressures of Transformation

José Neves and Luis Bento

Introduction

This paper will report the fundamentals of Organisational Social Responsibility (OSR) as it occurs in Portugal based on the authors' reflection and knowledge. It will start by presenting a brief proposal of a theoretical framework, that comprehends the problem of social responsibility, and then will summarise the involvement and contributions of national partners (companies, government, social partners, unions, employers associations, etc.) within this subject. The first concern will be to identify a definition of OSR that creates a base of understanding that promotes an appropriate aggregation of ideas. The text continues with considerations on the Portuguese reality regarding the area of regulation and implementation, and it concludes with a note on comparative analysis of Portuguese organisations, referring to examples of best practices in social responsibility. Some final notes about motivations, obstacles and trends will complete this reflection.

CSR Concept

The Green Book presented by the EU (2001) defines CSR[1] as "the voluntary integration of social and environmental concerns by companies in their operations and interactions with other interested parties". Notwithstanding the wide range of OSR approaches, certain features are consensual, e.g. a behaviour: a) adopted by the organisations on a voluntary basis beyond the legal obligations, b) closely associated with the concept of sustainable development, integrating the economic, social and environmental impact, c) which is not an optional "extra" added to the organisation core activities but pertains to the way it is managed, and d) is specific to each organisation regarding the importance attached to it and the way it is applied (Bransal, 2002). This set of ideas will be briefly structured in Table 1.

There is high consensus on the idea that the main function of an organisation consists of creating value through the production of goods and services that society needs, thus generating profits for its proprietors and well-being for society,

Table 1. Dimensions and aspects of the OSR concept

Aspect/dimension	Social	economic	environmental
internal	Social climate Employability People management and development	Adequacy Sustainability Perenity	Workplace hygiene and safety Working conditions Occupational health
external	Socio-cultural support	Socio-economic support Sponsorship	Environmental conservation

especially, through a continuous process of employment creation. However, the emergence of new social and market pressures is altering progressively the values and the temporal horizons of the activities of each organisation.

Currently, organisations are conscious that they can contribute to sustainable development by managing its operations in order to consolidate economic growth and increase competitiveness, while assuring concomitantly the protection of the environment and promoting social responsibility, including consumers' interests (Waddock, Bodwell & Graves, 2002). In Portugal, a series of legal charters of mandatory application are intended to regulate aspects that promote more information of a social nature, more health and safety at work, better family-work life balance and better connection of the organisation with the environment (Neves, 2002, 2004).

However, in spite of this normative framework, OSR is something that goes beyond the demands of the law or of any other administration and control system. The different stakeholders consensually accept the idea that the organisation needs to go further, and promote supplementary measures to those stipulated by law with regard to social responsibility (Université Européenne du Travail, 2001).

But this consensus, largely anchored in philanthropy and in ethics, that the law intends to incorporate and to reinforce (see e.g. the Sponsorship law and the IRC law), is weakened whenever it is important to know the impact of the OSR practices upon the strategy and competitiveness of the organisation (Stanwick, 1998; Roman, 1999). There is often a lack of connection between the practices and the stakeholders' expectations, that occasionally leads to minimum benefits being derived from the OSR practices both for the organisation and the beneficiaries. This happens because practices are conceived essentially in the perspective of the organisation and not in the beneficiaries' perspective. Making donations, upholding the law or the ethics codes generate reduced benefits that have a limited temporary impact if these practices are not consonant with the organisational strategy and if the strategy itself does not reflect the genuine expectations of the stakeholders. For example, shareholders want the return of their investment to be an appropriate answer of the organisation to the expectations of the stakeholders; Governments want the activities developed by the organisations to result in significant contributions for the social and economical development of the countries; NGOs and other groups of civil society call for the integration of principles of environmental protection and human rights in the organisations' activities.

To have a fixed budget for social responsibility activities and to scatter it among the several beneficiaries dilutes the real impact of such an effort. To allocate resources to social projects, disregarding the way the application of such resources translates into direct or indirect benefits from the organisation's activities and not to measure its impact, generates results of reduced value and reach (Waddock & Graves, 1997). The considerable percentage of Portuguese SMEs (79%) mentioned in the EU report (The European Observatory of SMEs, 2002) that occasionally or regularly allocates resources to social activities disregarding any strategic framework, that doesn't value social responsibility practices (24%) because they possess reduced knowledge of what it is, or simply because they fail to foresee any benefit coming from its social investment (36%), is a matter of concern. This is why it becomes important to know the level of integration, within OSR management and practices systems, as well as its transparency, standardisation and verification by third parties.

In some organisations and industries there is a long tradition of socially responsible initiatives adopted by managers. What currently distinguishes the meaning of OSR from the initiatives of the past is the attempt to manage it strategically, developing with this purpose the appropriate instruments. This implies an approach that places in the core of organisational strategies the expectations of all parties concerned as well as the principle of innovation and continuous improvement. The several facets of OSR depend on the particular situation of each organisation and the specific context in which it operates and is embedded.

The OSR concept was mainly developed by and for large multinational organisations but it must be adapted in terms of practices and of instruments to the specific situation of SMEs as they constitute the great majority of the national organisations. By virtue of their reduced complexity and of the strong influence exerted by their owners, SMEs often manage their social impact in a more intuitive and informal way than bigger organisations. In fact, many SMEs have already implemented social and environmental responsible practices without being familiar with the concept of OSR or communicating their activities[2].

It can be said that SME social commitment in favour of the communities has a local scope, an occasional nature and is not associated with any managerial strategy. Main driver is the owner's ethical attitude, although a significant number of SMEs also recognises advantages for the business. The lack of sensibility of the companies seems to constitute the largest obstacle to a socially committed attitude, especially among SMEs of smaller dimension with more limited resources.

Unlike big organisations, SMEs do not maximise the current advantages of their social performance. It is therefore important that they receive support to be able to adopt a more strategic approach. Understanding the motives for the different types of SMEs operating in different cultural contexts is crucial to a better understanding of the concept and higher SME participation[3]. As in the domain of quality, which an organisation has to show in order to supply a product or a service to another organisation, also in the social domain, the need to demonstrate social responsibility can contribute to the implementation of socially responsible policies in cultural and strategic terms. The support of national initiatives in the encouragement of social and environmental responsibility in SMEs can constitute a strong incentive to the implementation of a culture of social responsibility[4].

The convergence and transparency of OSR practices and instruments will constitute one of the crucial elements of the present and future debate on this issue. The set of guidelines, principia and codes of ethical-social nature presented throughout the last 15 years, lack a larger generalisation, transparency, verification and external validation. Some of the domains in which a larger convergence and transparency will be likewise desirable are: a) codes of conduct, b) evaluation, reports presentation and validation, c) social labels and d) politicisation of organisational administration.

The voluntary nature of OSR; its integration into the context of sustainable development; the need to deepen its content at a global level; the fact that one cannot expect to find universal one-fits-all solutions; the diversity of interests on the part of the social partners, investors and consumers – all this creates difficulties in the production and administration of such indicators. Now that the stage of the construction and consensus around the OSR concept is surpassed, it is necessary to unite efforts in the sense of finding practices that can equally gain the consensus of the people with regard to ethical-social indicators which one can generalise, verify externally and in an independent way.

General Aspects of the Portuguese Reality with Regard to OSR

In this section, we will make a reference to 1) some individual and institutional initiatives related to the sensibility campaign of OSR, 2) the series of national norms regulating important aspects of OSR, but not covering all, and 3) some information related to OSR practices implemented by SMEs and large-scale Portuguese organisations.

In Portugal, the passive attitude and the low priority given to OSR by the governmental bodies explains the incipient character of OSR divulgation and the highly differentiated ways in which it has been implemented. However, the situation is changing and in the last couple of years a group of events within OSR have taken place in Portugal to promote the concept and socially responsible practices. These were:

1. the international project[5] in which Portugal participated through IDICT La responsabilité sociale des entreprises et des partenaires sociaux dans les systèmes de relations professionnelles des pays de l'Union Européenne: du bilan social et environnemental à l'action sociétale et éthique (outils d'information, systèmes de représentation, pratiques de participation et de retour sur investissement),

2. the seminar on OSR organised by IDICT in 2003 and intended to promote the debate on OSR principles and practices, involving both the Business Owners Association (CIP – Confederation of the Portuguese Industry and CCP – Portuguese Confederation of the Trade and Services) and Union (UGT – General Worker Union and CGTP – General Confederation of the Portuguese Workers) as the main protagonists of the debate and

3. the 28th National Quality Congress promoted by APQ – Portuguese Association for Quality in 2003 having as a theme Quality, Sustainability and Social Responsibility. Herein, individual presentations and round tables explored the OSR issue and many other forums took place that developed technical-scientific discussion about OSR.

Thus, small, medium-sized and large organisations that opt for a culture of social responsibility are progressively increasing in Portugal[6]. At the associative level, there are two recent associations: APEE – Portuguese Association of Managerial Ethics, that was recognised as qualified to exercise functions of Sectoral Normalisation in the domain of Ethics and Social Responsibility, and APRSE – Portuguese Association for Corporate Social Responsibility. These are both framed by medium-sized and big national and multinational companies, that have been promoting the discussion and implementation of Social Responsibility best practices among their associates and others interested. At governmental level, the XV Constitutional Government adopted a more active attitude, giving high priority to this issue, attributing the highest importance to the preparation of a National Strategy for Sustainable Development (ENDS).

This National Strategy's main purpose is "to make of Portugal, within the horizon of 2015, one of the most competitive European Union countries, regarding environmental quality and social responsibility".

It is in this context that some elements of the academic community also reveal interest in this subject. At the beginning, the interests were more individual than institutional (Neves, 2002, 2004; Bento, 2003; Moreira, Rego & Sarrico, 2003; Moura et al., 2004), but progressively, the theme of OSR occupied the agenda of some academic institutions, both by creating research lines at the postgraduate level and by curricular contents related to business ethics within the courses of Management and related areas. Thus, there are conditions to increase and generalise concern with OSR and to minimise the influence of some of the obstacles previously mentioned.

Portugal has some regulations of a prescriptive character with regard to reports on social balance (Law n°. 141/85, Decree n°. 9/92, Decree n°. 155/92 and Decree n°. 190/96). In the social plan, Decree n°. 392/79 that guarantees equal opportunities to women and men regarding work and employment, Decree n°. 111/2000 aimed at the prevention and prohibition of discrimination, Law n°. 105/97 guaranteeing the right to equal treatment at work and employment and Decree n°. 70/2000 that regulates maternity leave and paternity rights within the context of work constitute evidence of this. Alongside the same line of social concern and improvement of hygienic, sanitary and health conditions, one can mention legal instruments related to the framework for work health, hygiene and safety (Decree n°. 441/91 and Decree n°. 133/99), also related with the organisation's security services (Law n°. 7/95, Decree n°. 26/94, Decree n°. 109/2000, Regulation n°. 1179/95 and Regulation n°. 53/96), with the exercise of the industrial activities (Decree n°. 109/91, Decree n°. 282/93, Ruling decree n°. 25/93 and Ruling decree n°. 17/95), with the organisation of work (Decree n°. 347/93, Regulation n°. 987/93, Decree n°. 331/93, Decree n°. 82/99, Decree n°. 349/93, Regulation n°. 989/93, Decree n°. 348/93, Regulation n°. 988/93, Decree n°. 330/93, Decree n°. 141/95 and Regulation n°. 1456 – A/95) and other specific legislation related to hygiene and safety regulations at work (Regulation n°. 702/80, Decree n°. 243/86 and Decree n°. 61/90) and with the conditions of work for youngsters under 16 years (Decree n°. 107/2001) and to pregnancy (Decree n°°. 70/2000). Although important, such regulatory instruments can only guarantee the execution of the minimum requirements in social matters, lacking other incentives for an enlarged concern with social responsibility.

In the environmental plan one should mention Law n°. 11/87 that establishes the basis for environmental policies, Regulation n°. 374/87 that controls industrial residues and Decree n°. 259/92 that establishes the regime of bodies in the domain of environmental quality. The communication of the organisation with consumers and users was also improved by means of Decree n°. 234/93 that defines the Portuguese system of quality.

The legislation mentioned has as common denominators the intention to regulate aspects that contribute to more information (case of the social balance report); prescriptive norms as to hygiene, safety and health at work; the balance between family life and work; and the connection of the organisation with the environment.

Similarly, they are characterised for having a public body as a regulator agent that implies a mandatory application.

However, in spite of these norms, the law does not cover the entirety of OSR. The specificity of each organisation with regard to history, activity, purpose, location, integration within the community, power, etc.; the dynamism associated with the development of society and work, and the globalisation of business and activities, impose new demands with regard to social responsibility. Such demands have manifested traditionally, in many cases, as paternalist attitudes or show-off behaviours rather than true strategic orientations. However, the consciousness of the systemic functioning of organisations, the recognition of the existence of a multiplicity of interdependent actors which are empowered, the acceptance that the organisations are required to be socially responsible, and the identification of the added value of a socially responsible behaviour, push actors to the acceptance of the idea that the organisation needs to go beyond what is legally established as social responsibility.

Several administration and control systems have been developed to aid the organisations to assimilate the principles of social responsibility and to go beyond what is required by law. In the environmental area, it is the ISO 14001 norm, in the social area there are the SA8000 or the AA1000 norms, modelled, monitored and certified in identical ways to ISO norms for quality. Lastly, for hygiene and occupational health there are the OHSAS18001 norms. But the pressures of social responsibility are not just based on these normalised patterns that the organisations adopt on a voluntary base. Other ways of social or institutional pressure contribute to reinforce the assimilation of such principles. We intend to mention the numerous evaluation systems, rankings and awards that a diversity of institutions promote to stimulate the organisational commitment in the assimilation and practice of such values.

In the plan of the implementation, organisations differ in the way they implement social responsibility. Size, industry, culture and commitment of management constitute some of the factors that contribute to the differences, regarding main emphasis (workers, stockholders, customers, vendors, local community, environment, etc.), regarding policy (formalised and with a deferred impact, the casuistic and informal), and finally regarding practice (aligned with organisational strategy and monitored in terms of impact, tacit and implicit) (The European Observatory of SMEs, 2002).

In order to illustrate the diversity of indicators used for the practice of social responsibility, the degree of integration of administration systems and transparency, standardisation and verification of practices of social responsibility by third parties, we analysed a group of Portuguese industrial and services firms and we found evidence of differences and similarities in the ways they exercise social responsibility. Almost all lack proper measures with regard to the demands of external verification, the necessary requirements of benchmarking practice and of external validation. As to similarities, it is worth noting the role that quality has in creating conditions for the integration of these concerns in the administration system as well as in emphasising the involvement of internal actors (managers and workers) and in the focalisation of the social and environmental dimensions inherent to social responsibility. The economic dimension manifests itself mainly in its external aspects (Neves, 2002, 2004).

This seems to sustain the idea endorsed by some authors about the advantage of standardising contents and procedures, thus facilitating an external evaluation and verification[7]. In spite of the particularities of each organisation, we think that organisations would benefit from the existence of such systems, as they would become protected from criticism associated with paternalism, the "show-off", or similar, and will also assimilate more easily the principles of social responsibility.

Conclusions

The results mentioned by the organisations that we studied, relate to the existence of a good social climate and of a good social dialogue. These were translated in the absence of strikes, in a closer connection with the community as shown by collaborations in socio-cultural affairs, sponsorship and the interest in preventing the negative environmental impact of their activities. They also contribute to the modelling of expectations of some of the internal and external stakeholders.

But the question remains whether the expectations created within the organisational administrative system have a strategic status or whether they are merely instrumental. Does the management of expectations follow a paternalistic reasoning, of image management and reputation, or is it part of strategy components?

We think that each organisation's unilateral declaration that such expectations constitute, within the management framework, one of the fundamental pillars of the organisational strategy, is insufficient to realise the validity and credibility of such declarations. The normalisation of contents in terms of indicators and procedures complemented by an external validation and verification, constitute important conditions of validation, transparency and credit to OSR behaviours. It is our opinion that this constitutes one of the main challenges for organisations. Another challenge lies in the permanent evaluation of the impacts of OSR behaviours in the life of the organisation.

But without a long-lasting organisation there is no development, wealth creation, employment, distribution and share of benefits, quality of life, in a word, sustainable development. The economic dimension of OSR in its internal aspect should be an object of special emphasis in the definition, implementation and control of the social responsibility indicators. Nowadays, the ease with which businesses declare bankruptcy and throw workers into unemployment, is a symptom that the economic aspect of OSR is not being adequately developed, in spite of evidence in the social and environmental realms that organisations do show some concern. It will be perhaps a symptom that in some cases, the OSR behaviours that organisations allegedly claim still lack a strategic dimension regarding conception, application, development, and control.

What about the future? One should expect that organisations, either due to a better developed citizenship awareness or due to stronger pressures from commercial, financial, and institutional stakeholders and the public in general (experienced in a variety of territorial levels: local, regional, national and international), will increase their practices of social responsibility and progressively relate them to its activity and business strategy. This will be done intending to detect the added value both for donor and receiver beneficiaries. However, two obstacles can undermine the motivation for social responsibility, especially in the case of SMEs: a) the economic costs associated with the definition, implementation, substantiation, registering, popularisation and control of social responsibility practices and b) the weakened conscience of social responsibility on the part of many of the economic agents.

Public support regarding information, co-financing consulting and intervention costs and intervention at academic training level regarding social responsibility contents, can help overcome these obstacles. The set of events previously mentioned regarding OSR sensibility, underlines the growing interest manifested by Portuguese society. Many organisations implement OSR practices, sometimes without the knowledge of the public, at other times integrating those practices formally into the operational activities reports. However, quite often, for several reasons, they do not develop enough sensibility regarding the importance and advantage of such practices. Greater commitment on the part of the institutional authorities is, therefore, mandatory so that these organisations become aware of OSR through awareness campaigns, more information, popularisation, support and promotion of such practices.

Notes

[1] CSR (corporate social responsibility) is an extremely restrictive expression because it refers only to a generic concept of company. It disregards many other appropriate forms where structured activities take place and that have a nature that surpasses mere profit seeking. Among these are for example social support organisations, public services organisations, cooperative organisations, etc., where one may find subordinate work, asymmetry of statutes and of powers, activities that are structured and regulated by operation norms, customer relationships, etc. The inherent content of the expression CSR, also applicable to several types of organisation, does not express adequately the above mentioned types of organisation. It is therefore advantageous, in our opinion, to find an alternative wider and

comprehensive expression, capable of extending to any type of organisation the content of the concept; perhaps OSR (organisational social responsibility) helps overcome such inadequacy and avoid ambiguity. It is in this sense of the concept "organization" that we generalise and start to use integrated in the expression OSR.

2 In correspondence with the same report, SMEs are characterised, in the majority of the cases, by ownership and management being concentrated in the same person, by that person(s) being well integrated at a local place, by often lacking human, financial and time resources, and by the interpersonal relationships being frequent and very personalised. Such characteristics help explain not only the degree of implication of SMEs with regard to social responsibility, but also the modality of the social support adopted (sports sponsorship, cultural activities, health and well-being activities, training and education activities, environmental activities, support to socially disadvantaged groups, etc.).

3 In correspondence with the previously mentioned report, ethical reasons, improvement of the relationship with the community, increment of the customers' loyalty, improvement of the relationship with partners and investors, increase of employee satisfaction and improvement of the economic result, constitute the main reasons for the adoption of social responsibility practices (varying between 55% and 13% in terms of frequency of the motivation). Third-party pressure, application of codes of conduct and use of public incentives are also motivations, which, however, account for less than 8%. In the same way, the main reasons for not adopting social responsibility practices are the lack of sensibility or the ignorance regarding the subject (24%), shortage of time and money resources (19% and 16% respectively) and the lack of connection with the activities of the company (17%). SMEs with growth, quality and innovation strategies are those that foresee an increase in their participation with regard to social responsibility. Environmental responsibility motives differ from social responsibility motives both in structure and degree of importance. Adaptation to the law, third party pressure, demands of the market, advantage over competitors, improvement of reputation and avoidance of legal sanctions, are the invoked reasons for implementing environmentally responsible practices.

4 With reference to the previously mentioned report, the matter of social responsibility is receiving (although in varying degrees) a growing attention on the part of the public authorities in the different European countries. Although the environmental dimension has been the object of more public initiatives, it is in the domain of the social dimension that the national positioning differs the most: some are more active (the case of Denmark and England) and others more passive and of low priority (Southern Europe countries). In practical terms, England, for example, adopted a group of political initiatives promoting OSR, in which the more paradigmatic is the creation of a Ministry for the social responsibility of companies in March 2000.

5 The project (Social responsibility of companies and social partners within the professional relations systems of EU countries: From the social and environmental plan to societal and ethical action – information instruments, representational systems, participation practices, and return on investment) results of an initiative from the national social partners within the ambit of a European session on the Green Book entitled: "Partnership for a new organization of work" promoted in 1999–2000 for the Strasburg CEES and the INTEP (France) with the support of the European Commission's Employment and Social Affairs Directorate and in collaboration with the Portuguese IDICT (Institute for the Development and Inspection of Work Conditions), VAB (Austria), HAUS (Finland) and AGFOL (Italy). The project pursued the following goals:

- To compare the legal frameworks and the models of social relations concerning the information and consultative instruments in terms of social and environmental affairs, evaluating its pertinence.

- To identify the existing obstacles and the initiatives favouring the development of corporate social responsibility and to confront the existing innovative practices about this matter.

- To enrich the competences of the social actors involved according to the diffusion and transfer of best practices.

[6] From big Portuguese organisations there are good examples of socially responsible practices that have been disclosed within their activity reports. These are even used as advertising messages in marketing campaigns. The above-mentioned EU report on European SMEs reveals that half of European SMEs is committed in varying degrees to social responsibility. In the Portuguese case and in global figures, Portuguese SMEs reveal a degree of superior commitment as compared with the European average, that is to say, 66% against the European average of 49%.

[7] In 2003 an OSR group was created in Paris. It is an informal network constituted by four universities from France, Holland, UK, and Germany, by professional associations of managers and HR experts (APG from Portugal and ADNCP from France), by quality and production technologies institutes from Berlin, Amsterdam, Rotterdam, and by companies (Danone and AGF – Allianz Group), by trade union institutions (Centre for Trade Unions Rights), and by social auditors certification institutions (CCIAS). The group has the purpose of developing an OSR European vision, to prepare ORS auditors' certification models, and to elaborate and promote the adoption of auditing models in OSR.

References

Bento, L. 2003. Da CSR – Corporate Social Responsability à RSO-Responsabilidade Social das Organizações – Alguns contributos para reflexão. *Sociedade e Trabalho,* No. 17/18. Lisboa: MTSS.

Bransal, P. 2002. The corporate challenges of sustainable development. *Academy of Management Executive,* 16(2): 122–131.

Commission of the European Communities. 2001. *Green Paper: Promoting a European framework for corporate social responsibility.* Brussels: EU Commission.

Moreira, J. M., Rego, A., & Sarrico, C. 2003. *Gestão ética e responsabilidade social das empresas.* Cascais: Principia.

Moura, R. et al. 2004. *Responsabilidade Social das Empresas: emprego e formação profissional.* Lisboa: MundiServiços.

Neves, J. G. 2002 – *Corporate social responsibility: The Portuguese national report.* Projet ligne B3 – 4000. Lisboa: IDICT.

Neves, J. G. 2004. Responsabilidade social da organização (RSO): conceito e aplicabilidade. *Recursos Humanos Magazine*, 5(30): 52–63.

Roman, R. M. 1999. The relationship between social and financial performance. *Business and Society,* 38(1): 109–126.

Stanwick, P. A. 1998. The relationship between corporate social performance and organisational size, financial performance and environmental performance: an empirical examination. *Journal of Business Ethics*, 17(2): 195–205.

The European Observatory of SMEs. 2002. *Les PME européennes et les responsabilités sociale et environnementale.* Brussels: Publications DG Entreprises, European Communities.

Université Européenne du Travail. 2001. *Socialement responsable ? Contribution à la réflexion sur la responsabilité sociale et ses pratiques en Europe.* Liaisons Sociales, Paris.

Waddock, S. A., & Graves, S. B. 1997. The corporate social performance-financial performance link. *Strategic Management Journal*, 18(4): 303–319.

Waddock, S. A., Bodwell, C., & Graves, S. B. 2002. Responsibility: the new business imperative. *Academy of Management Executive*, 16(2): 132–147.

Pan-European Approaches

24 Some Implications of National Agendas for CSR

Nigel Roome

Introduction

An increasing number of businesses are embracing the concept of corporate social responsibility (CSR) as they recognise that the world they confront presents a growing array of demands and pressures that are not signalled through markets or the traditional political processes on which they have relied for so long. By its very nature CSR is a complex, multi-faceted phenomenon arising at the interface of business and society. Moreover, the issues covered by the CSR agenda raise important questions about the role and responsibilities of business and the capacity of managers and companies to respond to the challenge of those new roles and responsibilities. The perspective taken in this paper is that CSR involves companies in organisational change as they learn ways to interact with new and enlarged sets of stakeholders and develop responses to their concerns, pressures and expectations.

CSR can be seen to involve generic as well as context-specific aspects. Generic aspects of CSR centre on the notion that the adoption of new roles and responsibilities demands a process of organisational change and the development of routines to manage those demands. This process implies a need to appreciate the demands and pressures on the organisations, to acknowledge, make sense of, and prioritise the areas for change, and, gain the commitment of members of the organisation to that process and the new ways of thinking and routines it demands. This in turn requires the direction of change to be signalled and communicated through some statement of vision of what the organisation needs to become, and, to prepare for that change through a strategy or plan which sets targets, allocates resources, provides for the managerial and organisational competence and sets in motion a process to move the organisation and its members toward the chosen vision. This strategy is then implemented through action programmes, which are supported by a system to monitor and review progress toward specific targets and the broader vision as a basis for the development of new plans and/or to review the vision itself. These aspects of CSR as organisational change are not held to be controversial. Identification of the elements of a vision, making commitment and gaining commitment of others, formulating and implementing a strategy leading to performance on CSR issues (and other unintended outcomes) that feed into a cycle of review and reflection is well established in business.

The source of fascination (and frustration) for researchers and managers stems less from the elements of this generic model and more from the specific issues in managing CSR as organisational change. These issues focus around questions such as:

1. How does the practice of CSR differ from the generic model outlined above?

2. What processes for stakeholder engagement are effective?

3. What institutional and other factors influence the adoption of CSR practices by companies?

4. What processes are effective in gaining commitment to CSR as organisational change?

5. Why do some organisations effect change better than others?

6. How do managers make sense of, rationalise, or develop a business case for CSR?

7. What capabilities and competencies support organisational performance in CSR?

8. How do companies integrate CSR with mainstream business practices?

9. How are choices made when there are conflicts between CSR issues and more conventional business choices?

Although these questions about the rationale, process and repertoires of CSR are critically important for research, policy and practice the purpose of this paper is to address more basic context-specific issues. To this end the paper explores what constitutes the overall field or agenda of CSR and how far this agenda and the response it elicits from companies, is shaped by national culture and institutions as norms, values, customs and rules. It is proposed that this most basic line of inquiry is a cornerstone to understanding the phenomenon of CSR and its managerial, organisational and social implications in a pan-European or international context.

Indeed, the paper addresses two intersecting themes of this book. The first is the great variety of issues, managerial choice and practices, which defines corporate social responsibility (CSR) in European firms. The second is the extent to which it is possible to detect patterns in the issues of and approaches to CSR in Europe and how far these are accounted for by the national (cultural and institutional) origins of firms and their senior managers.

While CSR practice reflects the fact that companies are assuming new roles and responsibilities, when viewed from a European perspective, the CSR agenda contains a wide set of issues. This is not a trivial issue. CSR is a complex, dynamic agenda. It has so many different dimensions that no company can claim mastery of these issues, making it an extremely difficult phenomenon to research.

With this background the paper is structured in three sections. The first section reviews different perspectives on CSR and how they relate to notions such as the socially, environmentally and financially sustainable enterprise. This section seeks to demarcate the overarching agenda of CSR issues. The second section reviews the factors that influence this agenda and how these issues appear to translate into company practices in different European countries. The paper concludes with a call for the development of a research framework for empirical comparative research that provides a basis to measure and compare CSR practices within European firms.

Perspectives and Definitions of CSR

The concept of corporate social responsibility has been subject to increasing debate since the suggestion by Milton Friedman that the responsibility of firms and their management is singularly defined by reference to the need to make choices that maintain and enhance shareholder value within the framework of the law (Friedman, 1962). Others, notably Ansoff (1979), Carroll (1989), Freeman and Gilbert (1988) and Sethi (1975) have suggested that firms have broader (social) responsibilities than those described by Friedman. They suggest that firms have an obligation to meet the requirements of the law but that firms should voluntarily accept responsibilities to society that go beyond those requirements.

Roome (1997) argues that the debate between those who say companies should adopt an explicit stance on CSR and those who say they should not is sterile and unhelpful because, in practice, there are firms that have chosen to interpret their responsibilities to shareholders and owners in terms of their relationships or responsibilities to a wider set of stakeholders. That is to say these companies have accepted that a way to secure value for shareholders is through CSR. This proposition, the business case for CSR, is argued in many ways. For example, CSR is seen as part of organisational/corporate leadership. It is about the development, presentation or maintenance of the value of the company and its "brands". It is part of an approach to risk management. It is consistent with enlightened corporate self-interest. It helps companies secure a continuing licence to operate. It is a potential source of innovation. It is the basis for developing knowledge or relationships that are difficult for others to replicate and therefore a source of competitive advantage. It is necessary in fulfilment of corporate principles or to meet the interests of owners and/or senior managers. It is a clear response to the issues arising from a company's previous exposure to bad publicity or poor practices. It is necessary for company survival.

Irrespective of the arguments used to support CSR it is observed that an increasing number of companies are adopting CSR practice. This has contributed a significant range of experience in terms of the way companies rationalise that practice, develop structures, systems and routines that help in understanding the needs and interests of the stakeholders in their social context, choose appropriate responses to those needs and interests, and, integrate those responses with other business processes and choices. Experience suggests that most companies and their managers approach this in a rather haphazard way.

In addition to the efforts by the more mainstream businesses to adopt CSR, there are others that have chosen to use CSR to establish a distinct position with respect to their role and/or responsibilities in society. This is, for example, the case with the long established co-operative movement or businesses, which combine a commercial approach with a social mission, as is the case with some fair-trade organisations. This is also the situation for privately or family-owned companies where CSR is part of the values or vision of their owners' interests.

That said, the overall agenda for CSR is confused and fragmented. Historically, while more and more companies have developed an explicit position on CSR over the past 40 years, at the same time the issues that make up the agenda of CSR have proliferated and changed. There is a significant dynamic in the issues to which companies (might) respond, as new issues are brought forward and new stakeholders enter discussion with companies about acceptable practices. For example, in the early 1970s there was concern over the functionality and safety of products. This was expressed through the development of the consumer movement upholding the interests of consumers. At the same time there was concern among social activists about the involvement of companies in countries, which were governed by repressive or oppressive regimes. This movement gave rise to calls for companies to disengage from these countries. From the 1980s this early CSR agenda was complemented by concerns about the wider environmental and social implications of company activities. The focus was on the way products were made, distributed and used, or, even more fundamentally, it addressed the environmental and social consequences of the technologies on which products and/or production processes were based. This led companies to adopt management systems to measure and monitor their environmental impacts and to develop and design new products or even new business models with lower environmental impact.

CSR concerns expanded again to include employment issues and conditions (that go beyond legal requirements) especially the fair treatment of employees and other workers irrespective of gender, race, religious orientation, age and disability. Concern for employees also extended to the responsibilities employers might have when closing plant or offices or replacing staff. Employee concerns also include education and training. More recently corporate attention began to include the responsibility to ensure that their suppliers conform to good labour standards and conditions, especially the use of child labour in developing economies. At about the same time the environmental agenda began to take account of the environmental effects of activities in supply chains rather than simply in individual companies and it addressed the role of leading companies in setting standards of practice in their sector or supply chain. Yet more recently, there has been a discussion about issues such as bribery and corruption and the moral hazard for senior managers and company boards when setting the financial rewards of senior managers by reference to share price, and the potential it creates to manipulate earnings and hide or minimise liabilities. This has become a serious issue for management practice and corporate governance along with many other examples of managerial malfeasance such as the abuse of company funds or the appropriation of privileges. This too is now part of the CSR agenda in some countries. So too is the long-standing practice of corporate philanthropy or charitable giving and partnerships with charities.

As the CSR agenda has developed and the topic increased in maturity so has the demand for, and supply of, ethical, social and environmentally responsible investment products available to shareholders whether they are socially and environmentally conscious or not.

While the overall field of CSR to which companies might respond is highly dynamic, fragmented and complex, four main agendas are detected within the broad debate and practice concerning the role and responsibilities of firms in society. First, there are demands on companies and their managements to set and uphold practices, which contribute to the development of high standards in business – for example in areas of employment, health and safety, plant and office closure and staff outplacement, salaries and conditions of labour of suppliers, financial accounting and reporting to shareholders. We call this area responsible business practices.

Second, there are the responsibilities to consumers to provide products and services that are safe, useable and functional and come from safe and reliable supply chains. This area is called consumer responsibility.

Third, companies are increasingly expected to acknowledge the need to restructure their activities in line with the objectives of sustainable development. That is to strive to ensure that their economic activities do not jeopardise the capacity of the environment to sustain the demands and pressures arising from those activities while taking account of social well-being and social concerns – this is the agenda for the sustainable enterprise.

Finally, there are companies that contribute their knowledge, technologies, products, services and other resources to a wide range of social ills such as the regeneration of communities and neighbourhoods, illiteracy, the provision of education and training, the alleviation of illness and disease, the improvement of living conditions, poverty or social inequities and the provision of, or access to, these human needs. These activities can have a very strong alignment with business interests, as is the case when publishing companies provide support for literacy campaigns. Sometimes, however, the rationale for these contributions is not so clear cut, as exampled when companies offer their staff the opportunity to participate in community-secondment programmes. We call this second area corporate philanthropy and corporate community involvement.

In addition an important and valuable distinction can be made in CSR between taking responsibility (for the intended and unintended outcomes of choices and actions) and acting responsibly. Taking responsibility for actions and choices implies something about the transparency and accountability for the processes and structures that are used to guide and make choices. This ultimately concerns the ways choice is governed. Whereas acting responsibly is more concerned with the issues in which action is taken.

These comments and distinctions are helpful in considering the relationship between CSR and sustainable enterprise. It is suggested here that a firm, which strives to be sustainable, has to take responsibility as well as act responsibly. However, it is also possible for firms to take responsibility for activities without an explicit commitment to be sustainable. It is also possible for companies to act responsibly (say by developing their corporate community involvement practices and philanthropy) without necessarily striving to be sustainable.

It is also understood that CSR practices vary between companies and between different sectors, as some sectors (mining, oil exploration, metals manufacture) create more significant social and environmental impacts than others. Often companies in these sectors have been subject to stronger, more enduring, pressure from stakeholders and other interests to take action to solve those problems. It is also observed that while some companies have made significant managerial commitments to CSR practice and performance, many others have not.

Cultural Factors Influencing CSR in a National and European Context

In the previous section the broad field of CSR was set out. It is observed that the CSR agenda has developed in a piecemeal fashion over time, that the developing agenda has affected sectors in different ways, and that companies have many ways to rationalise their approach to CSR and organise their response (or lack of response). It seems evident that no single company has mastered the whole field of CSR issues and practice.

It is also understood that the CSR agenda and the response by companies is not uniform across the countries of the European Community – the UK and Ireland, continental Europe, and the Nordic countries – let alone the enlarged Europe. This observation informs the central hypothesis of this paper – the CSR agenda, followed by leading companies in a country, is influenced by many context–specific factors, but, specifically by the cultural norms, traditions, rules and formal institutions of the country within which the company has its headquarters and by the historical development of societal governance operating in that country. It is suggested that these factors have a strong influence over the CSR agenda pursued by companies as well as affecting the approaches, norms and structures of corporate governance, and the capabilities of companies to manage CSR.

Although these ideas had not been widely applied to the field of CSR their logic stems from established management literature concerning management of organisations in international settings, and the relative capacity for organisational competitiveness or innovation in different national settings. In the case of cultures and organisations Geert Hofstede's pioneering work has established the nature of the different endowments for organisations arising from national cultures (Hofstede, 1991). More critically to our work we draw on the notion that the competitiveness of firms is partly a function of the complex interaction between firms, and between firms and non-economic actors in local settings, whether the "industrial districts" described by Marshall (Marshall, 1961), or the idea of (local) industrial clusters (Best, 1990; Porter, 1990) and their relation to the competitiveness of nations (Porter, 1990).

Similar arguments apply to the differential capacity for industrial innovation, which underpin Dosi et al's (1988) ideas about national systems of innovation. Their argument is that national differences in the institutional embeddedness of innovation processes can be observed. This means that (national or regional) institutional contexts give rise to specific types of innovation (Whitley, 2000) and foster different capabilities and capacities to support the processes of innovation. In short, the south of England UK is observed to have strong capabilities, experience and leadership in financial services, Germany a strong advanced automotive sector, Silicon Valley primacy in the design, development and application of computers and computer systems.

This work on systems and inter-relationships that are locally specific is based on the idea that networks of firms are embedded in national systems and institutions. These influence a firm's ability to compete, innovate and manage. This work acknowledges that performance in mainstream business activities differs between nations. The analysis suggests that organisations are influenced by the competencies at their disposal, by the networks, structures and systems that enable the transfer of tacit and explicit knowledge (between firms, between firms and educational institutes and between firms and other social entities) and by the institutions, as rules and belief systems, that support and guide organisational and managerial behaviour. It is suggested here that the ability of firms to develop and manage responses to the CSR agenda is affected by, and derivative of, what we might term "national systems of corporate social responsibility". However, unlike success in competitiveness, national systems of corporate responsibility not only affect the capacity to govern and manage CSR, they also exercise strong influence over the agenda that makes up the field of CSR. It is more appropriate, then, to talk in terms of "national systems and agendas for CSR".

The following provide some simple illustrations of how these national systems and agendas might affect companies. The social and political history of a country will affect the expectations in terms of dialogue, democracy, and participation. The way that stakeholders in civil society and the non-governmental sector are organised and their position in society will affect the governance of CSR because it influences the ease of engagement between firms and stakeholders that is a key part of CSR. The system of management education and training, the ability of managers to move between sectors and the expectations on senior managers to participate in community and/or local government initiatives will affect the capacity of individual managers to make sense of the motives of other actors engaged through corporate CSR. The social and environmental context, circumstances, and, concerns both past and present affect the CSR agenda to which companies are expected to respond. These elements of CSR are of course interconnected as the social and environmental conditions and concerns often provoke societal responses such as the development of particular expertise and institutional regimes and infrastructure. For example, the long history of concern for wildlife and nature conservation in Britain has become established as a key part of the British education systems, has created environmental pressure groups and led to partnerships involving business, which began in the early 1980s, such as "Industry and Nature Conservation Associations" or Groundwork Trusts (see Nature Conservancy Council, 1989).

The hypothesis that the agenda of CSR and the competence to govern CSR are strongly influenced by national characteristics was considered at a workshop held at the CSR conference "Managing on the Edge" in Nijmegen in September 2003. It was explored qualitatively through a comparison of CSR in Germany and the UK. Professor Dr. Habisch (Germany) and Professor Dr. Moon (UK) were invited to comment on, and discuss, the agenda for CSR and the response to that agenda by leading companies in their respective countries. Their inputs to the workshop were organised around a set of questions in a prescribed format. The format covered the identification of societal concerns in relation to: environmental issues and business; social issues and business; and areas of corporate community involvement. The commentators were also invited to structure observations on the extent to which the management and governance of CSR was subject to the characteristics of the modality of societal governance operating in their country. Again a prescribed format was developed based on the following nine points:

1. Political structure (e.g.: centralised, decentralised)

2. Political style and processes (e.g.: consensus, participative, hierarchic)

3. Social structure (e.g.: elite, egalitarian, meritocracy)

4. Strength of commitment to "voluntarism" as opposed to acceptance of the rules and controls of the state

5. Description of the role of companies in local and national society

6. Description of the role and position of non-government organisations & citizen groups in society

7. Characteristics of educational system (e.g.: valued skills & training)

8. Societal expectations on leaders (e.g.: to direct, to guide, to facilitate)

9. Historical traditions (e.g.: German apprentice/crafts guild system)

The workshop showed that there were marked differences between Germany and the UK in terms of the priorities attached to issues within the overall CSR agenda. The presentations also illustrated qualitatively different approaches to the governance of companies and the management of CSR.

It was clear that no account of CSR could be complete without a strong reflection on historical developments and the dynamics in the relationship between business and society as mediated by, among other factors politics and government. For example, the historical strength of the German tradition in Craft Guilds provided a context to the participation of present-day German companies in education and training initiatives within the theme of corporate-community involvement. There was no similar historical commitment in the UK, although there were politically inspired attempts in the early 1980s to develop company participation in the regeneration of decayed industrial areas including the provision of training and education for unemployed youth and minorities.

This analysis can be extended anecdotally to illustrate some of the important and complex relationships that surround CSR practice across Europe by drawing on four countries – UK, Germany, the Netherlands and Sweden. These are shown in the Table 1 below. Table 1 is organised according to the four fields discussed in the previous section – business responsibility, consumer responsibility, sustainable enterprise, corporate community involvement and philanthropy. Taking each country in turn.

In the UK the suggestion is that companies are involved in all four areas of CSR in the sense that it is possible to isolate companies with a history of leadership in each area. For example there is a particular commitment to sustainable enterprise among leading businesses as well as commitment to areas of corporate community involvement. During the past 20 years both parts of the CSR agenda were developed and promoted, initially within the context of Thatcher Britain's and more recently by the Labour government. The role and position of central government in Britain is critical in shaping this agenda. Government in the UK is relatively highly centralised and adversarial. This stems from a party political and electoral system in which there were strong traditional connections between political parties and interest groups. Elected governments develop policies that are designed to appeal to the "interests" they looked to for political support. Governments therefore had connections with the whole range of economic and social actors, but some actors were closer to power than others. For many years the system was polarised between the interests of "labour" and interests of "capital". While this system is now less strong its legacy is that the main channels of communication between actors was through bipartite relationships with the state. The system resembled a hub and spoke with government at the centre and interest groups and actors on each spoke. As a consequence the dominant pathway for decisions was through the agency and forums of government rather than through more plural forums and loose alliances of interests. The continental European tradition of consensus seeking is weak in the UK.

In the case of corporate community involvement the Thatcher government's involvement in privatisation and the rolling-back of the state in the early 1980s coincided with a period of social unease. The cathartic events around rioting in decayed, inner city areas and the gap of social governance in these areas encouraged government to push for greater business participation in the process of regenerating Britain's older industrial areas and in taking on responsibilities in a range of partnerships commercial and otherwise. This led to calls on business to remember the period of benevolent capitalism that operated in Britain in the 1880s through to 1910 when companies like Cadbury's, Rowntree, Pilkington's and Lord Leverhulme's Port Sunlight factory contributed to the social conditions of the communities in which they were based. These political imperatives were boosted by the patronage of the Prince of Wales for the organisation Business in the Community. On the sustainability side of CSR from the early 1990s, leading companies were involved in sustainability through their participation in voluntary environmental management systems, the promotion of better supply-chain management (British Telecom, B&Q) and new technologies (BP). A bridge between corporate community involvement and environmental issues flourished through the Shell Better Britain Campaign, which involved Shell in sponsorship of community-led environmental initiatives. These same concerns about local communities and environmental concerns began to affect companies with major overseas operations (BP, RioTinto Zinc).

The issues addressed under business and consumer responsibilities similarly arose from the geo-political history of the UK. Britain is a mature, multi-racial society, with a long history of immigration by British citizens of different ethnic origins and religious persuasions from the old Commonwealth countries. This brought forward equality in the work place as a political and social issue. Yet companies, such as Littlewoods, have provided corporate leadership in this area. In terms of consumer responsibilities there has been a long history of consumer activism in Britain, which can be traced back to the development of the cooperative movement as a way to secure consumers' interests in the quality and provenance of products (Cooperative Society). More recently, profound concerns over the integrity of food and food safety arose with the outbreak of BSE. This translated into a highly attuned concern in Britain about the responsibilities to consumers and others arising from the food supply chain. Food retailers (Sainsburys, Tescos), and food processors (Unilever) led this but it also involved food producers. In addition there has been public and consumer concern about the possible implications of a range of new technologies that surround genetic engineering. There were also significant consumer concerns about practices in the financial services sector over the way companies represent the risks associated with a range of financial products. Some of these issues arose when pension plans moved from the state to a mix of state, private and company schemes and also when equity-based mortgage endowment plans were sold based in the inflated returns of the late 1990s.

In Germany the modality of democracy and participation is very different than in the UK. Notions of democracy, based on proportional representation, a strong Federal and local state both involved with companies in the maintenance of a social market has been a dominant feature of post-war Germany. Moreover, this political character, together with the institutionalised participation of labour interests in the governance of firms, has created the setting for a rather different, more plural form of social and corporate governance. Governance in society and business, then, is through the balance of interests – between central and local, left and right, labour and capital. It is a system where the right to speak and the responsibility to listen are valued equally. It is a system where senior managers in companies are expected to remain in contact with the people as employees, or neighbours. Here, corporate community involvement has been a principal part of the CSR agenda more than sustainability and more than labour issues, which have been highly codified in German law.

The sustainability issues that affect German business seem to connect more with the role of German business as "local good neighbours" than the restructuring of business and its technologies. This helps to explain why so many German companies accepted the local reporting requirements of the Environmental Management and Auditing Scheme (EMAS) rather than opting for ISO 14001. It seems that a much stronger emphasis is to be found in German business on their contribution to a range of national and local social concerns. German businesses also participate strongly in education and training initiatives and in a range of company-specific community ventures (see for example betapharm GmbH). This follows the good-neighbour philosophy in Germany and the fact that environmental issues have been heavily dominated by detailed German legislation and public policy. In the same way consumer rights have been subject to protection while the quality and purity of food was, until recently, an unquestioned value in German society. A particular issue is that the corporate governance model operating in Germany involves supervisory boards for companies, which include labour interests directly in company strategy. This has created a context in which labour issues have been less significant as part of (voluntary) CSR practice than in say the UK.

The issue of sustainability dominates the CSR agenda in the Netherlands. In practice the two concepts are used virtually synonymously. Corporate community involvement and corporate philanthropy are not really on the CSR agenda. The exception is that there is extensive liaison or engagement between companies and stakeholders such as civic groups, pressure groups and regulators over the use of land and resources and company practices in a highly populated, congested country. This builds on a long tradition of community centred consensus building and discussion between groups over the development of resources as characterised in the Dutch polder-model. The key issues in the sustainability activities of companies are the licence to operate in the Netherlands (Royal Dutch Shell, DSM, Rotterdam and Amsterdam Ports, Schiphol Airport Amsterdam) and overseas (Royal Dutch Shell, Unilever), the management of supply chains (Unilever, Van Melle), which follow strongly from the trading history of the country, and the concern to be involved in developing new technologies that meet the needs of a more sustainable world (Philips, Essent, Royal Dutch Shell). This owes much to the Dutch tradition of strength in engineering and technological education. And to the role of education and research in pushing the sustainability agenda. Similarly, there is a CSR fringe area based on corporate community involvement and capacity building through social projects in developing countries, which links together the traditional role of Dutch companies in commodity chains and financial services (Triodos, RaboBank) to the social and environmental needs of producers and communities in developing economies.

In Sweden the physical demands of climate and geography, an enduring sense of community spirit and collective support and care for those most in need created a system of societal governance that placed store on pluralism and consensus. This brought high levels of state provision for many aspects of social welfare. High standards of living and social welfare provision mean that corporate community involvement in Swedish companies has been directed less toward Sweden and more toward community involvement and to the fostering of high labour standards in developing economies. Moreover, Sweden has traditionally been very active in overseas development, technology transfer and capacity-building and there is continuous social pressure on companies operating overseas to ensure their activities respect the interests of local communities and adopt high standards of business practice. By the same token employment and consumer issues are less significant parts of the CSR agenda and the involvement of business in education and training or health and well-being of Swedish society has not been an issue for CSR.

Table 1. Comparison of CSR agenda by country

Issues \ Country	UK	Germany	Netherlands	Sweden
Responsible Business Practices	• Racial & gender equity • Emerging issues around financial accountability & governance	• Emerging issues around financial accountability & governance, executive rewards	• Emerging issues around financial accountability & governance	• Practices in Developing Countries – corruption, child labour • Emerging issues around financial accountability & governance, executive rewards
Consumer Responsibility	• Food safety & provenance • Financial services products	• Food safety & provenance	• Quality for low price	
Sustainable Development	• Protected areas and species • Supply-chain issues & auditing • Management systems & reporting	• Waste recycling • Resource efficiency • Neighbourhood reporting and liaison	• License to operate • Community liaison • Supply-chain management • Product innovations	• Resource & energy efficiency • Product innovation & technology • Forest products • Development issues
Corporate-Community Involvement & Philanthropy	• Area regeneration • Community projects • Public/private partnerships	• Strong commitment to education/ training • Company-specific CCI	• Not really an issue except a minor concern for community issues in developing economies that provide commodities	• Corporate/ community involvement in developing countries

More recently the historical concern for frugality in the use of resources and the emphasis in the structure of industry around natural resources – timber and wood products and now high technology – has created pressure for resource efficiency and sustainable enterprise. Leading companies in the pulp and paper products sector (Stora-Enso), in telecommunications (Ericsson), electrical goods (Electrolux), domestic and office products (Kinnarps and Ikea) and construction (Sandvika) have a reputation for efficiency and the search for more sustainable applications of technology. This has been boosted by the emergence of the Natural Step movement, which itself emerged through a consensus process in Sweden and has had significant influence on the thinking of many Swedish companies.

The author of this paper recognises that a much deeper analysis of these issues is necessary than is permitted here. Nevertheless these preliminary observations make clear a number of points:

1. The CSR agenda has developed over time in line with the changing social, political and environmental context of countries.

2. The CSR agenda impacts companies in different sectors in different ways.

3. As the CSR agenda is discretionary for companies so the issues they choose to respond to as part of their approach to CSR are often specific to the company context, its values or business principles, technologies, resources, capabilities, products and markets.

4. Leading companies in CSR adopt a more or less generic approach to managing CSR issues.

5. Notwithstanding the variation between companies and sectors the CSR agenda is conceived differently in different countries in Europe and internationally.

6. The governance structure of companies, together with the company's national context appears to influence the way that CSR issues are managed as well as the set of issues that are managed.

Conclusions

The observations in this paper have a number of important implications for research, policy and managerial practice. It is recognised that a particular problem arising for researchers, managers and policy-makers in using the term CSR without any further qualification is that the meaning of the concept does not travel well. Put simply CSR to a Dutch researcher or manager seems to involve a different set of issues, with different priorities and practices than it does in the UK, Germany or Sweden. The only issue that unites these four national perspectives is that CSR involves business organisations in voluntarily taking on new roles and responsibilities that go beyond legal requirements in terms of the impacts of the company on shareholders, the environment, communities, businesses or consumers both locally and/or internationally. CSR in that sense is about organisational change, which involves the development of new relationships with a much more complex mix of stakeholders than has hitherto been the case.

In terms of research the variety of practice in CSR in Europe raises the need better to understand this diversity, together with its causes and consequences. In particular, we need to see more clearly what issues and approaches contribute to the overall field of CSR. Appreciate how company practices differ by organisational and national culture. Recognise the organisational structures, routines and managerial competences that shape the managerial practices around CSR, and, have some sense of the way that ideas and practice diffuse between companies, and, within nations and regions, under the pressure of internationalisation of business.

The commitment of the European Commission to promote higher standards of corporate social responsibility among European firms also raises issues of policy. These include questions about whether a European benchmark for CSR practices is appropriate? The extent to which the variation in practice between firms is acceptable to a policy within Europe that seeks to encourage high standards yet supports diversity? And, to what extent, can policies and actions identify and diffuse best practices, within the overall field of CSR, and encourage the development of a pan-European approach to CSR that builds constructively on this diversity?

In the case of practice, many European companies are raising their market and production horizons from the national level to the pan-European level and beyond. One implication of this process of internationalisation is that firms move from markets and locations with which they are familiar to territories that are less familiar. At the same time all aspects of a firm's activities, including CSR, are increasingly subject to international comparison. It is equally clear that what groups of stakeholders might regard as important CSR issues in one country are not necessarily the same issues that groups would regard as important in other countries or locations.

This brings forward a very practical issue for many leading companies namely: what constitutes good CSR practice in one country or sphere of operation might not be regarded in the same way in other countries. This implies that CSR is increasingly a strategic consideration in the positioning of companies in society and the process of internationalisation.

The dilemmas for companies that operate internationally particularly affect them when they are concerned about the sustainability of global commodity or supply chains. While there is significant variation in the agenda for CSR in Europe, that variation is even greater between Europe and developing economies. Developing economies often place more emphasis on employment opportunities and the development of economic and social conditions through the addition and retention of added-value, while developed economies place more emphasis on environmental concerns and the avoidance of child labour and bad employment practices and the avoidance of bribery.

A difficult task for companies is found in the choice about which priorities: which groups in which settings have claims that make sense to a company and its CSR practices. And this choice itself implies either a method for weighing priorities or decentralising responsibility for setting CSR agendas to the local level. Consequently, the need to be able to construct a more informed picture of the CSR issues by country is an increasingly important issue in managing business in their international setting.

The main implication of this paper is the call for the development of a concerted comparative research programme on national agendas and approaches to CSR within Europe. There is need for the development of an empirical methodology that enables an understanding of the (local) national variations in the agenda of CSR, is able to detect whether companies in different countries have different capabilities in managing these issues, and, places these variations in a pan-European or more global context.

This research needs to be developed around a methodology, which acknowledges that the European CSR agenda is more expansive than any one national agenda and that other world economic regions – North America, South East Asia, China, South and Central America, Africa, India and Russia – do not necessarily share the European CSR agenda as a whole. There is much that researchers can learn and managers need to learn from the diversity of issues, approaches and practices that are available in these other countries and regions.

References

Ansoff, H. 1979. Strategy and strategic management: the changing shape of the strategic problem. In: D. Schendel, & C. Hofer (Eds.), *Strategic Management.* Boston: Little, Brown and Company.

Friedman, M. 1962. The responsibility of business is to increase profits. *New York Times Magazine,* September 13: 12.

Best, M. 1990. *The new competition.* Cambridge: Polity Press.

Carroll, A. 1989. *Business and society: Ethics and stakeholder management.* Cincinnati: South Western Publishing Company.

Dosi, G. et al. 1988. *Technical change and economic theory.* London: Francis Pinter.

Freeman, R., & Gilbert, D. 1988. *Corporate strategy and the search for ethics.* Upper Saddle River, NJ: Prentice Hall.

Hofstede, G. 1991. *Cultures and organizations: Software of the mind.* New York: McGraw-Hill.

Marshall, A. 1961. *Principles of Economics,* 9th Edition. London: MacMillan.

Nature Conservancy Council. 1989. *Partnership Review.* (Eds.), A. Vittery & Roome, N. Peterborough: Nature Conservancy Council.

Porter, M. E. 1990. *The competitiveness of nations*. New York: The Free Press.

Porter, M. E. 1998. Clusters and the new economics of competition. *Harvard Business Review*, Nov-Dec: 77 – 90.

Roome, N. 1997. Corporate environmental responsibility. In: T. Bansal, & E. Howard (Eds.), *Business and the natural environment*. Oxford: Butterworth-Heinemann MBA Series.

Sethi, P. 1975. Dimensions of corporate social performance: an analytical framework. *California Management Review*, Spring: 58 – 64.

Whitley, R. 2000. The Institutional Structuring of Innovation Strategies: business systems, firm types and patterns of technical change in different market economies. *Organization Studies,* 21: 855 – 886.

25 A Conceptual Framework for Understanding CSR

Dirk Matten and Jeremy Moon

Introduction

In recent years the concept of corporate social responsibility (CSR) has gained unprecedented momentum in Europe. Even the sceptical Martin Wolff, Chief Economics Correspondent of the *Financial Times* commented that "CSR is an idea whose time has come" (Wolff, 2002: 62). CSR is a cluster concept which overlaps with such concepts as business ethics, corporate philanthropy, corporate citizenship, sustainability and environmental responsibility. It is a dynamic and contestable concept that is embedded in each social, political, economic and institutional context.

Notwithstanding this recent flurry of CSR activity in Europe, business social responsibility was traditionally regarded in Europe as a peculiarly American phenomenon, reflecting American traditions of participation, self-help and small or at least indirect government. There is, however, no evidence that those taking a comparative view of business-society relations on either side of the north Atlantic over the twentieth century would necessarily argue, by virtue of the relative low salience of CSR in Europe, that its businesses were socially *irresponsible*. Indeed there is evidence to the contrary. Vogel concluded that UK business is "more susceptible to social pressure both from government officials and from other forums to behave 'responsibly'" (1986: 50). This raises broad questions about the changing nature of, and the reasons, for European corporate social responsibility. In particular it raises a conceptual paradox: was it possible for business in Europe to be socially responsible in the absence of a language of CSR in Europe. And, to what extent does the recent adoption of a language of CSR in Europe reflect a fashion in management, or something genuinely new in the European corporate landscape. We reserve the term "genuinely new" to describe a situation in which the advent of modern CSR implies a previous disregard by corporations in Europe to live up to a set of responsibilities towards society, however defined.

Our argument developed in this chapter is that CSR in Europe, as defined by the majority of recent academic writings and corporate publications, is only "new" in the sense that it represents an innovation in *corporate policies*. While we would maintain that there is a long tradition of business involvement in many of the issues associated with modern CSR. These have been tackled by corporations in Europe for most of the last century (in some cases even longer). However, this company-social engagement was understood, articulated and performed in different ways.[1]

We seek to reconcile this contradiction by proposing a distinction between *"explicit"* and *"implicit"* CSR. We conceptualise CSR as a way of thinking and a set of practices enacted and addressed by – mostly voluntary – corporate policies, which *explicitly* circumscribe the responsibilities towards society, which corporations seek to address. On the other hand, the majority of issues which count as corporate responsibilities towards society in a European context are not part of the corporation's explicit policies but they are *implicitly* codified in the norms, standards and legal framework of Europe and its nations.

We use the distinction between explicit and implicit CSR to make sense of:

1. the rise and role of the new CSR in Europe, and

2. the way this approach to CSR interacts with deeply embedded national institutional contexts as CSR transforms from an implicit to an explicit form; and

3. the contextualisation of CSR in different national cultures, particularly those without a history of the Anglo-Saxon system of capitalism.

As background, we recognise that twentieth century Europe has experienced a wide range of political and economic systems including systems in which business motivated by profit and open and democratic forms of civil society have been suppressed; those with no independent business sector; those where corruption and irresponsibility flourished. However, we would argue that there are certain similarities between European countries, which manifest themselves in the way CSR is understood and practised and that this understanding is different from, for instance, the USA. We also acknowledge that there are still significant differences among European countries and that most of our thinking is informed by the experiences of CSR in west and north European countries and only to a lesser degree Central and Eastern Europe. The first group of countries have enjoyed extended periods of liberalism, democracy and regulated capitalism in a mixed economy and which, all things being equal, we would expect to resemble American business–society relations.[2] Secondly, we recognise that some features of American societal governance have similarity with features of the European model. Indeed in some cases the USA pioneered regulation for social responsibility (e.g. the post-civil war pensions and public sector employment, the New Deal, the regulatory work of the Environmental Protection Agency in the 1960s).

What is CSR?

A wealth of literature has been published on CSR over the last 30 years, many containing their own definition of CSR and related concepts (see for an overview Crane & Matten, 2004a: 37–71). Despite the variety of definitions, probably the most widely accepted and referred to conceptualisation of CSR found in the business and management literature is that of Archie Carroll, who sees CSR as a construct relating to four different areas of business-society relations (Carroll, 1979, 1991).

- **Economic responsibility.** Companies have shareholders who demand a reasonable return on their investments; they have employees who want safe and fairly paid jobs; they have customers who demand good quality products at a fair price etc. By definition this is the reason why businesses are set up in society and their first responsibility is to function properly as an economic unit and to stay in business. All subsequent responsibilities are based on this first layer of CSR. According to Carroll, the satisfaction of economic responsibilities is thus *required* of all corporations.

- **Legal responsibility.** The responsibility of corporations in relation to law demands that they abide by its provisions and "play by the rules of the game". Carroll suggests that the satisfaction of legal responsibilities is *required* of all corporations seeking to be socially responsible.

- **Ethical responsibility.** This responsibility obliges corporations to do what is right, just and fair, even when they are not obliged to by the legal framework. Carroll argues that ethical responsibilities therefore consist of what is generally *expected* by society over and above economic and legal expectations.

- **Philanthropic responsibility.** The fourth level of CSR looks at the philanthropic responsibilities of corporations. This aspect of CSR addresses a great variety of issues, including things such as charitable donations, the building of recreation facilities for employees and their families, support for local schools, or sponsoring of art and sports events. According to Carroll philanthropic responsibilities are merely *desired* of corporations.

A core debate in CSR is the idea of voluntary initiative by the corporation. This certainly applies in the areas of ethical and philanthropic responsibilities, but would also apply to the first two levels. The underlying rationale of explicitly stating economic and legal "responsibilities" as "requirements" of corporations assumes that – certainly on a short term basis – corporations have discretion in the way they live up to these responsibilities. Businesses can choose to, or by virtue of neglect, fail to meet responsibilities to the major stakeholders of companies, shareholders and employees.

However, the more familiar face of CSR does not centre on economic obligations to shareholders and employees or obligations to obey the law but to voluntary initiatives, programmes, policies and strategies of corporations to assume responsibilities towards society based on some ethical or philanthropic motivation. A plethora of other definitions and views on CSR have been suggested and discussed over the years but we would argue that Carroll's definition captures probably the lowest common denominator of CSR.

CSR in a European Context

Carroll also sets CSR and the development of related concepts, such as corporate social performance, business ethics, corporate citizenship, in an American context (Carroll, 1999). The corporate world and the academic literature suggest that the notion of corporations adopting CSR policies in order to live up to their "responsible" role in society derives first and predominantly from the United States. Given the recent attention to CSR in Europe this leads us to ask:

- Why has the US been ahead?

- How has it been possible that European corporations could have neglected the important issue of their responsibility to society?

- Why is it that European corporations are only now discovering their responsibilities towards society and are, as it were, catching up?

Our argument is that CSR as a voluntary corporate policy is a fairly recent and still scattered phenomenon in a European context. Corporations in most European countries are adopting CSR policies while the need to address and define a European approach to CSR has been more clearly felt on a political level. This has led the Commission of the European Communities (2001: 6) to define CSR as "a concept whereby companies integrate social and environmental concerns in their business operations and in their interaction with their stakeholders on a voluntary basis". This echoes the Anglo-American view of CSR. However, the fact the European Commission should make this statement in 2001 does not imply that CSR was previously neglected in Europe.

Table 1 provides some examples of issues, which would be the subject of CSR policies in an American and European context. While there is more granularity at the level of individual firms and countries, our intention here is to make a broad contrast.

We suggest that the key reason CSR has not been discussed to the same extent in Europe as it has been in the US is that the legal framework and institutional fabric in Europe has been inclusive of many of the issues that arise under CSR. These derive from historically different models of trust and authority relations from

Table 1. CSR issues in the American and European contexts (examples)

	American Context	**European Context**
Economic responsibilities	Corporate policies with regard to "good corporate governance", "remuneration" or "consumer protection"	Legal framework, codifying corporate constitution ("Betriebsverfassungsgesetz"), the 35h-week, minimum wage legislation or lengthy and elaborate legislation for developing and testing pharmaceuticals
Legal responsibilities	Relatively low level of legal obligations on business	Relatively high levels of legislation on business activity
Ethical responsibilities	Corporate policies with regard to local communities	High level of taxation in connection with high level of welfare state provision of local public services
Philanthropic responsibilities	Corporate initiatives to sponsor art, culture or fund university education	High level of taxation sees governments as the prime provider of culture, education etc.

those that prevail in the more liberal USA. This is captured in Albert's (1991) vivid conception of the "Rhenish model" of capitalism – a model in which formal institutions integrate and embed the social responsibility of corporations (such as laws, regulation, mandatory requirements) but have also given rise to less formal institutions, values, attitudes, customs or traditions which locate the role of the corporation in society much closer to societal goals and agendas than is found in the American system.

The precise nature of these formal and informal institutions and the drivers behind their development clearly varies among countries. Sweden's nineteenth century constitutional monarchy always stressed the need for consensus-seeking procedures among the estates and set a ground on which the democracy that emerged in the twentieth century was founded. The German guild tradition informed the habits of employers for over four hundred years through the guild providing apprenticeships for the good of society as well as business. This continues to underpin the German industrial training system. From the early nineteenth century the British parliament developed a regulatory framework and inspectorates to address the most anti-social manifestations of industrialisation – from slavery, to child-labour, working conditions, industrial location and pollution.

More recently, while the foundation for European post-war settlements differed between nations, they set much of Europe apart from the USA in terms of today's public policies and private duties. In the post-war UK, a shared desire to avoid the political and social divisions of the 1930s meant that key aspects of Labour's health and welfare reforms were sustained by the Conservatives. The main provision of post-war public housing was under Conservatives. Conservatives and Labour alike developed a tri-partite (government-business-labour) approach to a range of policy issues from prices and incomes policy to education, training and technology. For its part Sweden continued to build on its historic consensus-seeking neo-corporatist approaches to public issues. In West Germany, the imperative of developing a mainstream consensus to isolate fascist and communist groups as a political force resulted in a system of corporate governance, which provided employees with a legal status of equal standing to shareholders. These legal mechanisms in Germany were supported by a consensus mentality and informal institutions which have influenced the discretion of corporations which impact wider society's social and environmental interests and concerns (e.g. Lane, 1989, 1992; Lane, 1994).

Our point is that the social responsibilities of European corporations have been less a matter of their individual discretion than their USA counterparts. The social responsibilities of European business have been played out in a context with more deeply entrenched and embedded relationships between business, society and the state.

In the literature (Whitley, 1997, 1999) we can identify typical areas which constitute national specific elements of a particular national business system which all closely relate to CSR:

- *The role of the state in risk sharing/economic activity*

    The involvement of European governments in large and mandatory insurance systems for health, pensions and other social commodities gave rise to pressure on corporations to take over significant responsibility for these issues as a result of mandatory regulation. Governments with stakes as major shareholders or sometimes owners of corporations place issues of social risk at the top-level of corporate concerns. In the US social commodities and risks are a much more discretionary issue. The main impact of government in America is the provision of incentives to employers through negative tax expenditures. Corporations may well provide pension schemes, not as a result of compliance but of calculation of labour market factors, employee relations and CSR profile.

- *Less stronger influence of capital markets*

    In credit-based systems of corporate capital sourcing there is an institutionalised propensity of corporations to regard stakeholder claims other than those of shareholders as more legitimate than in market-based systems. For example corporations already seek to safeguard the employment part of their corporate policies and regard it as legitimate to "sacrifice" some degree of profitability to these policy goals.

- *Regulation of labour markets, role of trade unions and industry association*

  A particular area of CSR policies would be the role of employees and the position of labour as a production factor. Many of the firm-based policies, which are described as CSR in America, are redundant in a European institutional setting as it is mandatory for corporations to fulfil such measures.

Explicit and Implicit CSR – A Definition

The conclusion of our discussion so far is that CSR as a policy of voluntary engagement to meet the corporation's obligations towards society has not been an overt feature of European economies. Nevertheless, corporations in Europe have participated in activities and policies with a similar orientation not so much on a voluntary basis but as a result of requirements of their social environment, enacted by the institutional framework of business. Moreover, in Europe business associations have normally participated with other social and political actors in the design, review and re-design of such systems. This legitimises the obligations in the eyes of most corporations.

It could be asked why conformance with the law would count as *corporate* social responsibility? Much of the CSR literature argues that this could not be regarded as CSR as it is not a discretionary activity at the level of the corporation (e.g. Friedman, 1970; McWilliams & Siegel, 2001), notwithstanding the fact that corporations are part of a system which is responsible to society. Yet other authors (e.g. Carroll above) would recognise that business participation in such a regulatory system could be regarded as corporate social responsibility as it entails obedience to the law.

Our analysis of the character and modality of social responsibility in North America and Europe leads us to distinguish between implicit and explicit CSR. We propose the following definitions:

Explicit CSR refers to *corporate policies* that lead companies to assume responsibility for some interests of society. Explicit CSR would normally involve voluntary, self-interest driven policies, programmes and strategies of corporations to address issues perceived by the company and/or its stakeholders as part of their social responsibility.

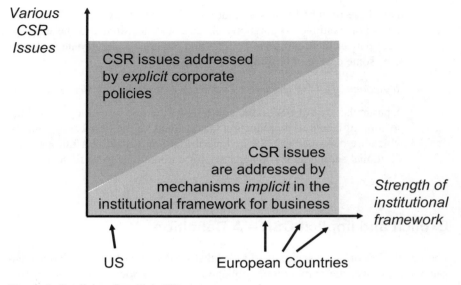

Figure 1. Implicit and explicit CSR

Implicit CSR refers to a country's *formal and informal institutions* through which the corporations' responsibility for society's interests are agreed and assigned to corporations. Implicit CSR normally consists of values, norms and rules, which result in (mostly) mandatory requirements for corporations to address issues, which social, political and economic interests consider a proper and reasonable obligation upon corporate actors.

Figure 1 shows how explicit and implicit CSR relate to each other. Implicit and explicit CSR are both approaches to deal with the same kind of issues, namely social issues in the relations of corporations to their stakeholders in the broadest sense. Both types of CSR represent competing approaches and – as the figure indicates – are present in most societies at the same time. The significant difference though lies in which approach assumes dominance. So, for instance in the US, while the general approach seems to be that the majority social issues are dealt with in the form of explicit CSR policies of corporations, there are still significant elements of (implicit) corporate social responsibilities regulated by the legal framework, for instance worker's rights issues and the role of trade unions. Similarly, in Europe, despite a strong emphasis on implicit CSR there is and has always been quite a substantial amount of explicit CSR in the form of philanthropy.

This distinction can be fleshed out further. *Implicit* CSR is embedded in the business-society-government relations within a political system. It may result from strong norms, which all parties recognise and in which all participate. These norms may inform regulation whose legitimacy is confirmed by its democratic context or prevailing approach to policy-making, such as participatory consensus-seeking practices. In these circumstances we would expect strong systems of social capital to grow up around the development and performance of the norms and the regulation.

Explicit CSR represents a departure from the more implicit CSR through its special focus on the corporation; the imperatives and drivers for social responsibility acting on corporations; and the tools for social responsibility that corporations can deploy. This special focus on the corporation can be encouraged by: corporations themselves, other business drivers such as public policy and government ideology, business associations and societal representatives.

Our point in making this distinction between implicit and explicit CSR is not simply to enable a better theatrical base for trans-Atlantic comparisons of CSR but also to make sense of the recent evidence of a move toward a more explicit form of CSR in Europe.

Evidence of More Explicit CSR in Europe

There are various factors that have contributed to a shift in the balance between implicit and explicit CSR in Europe toward the explicit. The first is the emergence and growth of CSR business associations or umbrella organisations. At the European level CSR Europe was established in 1996 consisting of 60 member companies and 18 national partner organisations from sixteen different countries. The most prominent and longest standing of the national partners is the British Business in the Community with a membership of over 700 firms accounting for 20% of the national private sector employment mainly based in the UK.

Secondly, there is a wide range of other organisations that have grown up around the theme of CSR. These include CSR "vanguard" organisations, which are dedicated to raising standards of corporate practice. There is also an emerging industry of CSR consultants who work to assist corporations with their CSR policies, stakeholder relations and CSR reporting (Fernandez Young, Moon & Young, 2003). Some of these are general consultants who have developed a CSR portfolio whereas others are dedicated entirely to CSR. Yet other organisations have come into operation to provide services to the CSR industry such as conferences and newsletters.

Thirdly, CSR has a more explicit status within companies, particularly in the form of dedicated board level responsibilities, senior managers, CSR professionals, organisational sections, processes, codes, programmes and budgets. Companies are increasingly likely to report their CSR policies and position within their annual reports, in freestanding reports or in their general corporate communications.

CSR is also the subject of increasing attention outside companies and the CSR organisations. Concern about CSR has now increased in the investment community with the growth of socially responsible investment funds, particularly in the UK but also in many other European countries. CSR has become a subject of increasing media attention, both as exposure to poor performance and also in the call for better and more explicit standards. In business education CSR appears to have a significantly more explicit profile in European universities and business schools, with new centres and dedicated teaching and research programmes (Matten & Moon, 2004). Finally, CSR is increasingly a concern of governments who are deploying various means encouraging companies to raise their CSR standards at home and abroad. This is specifically true of the European Union which has contributed to the debate on CSR in various documents and initiatives (e.g. Commission of the European Communities, 2001, 2002).

Why Explicit CSR in Europe?

The earlier discussion identifies the trend toward a more explicit CSR in Europe but it does not really explain the shift from implicit to more explicit CSR.

We hypothesise that this shift could be expected to result from some disjuncture in the wider system of social governance or national business system resulting from government/governance failures, new market imperatives or new social demands. In practice these conceptualisations are usually related, but for present purposes it helps to distinguish them.

The most dramatic example of government or institutional failure is where there is a complete breakdown of systems of societal governance, as was the case in the former Eastern Europe. In these circumstances, new systems emerge although their development is necessarily slow and tentative, especially in the absence of the sort of social capital predicated upon a well established civil society and long-standing habits of business responsibility which many of these systems face. However, explicit CSR may prove one among a range of governance solutions here and there is evidence that this is the case in Poland, Hungary and the Czech Republic (coincidentally countries which retained some vestiges of civil society through the periods of communism).

For all their well-established governance systems, even the west European countries can face deficits in governance. Perhaps the most dramatic has been the case of mass unemployment, urban unrest and fiscal stress experienced in the UK in the late 1970s and early 1980s. This is more or less the case for most Western European countries where corporate decisions on downsizing, relocation and mechanisation of production processes have been met by heated debate on the responsibility of corporations for a particular town, region or country. Interestingly, in the case of Denmark, record levels of unemployment and dependency on government in the 1990s prompted the Social Democratic Minister for Social Affairs to encourage various forms of CSR alongside government responses (Jespersen, 2003). In a similar vein, there is a broad literature arguing that corporations have increasingly stepped into a "sub political" (Beck, 1997) role in the area of environmental (in the sense of ecological) issues as governments have blatantly failed to avoid or handle the undesired side-effects of an energy intensive form of production and consumption (e.g. global warming, nuclear power), new technologies (e.g. GM food) or scandals (e.g. mad cow disease), just to name a few examples (Matten, 2004).

Similarly, new market imperatives may prompt business to adopt a more explicit CSR. At the most basic level the new imperative may concern the social licence of business to operate. Again, this was clearly articulated in the context of the UK governance crisis alluded to above. As *The Economist* commented of Marks & Spencer's expenditure on community work and charity, the firm was "making a sensible investment in its market place. If urban disorders become a regular fact of life, many of its 260 stores would not survive." (20.2.1982)

Another motivation for business may concern the perceived threat of new and unwelcome regulation. This was expressed by the leading UK business association, the Confederation of British Industry, in the context of the UK governance crisis: "companies fear that if they make no attempt to find solutions to community problems, the government may increasingly take on the responsibility itself. This might prove costly to employers both in terms of new obligations and greater intervention in the labour market. Many companies prefer to be one step ahead of government legislation or intervention, to anticipate social pressures themselves and hence be able to develop their own policies in response to them" (CBI 1981 quoted in Moon, 2004b).

Another relevant market imperative may be the growing importance of financial markets for business success. In this context explicit CSR may be regarded as a prerequisite for attracting global capital and the more European companies source their capital globally the more they have to comply with the requirements of international investors, particularly in the US. In a similar vein, CSR has been encouraged by a particular group of investors which integrate social and ethical criteria into their rationale, leading to developments such as the Dow Jones Sustainability Index or, in Europe, the FTSE4Good index (further reasons for an increase in CSR in Europe are discussed by Crane & Matten, 2004b).

Specifics of "Explicit" CSR in Europe

Though we argue that explicit CSR is gaining momentum in Europe and as such can be seen as part of a growing evidence about a potential Anglo-Saxonisation of

European businesses (Mayer & Whittington, 2002) there are, however, distinctly European features in the CSR engagement of European companies. Traditionally, the key issues in business-society relations have been played out around the question of the roles and the rights of employees. During the 1970s and 1980s, however, green issues and environmental protection became a key political issue in Europe and entered the business agenda relatively early. So, for instance in Germany, the first textbook for environmental management education in business schools was published already in 1980 (Strebel, 1980). Though the issues quickly became part of the "implicit" framework for CSR, the styles and approaches in tackling green issues in European societies remain distinct, most notably from the USA (Lofstedt & Vogel, 2001). This particularly applies to "new" issues such as genetic engineering, BSE and other risk related issues (Levidov & Carr, 2000; Wynne & Dressel, 2001). A recent manifestation of these changes became visible in the decision of Shell and BP to leave the Global Climate Coalition, a group of mainly American oil companies, set up to lobby against the implementation of the Kyoto Protocol and other measures of environmental protection (Levy & Egan, 2000; Levy & Kolk, 2002).

While we stressed the importance of implicit elements in the CSR framework in Europe one might also argue that part of the explicit CSR activities of companies consists in an active participation in changing and innovating the negotiated legal framework. In contrast to the US, where lobbying would be the key "weapon of choice" for corporations (McGrath, 2002) many European corporations have become active and key players in various efforts of self-regulation, reflexive regulation and other regulatory efforts (Orts & Deketelaere, 2001). On the other hand, European corporations are less inclined to engage in philanthropy than their North American counterparts (Palazzo, 2002). The most consistent explanation for this could be the fact that in Europe, relatively high levels of taxation in conjunction with a somewhat more developed welfare state infrastructure causes corporations to perceive issues such as funding of education or arts as being more in the responsibility of governments.

Interesting differences also seem to emerge in the field of actors in CSR in Europe. Next to corporations, CSR activities seem to be embedded in multi-stakeholder coalitions including trade unions[3], business associations[4] and NGOs[5]. One finding of Maignan and Ralston's (2002) comparison of US and European CSR is the greater preponderance of the European corporations to describe their CSR in stakeholder terms.

Most significantly, however, is the role of the government in European CSR. Although by conventional definition, CSR is regarded as incompatible with governmental regulation, explicit CSR as defined above in Europe is a key issue for regulators. The general approach seems to facilitate a new trend in business and encourage companies to assume more responsibilities, as most welfare states in

Europe are increasingly facing limits to their capacities of tackling social issues in the way they traditionally did. This political activity can be observed on all levels: There are significant efforts by the European Commission, both in terms of funded projects as well as Green Papers and other publications with the intent of defining and shaping CSR in a European context (Commission of the European Communities, 2001, 2002). On the national level, many governments have attempted to shape the CSR debate, most notably and advanced in the UK, which even has a governmental minister for CSR (Moon, 2004a). Even on the sub-national level, there is meanwhile quite a number of governmental initiatives on a local and regional level to facilitate CSR and encourage corporate involvement in society[6]. Apart from these initiatives as a key actor in promoting explicit CSR in Europe government still plays a significant role implicitly as they are deeply embedded in economic activities of business. So, for instance, governments in Germany, France or Italy directly intervene with credits, subsidies and other measures in corporations, particularly if there is the risk of mass lay-offs. Furthermore, governments still tend to own substantial amounts of shares in large European companies, Renault and Volkswagen perhaps being the most prominent examples. Consequently, governmental influence on the corporate attitudes towards social responsibility also remains implicitly strong notwithstanding the new interest in explicit CSR.

Implicit and Explicit CSR: Towards a New Research Agenda

We argue that a dual view of CSR as consisting of implicit and explicit elements does not only offer a better descriptive model of CSR but that this approach also opens the way to a more theorised research agenda in CSR.

In particular, contemporary European and American institutional theory sheds an interesting light on the global spread of CSR and its societal contexts beyond its American origins. It enables us to frame CSR as a research topic in a broader context of inquiry which is currently on the agenda in organisation studies as well as international management (Tempel & Walgenbach, 2005). On the one hand, explicit CSR is part of a broader movement of the global spread of management concepts, ideologies and technologies which mostly result in some sort of "Americanisation" of management practices. On the other hand, implicit CSR is part of the institutional framework of countries' regions and thus is considerably different from country to country. This debate about the convergence and divergence of management practice has been on the agenda in business studies for quite some time (Child, 2000), in particular in a European context (Geppert, Matten & Williams, 2002), and we would suggest institutional theories as the most propitious framework to explain "implicit" and "explicit" CSR.

Implicit CSR and the National Business Systems Approach

Starting with implicit CSR we would argue that its occurrence, forms and specific national differences can be explained by perspectives discussed for more than 30 years in the "national business systems" or "societal effect" approach (Maurice & Sorge, 2000; Maurice, Sorge & Warner, 1980; Sorge, 1991; Whitley, 1992, 1999, 2002a, 2002b). The basic theoretical construct of this perspective is depicted in Figure 2.

European institutionalists, as this school of research is sometimes referred to, argue that every country has a specific, historically grown institutional framework which shapes and constitutes what they call a "national business system" (Whitley, 1997) or "social system of production" (Hollingsworth & Boyer, 1997). We argue that this national business system (NBS) precisely encapsulates the underpinnings of what we termed "implicit CSR" earlier on in this paper. Let us have a look at some examples, analysing Whitley's three key areas of NBSs:

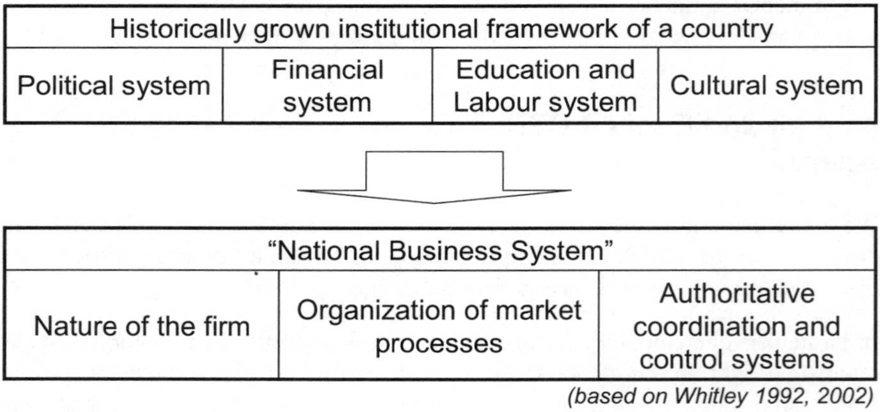

Historically grown institutional framework of a country			
Political system	Financial system	Education and Labour system	Cultural system

"National Business System"		
Nature of the firm	Organization of market processes	Authoritative coordination and control systems

(based on Whitley 1992, 2002)

Figure 2. Key elements of national business systems

- *Nature of the firm*: this aspect focuses primarily on forms of ownership coordination in an economy. While Anglo-Saxon countries tend to rely more on market based forms of contract based ownership, continental European countries still have a large amount of direct ownership or alliance ownership, most notably through networks of banks, insurance companies or even governmental actors. It is evident, that the nature of the firms then directly impacts on various CSR issues, such as the role of stakeholders beyond shareholders, the mechanisms of corporate governance, the accountability of corporations to wider constituencies etc.

- *Organisation of market processes*: a decisive feature of a NBS is how the economic relations between actors are organised and which coordination measures an economy prefers, the two extremes here being markets and alliances. The way these relations are organised touches on a significant number of CSR issues, such as consumer protection, product stewardship, liability for production and products, labour issues.

- *Authoritative coordination and control systems*: NBSs differ considerably in the way: employer-employee relations are organised and to which degree delegation takes place; trust governs relationships; and the discretion in the task environment granted to employees. Again, a large amount of CSR policies focuses on these issues and we would argue that the implicit framework of European CSR covers a significant number of issues which would be part of explicit CSR policies in different NBSs.

These elements of the NBS are shaped by political, financial, educational and cultural institutions, and as these institutions differ from country to country, NBSs also differ cross nationally. As we contend, that "implicit" elements of CSR are embedded in and part of the NBS, we argue that differences in what CSR actually means differ from country to country: implicit CSR, such as industrial relations, labour law or governance legislation are different from country to country which not only makes implicit CSR different cross-nationally but also the shape of explicit CSR policies: while, for instance, employee participation in corporate governance might be part of the explicit CSR policies of an American corporation, a German CSR policy would not have to address these issues as they are already predisposed by the (implicit) institutional framework of the NBS.

We suggest the NBS-approach also because it looks back on quite a rich tradition particularly in Europe (Whitley, 1992; Whitley & Kristensen, 1996, 1997), but increasingly so also in other parts of the world (Choi, Hilton & Millar, 2004). The research in this area is particularly rich in the field of comparing continental European NBSs with Anglo-Saxon versions (Lane, 1989; Sorge & Warner, 1986) which provides a fruitful basis for the analysis of (explicit) CSR as a predominantly Anglo-Saxon concept being applied increasingly in Europe. Furthermore, one of the key arguments of this school of research is that despite ongoing processes of globalisation in the sense of harmonisation and standardisation of management processes and structures, NBSs still remain distinctly different, and thus stress what empirically has been result of many studies in the area of CSR so far, that Europe (as compared to other continents) as well as different countries within Europe, provides a rather diverse picture of CSR challenges, practices and policies.

Explicit CSR and Institutional Legitimacy

On the other hand, as we have argued above, there is ample evidence that CSR in the "explicit" sense is gaining momentum and spreading all over Europe (and beyond). We would suggest that the theoretical approach of "new" or "American" institutionalism (DiMaggio & Powell, 1983; Meyer, 2000; Meyer & Rowan, 1977) provides a helpful theoretical perspective on the understanding of these processes. The central focus of this school of institutionalism has been to analyse how homogenisation of institutional environments across national boundaries takes place and how regulative, normative and cognitive processes lead to more and more standardised and rationalised practices in organisations across industries and national boundaries. We would argue that new institutionalism helps to understand why and how explicit CSR is gaining momentum as a new management element or concept. The key argument of this theoretical school is that organisational practices change and become institutionalised because they are considered as legitimate. Legitimacy – as opposed to economic efficiency for instance – is regarded as the key driver of institutionalisation. This legitimacy is "produced" by three key elements or processes (DiMaggio & Powell, 1983):

- *Coercive isomorphisms*: externally codified rules, norms or laws assign legitimacy to practices. In the case of CSR in Europe one could argue that governmental initiatives, such as EU Green Papers, or the initiatives of the UK Department of Trade and Industry count among those coercive isomorphisms which foster the spread of CSR across Europe. Similarly, self-regulatory and voluntary initiatives which refer to codes and norms could be counted among these isomorphisms. So, for instance, various codes of conducts for multinational corporations issued by bodies such as the UN, the OECD, the ILO and others can be counted among drivers of CSR, certainly for MNCs, in Europe. Also the compliance with certain environmental standards, such as ISO 14000 or the EMAS scheme – often supply chain driven – coerce companies to adopt particular CSR policies. An increasingly important role here is also played by the socially responsible investment community. Indexes such as the FTSE4GOOD or the decision criteria of certain investment funds play a similar role for corporations if they want to gain or sustain access to these sources of capital. Most recently, the UN Global Compact could be seen as another driver of explicit CSR as it also externally codifies some fundamental basics of responsible corporate behaviour. However, as the membership of the UNGC is voluntary there is another element leading to legitimacy to be considered:

- *Mimetic processes*: in a business climate of increased uncertainty and increasingly complex technologies managers tend to consider certain practices as legitimate just because they are considered to be "best practice" in other parts of the organisational field. These processes would also account for the upcoming of "management fashions", such as the recent wave of "business re-engineering". In the area of CSR, particularly in large European MNCs, this can certainly be considered an important driver for CSR. Regular CSR reports – often in the form of "corporate citizenship" or "sustainability" reports – or flagship projects in the area of philanthropy could be considered as prominent examples here.

- *Normative pressures*: a particular role has been identified for educational and professional authorities which directly or indirectly set standards for "legitimate" organisational practices. A particular role has been identified for educational institutions, in particular for the degree of an MBA which increasingly becomes the standard formal education for decision makers in most companies in the industrialised world. With regard to CSR and its spread in Europe, we can certainly identify some significant rise of pressures from this angle. Not only have global initiatives such as for instance the "global business coalition against AIDS" or other initiatives in connection with the World Economic Forum recently encouraged CSR for its member organisation. In particular in Europe, with the foundation of the "European Academy of Business in Society (EABiS)" in 2002, or similar initiatives at national level, a growing number of professional associations exert normative pressures on business to adopt CSR. Furthermore, as recent research among the 166 leading business schools or institutions for higher education in business has surfaced, CSR is now at least an optional, in many cases a compulsory part of business education (Matten & Moon, 2004).

This particular theoretical angle has quite a rich tradition in management research and also in particular in CSR related topics. In the area of environmental management practices there is a rich stream of research which has analysed the spread of more environmentally friendly corporate practices through the lens of new institutional theory (Hoffman, 2001; Hoffman & Ventresca, 2002). We would argue, that this lens is also particularly proficient and helpful in understanding explicit CSR in a European context.

Conclusion

This paper has sought to identify CSR as a complex social and business phenomenon, which depends on more dimensions than just voluntary corporate policies. We argue that CSR is increasingly focusing on problems, which are tackled by a broader plethora of actors than companies and business interests. Our conceptualisation would then lead us to argue that the transfer of CSR out of the Anglo-American context unveils that voluntary corporate policies are just one among several ways of addressing social issues and problems in the relation of business and society.

This view leads to a number of consequences: First, it reassesses the societal context of corporate CSR policies and opens the circle of potential actors in CSR beyond the corporate sphere. Secondly, it has some provocative policy implications as it presents CSR as a phenomenon, which can either be tackled by corporations or by other institutions, most notably governments. Thirdly, the differentiation into CSR as a more multifaceted phenomenon entails a number of challenges for research in CSR, both on the level of theoretical conceptualisations as well as research agendas on the empirical level.

Notes

[1] A recent study of CSR in Japan echoes this puzzle of reconciling a traditional and a new CSR. Fukukawa, K., & Moon, J. 2004. A Japanese Model of Corporate Social Responsibility?: A study of website reporting. *Journal of Business Ethics*: forthcoming.

[2] The comparison of business-society relations of pre-democratic Spain and Portugal and communist Eastern Europe with those of the USA would be a very different exercise. It is noteworthy that following democratisation and market liberalisation Spain and Portugal have witnessed increases in the welfare state, economic regulation and CSR, and following the reduced scope of state welfare and regulation, some of the former communist countries have witnessed an interest in CSR.

[3] An example are the activities of the European Trade Union EUROCADRES which has recently actively encouraged CSR as a trade union topic in its member organisations across Europe, see www.eurocadres.org .

[4] A prominent and longstanding organisation is the British "Business in the Community" (BITC), which facilitates a plethora of CSR activities by corporations, see www.bitc.org.uk.

[5] For examples see Bendell. Bendell, J. (Ed.). 2000. *Terms for endearment: business, NGOs and sustainable development*. Sheffield: Greenleaf.

[6] As example see the initiative of the regional government of the province of North-Rhine Westphalia at www.corporate-citizenship.nrw.de.

References

Albert, M. 1991. *Capitalisme contre capitalisme*. Paris: LeSeuil.

Beck, U. 1997. Subpolitics, ecology and the disintegration of institutional power. *Organization & Environment*, 10(1): 52–65.

Bendell, J. (Ed.). 2000. *Terms for endearment: business, NGOs and sustainable development*. Sheffield: Greenleaf.

Carroll, A. B. 1979. A three dimensional model of corporate social performance. *Academy of Management Review*, 4: 497–505.

Carroll, A. B. 1991. The pyramid of corporate social responsibility: toward the moral management of organizational stakeholders. *Business Horizons* (Jul-Aug): 39 – 48.

Carroll, A. B. 1999. Corporate social responsibility – evolution of a definitional construct. *Business & Society*, 38(3): 268 – 295.

Child, J. 2000. Theorizing about organizations cross-nationally. In: J. L. C. Cheng, & R. B. Peterson (Eds.), *Advances in international comparative management*, Vol. 13: 27 – 75. Stamford, CN: JAI Press.

Choi, C., Hilton, B., & Millar, C. 2004. *Emergent Globalization*. Basingstoke: Palgrave.

Commission of the European Communities. 2001. *Green Paper: Promoting a European framework for corporate social responsibility*. Brussels: EU Commission.

Commission of the European Communities. 2002. *Communication from the Commission concerning corporate social responsibility: A business contribution to sustainable development*. Brussels: EU Commission.

Crane, A., & Matten, D. 2004a. *Business ethics – A European perspective*. Oxford: Oxford University Press.

Crane, A., & Matten, D. 2004b. Questioning the domain of the business ethics curriculum. *Journal of Business Ethics*, forthcoming.

DiMaggio, P. J., & Powell, W. W. 1983. The iron cage revisited: Institutional isomorphism and collective rationality in organizational fields. *American Sociological Review*, 48: 147 – 160.

Fernandez Young, A., Moon, J., & Young, R. 2003. *The UK Corporate Social Responsibility consultancy industry: a phenomenological approach*. Nottingham: Research Paper Series of the International Centre for Corporate Social Responsibility, No 14.

Friedman, M. 1970. The social responsibility of business is to increase its profits. *The New York Times Magazine*, 13. Sept. 1970.

Fukukawa, K., & Moon, J. 2004. A Japanese Model of Corporate Social Responsibility?: A study of website reporting. *Journal of Business Ethics*: forthcoming.

Geppert, M., Matten, D., & Williams, K. (Eds.). 2002. *Challenges for European Management in a Global Context – Experiences from Britain and Germany*. Basingstoke: Palgrave Macmillan.

Hoffman, A. J. 2001. *From heresy to dogma: an institutional history of corporate environmentalism* (Expanded ed.). Stanford, Calif.: Stanford University Press.

Hoffman, A. J., & Ventresca, M. J. 2002. *Organizations, policy and the natural environment: institutional and strategic perspectives*. Stanford, Calif.: Stanford University Press.

Hollingsworth, J. R., & Boyer, R. 1997. Coordination of economic actors and social systems of production. In: J. R. Hollingsworth, & R. Boyer (Eds.), *Contemporary capitalism: the embeddedness of institutions*: 1 – 47. Cambridge: Cambridge University Press.

Jespersen, K. 2003. Social Partnerships: The Role of Government in Denmark. In: M. Morsing, & C. Thyssen (Eds.), *Corporate Values and Responsibility: The Case of Denmark*. Frederiksberg: Samfundslitteratur.

Lane, C. 1989. *Management and labour in Europe. The industrial enterprise in Germany, Britain and France*. Aldershot: Edward Elgar.

Lane, C. 1992. European business systems: Britain and Germany compared. In: R. Whitley (Ed.), *European business systems*: 64 – 97. London: Sage.

Lane, C. 1994. Industrial order and the transformation of industrial relations: Britain, Germany and France. In: R. Hyman, & A. Ferner (Eds.), *New frontiers in European industrial relations*: 167 – 195. Oxford: Blackwell.

Levidov, L., & Carr, S. 2000. Precautionary regulation: GM crops in the European Union. *Journal of Risk Research, Special Issue*, 3(3): 187 – 295.

Levy, D., & Egan, D. 2000. Corporate politics and climate change. In: R. A. Higgott, G. R. D. Underhill, & A. Bieler (Eds.), *Non-state actors and authority in the global system*: 138 – 153. London: Routledge.

Levy, D. L., & Kolk, A. 2002. Strategic Responses to Global Climate Change: Conflicting Pressures on Multinationals in the Oil Industry. *Business and Politics*, 3(2): 275 – 300.

Lofstedt, R. E., & Vogel, D. 2001. The changing character of regulation: A comparison of Europe and the United States. *Risk Analysis*, 21(3): 399 – 405.

Maignan, I., Ralston, D. A. 2002. Corporate Social Responsibility in Europe and the U.S.: Insights from Businesses' Self-presentations. In: *Journal of International Business Studies*, 33(3): 497 – 515.

Matten, D. 2004. The impact of the risk society thesis on environmental politics and management in a globalizing economy – principles, proficiency, perspectives. *Journal of Risk Research*, 7(4): forthcoming.

Matten, D., & Moon, J. 2004. Corporate Social Responsibility Education in Europe. *Journal of Business Ethics*: 377 – 398.

Maurice, M., & Sorge, A. (Eds.). 2000. *Embedding Organizations: Societal analysis of actors, organizations and socio-economic context*. Amsterdam: John Benjamins.

Maurice, M., Sorge, A., & Warner, M. 1980. Societal differences in organizing manufacturing units: A comparison of France, West Germany and Great Britain. *Organization Studies*, 1(1): 59 – 86.

Mayer, M., & Whittington, R. 2002. The evolving European corporation: strategy, structure and social science. In: M. Geppert, D. Matten, & K. Williams (Eds.), *Challenges for European management in a global context*: 19–41. Basingstoke: Palgrave.

McGrath, C. 2002. *Comparative lobbying practices: Washington, London, Brussels*. Paper presented at the Political Studies Association annual conference, University of Aberdeen.

McWilliams, A., & Siegel, D. 2001. Corporate social responsibility: a theory of the firm perspective. *Academy of Management Review*, 26(1): 117–127.

Meyer, J. W. 2000. Globalization – Sources and Effects on National States and Societies. *International Sociology*, 15: 233–248.

Meyer, J. W., & Rowan, B. 1977. Institutionalized organizations. *American Journal of Sociology*, 83: 340–363.

Moon, J. 2004a. CSR in the UK: an explicit model of business – society relations. In: A. Habisch, J. Jonker, M. Wegner, & R. Schmidpeter (Eds.), *CSR across Europe*: 51–65. Berlin: Springer.

Moon, J. 2004b. *Government as a Driver of Corporate Social Responsibility. The UK in Comparative Perspective*. Nottingham: Research Paper Series of the International Centre for Corporate Social Responsibility, No. 19.

Orts, E. W., & Deketelaere, K. (Eds.). 2001. *Environmental Contracts*. Dordrecht et al.: Kluwer.

Palazzo, B. 2002. U.S.-American and German business ethics: an intercultural comparison. *Journal of Business Ethics*, 41: 195–216.

Sorge, A. 1991. Strategic fit and societal effect – interpreting cross-national comparisons of technology, organization and human resources. *Organization Studies*, 12(2): 161–190.

Sorge, A., & Warner, M. 1986. *Comparative factory organisation. An Anglo-German comparison of management and manpower manufacturing*. Aldershot: Gower.

Strebel, H. 1980. *Umwelt und Betriebswirtschaft*. Berlin: Erich Schmidt.

Tempel, A., & Walgenbach, P. 2005. Global standardization of organisational forms and management practices? Combining American and European institutionalism. *Journal of Management Studies*, forthcoming.

Vogel, D. 1986. *National Styles of Regulation: Environmental Policy in Great Britain and the United States*. Ithaca NY, London: Cornell University Press.

Whitley, R. (Ed.). 1992. *European business systems*. London: Sage.

Whitley, R. 1997. Business systems. In: A. Sorge, & M. Warner (Eds.), *The IEBM handbook of organizational behaviour*: 173–186. London: International Thomson Business Press.

Whitley, R. 1999. *Divergent capitalisms. The social structuring and change of business systems*. Oxford: Oxford University Press.

Whitley, R. 2002a. Business Systems. In: A. Sorge (Ed.), *Organization*: 178–212. London: Thomson Learning.

Whitley, R. (Ed.). 2002b. *Competing Capitalisms: Institutions and Economies*. Cheltenham: Edward Elgar.

Whitley, R., & Kristensen, P.H. (Eds.). 1996. *The changing European firm*. London: Routledge.

Whitley, R., & Kristensen, P.H. (Eds.). 1997. *Governance at Work*. Oxford: Oxford University Press.

Wolff, M. 2002. Response to "Confronting the Critics". *New Academy Review*, 1(1): 230–237.

Wynne, B., & Dressel, K. 2001. Cultures of uncertainty – transboundary risks and BSE in Europe. In: J. Linneroth-Bayer, R. Löfstedt, & G. Sjöstedt (Eds.), *Transboundary risk management*: 121–154. London: Earthscan.

26 The Role of Business in Society in Europe

Gilbert Lenssen and Volodja Vorobey

Introduction

This contribution explores theoretical models and empirical data to compare the different roles of business in European societies. We will argue that the depth of these differences needs better understanding before considering the case for convergence of these roles as a basis for Europe-wide policies on "CSR" by companies and government policymakers alike. We mention "CSR" between inverted commas because it appears to us as an ill-defined concept with different interpretations. Its emergence can be better studied by considering the changing role of business (and government) in society.

In part 1, we will propose that the central theoretical concept for the comparative study of the role of business (and government) in society is *social contract*, but that this concept needs to be underpinned by legitimacy theory and stakeholder theory in order to operationalise research into social contracts.

In part 2, we will demonstrate how Hofstede's research (and follow-up research by others) have provided the empirical data that allows a certain explanation of the differences in the behaviours of different stakeholders with respect to corporate roles and responsibilities in different European societies.

In part 3, we show how the comparative analysis of socio-political systems further explains these differences and provides a better understanding of why "CSR", as an Anglo-Saxon concept might get rooted in Germany and France, albeit in different ways.

In part 4, we will provide a comparison of corporate governance systems in Europe which is crosslinked to the national culture profiles and national socio-political systems, building towards our proposed model of four main systems of the role of business (and government) in societies in Europe.

In part 5, we will argue that corporate reputation research seems well fitted to explore differences in processes of gaining and maintaining legitimacy within different cultural and socio-political environments. We argued in part 1 that also legitimacy theory is needed to underpin comparative research of social contracts in Europe.

Part 1: Social Contract Theory, Legitimacy Theory, and Stakeholder Theory

We propose that the cornerstone theory, explaining the role of business is *social contract theory*. It states that each society has a set of defined relations between society, business and state and modalities of relations are specific to each society. Such contracts between society and state, society and business could be formal/explicit by taking the form of laws, regulations, rules and procedures or informal/implicit through commonly accepted traditions. At the firm level, Sacconi (2004) defines social contract as the agreement that would be reached by the representatives of all the firm's stakeholders in a hypothetical situation of impartial choice.

Multiple factors could have contributed to the process of defining social contract in any particular society. A social contract is intrinsically present in every society as an expectation of society towards business, of society towards state (government) and vice versa. Due to the complicated and multi-facetted process of creating a social contract and the way a social contract is embedded in institutions, none of the sides in the state-society-business triangle could drastically influence social contract status quo in the short term. It provides a reference point for companies on how business processes and policies are maintained and what the expectations of business in a given society are in a long-term period.

Social contract theory deals with abstract entities of society, state and business, making it possible to extrapolate it to other levels of complexity of social arrangements.

Donaldson and Dunfee (1999) developed an Integrated Social Contracts Theory with clear differentiation of macrosocial contracts (expectations of community) and microsocial contracts (specific form of involvement). Although this theory sets the context for managers to take decisions, it does not provide a framework to analyse the dynamics of macro- and microsocial contracts in line with changing demographics of population in Europe, increased mobility and information flows. Moreover, whilst social contracts theory could explain the initial motivation of companies to engage with communities, it might not explain the totality of their involvement.

This highlights the underlying ambiguity of the social contract theory with regard to defining the object of research with which it deals. It is hard to define a dynamic entity such as society in static descriptive terms of micro- or macro-levels, geographical or historical boundaries etc. Applicability of this theory becomes even more ambiguous with the higher level of complexity of societal arrangements, for instance when communities of different ethnic, cultural and economic background mix in a given territory. A social contract attributed to a local community operates with different norms compared to one of the European community if one endeavours to apply social contract theory on a wider European scale. Following Gray, Owen and Adams (1996) it can be stated that society and business transform into a complex series of societal contracts of individual particles of state, society and business.

Legitimacy theory anchors the social contract arrangements in the state-society-business triangle to a business sector perspective and the same concerns could be addressed to this theory. For example, Suchman (1995) defines legitimacy as "a generalised perception or assumption that the actions of an entity are desirable, proper, or appropriate within some socially constructed system of norms, values, beliefs and definitions." He identifies three types of organisational legitimacy (pragmatic, moral, and cognitive) and three key challenges of legitimacy management (gaining, maintaining and repairing legitimacy). Suchman points out that "legitimacy management rests heavily on communication" – therefore in any attempt to involve legitimacy theory, there is a need to examine some forms of corporate communications. Whilst social contract theory remains abstract and static, and difficult to operationalise, legitimacy theory emphasises the dynamic process of gaining legitimacy by a company by concrete actions and communications.

As we will explore in part 4, corporate reputation indices in different countries can shed light on the different legitimation processes companies need to adopt in each country, in order to be perceived as living up to its social contract.

Legitimacy is attributed to a purpose or goal that a company has. Clear and consistent communication is essential to transmit a company's efforts in legitimacy management to other sides of the triangle, i.e. to society and the state. While in the long-term business could refer to the social contract attributed to a given society at large, in the short term business requires far better understanding of such diverse groups that make up society.

This is where stakeholder theory can help define the parties of social contract in better terms. In his classic book, Freeman (1984) describes the firm as a series of connections of stakeholders that the managers of the firm attempt to manage. Freeman's classic definition of a stakeholder is "any group or individual who can affect or is affected by the achievement of the organisation's objectives" (Freeman, 1984: 46). Clarkson (1995) furthers developed stakeholder theory by defining primary and secondary stakeholders based on stakeholders' level of engagement in transactions with the corporations and their importance for the corporation's survival.

However, stakeholder theory does not provide an answer on how social, historical and cultural factors influence such interactions. Depending on time and space in De Bettignies' terms, the notion of *stakeholder* could vary significantly in its meaning, especially if the dynamic of interaction between stakeholders is considered. Mitchell, Agle and Wood (1997) developed a model of stakeholder identification and salience based on stakeholders possessing one or more of the attributes of power, legitimacy and urgency. Agle, Mitchell and Sonnenfeld (1999) confirm that the three attributes do lead to salience. All three attributes are subject to cultural and historical interpretation within a particular context.

Part 2: Cultural Differences Affecting "Corporate Social Responsibility"

Theories of cultural differences can provide an explicative framework for analysing descriptive evidence of differing roles of business in different societies. Hofstede's seminal work provided an empirically-derived theory of culture delineating cultural differences between countries using five value-oriented, bipolar dimensions (Hofstede 1984, 1991). These are:

1. Large vs. small power distance (PDI)

2. High vs. low uncertainty avoidance (UAI)

3. Individualism (IDV)

4. Masculinity (MAS)

5. Long-term vs. short-term time orientation (CDI)

Katz, Swanson and Nelson (1999) adopted it to present a framework that assesses how cultural factors influence expectations of CSR amongst the aforementioned stakeholders. His conclusions on influence of culture on social issues in management are:

1. Consumer activism will be more likely to occur in cultures exhibiting lower levels of power distance, lower levels of uncertainty avoidance, higher levels of individualism and lower levels of masculinity.

2. Environmental activism will be more likely to occur in cultures exhibiting lower levels of power distance, higher levels of uncertainty avoidance, lower levels of individualism and lower levels of masculinity.

3. Employee activism will be more likely to occur in cultures exhibiting lower levels of power distance, lower levels of uncertainty avoidance, higher levels of individualism and lower levels of masculinity.

4. Governmental activism will be more likely to occur in cultures exhibiting lower levels of power distance, higher levels of uncertainty avoidance, lower levels of individualism and lower levels of masculinity.

5. Community activism will be more likely to occur in cultures exhibiting lower levels of power distance, lower levels of uncertainty avoidance, lower levels of individualism and lower levels of masculinity.

Table 1 provides the relative scores on the Hofstede dimensions for a selected group of European countries.

Table 1. Cultural factor profiles for selected European countries

Country	PDI	UAI	IDV	MAS	CDI
Germany	low	high	medium/high	high	low
France	high	high	High	medium	low
Netherlands	low	medium	High	low	medium
Sweden	low	medium	High	low	medium
United Kingdom	low	low	High	high	low

The United Kingdom exhibits below average on power distance and uncertainty avoidance, relatively high levels of masculinity, and high levels of individualism in combination with short-term orientation. In this context, one would expect consumer activism to be very high. Consumers trust information from external sources and there is a strong tendency to engage in political activism, i.e. to putting pressure on firms. Employee turnover is high and loyalty to employers is low. Salary and public recognition are relatively more important factors in employees' utility functions. Business tends to be given prominence over the public sector, with the government seeing its role as creating an enabling corporate environment for social responsibility.

The welfare of the close family and friends may be considered more important than wider social goals and environmental protection. All stakeholders have a short-term orientation. Companies in Great Britain also consider public acceptance a key determinant of their "licence to operate" (i.e. legitimacy).

France differs significantly from Great Britain in three of Hofstede's dimensions. This suggests a contrasting view of corporate social conduct. France ranks high in power distance and especially uncertainty avoidance, relatively lower in masculinity and has similar levels of individualism. In this context, the likelihood of consumer activism is ambiguous. On the one hand, there is low tolerance of consumer protests (high UAI), whilst on the other hand, consumers are likely to express their opinions about products and services (high IDV). Employees accept a very hierarchical structure and open employee conflict is unlikely (high PDI and high UAI). The government is relatively centralised (high PDI) and has a very strong preference for formal and written structures and rules (high UAI). This is indeed consistent with reality. France is the only European country, in which social reporting is obligatory by law.

Businesses in France are less likely to consider the interests of their wider stakeholders. Their primary concern may be government regulation.

With low scores on PDI and a significantly high uncertainty avoidance index, Germany has a propensity to provide legal frameworks for companies as a response to public concerns. Such frameworks are the result of a consultation process where representatives of the community play a crucial role (low PDI). To some extent, low PDI and a designed process of integrating public expectations into legal frameworks mitigates the tendency of business to obey authorities, as opposed to expectations of the public (as would be the case with high UAI). Sophisticated regulatory frameworks for the operations of companies at the level of Federal States (*Bundesländer*), even communities, together with the consensus-based federal legislation provides evidence for the validity of the model.

In Holland and Sweden (largely representative for all Scandinavian countries) we can still see another profile. Environmental activism is high as well as consumer activism (low PDI, high IDV, medium UAI, low MAS) but the medium UAI explains the extent of legislation and regulation in environmental matters and consumer protection. Medium levels of UAI coupled with low levels of MAS and medium levels of CDI might explain the extent of the provisions of the welfare state.

From the above analysis based on the framework by Katz et al and by comparing the scores on cultural dimensions from all European countries (Hofstede, 1984), we can identify four cultural clusters in Europe which correspond to four clusters on the role and expectations of business, government and societal stakeholders and activists:

1. The Anglo-Saxon system (UK, Ireland)
   Cultural model of society: Market (high IDV, high MAS, low UAI, low PDI)
   Central concept: mutual adaptation by competition

2. The Dutch/Scandinavian system
   Cultural model of society: Network (high IDV, low MAS, medium UAI, low PDI)
   Central concept: mutual adaptation by consensus building

3. The Latin system (France, Belgium, Italy, Spain)
   Cultural model of society: Pyramid (high IDV, high MAS, high UAI, high PDI)
   Central concept: coordination by hierarchy and bureaucracy

4. The Germanic system (Germany, Austria, German-speaking Switzerland)
   Cultural model of society: Machine (Medium/high IDV, high MAS, high UAI, low PDI)
   Central concept: coordination by ordered community

These four main systems in Europe linking cultural differences to the roles of business, government and society seem to be reflected in corporate governance systems as we will explore in part 4.

From the above analysis, one can conclude that cultural tendencies shape a nation's expectations of the role of business (and government) in society. Aligning business practices with prevailing cultural norms will help to minimise potential conflicts that stem from cultural expectations. Katz et al talk about *cultural citizenship*, that is, business practices should be aligned with prevailing cultural norms, and managers should anticipate and minimise the conflicts, which can stem from cultural differences.

Part 3: Socio-Political Systems and "Corporate Social Responsibility"

In his description of culture, Trompenaars (1997) refers to mental reinforcement of culture via institutions and tangibles of a society. When culture becomes crystallised in the institutions, it affects the distribution of roles and responsibilities of business, government and societal actors.

Socio-politcal systems embody the balance of power between society, state and business. When the social functions of the state are firmly embedded in institutions of e.g. national social security, business has a defined framework to utilise its organisational competencies, for instance by contributing to areas where services provided by state institutions are not sufficient and not mitigating national social security services where they work.

Changes in the role and responsibilities of business need to be understood within the context of the changing role of government in society at large and in regulating the relationships of companies with its stakeholders in society in particular. Recently the debate was concentrated on *better state* vs. *less state* but not on the *more state*. Underlying this debate is the perception that individual governments are increasingly inhibited in their autonomy by the international forces of globalisation and supranational commitments like e.g. the EU growth and stability pact within EMU. This affects all countries in similar ways and the resulting change is likely to contribute towards degrees of convergence of the role of government, with possible converging effects on the role of business.

Segal (2004) provides an analysis of the place of "CSR" in Anglo-Saxon, German and French socio-political systems. In his analysis he deliberately avoids references to public opinion on the role of business as well as debate on pros and cons of state intervention to market economy. Instead, Segal defines three models of role of business in society: the Anglo-Saxon (where, in his interpretation the concept of "CSR" originates), the French and the German model.

He begins with the proposition that the concept of "CSR" is in origin and by nature a protestant Anglo-Saxon concept, in which liberty is the primary value, but where freedom requires taking voluntary responsibility. He illustrates how the concept of "CSR" fits well within the UK, where it is well rooted, how the main questions around "CSR" are addressed and how the concept is received and might be taking roots in France and Germany (in the context of the above-mentioned currents of convergence of the role of government).

The main question of the Anglo-Saxon model is whether "CSR" contributes to the profitability and competitiveness of the company. There is a strong conviction among promoters of "CSR" in the Anglo-Saxon countries that there is a direct link between profitability and the level of the company's engagement in "CSR". Corporate reputation, an essential element of a company's capital in Anglo-Saxon countries, provides such a link. A company has to engage in "CSR" practices to avoid the risk of damaging its reputation because of the company's stakeholders' ability to utilise communication channels effectively and stategically. The Anglo-Saxon model is characterised by a far-reaching power of media, which shows an aggressive approach towards the transparency of a company's operations and low reverence to persons in power, politicians and corporates alike. Thus, the company has to enable a measurement mechanism to be able to prove any claims it makes in public. A reporting system has to be built and formal procedures defining different aspects of "CSR" and clarifying the different commitments of the company are to be constantly improved. The company is expected to produce limited but tangible results but to be committed to continuous and measurable progress. Formal verifiable rules are an indispensable part of the Anglo-Saxon model. Such rules frame companies' efforts to build their reputation in the community. In the Anglo-Saxon model, "CSR" is not perceived as a keystone in the moral contruction of the company. It is a structured field for engagement with the company's stakeholders in order to avoid harmful effects of stakeholder activism on corporate reputation. It is therefore often coincided with "enlightened self-interest" by firms.

It should be noted that the role of the UK government in society has become more active during the last decade in areas such as education, health, income redistribution and public infrastructure. The roles of business and government in actively shaping the common good in general and through specific "PPP's" (Public-Private Partnerships) in particular seem to have become part of the fabric of society.

The German model of "CSR" is centred on the principle of an organised community. The term "CSR" is somewhat alien in Germany and it should be no surprise that the term "Corporate Citizenship" is preferred. The German tradition values order where each member has a voice on matters of joint interest but also agrees on a certain collective discipline. In return, all accept collective discipline as it was freely discussed and not imposed. Underlying such common order is the principle that clear responsibilities are assigned to every player. That is why companies have a problem accepting the legitimacy of NGOs that want to insert themselves freely into a properly functioning system. They can accept NGOs but only if NGOs will be co-responsible and not merely protesting. Such logic empedes the acceptance of a wider stakeholder model of "CSR" because in this model interconnections between all players are not important while in the Germanic model stakeholders should have assigned interdependent roles.

In the Germanic approach, decisions are meaningful if everyone was consulted, in the Anglo-Saxon model an executive could decide more autonomously. In Germany, "communitarian law" is the cement that maintains efficiency but is not necessarily a threat to individual initiatives and entrepreneurship. Society will probably not embrace a "CSR" model as an integral part of the strategic market positioning of individual companies. This does not mean that there is no space for companies to take some individual initiatives of *bürgerliche Verantwortung* and then collect the public rewards in demonstrating their good citizenship.

It can be reasonably expected that, in the wake of the reforms of the welfare state and of the levels of public provisions, and the implicit reduction of the guarantees by the state at all levels (federal, state and local) to its individual citizens, corporate citizenship by companies will spread and intensify. This will predictably happen through a slow communitarian process establishing new common rules for an extension of the role and responsibility of business in society.

The French socio-political model resembles somewhat the German model, though the reasoning behind the adoption of this model is different. The idea of the higher ideal (*grandeur*), serving the general interest is at the heart of French culture and politics. The public and state perceive a company as an entity engaged in a quest for maximisation of its profits which needs to be regulated or, in key industries, even controlled by the state. Intentions of a company to engage in "CSR activities" beyond those legally required are met with scepticism as acts of manipulation of the public opinion. Segal identifies major obstacles in the way of companies engaging in "CSR" in French socio-political model:

- The law is an expression of general/common interests in the French model. In the French model, companies willing to go beyond legal requirements and engage in "CSR" to act to the benefit of common interests will face challenges. Segal concludes that there is no certainty that France is ready to assign to companies a legitimate role to "interfere" in the building of the common social good.

- Historically, secularism is an important issue in France. In such circumstances, attempts by companies to introduce moral codes of conduct or to implement organisational values programmes are perceived as dangerous substitutes for citizens' own consciousness and "individual good education". Companies as part of the public system should be ethically neutral.

Nevertheless, the concept of *la responsabilité societal des entreprises* ("RSE") is gaining ground in France albeit on a different basis than in the UK or Germany. Some firms however prefer to label their efforts as *développement durable* and *responsabilité globale de l'entreprise*. This might fit well with the old common belief that France should be the shining light in the world (*La France est la lumière du monde*) and the more recent belief that France should challenge the model of American inspired global "turbo capitalism".

Though the concept of "CSR" originated in Anglo-Saxon countries, the French and German models described by Segal point to evidence that there is more than one model of it. Privatisation, deregulation, reforms of the welfare state, reductions of public provisions and consequent appeals to more individual and corporate responsibility are however likely to continue in both Germany and France. With these, medium-term convergence of the roles of business and government in society between the UK (where government activism and spending is on the increase), France and Germany is likely to be created.

The comparative analysis of socio-political systems indicates that the study of the (changing) role of business in European societies should not be divorced from the (changing) role of government in these societies incuding economic and social policy. This points to a major deficiency in EU policymaking on CSR, which seems divorced from the process of creating economic convergence.

After exploring European diversity of the roles of business in society by social contract/legitimacy theory and by analysing cultural and socio-political differences between European societies, we will now explore how these differences are reflected and manifested in two domains at the level of business: corporate governance and corporate reputation.

Part 4: Corporate Governance in Europe

A system of corporate governance is defined as a more or less country-specific framework of legal, institutional and cultural factors shaping the patterns of influence that stakeholders (investors, creditors, employees, customers, suppliers and the government) exert on managerial decision-making (Van den Berghe & De Ridder, 1999; Van den Berghe, 2002). To derive a taxonomy of corporate governance systems, we will refer to two reference factors, the definition of accountability and the definition of responsibility.

Such an approach enables corporate governance issues to be integrated with the wider debate on "CSR". Differences in the scope of accountability and responsibility of a company define national systems of corporate governance. Whereas accountability of the company is addressed by national legislation, responsibility of the company is an implicitly addressed issue without being necessarily integrated in the law, this in accordance with legitimacy theory and stakeholder theory.

Albert (1991) and De Jong (1996) distinguish "market-oriented" (Anglo-Saxon) and "network-oriented" (Rhineland) systems of corporate governance. In the Anglo-Saxon countries, one specific stakeholder can be identified which can exert a substantial influence on managerial decision-making: the influence of *shareholders* is strongly institutionalised in these countries. Companies are accountable and responsible towards shareholders in this model. The major (paradoxical) characteristics of this system are:

- Active external market for corporate control often referred to as "the takeover market".
- An active market for corporate ownership: the wider corporations are held, the less mechanisms shareholders can use effectively to influence managerial decision-making directly.
- Prevalence of "one share, one vote" principle but with many restrictions.

The system is often referred to as the "outsider model" as it is based on widespread shareholding and on a liquid stock market.

In the Rhineland system, the corporation is considered as an autonomous socio-economic entity constituting a coalition of various participants, such as shareholders, corporate management, employees, suppliers and customers, striving for the continuity of the firm as a whole (Moerland, 1995a). Responsibility of the company extends to all stakeholders and not predominantly only to shareholders as in the Anglo-Saxon model. However, the company is still accountable to shareholders or investors only: when conflicts of interest appear, the decisive criterion is the financial interest of the enterprise. The Rhineland system of corporate governance prevails in Germanic countries (Germany, Switzerland, the Netherlands) and Nordic countries (Norway, Sweden, Denmark, Finland) and can be typified as an "insider model".

Major characteristic of Rhineland system:

- Stock markets play a less important role in the economy

- Two-tier board system

- The "one share, one vote" principle pursued in the Anglo-Saxon countries does not prevail in the Germanic countries. German companies can issue non-voting shares up to an amount equal to that of all voting shares issued and can limit the voting power of an individual shareholder irrespective of the number of shares held (Franks & Mayer, 1990). Similar restricting measures apply in e.g. Holland

To explain the difference between Rhineland and Anglo-Saxon models, reference can be made to Hofstede's differences in value dimensions. Differences in the uncertainty avoidance (UAI) dimension explain short-term orientation in the Anglo-Saxon model and long-term orientation of the Rheinland model. In the Anglo-Saxon system unrestricted markets for capital, labour, goods and services ensure rapid adjustment to changing circumstances, thereby disfavouring long-term and stable relationships (Gelauff & Den Broeder, 1996) which typify the Rhineland model.

These categorisations obviously oversee some differences between individual countries within one system of corporate governance. Furthermore, a third group of countries form a distinct system of corporate governance (Weimer & Pape, 1999). The so-called Latin countries (France, Spain, Italy, Belgium) take a middle approach towards understanding a company: between the instrumental approach of the Anglo-Saxon outsider model and the institutional approach of the Rhineland insider model. In the Latin model, the accountability of the company is firmly linked to shareholders while the company is responsible to both shareholders and some of its stakeholders. It is labelled as the "shareholder reference model".

The Latin shareholder model of corporate governance has the following characteristics:

- Companies have the choice of using either a one-tier or a two-tier board system (France).

- The authority of the company's PDG (Chairman/CEO) is very strong

- The "one share, one vote" principle does not apply in general. In France, up to 25% of shareholders' capital can, under certain circumstances, be issued as non-voting preferred equity (Franks & Mayer, 1990).

- Financial holdings and cross-shareholdings, government control and family control (De Jong, 1989; Moerland, 1995a, 1995b) are important features (with restrictions in Italy and Belgium). There is no active market for corporate control, but the number of hostile takeovers is higher than in the Germanic countries (Moerland, 1995b).

Shareholders in the Latin countries are probably more influential than in the Germanic countries since shareholders' sovereignty is viewed as an important concept, but their influence is not as decisive as in the Anglo-Saxon countries. One of the fundamental principles of French corporate law is that the shareholders can remove directors at will. This principle is known as revocabilité ad nutum (ICMG, 1995).

The limits in utilising the legitimacy/stakeholder theory become evident in applications to the Latin or reference system of corporate governance. It is not enough only to identify stakeholders and define towards which of them the company is accountable and how the social contract makes the company responsible to some of its stakeholders. It is also necessary to define how differences in power, legitimacy and urgency attributes of different stakeholders shape the corporate governance system. Historically, such attributes are adapted in the institutions of state, the political system and by legislation, which, if combined, represent a national consensus on power, legitimacy and urgency attributes of different stakeholders. In general approximation, the socio-political model of analysis of Segal defines the level of these attributes for salient stakeholders in different European countries. The French socio-political model with its strong emphasis on the role of the state and the law as caretakers of the interests of society explains why in the Latin model of corporate governance salient stakeholders exist. The model of organised community (German model) explains the responsibility of a company to all stakeholders in the Rhineland model of corporate governance, although cultural diversity theory needs to be applied to explain the differences between corporate governance systems of Germany and Holland, i.e. the differences on UAI and MAS.

Different theories are needed to explain the diversity in corporate governance models existing in Europe. Multiple factors define which groups of stakeholders companies are accountable towards and responsible for. This could range from just shareholders (Anglo-Saxon model) to all stakeholders' groups including shareholders, primary stakeholders (Latin model), secondary stakeholders and society at large (Rhineland model).

Our analysis so far demonstrates how social contracts on the role and responsibilities of business in society vary substantially between European countries. These variations can be explained by cultural clusters and socio-political systems which are reflected in corporate governance systems according to four groups as illustrated in Table 2.

Table 2. Linking cultural diversity clusters to sociopolitical and corporate governance systems

Cultural diversity clusters	Socio-political system (Segal)	Corporate Governance system
Anglo-Saxon system market/competition	UK	Anglo-Saxon market-oriented "outsider system"
Germanic system machine/community	Germany	Rhineland network-oriented "insider systems" with some variations between Holland/Scand. and Germany
Dutch/Scandinavian system network/consensus	(*)	
Latin system pyramid/bureaucracy	France	Latin "shareholder reference system"

(*) Segal does not provide for a separate analysis of the Dutch/Scandinavian socio-political system, which, it can be argued, shows strong similarities to the German system, albeit with some differences.

Part 5: Corporate Reputation in Europe

Another manifestation of the cultural and socio-political differences between European countries is in the differences between the drivers of corporate reputation in these countries and in the way companies build legitimacy within the specific social contract. The underlying logic of the "CSR" concept suggests that social and environmental effects (as deemed relevant by stakeholders and society at large) of economic decisions affect the reputation of the company. It is essential to verify if corporate reputations gauge the legitimacy of firms' actions.

Currently there are no reliable data available across European countries to study the effect of "CSR" programmes on corporate reputation. However, Fombrun and Foss (2001) have recently unfolded a research programme across Europe to examine the different drivers of corporate reputation in different countries. To do so, he relies on the *Reputation Quotient* research instrument to identify companies that are best-regarded and worst-regarded by the general public in each country. He then carries out quantitative and qualitative analysis of media content, corporate communications, social initiatives, investor reports, and workplace practices to identify differences in stakeholder positionings between the best-regarded companies and the least-regarded companies in each country. The overall objective is to identify sustainable practices that enable a convergence of economic, social, and reputational benefits in each country.

To ensure reliable cross-national comparisons, the same research instrument is used in all countries to measure corporate reputation and public perceptions of companies – the Reputation Quotient (RQ). The instrument measures corporate reputation on the basis of public perceptions about companies on six dimensions:

- *Emotional Appeal:* How much the company is liked, admired, and respected.

- *Products & Services:* Perceptions of the quality, innovation, value, and reliability of the company's products & services.

- *Financial Performance:* Perceptions of the company's profitability, prospects, and risk.

- *Vision & Leadership:* How much the company demonstrates a clear vision and strong leadership.

- *Workplace Environment:* Perceptions of how well the company is managed, how it is to work for, and the quality of its employees.

- *Social Responsibility:* Perceptions of the company as a good citizen in its dealings with communities, employees, and the environment.

One might expect more or less significant differences on the relative weight of the dimensions of workplace environment and social responsibility in the RQ in different European countries. Currently, research is underway in UK, France, Denmark, Germany, Italy. It will be interesting to test and link the research results into our Table 2.

In earlier publications, Fombrun, Gardberg and Barnett (2000) suggested that corporate reputations are built following (universal) principles, but derived from research mainly carried out in the US:

1. The Principle of Distinctiveness: strong reputations result when companies hold a distinctive position in the minds of resource-holders,

2. The Principle of Focus: strong reputations result when companies focus their actions and communications around a single core theme,

3. The Principle of Consistency: strong reputations result when companies are consistent in their actions and communications to all resource-holders,

4. The Principle of Identity: strong reputations result when companies act in ways that are consistent with espoused principles of identity. Spin is anathema to reputation building, and in time all efforts to manipulate external images that rely purely on advertising and public relations fail when they are disconnected from the company's identity,

5. The Principle of Transparency: strong reputations result when companies are transparent in the way they conduct their affairs. Companies with stronger reputations are more visible across all media. They disclose more information about themselves and are more willing to engage stakeholders in dialogue.

Our cultural and socio-political exploration of "CSR" already revealed major differences in the substance and style companies use in corporate communications as part of the process to maintain legitimacy. If transparency equals strong communication in the Anglo-Saxon system, providing for positive reputation effects, it provides a reason for suspicion in the French system. Differences in the RQ data might be expected in this respect, e.g. companies with a strong reputation in France might not necessarily be the ones most actively communicating to their stakeholders. Cultural differences will also play an important role as the RQ is reliant on the measurement of public perceptions, which are largely dependent on underlying cultural assumptions.

Fombrun's initial data show that the influence of perceptions of social responsibility on corporate reputation are considerably higher in Europe, albeit at different levels, at least in the countries where he tested the research model (e.g. higher in Denmark and UK, lower in France and Germany).

Kowalczyk and Pawlish's (2002) research cannot identify a link between externally perceived organisational culture and social responsibility component of the RQ. The Organisational Culture Profile (OCP) of O'Reilly, Chatman and Caldwell (1991) was used in this study. Chatman and Jehn (1994) note that the factors in the OCP are similar to the Hofstede dimensions of national cultures. More research is required to bring prevailing organisational cultures and values in countries and companies operating in these countries, into the comparative study of the different manifestations of "CSR".

Conclusions

In this contribution we argue that the case for diversity of the roles of business in European societies is strong and that the case for convergence seems feeble; although this case might be strengthening in the medium term and needs careful analysis of economic, political and social change.

We argue that if this diversity is ignored it is at the peril of policymakers. Even if the diversity is acknowledged, the level of analysis seems shallow. To simply state that "an Anglo-Saxon ethical approach to CSR, combined with French concerns for social issues, a German/Scandinavian concern for the environment and a Europe-wide worry about sound corporate governance is complementary and can provide the basis for a 'European CSR agenda'" (as heard in EC circles recently), is not a deep analysis of the prevailing diversities.

The central concluding argument of this contribution however is that, despite the fact that some pieces of empirical research are still missing, the need for integrated theorybuilding from across a number of theories and research angles is required to progress our understanding of the diversity in Europe and to identify the possibilities and opportunities for convergence.[1]

Only this depth of understanding will enable a thought-through approach to developing common European policies.

Note

[1] The European Academy of Business in Society (EABIS) has been commissioned by the EC to create a European research area on "CSR" to foster better integration of research efforts across Europe and to enhance the relevance of the research to all stakeholders: business, civil society, policymakers. More information on this programme can be found on www.eabis.org.

References

Agle, B. R., Mitchell, R. K., & Sonnenfeld, J. A. 1999. What matters to CEOs? An investigation of stakeholder attributes and salience, corporate performance, and CEO values. *Academy of Management Journal*, 42: 507 – 525.

Albert, M. 1991. *Capitalisme contre capitalisme*. Paris: Editions du Seuil.

Chatman, J. A., & Jehn, K. A. 1994. Assessing the relationship between industry characteristics and organizational culture: How different can you be? *Academy of Management Journal*, 37: 522 – 553.

Clarkson, M. B. E. 1995. A stakeholder framework for analyzing and evaluating corporate social performance. *Academy of Management Review*, 20: 92 – 117.

De Jong, H. W. 1989. The takeover market in Europe: control structures and the performance of large companies compared. *Review of Industrial Organization*, 6: 1 – 18.

De Jong, H. W. 1996. Rijnlandse ondernemingen presteren beter. *ESB*: 228 – 232.

Donaldson, T., & Dunfee, T. W. 1999. *Ties That Bind*. Boston: Harvard Business School Press.

Franks, J. R., & Mayer, C. 1990. Capital markets and corporate control: A study of France, Germany, and the UK. *Economic Policy*, 10: 191 – 231.

Freeman, R. E. 1984. *Strategic management: A stakeholder approach*, Boston: Pitman Publishing.

Fombrun C., & Foss, C. 2001. The Reputation Quotient. *The Gauge*, May. http://www. reputationinstitute.com/sections/rank/rank.html, accessed 20.05.2004.

Fombrun, C., Gardberg, N., & Barnett, M. L. 2000. Opportunity platforms and safety nets: Corporate citizenship and reputational risk. *Business and Society Review*, 105(1): 85 – 106. http://www.reputationinstitute.com/sections/rank/fombrunetal2002.pdf, accessed 20.05.2004.

Gelauff, G. M. M., & Den Broder, C. 1996. *Governance of stakeholder relationships; the German and Dutch experience*. The Hague: Centraal Plan Bureau.

Gray, R., Owen, D., & Adams, C. 1996. *Accounting and Accountability*. London: Prentice-Hall.

Harris International. 2004. *Guide to the Annual Reputation Quotient Methodology*. New York.

Hofstede, G. 1984. Cultural Dimension in Management and Planning. *Asia Pacific Journal of Management*, January: 81 – 99.

Hofstede, G. 1991. *Cultures and Organisation: Software of the Mind*. London: McGraw-Hill.

ICMG (International Capital Markets Group). 1995. *International corporate governance: Who holds the terms?* London: ICMG.

Katz, J., Swanson, D., & Nelson, L. 1999. *Culture Based expectations of Corporate Citizenship*. http://info.cba.ksu.edu/Katz/Working%20Papers/culture.pdf, accessed 20.05.2004.

Kowalczyk, S. J., & Pawlish, M. J. 2002. Corporate Branding through External Perception of Organizational Culture. *Corporate Reputation Review*, 5(2 – 3): 159 – 174.

Mitchell, R. K., Agle, B. R., & Wood, D. J. 1997. Toward a theory of stakeholder identification and salience: Defining the principle of who and what really counts. *Academy of Management Review*, 22: 853 – 886.

Moerland, P. W. 1995a. Alternative disciplinary mechanisms in different corporate systems. *Journal of Economic Behaviour and Organization*, 26: 17 – 34.

Moerland, P. W. 1995b. Corporate ownership and control structures: An international comparison. *Review of Industrial Organization*, 10: 443 – 464.

O'Reilly, C., Chatman, J., & Caldwell, D. 1991. People and organizational culture: A Q-sort approach to assessing person-organization. *Academy of Management Journal*, 34: 487 – 516.

Sacconi, L. 2004. Corporate Social Responsibility (CSR) as a model of "extended" corporate governance. An explanation based on the economic theories of social contract, reputation and reciprocal conformism. *Liuc Papers*, No. 142. Serie Etica, Diritto ed Economia 10.

Segal, J.-P. 2004. *Pluralité des lectures politiques de la responsabilité sociale de l'entreprise en Europe*. Unpublished paper. ENPC, CNRS, Gestion et Société.

Suchman, M. C. 1995. Managing legitimacy: Strategic and institutional approaches. *Academy of Management Review*, 20: 571 – 610.

Trompenaars, F. 1997. *Riding the Waves of Culture.* London: Nicholas Brealey Publishing Ltd.

Van den Berghe L., & De Ridder, L. 1999. *International Standardisation of Good Corporate Governance, Best Practices for the Board of Directors.* Boston: Kluwer Academic Publishers.

Van den Berghe, L. 2002. *Corporate Governance in a Globalising World: Convergence or Divergence? A European Perspective.* Boston: Kluwer Academic Publishers.

Weimer, L., & Pape, J. C. 1999. A Taxonomy of Systems of Corporate Governance. *Corporate Governance*, 7(2): 152 – 166.

Epilogue

Jan Jonker and René Schmidpeter

The intent to set out for the endeavour that finally has led to this book, was to create in one volume an overview of the various debates around the notion of corporate social responsibility (CSR). Trying to capture and value the richness of the developments, ideas and hopes expressed in the previous pages in hindsight appears to be an almost impossible task. Still, one thing becomes unmistakably clear; CSR is an umbrella notion that fits different purposes in a variety of national contexts. It is therefore not surprising that the collective image that rises out of the previous pages is complex and sometimes even confusing.

Many – if not all – countries across Europe seem to be engaged in processes of societal and institutional transition. In some cases societies are still searching for ways to reshape themselves after abandoning periods of former regimes. In other cases societies are searching for ways to reconfigure the institutions of the past with the pressing demands of a contemporary open society. This also requires novel ideas, approaches and concepts. This volume illustrates that variety is one of the true characteristics of Europe. Respect for this variety – trying to understand where people and nations come from and in which direction they are heading – must therefore be a basic value for shaping organisational and institutional processes across Europe.

Maybe one of the things this volume proves for the first time is that the debates regarding corporate social responsibility (and its affiliated notions and terms) should not be "downsized" in one definition, concept or mantra. When we set off for the endeavour to collect the various contributions across Europe, we were certainly aware of regional and national differences. As the European Union grows in size and deepens its common grounds it becomes increasingly important for business and governments to broaden knowledge concerning each other. Only if we learn to better understand how to construct Europe from its different concepts and beliefs, as well as achieving synergies wherever possible, will we meet the needs of a highly competitive future.

Against the background of all that has been presented in these previous pages we would like to draw attention to five significant aspects that are present in all cases regardless of their background.

The Dominant Role of Business

It needs no argument that in contemporary society the role of business is eminent. From north to south and from east to west the firm has become an established and influential institution in society. At the same time businesses are – sometimes reluctantly – searching for the role they want to fulfil in a changing societal context that has grown complex over the past decades. Not all businesses are willing to accept this sometimes still diffuse responsibility that implicitly arrives with a changing role. For many the business of business is still simply doing business, assuming that the licence to operate has a semi-permanent character. But if we accept that business is a dominant force in shaping contemporary society, certainly the times have arrived to critically assess its underpinning value systems in the light of the needs and expectations of various constituencies. Business is still about doing business, but it is not the only concern of business. The open character of markets and societies, the fast growing possibility to track and trace almost instantly what a company does, and the growing demands from a variety of audiences to be accountable, are fostering the need to re-value the business paradigm. *The concept of the firm has to be re-connected to a sound understanding of a society in transition.* Business does not operate in a vacuum. Due to its pure presence it is a player in the market and in the society it operates in. These two dimensions cannot be separated from each other. They are rather two sides of one coin.

In Search of a Societal Concept

Society – a human concept so masterfully crafted and embedded over the seventeenth and eighteenth centuries – no longer fits the demands it is facing. The concept developed with a national view in mind regulated the balance between the dominant institutions that shaped a specific country. Now all this is in turmoil: national boundaries have become obsolete, the EU is expanding in size and number of inhabitants, and what once was far away is now just around the corner. So the task lying ahead is to reshape, and to reinvent a strong and powerful concept that has served a great number of countries in Europe on a national basis over the past centuries. But how could that be approached? Do we need to review the work of philosophers such as Hobbes, Locke and Rousseau? Or should we let ourselves be inspired by influential Western thinkers such as Castells, Fukuyama, Putnam or Giddens? Whatever the possible routes to take, in the greater European context such a concept can never be shaped by just a few influential thinkers. That would in every respect deny the historical roots on which Europe is grounded. Despite all this, one thing remains clear: the sum of national concepts of society does not provide the answer to what society should look like in the decades to come. It will depend on all the different actors (business enterprises, public authorities, NGOs, trade unions, churches etc.) to work together in cross-sectoral partnerships and novel alliances in order to craft the institutional setting for our future. Through these partnerships and the exchange of ideas Europe can make use of its variety and its different resources as well as developing a common identity in the end. Maybe this identity is what needs to be crafted above all.

The Challenge of Pluralistic Societies

When reading through the various contributions, the limited importance of the role of citizens in society shines out. Still in a customised and individualised society in transition, the role of the individual citizen as a co-shaper of that society is certainly an issue. Neither in the abundant literature on CSR that has appeared in previous years, nor in the rich amalgam of developments, does the individual citizen's role and the social contract seem to be a clear-cut subject of concern. Why is the contemporary citizen primarily reduced to a consumer of goods and services? A consumer has the legitimate right to act beyond the boundaries of a national value system but at the same time is not accountable for these acts. This leads to a situation in which it is sufficient to act just in accordance with the law, a form of individual compliance. So what does that imply for the growing responsibility of that consumer? In a society in transition its citizens should not only be bound by law but also by common value systems. It is in those value systems that we have to recalibrate the individual responsibility and accountability that fit a context in transition.

CSR as the Missing Link

The different contributions also clearly demonstrate that drivers for CSR vary from country to country. Where in one country NGOs seem to be a key factor, in other countries public authorities can be a crucial driver. The cultural and the institutional context varies as well as the perception of business. In some countries this has led to a search for the business case of CSR, in others the public debate is deeply rooted in ethical questions. CSR as it emerges overall is a multi-faced economic, social and political concept. *As such it could turn into an important linking element on the way to a more united Europe*, without neglecting the differences and heterogeneous histories of the individual countries. As any other umbrella concept it is important to include different perspectives and national viewpoints and to avoid being exclusive at the start. The concept of CSR is deeply rooted in the idea of bridging sectors, traditions and political ideas. Thus, one of the strengths of CSR lies in its interaction compared to pure action. Interaction also leads to innovative outcomes that cannot be managed by one single institution or single player. Instead it brings together people from different sectors and countries around common issues. As such it is an open process where the main task will be to bring people together so they can engage in a dialogue: *elaborating CSR then means elaborating Europe.*

Social Capital as Fertile Ground

When looking at the big picture it appears that CSR cannot be a top-down concept. Its real success will come from the (regional) ground close to the operative level. Especially small and medium-sized enterprises (SMEs), NGOs and private interest groups play an important part in everyday life. Maybe the time has come to learn to take advantage of the new possibilities of a globalised world and at the same time strengthen local and regional cohesion. Through fostering the dialogue between the different actors at local level social capital can be built. Social capital in this regard can be understood as the level of trust, networks of collaboration and institutions which foster cooperation in society and thus help to overcome problems of collective action. Social capital will be an important asset not only for maintaining social cohesion but also for business success. The different contributions highlight that business relies on a rich and stimulating social environment and on the supply of common goods; as much as society relies on competitive and productive business enterprises that contribute to the wealth of society. Business success and social success are therefore not contradicting factors but rather reinforce each other. In the long term the success of business and social prosperity can only be achieved together. Consequently, it would be a mistake to underestimate the importance of the mutual investments in networks of trust and collaboration. If we decide otherwise, consuming the existing social capital created in the past, we will give away an important asset: the growing social cohesion that has served Europe as a successful political, social and economic concept.

It needs to be said that the endeavour of this book has led to a rich yet sometimes heterogeneous harvest. Despite ideas abounding, it might be wise to accept that the process of reconfiguring the balance of institutions in a wider society will take time. Europe is not the place for quick fixes and overnight solutions. We like what we have and we only know what we have lost when it is gone. Europe is a place of many cultures based on deeply rooted traditions.

Promoting further understanding and research in the field of CSR is a necessary investment in a common future. Only if we are successful in the task of making all the different traditions contribute to a common Europe will we foster a fabric of society which combines economic and societal needs. This can be the old as well as the new strength of Europe in an ever more complex world.

The Authors of This Book

Melsa Ararat is a faculty member at the Graduate School of Management of Sabanci University, Istanbul where she holds the position of Executive Director of Turkey's Corporate Governance Forum. She advises corporate boards and government on CG matters as well as being an external advisor to S&P's Governance Unit. She has previously held international management positions in Asia Pacific, Japan and Europe. Her current work focuses on the overlap of corporate governance, business strategy and CSR. She has published on CG issues, contributed to the CG Code for Turkey and co-authored the book of Risk and Corporate Governance by McGraw Hill.

François Beaujolin holds the chair in Corporate Social Responsibility at the Paris 12 University. He created a master "audit social et sociétal" on the management of CSR in organisations in 2001. He has written several books on the link between CSR, social relations and human resources management: *Vouloir l'industrie* (1982); *Gérer les compétences* (1999); *Vers une organisation apprennante* (2001). He has been working on the topic of CSR for 35 years as consultant, trade unionist, HR manager, head of different departments of the Ministry of Labour and researcher in France.

Luís Bento holds the Chair of Business Ethics at Autonomous University in Lisbon and is a member of the Paris Group on CSR. He is a management consultant specialising in human resources, vice-president of APG and past-president of IFTDO-International Federation for Training and Development Organisations. He is widely published in newspapers and Management magazines on topics related to business, management, HR, ethics and training, including books on Training Development. He has worked with trade unions, companies, public administration (as World Bank consultant and adviser) in several countries in Africa, Asia, Europe and South America. He is also a visiting professor at Bordeaux Business School.

Marie Bohata runs the Centre for Leadership & Governance at CMC Graduate School of Business, Prague. In her professional career, she has served as President of the Czech Statistical Office, senior research fellow at the Economics Institute in Prague and as a member of governing bodies of various international organisations including EBEN, ISBEE, IACC and IIPE. She is a founding member of the Czech chapter of Transparency International and has chaired its executive board since 1998. She has been publishing mainly on the Czech economic transformation including ethical aspects of transformation processes, SMEs, corporate governance and foreign direct investments.

Gheula Canarutto is a lecturer at Bocconi Business School and University, Milan, Italy. She is working in the Accounting and Control area and is conducting research in the area of corporate social responsibility external communication and business ethics. Her research examines corporate social responsibility and communication practices of the most famous world corporations in order to get a general social responsibility communication framework. She has written a book, *Business ethics and Jewish law,* which will be soon published in Italy.

gheula.canarutto@sdabocconi.it

Michel Capron is a professor in Business Administration at Paris 8 University in Saint-Denis and the director of a research centre on organisations management (LERGO). He is widely published on CSR topics, especially a book (with Françoise Quairel) entitled *Mythes et réalités de l'entreprise responsable* (2004). He was a member of the French official delegation at the World Summit on Sustainable Development in Johannesburg and is a member of the French Sustainable Development National Council. He is also an expert for UNESCO on economics and ethics issues and works with social economy organisations (like CECOP) on CSR evaluation tools.

Jacqueline Cramer holds the chair in Environmental Management in Organisations at the Erasmus Centre for Sustainable Development and Management, Erasmus University Rotterdam. Moreover, she manages the programme "Corporate Social Responsibility in international context" of the Dutch National Initiative for Sustainable Development and coordinates together with Jan Jonker the Dutch Research Programme on Corporate Social Responsibility financed by the Ministry of Economic Affairs. She has widely published on topics that relate to corporate social responsibility and strategic environmental management in companies, including *Towards Sustainable Business; Connecting Environment and Market* (1999) and *Learning about Corporate Social Responsibility; The Dutch Experience* (2003). She is a member of various (inter)national advisory boards of the government, industry and non-profit organisations.

jmcramer@xs4all.nl

Nikolay Dentchev is a doctoral student at the Department of Management and Organisation, Ghent University, Belgium. His doctoral research approaches the topic of corporate social performance (CSP) from a strategic management perspective. More specifically, he is concerned with the role of CSP for the competitiveness of organisations and with the process of integrating responsibility principles in business models.

László Fekete has been elected to the MOL Chair of Business Ethics at the Budapest University of Economic Sciences in 2001. He studied history, economic history, and sociology in Hungary, Germany and the USA and holds a PhD in philosophy. His research interests include the philosophical and ethical problems of business transactions, digital culture and the information society. His recent essays – *Man, Machines, and Communications*; *Rights, Rules, and Regulations in Cyberspace*; *The Networks of Philosophy*; *Ethics of Economic Transactions in the Global Network Society* – have been published in different philosophical and sociological reviews at home and abroad. He is co-author and editor of *Contemporary Ethics* to be published in 2004.

José Luis Fernández Fernández holds the *"Javier Benjumea" Chair of Ethics for Business and Economics* (Pontifical University Comillas, Madrid). He is a full professor of the ICADE Business Faculty and co-ordinator of Professional Ethics for the entire University. He has been President of *EBEN-Spain* since 1993. Since 2000 he has been a member of the Board of the *European Ethics Network*. He takes part in the Commission for Corporate Social Responsibility of AECA and is a member of the International Editorial Board of *Ethical Perspective*. He has written numerous articles and several books on business ethics.

jlfernandez@cee.upco.es

Wojciech W. Gasparski is director and founder of the Business Ethics Centre, a joint unit of the Institute of Philosophy and Sociology, Polish Academy of Sciences & L. Kozminski Academy of Entrepreneurship and Management, Warsaw, Poland. His areas of interest are philosophy of human action (praxiology), business ethics, organisational design, methodology, and systems theory. He has published several books and over three hundred papers, among them are: *Beyond the prose of business*, in: L. Zsolnai (ed.) *Spirituality and Ethics in Management* (2004); *European Standards of Business Ethics and Corporate Social Responsibility* (in Polish) (2003); *Human Action in Business: Praxiological and Ethical Dimensions*, with L. V. Ryan (1996).

wgaspars@wspiz.edu.pl

André Habisch is a professor for Social Ethics at the Catholic University of Eichstätt-Ingolstadt, Germany and visiting research professor at the International Centre for CSR at Nottingham Business School. He founded the Center for Corporate Citizenship (CCC), a cross-disciplinary research centre on CSR/CC. He was a member of the Commission "Zukunft des Bürgerschaftlichen Engagements" of the German Bundestag (1999–2002). Together with leading German business magazines regularly evaluates the CSR performance of German companies. Grounded on this empirical material he published *Corporate Citizenship* (2003) and *Responsibility and Social Capital* (with L. Spence and R. Schmidpeter, 2004). He is a member of the Editorial Board of the *Journal of Corporate Citizenship*.

andre.habisch@ku-eichstaett.de

Aimé Heene is an associate professor at Ghent University and at Antwerp University. At Ghent University he heads the Department of Management and Organisation and is the programme director for a master's programme in "management for public organizations". He focuses his research on competence-based strategic management in private and public organisations and on the development of a strategic rationale for stakeholder management. He recently published a textbook on strategic management, *The New Strategic Management* (2004), together with Ron Sanchez from the Copenhagen Business School. Since 1992 he has (co)chaired six international conferences and workshops on competence-based strategic management.

aime.heene@Ugent.be

Eleanor O'Higgins, PhD, is on the faculty of University College Dublin, Ireland. She specialises in teaching, research and publications in business ethics, corporate social responsibility, corporate governance and strategic management. She has published in scholarly journals, books and the professional and business media. She has organised and presented at major international conferences and carries out teaching and speaking assignments in countries in Europe, Asia and the Americas, addressing industry groups and academic audiences. She is a member of the United Nations Global Compact Learning Forum, and of the Business Ethics Faculty Group of the Community of European Management Schools (CEMS).

Jan Jonker is associate professor and research fellow at the Nijmegen School of Management, University of Nijmegen (Holland). He has run his own consultancy practice for over fifteen years. His research interest lies at the crossroads of management and corporate social responsibility, in particular in relation to the development of business strategies and implementation. He has written seven books alone or with others including the *Toolbook for Organisational Change* (1998). He has also published over a hundred articles. He has given a rich variety of (public) lectures and presentations in various parts of the world and was a visiting professor in Australia, France and England.

Jouni Korhonen, research professor at the University of Tampere Research Institute for Social Sciences (Finland), is the Editor-in-Chief of *Progress in Industrial Ecology – An International Journal* (PIE) and a subject editor of the *Journal of Cleaner Production*. He is on the editorial board of *Corporate Social Responsibility and Environmental Management* as well as *International Journal of Opportunity, Growth and Value Creation*. Dr. Korhonen has published over 30 articles on industrial ecology, corporate environmental management and corporate social responsibility in international scientific journals. He published *The Primal, The Modern, and The Vital Center – A Theory of Balanced Culture in a Living Place* (2002).

Mari Kooskora is the Director of Estonian Business School Ethics Centre and Editor-in-Chief of EBS Review at the Estonian Business School (EBS) where she teaches business ethics, organisational behaviour and negotiations and conflict management. She is a visiting lecturer at the International School of Management in Kaunas, Lithuania. As a researcher she participates in several interdisciplinary studies conducted at EBS. Continuing her doctoral studies at the University of Jyväskylä in Finland she investigates into "Leadership ethics in Transition Societies, case Estonia". She has also published in the mentioned fields of research. Mari Kooskora is president of the Estonian Ethics Educators' Association, member of EBEN, CSR Tutkimusryhmä and IESE alumni.

Konstantin Kostjuk is a research fellow and public relations officer at Konrad Adenauer Foundation, Moscow. His main activities are the organisation of conferences and publications on different subjects such as social ethics, business ethics, Christian social teaching, theory of institutionalism and institutional deformations, sociology of the information society, globalisation, theoretical sociology and modern social philosophy. His articles and contributions include *The Sources of Antiwesternism and Antimodernism in the Eastern Orthodoxy* published in *La nuova Europa* (2002) and in autumn 2004 his book *Der Begriff des Politischen in der Russisch-Orthodoxen Tradition: Zum Verhältnis von Kirche, Staat und Gesellschaft in Rußland* will be available.
kkostjuk@mtu-net.ru

Suzan Langenberg is a PhD student at Nyenrode University, The Netherlands. She studied philosophy and history at the University of Amsterdam and has worked as a senior advisor for Project 21 (profit) and Perspectief vzw (non-profit) since 15 years. She worked out student-participation programmes for primary and secondary schools and promoted them in Flanders during the 1990s. In addition, she built up management and leadership programmes based upon an ethical conflict-development concept, which were delivered in SMEs and multinationals. Since 2002 she has been working on a PhD concerning free speech and the impact on human judgement and organisational behaviour; *Critical stakeholders*, in: *Journal of Business Ethics* (2004).

Gilbert Lenssen is Professor of Business Environment at The College of Europe (Bruges, Warsaw) and of Organisational Behaviour at Leiden University. He directs the overall orientation and research content of EABIS. His research and teaching areas include corporate social responsibility; the implications of globalisation for business, government and society; intercultural management, and organisational transformation. He has written books and articles on management theory, management cultures, corporate responsibility and contemporary epistemology. Gilbert Lenssen is a member of the Editorial Board of the Corporate Governance Journal, the New Academy Review as well as of the European Foundation for Management Development (EFMD) Board.

Alpar Losoncz is a professor at the University of Novi Sad, Serbia. He also teaches at the Faculty of Philosophy in Szeged University, Hungary. He is a lecturer at the Faculty of Philosophy in Novi Sad, and initiator of the Specialist Academic Studies in Novi Sad and director of the course relating to Business Ethics. His major fields of interest are business ethics, ecological economy and social capital. His most important publications are *The European Dimensions* (2002); *Spiritual Motivation in Management,* in: *Spirituality and Ethics in Management* (2004); *Suffitientia Ecologica* (2004).
corna@eunet.yu

Dirk Matten is a professor of CSR and Business Ethics at the University of London (Royal Holloway). In 2004, he also was a Visiting Scholar at the Leonard N. Stern School of Business, New York University. His research interests are in business ethics, international management and corporate environmental management. His recent publications include the first European text on *Business Ethics,* with A. Crane (2004); *Corporate Citizenship: Towards An Extended Theoretical Conceptualization,* in: *Academy of Management Review,* with A. Crane; and *Can Corporations be Citizens?,* in: *Business Ethics Quarterly*, with J. Moon and A. Crane.
Dirk.Matten@rhul.ac.uk

Domènec Melé is professor and chairman of the Department of Business Ethics at IESE Business School, University of Navarra, Spain. He also chairs the bi-annual International Symposium on Ethics, Business and Society held by IESE since 1991. He has been working intensely on business ethics, corporate social responsibility, Christian thought in management, philosophy of management and organisational cultures. He authored or coauthored 15 books and about 50 articles in referred and specialised journals and chapters of collective works. Currently, he serves as a member of the editorial board of the *Journal of Business Ethics,* the *Philosophy of Management* and *La Società.*

Jeremy Moon is professor and director of the International Centre for Corporate Social Responsibility and a deputy director of Nottingham University Business School. His research interests include comparative CSR; government and CSR; and corporations and citizenship. His recent publications include *Business Social Responsibility and New Governance,* in: *Government and Opposition* (2002); *Corporate Social Responsibility Education in Europe*, with Dirk Matten, in: *Journal of Business Ethics* (2004); and *Can Corporations be Citizens?,* with Andy Crane and Dirk Matten, in: *Business Ethics Quarterly* (2004).

Mette Morsing is an associate professor at Copenhagen Business School (CBS), where she is also a director of CBS Centre for Corporate Values and Responsibility. Her research interests are corporate communication and corporate social responsibility. She has published a number of articles on these issues in for example *Cor-*

porate Reputation Review and *Journal of Communication Management,* and her latest books are *Corporate Values and Responsibility – the Case of Denmark* with Christian Thyssen (2003) and *Beyond Corporate Communication* with professor Lars Thøger Christensen (2004). In her research, Dr. Morsing has worked with international and Danish companies, trade unions and employer organisations.

José Gonçalves das Neves is associate professor of Social and Organisational Psychology at ISCTE (Instituto Superior de Ciências do Trabalho e Empresa) in Lisbon, where he teaches graduate and post-graduate students. His main interest of research, teaching and organisational intervention focuses on organisational culture, effectiveness, quality service and corporate social responsibility. He has published several papers and books on social and organisational psychology issues and has been involved in the design and implementation of change projects. Recent publications include *Changer la culture organisationnelle: du contenue au processus* in: C. Vandenberghe, N. Delobbe, G. Karnas (Eds.), *Dimensions individuelles et sociales de l'investissement professionnel* (2003).
jose.neves@iscte.pt

Claudio Nidasio is committed to research and teaching at SDA Bocconi University School of Management, Milan, Italy. His major fields of interest include Public Management and Governance and Corporate Social Responsibility. His research is primarily based on public sector policies for CSR, *Implementing CSR on a large scale: The role of Government* (2004), and Business-Government Relationships, *CSR role in Public–Private partnerships: Models of governance* (2003). He has studied Industrial Engineering and Management and holds an International Master of Science in Management of Production. He has previously worked in the United States and Europe in a multinational business environment.
claudio.nidasio@unibocconi.it

Nigel Roome holds the chair in Sustainable Enterprise and Transformation at the Erasmus Centre for Sustainable Development and Management, Erasmus University Rotterdam. He is widely published on topics that relate business and technology to the issues of environmental management, sustainable development, corporate responsibility and global change including books on sustainability strategies for industry (1998) and the ecology of information and communications technologies (2002). He has worked with companies, trade associations, professional institutes and the voluntary sector in Europe and North America and advised with the World Bank, the European Community and governments in Canada, UK and Mexico.

René Schmidpeter is a researcher at the Catholic University of Eichstätt-Ingolstadt, Germany. He is General Manager at the Center for Corporate Citizenship and international associate at BRESE, London. For the Anglo-German Foundation he conducted extensive field research concerning CSR in small and medium-sized enterprises. Other research projects referred to cross-sectoral innovation networks in Eastern Germany (for the Federal Ministry of Education and Research) and local social policy (for Deutsche Forschungsgemeinschaft). His publications include *Corporate Citizenship as Investing in Social Capital* (2001), with A. Habisch and H.-P. Meister and *SMEs, Social Capital and Common Good* (2003), with L. Spence.

Nina Seppala is a doctoral student at Warwick Business School, UK, where she is conducting research in the area of strategic management and international business. Her research examines the decisions, actions, and organisational modes that multinational companies adopt in order to engage in corporate social responsibility in emerging economies and developing countries. She has previously worked on democracy promotion for the International Institute for Democracy and Electoral Assistance, and on training in peace-making and preventive diplomacy for the United Nations Institute for Training and Research.

Alfred W. Strigl heads the Austrian Institute for Sustainable Development, Vienna. His activities focus on the management of sustainable development processes in organisations, companies and municipalities e.g. through development of guiding visions, strategic process management and sustainability reporting. He teaches at the University for Natural Resources and Applied Life Sciences. Alfred Strigl is President of the European Association for Sustainable Development (ESD) and member of the Austrian Council for Sustainable Development, the "Actors-Network Sustainable Austria" and the CSR working group at the Austrian Standards Institute.

Betty Tsakarestou is a lecturer in the Department of Communication, Media and Culture, Panteion University, Athens, and Head of the Laboratory of Advertising and PR. She teaches courses on "Business Ethics and Responsibility", "Theory of Advertising and Public Relations". She has published chapters in books on *Advertising in Greece (Springer 2002)* and *CSR and Responsible Consumption (2003)*. Her forthcoming book is on *Responsibility, Corporate Reputation and Social Innovation*. She has worked with companies and trade associations. Currently being a member of the Greek Institute of Communication she is Head of Research on CSR and Responsible Consumption.

btsaka@panteion.gr

Aleksandr Vasiljev is a Research Fellow in the Centre for Business Ethics in Vilnius University, Lithuania. He currently works on the issues of international business ethics, business ethics and corporate social responsibility, ethical dimensions of sustainable development, and participates in studies on ethical tools implementation in anti-corruption activities. He is also involved in the projects related to responsible tourism.

casa_alva@lycos.com

Nijole Vasiljeviene is an associate professor, Head of the Centre for Business Ethics at Faculty of Humanities, Vilnius University, Lithuania. She is strongly involved in theoretical and applied researches related to moral philosophy, professional and business ethics, ethics institutionalisation in organisations, business ethics teaching methodology. She is the author of more than 100 publications including the *monograph Business ethics and codes of conduct (2000)*.

nijalex@is.lt

Volodja Vorobey is a project coordinator at the European Academy of Business in Society, Belgium, where his responsibilities include Directory of Education, Training and Research on CSR, Business in Society Gateway and support for EABIS PhD Network. He is engaged in the promotion of CSR in Central and Eastern Europe, including the development of http://www.csr.org.ua portal for Ukrainian audience. He has previously worked for AIESEC International as a Global Foundation Coordinator and led the AIESEC delegation at the World Summit of Sustainable Development in Johannesburg (2002). Volodja has worked in non-governmental organisations and companies in Iceland, Germany and Ukraine.

Martina Wegner is a researcher at the Catholic University of Eichstätt-Ingolstadt, Germany. She holds a degree in philosophy focussing on business ethics and sustainability issues. Her research projects include a two-year 6-country comparative study on corporate sustainability for Allianz Group, the results of which were presented on several international conferences. For Bertelsmann Foundation she recently co-authored with André Habisch an investigation into the legal aspects of CSR in Germany. She is a research fellow at the Center for Corporate Citizenship and teaches Business Ethics and Sustainability Management at several universities. Her consulting work for various companies refers to the fields of business ethics, CSR and sustainability.

wegner1510@aol.com

Jan-Olaf Willums chairs the Foundation for Business and Society, Oslo, and heads InSpire, its social venture capital fund. He is adjunct professor at the Centre for Corporate Citizenship (Norwegian School of Management). He holds a D.Sc. from the Massachusetts Institute of Technology. He is presently interested in measuring intangible assets, and evaluating the impact of social and environmental factors. He heads a French-Norwegian research project in this field. His publications include *The Greening of Enterprise* (1990); *From Ideas to Action* (1992); and *The Sustainable Business Challenge* (1997).

Willums@online.no

different cultural and socio-political environments. We argued in part 1 that also legitimacy theory is needed to underpin comparative research of social contracts in Europe.

Part 1: Social Contract Theory, Legitimacy Theory, and Stakeholder Theory

We propose that the cornerstone theory, explaining the role of business is *social contract theory*. It states that each society has a set of defined relations between society, business and state and modalities of relations are specific to each society. Such contracts between society and state, society and business could be formal/explicit by taking the form of laws, regulations, rules and procedures or informal/implicit through commonly accepted traditions. At the firm level, Sacconi (2004) defines social contract as the agreement that would be reached by the representatives of all the firm's stakeholders in a hypothetical situation of impartial choice.

Multiple factors could have contributed to the process of defining social contract in any particular society. A social contract is intrinsically present in every society as an expectation of society towards business, of society towards state (government) and vice versa. Due to the complicated and multi-facetted process of creating a social contract and the way a social contract is embedded in institutions, none of the sides in the state-society-business triangle could drastically influence social contract status quo in the short term. It provides a reference point for companies on how business processes and policies are maintained and what the expectations of business in a given society are in a long-term period.

Social contract theory deals with abstract entities of society, state and business, making it possible to extrapolate it to other levels or complexity of social arrangements.

Donaldson and Dunfee (1999) developed an Integrated Social Contracts Theory with clear differentiation of macrosocial contracts (expectations of community) and microsocial contracts (specific form of involvement). Although this theory sets the context for managers to take decisions, it does not provide a framework to analyse the dynamics of macro- and microsocial contracts in line with changing demographics of population in Europe, increased mobility and information flows. Moreover, whilst social contracts theory could explain the initial motivation of companies to engage with communities, it might not explain the totality of their involvement.

This highlights the underlying ambiguity of the social contract theory with regard to defining the object of research with which it deals. It is hard to define a dynamic entity such as society in static descriptive terms of micro- or macro-

Index

- The law is an expression of general/common interests in the French model. In the French model, companies willing to go beyond legal requirements and engage in "CSR" to act to the benefit of common interests will face challenges. Segal concludes that there is no certainty that France is ready to assign to companies a legitimate role to "interfere" in the building of the common social good.

- Historically, secularism is an important issue in France. In such circumstances, attempts by companies to introduce moral codes of conduct or to implement organisational values programmes are perceived as dangerous substitutes for citizens' own consciousness and "individual good education". Companies as part of the public system should be ethically neutral.

Nevertheless, the concept of *la responsabilité societal des entreprises* ("RSE") is gaining ground in France albeit on a different basis than in the UK or Germany. Some firms however prefer to label their efforts as *développement durable* and *responsabilité globale de l'entreprise*. This might fit well with the old common belief that France should be the shining light in the world (*La France est la lumière du monde*) and the more recent belief that France should challenge the model of American inspired global "turbo capitalism".

Though the concept of "CSR" originated in Anglo-Saxon countries, the French and German models described by Segal point to evidence that there is more than one model of it. Privatisation, deregulation, reforms of the welfare state, reductions of public provisions and consequent appeals to more individual and corporate responsibility are however likely to continue in both Germany and France. With these, medium-term convergence of the roles of business and government in society between the UK (where government activism and spending is on the increase), France and Germany is likely to be created.

The comparative analysis of socio-political systems indicates that the study of the (changing) role of business in European societies should not be divorced from the (changing) role of government in these societies including economic and social policy. This points to a major deficiency in EU policymaking on CSR, which seems divorced from the process of creating economic convergence.

After exploring European diversity of the roles of business in society by social contract/legitimacy theory and by analysing cultural and socio-political differences between European societies, we will now explore how these differences are reflected and manifested in two domains at the level of business: corporate governance and corporate reputation.

Printing: Strauss GmbH, Mörlenbach
Binding: Schäffer, Grünstadt